American Psychosis

American Psychosis

A HISTORICAL INVESTIGATION OF HOW THE REPUBLICAN PARTY WENT CRAZY

DAVID CORN

TWELVE

NEW YORK BOSTON

Twelve
Hachette Book Group
1290 Avenue of the Americas, New York, NY 10104
twelvebooks.com

twitter.com/twelvebooks

First Edition: September 2022

Twelve is an imprint of Grand Central Publishing. The Twelve name and logo are
trademarks of Hachette Book Group, Inc.

The publisher is not responsible for websites (or their content) that are not owned by
the publisher.

The Hachette Speakers Bureau provides a wide range of authors for speaking events. To
find out more, go to www.hachettespeakersbureau.com or call (866) 376-6591.

Library of Congress Cataloging-in-Publication Data
Names: Corn, David, author.
Title: American psychosis : a historical investigation of how the Republican
Party went crazy / David Corn.
Description: First edition. | New York : Twelve, 2022. | Includes bibliographical
references and index.
Identifiers: LCCN 2022020667 | ISBN 9781538723050 (hardcover) |
ISBN 9781538723074 (ebook)
Subjects: LCSH: Republican Party (U.S. : 1854-) | Conspiracy theories—Psychological
aspects—United States. | Conspiracy theories—Political aspects—United States. |
Right-wing extremists—United States. | United States—Politics and government.
Classification: LCC JK2356 .C697 2022 | DDC 324.2734—dc23/eng/20220701
LC record available at https://lccn.loc.gov/2022020667

ISBNs: 978-1-5387-2305-0 (hardcover), 978-1-5387-2307-4 (ebook)

Printed in the United States of America

LSC-W

Printing 1, 2022

For Welmoed, Maaike, and Amarins

Contents

We know that the Furies do not come uninvited.

—Katherine Anne Porter

Two Mobs

N elson Rockefeller stared into a sea of hate.

Standing at the podium of the Republican National Convention of 1964, the fifty-six-year-old patrician politician who symbolized dynastic American power and wealth was enveloped by waves of anger emanating from the party faithful. Delegates and activists assembled in the Cow Palace on the outskirts of San Francisco hurled boos and catcalls at the New York governor. He was the enemy. His crime: representing the liberal Republican establishment that, to the horror of many in the audience, had committed two unpardonable sins. First, in the aftermath of Franklin Delano Roosevelt's New Deal, these turncoat, weak-kneed Republicans had dared to acknowledge the need for big government programs to address the problems and challenges of an industrialized and urbanized United States. Second, they had accepted the reality that the Cold War of the new nuclear age demanded a nuanced national security policy predicated on a carefully measured combination of confrontation and negotiation.

Worse, Rockefeller had tried to thwart the hero of the moment: Barry Goldwater, the archconservative senator from Arizona, the libertarian decrier of government, the tough-talking scolder of America's moral rot, and the hawkish proponent of military might who had advocated the limited use of nuclear arms. Rockefeller, a grandson of billionaire robber baron John D. Rockefeller, had competed for the presidential nomination against Goldwater, but his campaign had been subsumed by the right wing's takeover of the party. Still, at this late stage, on July 14, the second night of Goldwater's coronation, Rockefeller and other moderate Republican dead-enders were praying for a last-minute political miracle that would rescue their party from the conservative fringe—the *kooks*, as they were widely called. This evening they were taking one final stab at keeping those kooks at bay.

Clenching his square jaw, Rockefeller had hit the stage with an immediate task: to speak in favor of a proposed amendment to the Republican

Party platform denouncing extremism, specifically that of the Communist Party, the Ku Klux Klan, and the ultraconservative, Red-baiting John Birch Society. The platform committee, controlled by Goldwater loyalists, had rejected this resolution. Yet the moderates hadn't given up. On the opening night of the convention, Governor Mark Hatfield of Oregon had declared, "There are bigots in this nation who spew forth their venom of hate. They parade under hundreds of labels, including the Communist Party, the Ku Klux Klan, and the John Birch Society. They must be overcome."

That was not the predominant sentiment within the Cow Palace. Hatfield was met with a barrage of hisses and boos. He later called the response "frightening" and reflected, "It spoke to me not merely of strong political disagreement, but of a spiteful kind of enmity waiting to be unleashed to destroy anyone seen as the enemy—domestic or foreign."

The delegates were strident anticommunists—many feared evil Reds were subverting the government and the nation's most revered institutions—and for them, Goldwater was the leader of a do-or-die crusade against leftism. They would eagerly back a resolution reviling commies. And though the Grand Old Party—founded a century earlier by antislavery politicians—was now actively moving to court racist Southern voters opposed to desegregation and civil rights, they might disavow the Klan. But including the John Birch Society in this lineup of extremists to be deplored was a not-subtle-at-all dig at Goldwater and his fanatic followers. Everyone in the room knew what—and who—this resolution was aimed at.

Founded in 1958 by Robert Welch, a onetime candy manufacturer, the John Birch Society was the most prominent exponent of right-wing conspiratorial paranoia. It proselytized that the commies were everywhere, in secret control of the US government and subverting many of America's most cherished organizations: schools, churches, the media, and PTAs. Welch had even fingered Dwight Eisenhower, the World War II hero who served two terms as president, as a Soviet asset. Though many Americans might have looked upon it as a fringe outfit—the kookiest of the kooks—the John Birch Society and its members were mightily assisting the Goldwater effort as volunteers and funders. Though Goldwater, under much pressure, had distanced himself from Welch, he had not disavowed the society and its members. His once-improbable path to the GOP presidential nomination had been fueled by the paranoid passions of the Birchers and other far-right conservatives.

The Goldwater zealots in the Cow Palace—a project of FDR's Works Progress Administration originally built as a livestock pavilion—were sure as hell not going to let Rocky and those establishment Republicans vilify and ostracize this crucial component of the Goldwater coalition.

It was late in the evening when Rockefeller hit the rostrum for his allotted five minutes. As he had walked toward the stage, people threw paper at him. Senator Thruston Morton of Kentucky, the convention chair, claiming concern for Rockefeller's safety, asked him to postpone his remarks. Believing Morton was shoving him, Rockefeller snapped, "You try to push me again, and I'll deck you right in front of this whole audience."

As soon as Rockefeller proposed adding the anti-Bircher amendment to the platform, the crowd shouted, "No! No!" A rumbling of boos resounded through the hall. Rockefeller pushed on: "It is essential that this convention repudiate here and now any doctrine—" Another cascade of jeers interrupted him. He smiled and waited for it to subside. At least he was now showing the world the true nature of this new Goldwater-bewitched GOP. In Goldwater's command center, top campaign aides dispatched a message to their delegates: *Knock it off.* The Goldwater men despised Rockefeller, but they didn't want to stir sympathy for him or generate news stories suggesting the Goldwaterites were embracing the Birchers. But the heckling did not abate.

A defiant Rockefeller continued, assailing "any doctrinaire militant minority, whether Communist, Ku Klux Klan, or Bircher." The booing got louder. Rockefeller noted that Eisenhower, addressing the convention two hours earlier, had called on the GOP to reject radicalism of the left and right. He quoted himself—from a speech he had given a year before—warning that the Republican Party "is in real danger of subversion by a radical, well-financed, highly disciplined" minority that was "wholly alien to the sound and honest conservatism." More boos. He was clearly referring to the Birchers, and he urged his fellow Republicans to heed "this extremist threat" and "its danger to the party." Once more, jeers, catcalls, and the chant "We want Barry!" Morton tried to quiet the audience, but to no avail.

Rockefeller complained he had been the victim of these "extremist elements," pointing out that he had received "outright threats of personal violence." A young Goldwater volunteer shouted, "You goddamned Socialist!" Baseball legend Jackie Robinson, a Rockefeller supporter in the hall, called out, "C'mon Rocky"—and nearly got into a fistfight with an Alabama delegate.

As veteran political correspondent Theodore White, who was present, later put it, Rockefeller "was the man who called them kooks, and now, like kooks, they responded to prove his point," and the "kooks" were "hating and screaming and reveling in their own frenzy." A call for reasonableness, a plea to spurn the paranoid, irrational, and conspiratorial tenets of the far right—this was not what Goldwater's people wanted to hear. Some reporters feared Goldwater supporters were about to storm the stage and physically attack the governor.

Maintaining a wry and cocky smile, Rockefeller told the audience, "This is still a free country, ladies and gentlemen," and he condemned the "infiltration and takeover of established political parties by Communist and Nazi methods." He added, "Some of you don't like to hear it... but it's the truth." He declared, "The Republican Party must repudiate these people."

The Republican Party—those then in control of it—thought otherwise. On a voice vote, the nays overwhelmed. "God save the Union," Senator Tom Kuchel, a moderate Republican, remarked.

———

About noon on January 6, 2021, President Donald Trump took the stage at a "Save America" rally on the Ellipse, south of the White House, and surveyed a crowd seething with rage and animated by paranoia. Trump had lost his bid for reelection to former Vice President Joe Biden two months earlier. Yet in the intervening weeks, he had insisted that the results were fraudulent and that he had been denied a second term by a nefarious plot with a global reach. His political allies had promoted assorted and overlapping conspiracy theories involving voting machine manufacturers, China, Venezuela, the CIA, Italian hackers (who used military satellites), local Democratic operatives, and the media. It was all rubbish—bizarre, foolish, fact-free charges. Various courts had tossed out lawsuits from Trump partisans alleging vote-rigging. The Justice Department—overseen by Attorney General William Barr, a Trump loyalist—had found no evidence of meaningful election fraud.

Trump had long been a purveyor of outlandish conspiracy theories, and, in defeat, he was not going to stop. He had become a hero for conservatives by championing birtherism, the false and racist notion that Barack Obama had been born in Kenya. His volatile presidency had been marked by his never-ending promotion—through tweets and other statements—of dark, misleading, and false claims: The Deep State was out to destroy him. The investigations of Moscow's attack on the 2016 election—and of the troubling interactions between Trump's campaign and Russians—were a plot to subvert his presidency. News outlets were an unrelenting enemy conniving to crush him. Trump had painted a Manichean picture of the world for his supporters, asserting an array of sinister forces was bent on sabotaging his presidency. The 2020 election was the latest chapter in this saga, and during this post-election period, Trump had fed the paranoid right and his fellow Republicans outlandishly bogus claims of a stolen election.

Millions of Americans believed him—including many far-right extremists. In the crowd before Trump this day—and in bands roving throughout the nation's capital—were white supremacists, Christian nationalists (who thought the United States should be identified and organized as a Christian state), neo-Nazis, and adherents of the QAnon conspiracy theory. This theory held that the world was controlled by a cabal of Satan-worshipping, cannibalistic pedophiles (which included prominent Democratic officials, Hollywood celebrities, and the Pope) and that Trump was engaged in an all-out war to crush this evil power and save humanity. Some posters on QAnon sites had called for violence this day.

Certainly, among the people gathered for this rally—which was organized by a bevy of right-wing outfits controlled by Trump backers working in close coordination with the White House—were Republicans and Trump supporters who did not identify with QAnoners, Nazis, Christian bigots, and racists. These outraged people simply bought Trump's guff about a rigged election. But hate and paranoia—nurtured by Trump—pervaded the air. Members of self-styled right-wing militias had come to town ready for action, responding to Trump's tweet of December 19: "Big protest in D.C. on January 6th. Be there, will be wild!" One of these groups, the Oath Keepers, stashed weaponry at a Comfort Inn outside Washington, should Trump call on them to take up arms. Wearing body armor, they were ready to move in and apprehend members of the Deep State on Trump's signal. The Proud Boys, an extremist group with a history of street violence that referred to itself as "Western chauvinists" and promoted antisemitic, racist, and misogynistic views, were roaming the streets of Washington, eager to do battle for Trump. During a campaign debate the previous September, Trump had told the Proud Boys to "stand back and stand by"—and the group saw that as a message from Trump: Wait for my call.

When Trump, wearing a dark winter coat and gloves, hit the stage, he paced back and forth before fluttering American flags, as the P.A. system played "God Bless the USA." He told the crowd that "our election victory" was "stolen by emboldened radical-left Democrats" and "the fake news media" and that he had won in a "landslide." He vowed, "We will not take it anymore." The crowd chanted, "Fight for Trump!"

Vice President Mike Pence was soon to preside in the Capitol over the ceremonial certification of the Electoral College vote count. Before this crowd, Trump called on Pence to refuse to accept the votes from swing states Biden had won and halt that proceeding. This was not an option Pence possessed under the Constitution or federal law. But Trump's grand plan was to block the certification. Then Republican-controlled state legislatures in these states could overturn Biden's victory and appoint pro-Trump electors. And if those states failed to do so, the election would be thrown to the House to decide, with each state delegation casting one vote, a process in which the GOP had the advantage. "I hope Mike is going to do the right thing," Trump said. (About this time, Pence released a statement saying he would not do as Trump wished: "My oath to support and defend the Constitution constrains me from claiming unilateral authority to determine which electoral votes should be counted and which should not.")

Trump beamed as he spoke to his people. He said there was "extraordinary love" within the crowd. His followers chanted, "We love Trump!"

Trump was apocalyptic. Should Biden become president, he thundered, the "country will be destroyed." He derided "weak" and "pathetic" Republicans who were not taking action to stop the purported election theft: "You'll never take back our country with weakness. You have to show strength and you have to be strong. We have come to demand that Congress do the right thing." He cited allegations of irregularities that had already been disproven. Were the certification not blocked, he asserted, "You will have an illegitimate president...And we can't let that happen."

Though warned that a number of protesters were armed, Trump whipped up the crowd, as had previous speakers. Earlier in the rally, Donald Trump Jr. urged the demonstrators to "stand up and fight." Representative Mo Brooks, an Alabama Republican, told the gathering it was time to start "kicking ass." With a raised voice, he egged them on: "Are you willing to do what it takes to fight for America?" He declared that they had to "carry the message to Capitol Hill." Rudy Giuliani, the former New York City mayor and Trump's consigliere, who had challenged election results and lost court cases across the country, insisted the "election was stolen" via "crooked" voting machines. "Let's have trial by combat!" he yelled.

Many in the audience had been primed the previous day during premarch rallies in different Washington locations. These events featured speakers deemed too extreme by the main rally organizers to share the stage with Trump. At one of these well-attended kick-off events on Capitol Hill, paranoia and conspiracy theory ran rampant. Ali Alexander, who had dubbed himself the leader of the so-called Stop the Steal movement, told the crowd, "We are here to stop a coup that's going on in our country." He shouted, "This is our country, one way or another." He led the audience in chanting, "1776! 1776! 1776!" He concluded by a giving "a few shout-outs" to his "friend" Alex Jones, the notoriously loony conspiracy-monger. A red-faced, bellowing Jones then decried "globalists" who "brainwash and gaslight the public." He denounced "the satanists who run this system" and called Biden a "Chinese communist agent," claiming billionaire Bill Gates was "enslaving" the world and the ongoing COVID-19 pandemic was a "hoax." Jones exclaimed, "I want you to commit to total resistance."

The flood of paranoia continued to pour forth at this January 5 event. Joe Flynn, the brother of retired Lieutenant General Michael Flynn (Trump's first national security adviser, who was forced out of the job after lying to the FBI about his contacts with the Russian ambassador), blasted the "cowards" in the GOP. "Are we going to let them cower to these communists?" he asked. Roger Stone, the longtime underhanded political operative and Trump-whisperer convicted of lying to Congress (whom Trump had recently pardoned), insisted that Democrats and the media were mounting a "psy-op" against America to convince people Biden had won. "This is," he declared, "a fight for the future of Western civilization as we know it...It's a fight between the godly and the godless." Alan Hostetter, a leader of the Stop the Steal forces in California, proclaimed war was at hand: "We are at war tomorrow...They need to know we as a people, a hundred million strong, are coming for them...I will see you all tomorrow at the front lines." (A few weeks earlier, at a California protest, Hostetter had called for the "execution" of Trump's foes.) That day, Steve Bannon, Trump's former chief strategist and still an ardent Trump advocate, proclaimed on his website, "All hell is going to break loose tomorrow. It's gonna be moving. It's gonna be quick." Top Trump adviser Jason Miller zapped out a similar it's-time-to-fight message: "Everyone is going to remember who actually stands in the breach and fights tomorrow and who goes running off like a chicken."

It was within this highly charged atmosphere that Trump was addressing his supporters and feeding them a toxic brew of baseless charges and doomful suspicion, declaring the existence of the United States was threatened. He warned, "If you don't fight like hell, you're not going to have a country anymore." He gave his irate devotees marching orders: "We're going to the Capitol, and we're going to try and give...them the kind of pride and boldness that they need to take back our country." Trump was directing an armed mob toward Congress. His supporters shouted, "Take the Capitol!"

Music came on: "YMCA"—the gay anthem the campaign for some reason had adopted as a signature song. Trump pumped his arms and danced a bit. Though he had suggested he would lead the crowd as it moved on the Capitol, the Secret Service blocked him from joining the throng, and he returned to the White House to watch on television what would unfold.

As Trump was finishing, members of the House and Senate were gathering in the House of Representatives chamber to begin certifying the electoral vote. Around this time, pro-Trump rioters who had skipped the rally or left early began grappling with Capitol Hill police officers. Soon hand-to-hand fighting broke out, as thousands of Trump's shock troops—bolstered by rally attendees—stormed the symbol of American democracy. Proud Boys flashed a white power signal. Rioters carried Confederate flags. One wore a CAMP AUSCHWITZ sweatshirt; others had shirts proclaiming MAGA CIVIL WAR JANUARY 6, 2021. A QAnon "shaman" led one band of the Trumpers. Trump flags billowed in the air.

The mob breached the Capitol. Proud Boys were some of the first in. Members of the Oath Keepers militia helped guide rioters inside. Incensed Trump supporters stomped through the building, declaring their intent to halt the vote certification. Hours of insurrectionist terror and chaos ensued. Rioters brutally beat officers—sometimes with American flags. They ransacked the House and Senate chambers and other offices. Lawmakers barricaded doors. Pence and legislators were hurriedly evacuated, and the certification ceremony halted, as the marauders rampaged through the building, some searching for Pence and House Speaker Nancy Pelosi. "Hang Mike Pence," they shouted. The insurrectionists constructed gallows outside the Capitol, echoing a famous scene from the white nationalist novel *The Turner Diaries*.

As the riot—broadcast on live television—raged, Trump placed his own vice president at further risk by tweeting, "Mike Pence didn't have the courage to do what should have been done to protect our Country and our Constitution." Rioters battled police officers and yelled, "We're here for Trump!" They also chanted, "We love Trump!" Some shouted, "We are the storm"—the motto of QAnoners. One rioter, a QAnon fanatic, was shot and killed, as she tried to break through locked doors in pursuit of House members. Another collapsed outside the building and died.

This afternoon of hate and violence continued for about two hours. In the White House, Trump watched the melee on television with excitement. He ignored pleas from family members, advisers, and Republican legislators to intervene and instruct his followers to retreat. He was getting what he wanted: a delay in the electoral count certification. At one point he tweeted a request for "everyone at the U.S. Capitol to remain peaceful"—a statement his advisers forced him to issue. But it was too late for that, and Trump took no decisive steps to end the raid. He abandoned his responsibility to defend the Constitution and protect the nation.

As law enforcement officers began to regain control of the Capitol,

Trump finally released a video telling the raiders "to go home now." But he reiterated the lie that had triggered the assault: "We had an election that was stolen from us." He honored the violent mob of extremists and racists: "We love you, you're very special." Once the rioters were cleared, he posted a tweet referring to them as "great patriots," adding, "Go home with love and in peace. Remember this day forever!" By then, about 150 police officers had been injured. One officer who had been in the fighting died of two strokes the following day. In the months to come, four officers committed suicide.

At 8:00 p.m. Congress reconvened and certified Biden had defeated Trump.

A line runs from the 1964 convention to Trump's riot. It's not a straight line. It has zigged and zagged over the years. But there is a path. What happened on Capitol Hill was a continuation of the Republican Party's decades-long relationship with extremism. For years, the Party of Lincoln had encouraged and cashed in on paranoia, bigotry, and conspiracy theory. Trump took this to a new level, but this was not a new strategy.

More than half a century earlier, Nelson Rockefeller had tried and failed to tame a crowd of Republicans and distance the party from the Birchers and their conspiratorial right-wing swill. Trump, preying on similar conspiratorial sentiments, weaponized the delusions held by his supporters that he had originated and advanced. He incited thousands who came to Washington because of his big lie—who accepted his claim that malevolent and covert forces controlling the world rigged the 2020 election against him. He had assembled an army of extremists and conspiracy believers and unleashed it upon the nation's constitutional order to retain power. He was using the hatred, ignorance, and irrationality that gripped millions of Americans to subvert democracy.

There was madness within the mob. These enraged Trumpers lived in a false reality. The election was not stolen. Trump was not battling a secret cabal of pedophiles and cannibals. What they believed was wrong—extremely wrong. Yet facts no longer mattered. They were guided by what Trump adviser Kellyanne Conway once called "alternative facts." It was as if they were infected by a psychosis. That is a condition when the brain does not properly process information. This can lead to detachment from reality. A person undergoing psychosis might see, hear, or believe things that are not real. For many of the Capitol Hill assailants, Trump and his paranoia had become a theology. With his false assertions, Trump had engineered a distorted reality—as had all those Republicans who did not refute Trump's baseless claims about the election. He—and they—had encouraged the spread of this American psychosis.

————

Voting down an anti-extremism platform provision and violently attacking the Capitol are different forms of political activity. But they were related. Both were manifestations of this decades-long effort of the Republican Party and its leaders to capitalize on extremism and paranoia. In the years between the 1964 convention and the 2021 riot, the GOP fueled fanaticism and forged a relationship with peddlers of conspiracy theory and hawkers of the politics of hate and fear.

The strength of this bond varied through this time, but it was never renounced or severed. The Trump-incited January 6 riot was exceptional. The United States had never witnessed American domestic terrorists violently assault Congress to keep a defeated president in office. But Republicans had often sought to trade on the darkest of suspicions within the citizenry and the worst elements of the far right: conspiracism, racism, and paranoia. In 1964, observing the Goldwater movement, Pulitzer Prize–winning historian Richard Hofstadter identified a "paranoid style" in politics within the United States. In his seminal essay "The Paranoid Style in American Politics," he noted that "much political leverage can be got out of the animosities and passions of a small minority" for whom "the feeling of persecution is central…[and] systemized in grandiose theories of conspiracy."

Hofstadter wrote that this "paranoid style" was, in the United States, "the preferred style only of *minority* movements." That seemed to relegate this strain of politics to a limited role. But Trump had made the paranoid style a central element of his political force. He elevated the demagogic exploitation of fear and disorder to an extent no American president had ever attempted. It was the core of *his* movement, which controlled the Republican Party.

There are no Big Bangs in history. No events that materialize—or explode—out of nothing. January 6 seemed a break from the past and from the nation's political reality. But no one person—not even Trump—could have engineered such a profound rupture on his or her own. This was an instance of a man meeting a moment shaped by the actions and inactions of others over a lengthy stretch. The GOP had long played with and stoked the fires of extremism for political advantage. It had encouraged and exploited a psychosis. This sickness reached an apotheosis on that cloudy and chilly winter afternoon. Yet it had been years in the making.

CHAPTER 1

Backstory I
The Rise and Decline of the Grand Old Party

The origin story of the Republican Party is a noble tale. A small number of politicians banded together to thwart a horrific prospect: a white supremacist oligarchy seizing political and economic control of the United States of America. And they succeeded, saving the nation from a terrible fate. But after that, the GOP's history becomes far more complicated.

In 1854, the political atmosphere in the United States was charged, with the debate over slavery dominating the nation's discourse. As the country expanded to the west, a critical question was at hand: Would slavery be permitted in these new territories and states?

The slavery issue had recently wrecked the Whigs, one of the two major parties. Leading up to the 1852 presidential election, its Northern faction, composed mostly of antislavery advocates, went so far as to block the nomination of its own incumbent president, Millard Fillmore, a Whig who personally opposed slavery but had taken no steps to dismantle the barbarous system of bondage, believing that doing so would tear apart the union. After a grueling fifty-three ballots at the party's national convention, the Whigs settled on a former general named Winfield Scott, who was backed by the Northerners. Yet Southern Whigs pushed through a proslavery platform. Such a divided house could not stand. Scott was crushed by Democrat Franklin Pierce in the election, and the Whigs imploded as a party. The United States was left with one major partisan outfit: the Democrats, a party in favor of limited government and a friend of Slave Power.

Come early 1854, Congress was deliberating on organizing the Permanent Indian Territory—a huge swath of land west of the Mississippi River where President Andrew Jackson had brutally relocated Native Americans from Southern states—into Kansas and Nebraska. Up for debate was a law that would allow settlers in those areas to decide whether to permit slavery.

More than a moral question was at stake. This was a raw political brawl about economic influence. If new territories became slave states, that would bolster the already considerable might of the South—the richest region in the country and a racist oligarchy controlled by large plantation owners. The importation of slavery into these areas would also reduce economic opportunities for white men seeking work in the West. Small farmers would not be able to compete with vast plantations that functioned as slave labor camps. The Kansas-Nebraska Act threatened to lead to an America dominated by the racist dictatorship of the South that had subjugated millions of Black people.

In March 1854, spurred by the prospect of this legislation becoming law, a group of Whigs, antislavery Democrats, members of the Free Soil Party, and Know-Nothings (whose party believed Catholic immigrants posed the greatest threat to the nation) gathered in Ripon, Wisconsin, to discuss forming a new party to confront the menace of spreading slavery. It would be called the Republican Party, a name that harkened back to the Democratic-Republican Party of Thomas Jefferson.

Months later, the morning after Congress passed the measure, a group of about thirty House representatives from various parties assembled in a Washington, DC, boarding house. They committed to joining the burgeoning Republican Party to combat the exportation of slavery to the West. In Illinois, a onetime congressman who still considered himself a Whig (hoping the party could somehow get itself together) and who opposed the *extension* of slavery (but not slavery itself) declined invitations to join the new Republican Party. But about two years later—after "anti-Nebraska" candidates in the 1854 election wiped out members of Congress who had supported the law—Abraham Lincoln signed up with the Republicans, becoming one of the party's rising stars. Within four years, he would be elected the first Republican president.

The Republican Party of Lincoln would not only win the Civil War and free four million enslaved Americans; it would advance the idea that a strong national government was necessary to promote the public interest. Its 1860 platform opposed the expansion of slavery and reiterated "all men are created equal" (without urging the abolishment of slavery). The party also called for distributing land to farmers, protecting the rights of immigrants, and bolstering the nation's infrastructure with the construction of harbors and a transcontinental railroad.

Triumphing in the 1860 election, the new Republicans, as historian Heather Cox Richardson put it, "had fashioned themselves as the defenders of American liberty, the guarantors of economic fairness and equality." Republicans supported tariffs—a tax on goods from Europe—to protect workers and farmers and to finance an activist government that would create a national currency system, support public education (by establishing land-grant colleges), assist low-income Americans (through an ambitious homestead program), bolster the nation's leading industry (with the establishment of the US Department of Agriculture), and implement a progressive income tax. Its aim was to expand economic opportunity. (Democrats generally opposed using the federal government to boost economic development.) With the Thirteenth Amendment, Lincoln and the Republicans ended slavery.

Over the next hundred years, the party would seesaw between championing reform to benefit the citizenry and serving the interests of the wealthy and powerful, between advocating the rights of freedom and neglecting the plight of Black Americans. In 1961, Theodore White, the political journalist, would describe the Grand Old Party this way: "The Republican Party, to be exact, is twins and has been twins from the moment of its birth—but the twins who inhabit its name and shelter are Jacob and Esau: fratricidal, not fraternal twins. Within the Republican Party are combined a stream of the loftiest American idealism and a stream of the coarsest American greed." In the decades after the Civil War, White observed, "as America swelled with industry and new immigrants from Europe, these twins of the Republican Party, the good and the greedy, fought each other for control of the Party and the nation's power."

That internal battle began shortly before Lincoln's assassination, with Republicans disagreeing how far they should go in expanding the rights of Blacks in the South. That fight intensified, when Lincoln's vice president, Andrew Johnson, a pro-Union Democrat from Tennessee, succeeded him. Johnson unabashedly supported the South's postwar efforts to regain power and limit the rights of freed slaves. Opposing him, congressional Republicans fought to protect the gains won through the death and destruction of the Civil War—as the Ku Klux Klan and other white supremacists terrorized Blacks and Republican officeholders in the South. ("This is a country for white men," Johnson declared, "and by God, as long as I am President, it shall be a government for white men.") Yet divisions arose among the Republicans, pitting those who sought aggressive Reconstruction policies to provide political and economic assistance to Blacks against those who worried about radicalism. The party also split into a camp that backed the rise of labor unions and one that feared these new entities.

By the time Ulysses S. Grant won the White House for the Republicans in 1868, the war for the party's soul was fully underway. The party backed the Fourteenth and Fifteenth Amendments to the Constitution, which made freed slaves citizens and prohibited the denial of the right to vote due to "race, color, or previous condition of servitude." But there were personal spats among party leaders. Northeastern Republicans favored high tariffs to protect established business interests; Western Republicans representing developing areas were skeptical and more interested in easy credit.

After workers in France set up the Paris Commune in 1871, business interests and the affluent feared organizing among American laborers. Elements of the Republican Party became more attuned to bankers and businessmen and worried about the expanding power of workers and Black Americans. The party divided, with Liberal Republicans facing off against the Republicans in power, whom they viewed as corrupt politicians too eager to please the wealthy. Increasingly corporate interests held sway over the party, and voices within it started assailing social programs as "socialism" and "communism."

Even as the Democrats excoriated the GOP as the party of big government and fared well at the congressional level with that line of attack, the Republicans continued to win presidential elections. Rutherford B. Hayes, a Republican who triumphed in the contested election of 1876, dispatched troops to help the railroads beat back a strike and declined to use federal soldiers to protect Republican state governments in the South threatened by white supremacists. The Democrats, advocating small government, low taxes, and states' rights (the not-so-coded term for white supremacy), regained political control in the South.

In 1884, the Republicans lost the White House to Grover Cleveland, a Democrat, partly because the party had come to be seen as too cozy with the economic elites. The GOP had pulled a complete reversal since Lincoln's day, when he had focused on increasing economic opportunity. Still, the Republicans would win the presidency in the next five of six elections, relying on corporate money to finance their campaigns. After Republican Benjamin Harrison won the 1888 contest, one publication exclaimed, "This is to be a business-man's Administration" and "business men will be thoroughly well content with it."

The Republican Party was in charge for most of the Gilded Age. As the Democrats embraced populism and repeatedly nominated as their standard-bearer the fiery crusader William Jennings Bryan, who passionately denounced the well-heeled and the business trusts, the GOP established itself as the party of money—collecting and spending gobs of it to win elections. William McKinley, the Republican governor of Ohio, won the presidential contest in 1896, with industrialist Mark Hanna, his close friend and adviser, squeezing massive contributions out of tycoons and other corporate leaders fearful of Bryan's anti-establishment (and conspiratorial) populism.

During this stretch, the GOP largely showed indifference to the anti-Black violence and Jim Crow laws spreading in the South. And it became the party of imperialism, pushed in this direction by the young Theodore Roosevelt, who was appointed assistant secretary of the Navy in 1897 and who believed that for America to be a great nation it must conquer and claim overseas lands, just as it did with Native Americans at home.* This impulse led to the Spanish-American War—during which Roosevelt became a political celebrity by leading his Rough Riders regiment in Cuba against Spanish troops—and the subsequent cruel subjugation of the Philippines. At the same time, within the party grew a dissident bloc of Progressive Republicans—which included T.R.—who wanted to take on the corruptions of politics and regulate the excesses and growing problems of the new industrialized economy and robber baron capitalism.

Elected governor of New York in 1898, that upstart Roosevelt began implementing liberal initiatives. He bolstered civil service reforms, started regulating sweatshops, and pushed companies to pay corporate taxes. This did not endear him to the Republican establishment, which cooked up a plan to sideline Roosevelt by shoving him into the vice presidency. With Roosevelt as his running mate, McKinley won reelection in 1900, again defeating Bryan. In September the following year, McKinley was shot dead by an anarchist. "I told McKinley it was a mistake to nominate that wild man," Hanna complained, referring to Roosevelt, adding, "Now look. That damn cowboy is president of the United States."

Roosevelt reoriented the party. He championed an activist federal government that would oversee (not undermine) business, promote a "Square Deal" for the booming middle class, conserve large swaths of land in the untamed West, and pursue grand ambitions overseas, such as the Panama Canal. The old guard of the GOP grumbled, but to the American public, it looked as if the Republican Party, with Roosevelt in the saddle, had returned to the progressivism of Lincoln.

The twenty-sixth president enacted legislation to prevent the railroads from price-gouging and to clean up the meat industry. He called for greater

---

* In his 1896 book, *The Winning of the West*, Roosevelt laid out an unapologetic racist rationale for conquest: "All men of sane and wholesome thought must dismiss with impatient contempt the plea that these continents should be reserved for the use of scattered savage tribes, whose life was but a few degrees less meaningless, squalid, and ferocious than that of the wild beasts with whom they held joint ownership."

taxes on the wealthy, antitrust action, and federal oversight of the stock market. At a time when the United States was undergoing a profound transformation from an agricultural society to an industrialized powerhouse and expanding with new waves of immigration, T.R.—over the objections of leaders in the party—viewed government as a force to moderate the downsides of a rip-roaring, free-market economy. "I am not advocating anything revolutionary," Roosevelt once said, "I am advocating action to prevent anything revolutionary."

Then came William Howard Taft, Roosevelt's secretary of war and close political ally. He succeeded Roosevelt as president after the 1908 election but sided with conservative Republicans and adopted a more cautious approach toward reform and regulation. He supported a new tariff measure that favored the business interests of the East. Taft's stance infuriated Roosevelt. In a high-octane speech in 1910, he proclaimed the need for a "New Nationalism," under which a strong government would further challenge corporate power to protect workers and consumers. He railed against "a small class of enormously wealthy and economically powerful men, whose chief object is to hold and increase their power." He advocated abolishing corporate donations to political campaigns and called for laws to ensure a minimum wage and better working conditions.

Here was a new round in the fight for the soul of the Republican Party—and Roosevelt lost. The party rejected his comeback bid and renominated Taft in 1912. Roosevelt ran for president with the Progressive Party, aka the Bull Moose Party. This split gave the Democrats an opening, and their nominee, New Jersey Governor Woodrow Wilson, skated into the White House with far fewer votes than the combined totals for Roosevelt and Taft.

With Roosevelt out of the way, the Republican Party stayed with its default position: oppose reforms that checked corporate power. Such measures, party leaders warned, were socialistic. They said the same about the new progressive income tax Wilson and congressional Democrats enacted. They decried a new banking system that increased federal oversight of the financial industry. After the 1917 Bolshevik Revolution in Russia, Republicans declared that Democrats, with their reforms, were similarly plotting to overthrow American capitalism. Following World War I, they denounced the proposed League of Nations as a socialist conspiracy to destroy the United States under the banner of internationalism.

As labor unrest and agitation spread after the war, Republicans, during the first Red Scare, warned of a Bolshevik threat at home. At its 1920 convention, the GOP nominated Warren G. Harding, a second-rate, backslapping politician who relished playing poker. His running mate was Calvin

Coolidge, who as governor of Massachusetts had seized control of Boston during a police officers' strike and earned national acclaim for thwarting the supposed advance of Bolshevism in the United States.

Harding promised a return to "normalcy," which meant no more stirring the pot about American businesses screwing workers or consumers. During the campaign, Republicans courted Black votes in the North, as Harding assailed lynching but also defended segregation. He won in a GOP landslide. Voters were tired of the war and its aftermath. First-time women voters opted for the Republican.

The Harding White House stank of tobacco smoke and corruption. When Harding died suddenly, Coolidge became the chief executive. With Commerce Secretary Herbert Hoover and Treasury Secretary Andrew Mellon by Silent Cal's side, the party of business doubled down. They slashed government spending and cut taxes for the wealthy. Commerce was booming in the Roaring Twenties. The new technologies of radio and movies were spreading, as were automobiles and electricity. Consumerism and mass media were on the march. Wall Street was jazzed with speculation. The Republicans saw no reason to get in the way of this. They were the party of unfettered capitalism and triumphalism. When Hoover was nominated in 1928 as the party's presidential candidate, he declared, "We in America today are nearer to the final triumph over poverty than ever before in the history of any land."

American politics had long had an ugly side. (Thomas Jefferson and John Adams in 1796 and 1800 had waged bitter, smear-filled battles.) But the 1928 campaign, with Hoover running against Al Smith, the Democratic governor of New York, featured an expanded use of sleaze: religious bigotry. Smith was a Catholic, and the Republicans sought to exploit the widespread prejudice against Catholicism.

Anti-Catholic sentiment in part grew out of antagonism toward immigrants from Ireland, Italy, and elsewhere, but it also was inflamed by a conspiratorial notion. Catholics were suspected of being loyal—and secretly so—to the Pope, not America. Smith's nomination sparked panic in some Protestant quarters. Rumors spread: If Smith were elected, all Protestant marriages would be annulled. One Baptist leader declared a vote for Smith was a vote against Christ. Flyers showed a photograph of the Holland Tunnel and declared it was a secret passageway between Rome and Washington for the Pope to employ. A widely circulated cartoon depicted the Pope at the head of the table in the Cabinet Room of the White House, with priests and bishops by his side and Smith, dressed like a bellboy, in the corner.

Hoover and his campaign did not directly engage in Catholic-bashing, but state and local Republicans distributed pamphlets that denounced Smith and Catholicism. They also spread the word that Smith approved of interracial marriage. It was a strategy designed to capitalize on fear, bigotry, and religious paranoia. These smear tactics might not have been necessary for the GOP to prevail. With the economy still zipping along, Hoover won handily.

———

The GOP was fully entrenched as a conservative party—abandoning the progressivism of Lincoln and Roosevelt—and the two main parties settled into the fundamental roles that would exist for the next hundred years. The GOP was the party of business, opposed to government power (except regarding the national security state); the Democrats would challenge, to varying degrees, the prerogatives of the economically powerful, and at times they would wave the progressive banner but, at this point, not on race. (Some of the fiercest white supremacists of the South were Democrats.)

Yet after October 29, 1929—Black Tuesday—it was no longer an asset to be the party of big business. The stock market collapsed, and the Twenties ceased to roar. An immense depression and mass unemployment ensued. Hoover and the Republicans were at a loss as to what to do. They continued to revile big government and proceeded to slash spending (which threw more people out of work). For a decade, the Republicans had called the shots. They owned the system, and it lay in tatters.

Hoover's loss to Franklin Roosevelt in 1932 was no surprise. Once more, a Roosevelt wielded federal power to save American capitalism from itself. In response to FDR's New Deal, the Republicans fractured yet again. A camp led by Hoover, with its spiritual heart in the Midwest and rural areas, would play the Red card, assailing Roosevelt's moves as socialism. The competing wing, centered in the urban areas of the East, accepted that a modern industrialized economy required *some* degree of government oversight and a *limited* amount of social welfare programs. But in the first years of Roosevelt's era, the conservatives reigned within the GOP.

As Roosevelt steered the nation toward a society of grand public works, financial regulation, organized labor, and social protection, Republicans tended to bitterly oppose "that man" in the White House and his programs. Their first attempt to boot him out of the office—with Kansas Governor Alf Landon, a former oil executive, as the GOP nominee—was an abysmal flop. Landon declared that the nation's existence was at stake and that only his election would preserve "the American form of government." The business community was on his side and pumped millions into the Landon campaign. Roosevelt, supported by urban voters and Black Americans who had moved into Northern cities after World War I during the Great Migration, swamped Landon, winning 46 out of 48 states, and Republicans dropped to near-irrelevant numbers in Congress, 88 members in the House and 19 in the Senate.

Still, conservatives remained the dominant force within the GOP, and as Nazi aggression in Europe set off a second world war, leading Republicans became key voices of isolationism. Yet when it came time to pick a champion to go up against FDR in 1940, the conservatives, who were pushing Senator Robert Taft, the son of President Taft and a steadfast isolationist who embodied the party's small-government and pro-business values, ran into the campaign of Thomas Dewey, the thirty-seven-year-old crusading district attorney of New York, who had earned a national reputation battling the mob.

Though a stiff campaigner, Dewey attracted support from the liberals within the party and became the front-runner. Yet neither side could win the day at the party's convention, and an improbable candidate snatched the nomination: Wendell Willkie, a Wall Street lawyer, former Indiana utility executive, and onetime Democrat who had never held or run for public office and who was backed by the party's moderates. Willkie criticized the New Deal's "antibusiness philosophy." Roosevelt campaigned against him by both decrying the isolationism of the GOP *and* vowing to keep American "boys" from being "sent into any foreign war." With the Democrats still holding the South and scoring big in the cities, Roosevelt clobbered Willkie to win an unprecedented third term.

Within the Republican Party, a resentment began to simmer, as conservatives groused that the Eastern establishment had forced a moderate (who had registered as a Republican only the year before!) upon them as a nominee. The grand pooh-bahs had sold out the party's heart and soul. A slow fuse was lit.

As the nation pondered how to respond to Adolf Hitler's conquests in Europe and the widening conflict overseas, conservative Republicans led by Taft continued to champion isolationism. With the attack on the US naval base at Pearl Harbor on December 7, 1941—in which more than 2,400 Americans were killed—the debate became moot. Over the previous twelve years, the Republicans had ended up on the wrong side of both economic policy and national security policy. Its prospects were not promising.

Following several years of war that generated government spending that helped bring the Great Depression to an end, the GOP had a fourth shot at Roosevelt in 1944. Dewey, now governor of New York, secured the nomination without much of a fight, and the party adopted moderate and even progressive policies: endorsing the Equal Rights Amendment that would enshrine women's rights, favoring the extension of Social Security, and acknowledging the need for labor protection laws. It looked as if the Republican Party had finally made its peace with the modern welfare state, and it adopted a moderate stance of internationalism. Dewey called himself a "New Deal Republican." The party's main line of attack was a personal slam against Roosevelt. Four more years of *that man*, its platform warned, "would centralize all power in the President, and would daily subject every act of every citizen to regulation by his henchmen; the country would remain a Republic only in name."

During the campaign, Dewey and the Republicans expanded on this apocalyptic rhetoric and deployed what would soon become a common tactic for the party: baseless Red-baiting. Dewey declared "the Communists are seizing control of the New Deal through which they aim to control the government of the United States." The enemy within, subversion, treason— the Republicans were endeavoring to stir up suspicion and fear. But with the war still on—and with Russia helping by battling Hitler's armies—the scare tactics didn't stick. Not yet. Roosevelt decisively defeated Dewey.

After Roosevelt's death in 1945 and Vice President Harry Truman's ascension to the highest office, the Republicans, blasting the Democrats for the administration's postwar policy, won control of both houses of Congress in 1946 and throttled Truman's legislative agenda. (Representative B. Carroll Reece of Tennessee, the Republican Party chair, had called the midterm campaign a contest of "Communism vs. Americanism.") Working with Southern Democrats, they beat back the civil rights legislation and taxes of the New Deal. They also weakened labor law to benefit corporations. And the Republicans ramped up the anticommunist crusade.

In Republican hands, the House Un-American Activities Committees— often referred to as HUAC—intensified its hunt for subversives. The committee held hearings designed to show communists had taken hold of Hollywood. One friendly witness was an actor named Ronald Reagan. He testified that he abhorred communists and their underhanded tactics but noted he didn't think they could get too far in the movie industry. He added an important caveat: "I never as a citizen want to see our country become urged, by either fear or resentment of this group, that we ever compromise with any of our democratic principles."

Fear, though, was becoming the main currency of the party Reagan would one day lead. Serving on HUAC was a freshman Republican from southern California named Richard Nixon, who had won his seat in the Republican sweep of 1946 by decrying the liberal Democratic incumbent as "more Socialistic and Communistic than Democratic." He assumed a prominent role when HUAC, in hearings covered by the new medium of television, examined the explosive charge from Whittaker Chambers, a self-confessed former communist operative, that Alger Hiss, a past State Department official, had been part of his secret spy ring in the 1930s—an accusation Hiss vehemently denied. The Hiss controversy would turn Nixon into a political star and bolster the dark conspiratorial narrative Republicans increasingly relied upon: Subversion from within was a clear and present danger, and the Democrats were too soft to stand up to the enemy or, worse, were secretly allied with it.

This ploy wouldn't be enough for the GOP to win the White House. In 1948, the Republicans again nominated Dewey—once more aggravating the Taft conservatives, who believed Taft's turn had come—and quilted together a platform that included New Deal notions (such as expanding Social Security), calls for lower taxes, and strident anticommunism. The Democrats were racked by a three-way split. Truman had the party's nomination, but progressive Democrats nominated Henry Wallace, Roosevelt's second vice president, and Dixiecrat Democrats, enraged by Truman's civil rights measures, ran South Carolina Governor Strom Thurmond, a staunch segregationist. With the Democrats divided, Republicans had cause for optimism. (Thurmond claimed that Truman was hiding "the extent to which Communists and Communist sympathizers have honeycombed the Administration and dictated its policies.")

On the campaign trail, Dewey avoided all-out denunciations of the New Deal or slashing attacks on Truman—which disappointed conservatives in the party. He also developed a reputation for dishing out banalities; he told one audience, "Your future is still ahead of you." Truman ran a "Give 'em Hell" campaign against the "Do Nothing" Republican Congress and called for a national health insurance program. He slammed Dewey as a "front man" for fascism.

The polls looked good for Dewey. Before the results were in, the *Chicago Daily Tribune* printed an edition declaring "DEWEY DEFEATS TRUMAN." He did not, and Truman's win helped the Democrats regain control of Congress. This was the fifth presidential loss in a row for the GOP. For Taft and his fellow conservatives, a deepening resentment was reaffirmed: the Eastern moderates had again prevailed in selecting a nominee too willing to accept big-government activism, and this Me Too approach had resulted in another failure. Taft believed the Rs had to take a hardline approach to the New Deal Democrats and draw a firm distinction.

For decades, the Republicans had accused the Democrats of being anti-American, traitors to the republic (see the Civil War), or in league with socialism and labor unrest imported from overseas. The party's embrace of Red-baiting had not yet paid off. But events would conspire to render this attack more profitable.

In August 1949, the Soviets conducted their first atomic test. The American nuclear monopoly evaporated, and an arms race began. Weeks later, the Chinese Communists claimed victory in their civil war against the Nationalists and declared the establishment of the People's Republic of China. With communists assuming power in China and developing the bomb in Russia, many Americans were unnerved by this new global order. The war against fascism had been won, yet the nation still faced dire threats. On February 3, 1950, Klaus Fuchs, a British physicist who had worked at the Manhattan Project, was arrested for having spied for the Soviet Union. Two weeks earlier, Alger Hiss had been found guilty of perjury and sentenced to five years in prison. For the Red-chasers, here was evidence of a threat from within that was in cahoots with the threat from abroad. The Republicans seized the opening.

Five days after the Hiss verdict, Nixon, then running for the US Senate, delivered a four-hour speech on the Hiss case on the House floor. He said that the episode had revealed a "sinister type of activity" that permitted "the enemy to guide and shape our policy." Nixon was fearmongering about a vast conspiracy without providing clear details—and calling for a crusade against subversion. He would go on to win his Senate race by Red-baiting his opponent, Representative Helen Gahagan Douglas, who, he brayed, was "pink right down to her underwear."

One Republican, though, was about to elbow past Nixon to lead the Reds-under-the-beds pack. On February 9, Senator Joe McCarthy, a first-termer from Wisconsin, was slated to give a speech at a Lincoln Day event organized by the Ohio County Republican Women's Club in Wheeling, West Virginia. He had brought with him two speeches: one on housing policy, the other on communist subversion. Undecided on which one to deliver, he asked a former Republican congressman for advice. Communism, the fellow said.

Soon after, in the Colonnade Room of the McLure Hotel, McCarthy declared to those GOP ladies that he had in his hand "a list of 205 . . . names that were made known to the secretary of state as being members of the Communist Party and who nevertheless are still working and shaping policy in the State Department." That was a lie. McCarthy apparently was referring to a 1946 letter from then–Secretary of State James Byrnes noting that the department's screening of 4,000 employees transferred into the agency had found 284 employees who were deemed not suitable for permanent employment and 79 of them had been dismissed. That left 205. But it was unclear if these employees were members of the Communist Party or what had happened to them in the subsequent years. Many of the men who had been fired by the State Department in the late 1940s for supposed security reasons were canned because they were homosexuals, not communists.

The truth didn't matter to McCarthy. He hit on a theme that would resonate for years: "The reason why we find ourselves in a position of impotency is not because our only powerful potential enemy has sent men to invade our shores, but rather because of the traitorous action of those…who have had all the benefits that the wealthiest nation on earth has had to offer—the finest homes, the finest college education, and the finest jobs in government we can give." The *true* threat, McCarthy alleged, came from inside. From the elites. From the people in charge. From fellow Americans who were disloyal.

Other Republicans in recent years had attacked the Truman administration and Democrats for coddling and encouraging communists. But with his phony list, McCarthy had broken through. Front-page headlines alerted the world to his frightening accusation. Basking in the attention, he sent a letter to Truman demanding Secretary of State Dean Acheson provide a list of all the "bad security risks" in the department who had "communist connections." He added, "Failure on your part will label the Democratic Party of being the bedfellow of international communism."

The details didn't matter for McCarthy. He was widely regarded by the Washington press corps and other politicians as a fabulist (and well-known as a gambler and an excessive drinker). Though Republican politicians—and some conservative Democrats—had for years endeavored to exploit popular fear of communism, McCarthy had succeeded in finding a way to manipulate and heighten an unease that had been creeping through the land. With his stunt, McCarthy had solidified his party's relationship with paranoia and started a political streak that would stretch for decades.

CHAPTER 2

Backstory II
Fear and Loathing in America

Paranoia, conspiracy-mongering, and hysteria have been part of American public life since before the nation was born.

The Salem witch trials of the 1690s marked a delusional panic that occurred in the Massachusetts colony during a time of economic tension and increasing rivalry between Salem Village and the more affluent Salem Town. More than two hundred people—mostly women—were accused (often based on the "spectral evidence" of dreams and visions) of scheming with Satan. It turned out to be just a big mistake. Within a few years, the local authorities proclaimed the affair a tragic error and declared the trials unlawful—too late for the nineteen unfortunates who had been hanged and the eighty-one-year-old man pressed to death by stones. The colony moved on.

The American Revolution itself was driven, at least in part, by conspiratorial thinking. In his classic and Pulitzer Prize–winning work, *The Ideological Origins of the American Revolution*, historian Bernard Bailyn, who had studied years' worth of colonial pamphleteering, noted that colonists widely shared the belief that England's repressive policies were "a deliberate assault launched surreptitiously by plotters against liberty both in England and in America." A small band of wicked schemers across the ocean were apparently conniving to destroy England's constitutional order and suppress freedom there, as well as to enslave the people of the New World. Literally. Samuel Adams, for one, claimed the British intended to turn all the white colonists into slaves. In this view, the colonists were not in a power-play policy dispute with King George III; they were the victims (as were English citizens) of the machinations of a nefarious cabal. As Bailyn put it, "It was this—the overwhelming evidence, as they saw it, that they were faced with conspirators against liberty determined at all costs to gain ends which their words dissembled—that was signaled to the colonists after 1763, and it was this above all else that in the end propelled them into Revolution."

Conspiracy and politics would forever intermix in the new nation. Less than a decade after the establishment of the US government, a major conspiracy theory shook the American republic—one that was brazenly fed and crassly exploited by prominent politicians.

————

In May 1798, Jedidiah Morse, the stern-looking pastor of First Congregational Church in Charlestown, Massachusetts, took to the pulpit and delivered the first of several fiery sermons that would set off a tidal wave of paranoia and fear. At that time, the young country was close to war with France, which had seized American ships in response to the United States' support of Great Britain in its ongoing clash with the First Republic of France. The US-France conflict—called the Quasi-War—was transpiring with the nation bitterly divided between Jeffersonians, who leaned toward France and admired the populist values of the revolution, and the Federalists, who favored royalist England and a more orderly power structure.

Morse, a Federalist and supporter of John Adams, the current president, had an explanation for the discord and rancor infecting American society. He pointed to a book published the previous year by a Scottish scientist named John Robison that carried an unwieldy title: *Proofs of a Conspiracy Against All the Religions and Governments of Europe, carried on in the Secret Meetings of Free Masons, Illuminati, and Reading Societies.* It was a crank job.

Robison described the shocking details of a secret Masonic society called the Illuminati that had emerged in Bavaria in 1776 purportedly with the dastardly goal of "rooting out all the religious establishments, and overturning all the existing governments of Europe." He maintained it was behind the French Revolution of 1789—a societal upturning that had scared the hell out of ruling elites and god-fearing people in Europe and the new United States. Even more alarming, this sinister group aimed to cultivate sensual pleasures, corrupt women, and undermine property rights. Its members were concocting a tea that would cause abortion and a substance that "blinds or kills when spurted in the face." Robison's claims about the secret society's ultimate aims were a bit confusing. He contended that the Illuminati were a danger to Protestantism and posed "the threat of both 'popery' and 'atheism.'" It could, he said, lead to either religious "absolutism" or "radical democracy."

At the time, some evangelical Federalists worried about the preservation of the United States as a Christian nation. Using Robison's book as his text, Morse declared the present trouble in the land was the handiwork of this clandestine crew tied to France that was conniving to overthrow all government and "abolish Christianity." Timothy Dwight IV, the president of Yale University, endorsed Morse's contention, and anti-Illuminatism raged through Protestant New England, with Federalists accusing Thomas Jefferson and the Democrats of being in alliance with this vast and insidious conspiratorial network.

During a Thanksgiving sermon, Morse blamed the Illuminati for a long list of American ills, including political division and inefficient government, and he identified it as the force that destroyed the Greek and Roman empires and the French monarchy. To the published version of the sermon, he attached a forty-five-page appendix with purported evidence of all this devious intrigue. The publication was a hit. Clergy across New England took up Morse's diatribe against the Illuminati. Federalist officeholders cited it. John Jay, the first chief justice of the Supreme Court, wrote to Morse to cheer him on. Adams himself echoed Morse when he declared the nation was threatened by the "hostile designs and insidious acts of a foreign nation" that was "subversive of the foundations of all religious, moral, and social obligations."

Americans, at least those loyal to the Federalists, were buying Morse's bizarre ravings. In 1799, he announced he had come into possession of proof "that secret societies under the influence and direction of France, holding principles subversive of our religion and government, existed somewhere in this country." This was a not-so-veiled reference to the secretive Jeffersonian Democratic-Republican clubs that had sprung up in favorable response to the French Revolution and embraced radical democracy. Morse claimed he even had a list of one hundred officers and members of the Illuminati organization in Virginia, "secret enemies" determined to spread "infidelity, impiety, and immorality." (Who was from Virginia? Thomas Jefferson.)

Before Morse kicked off this craziness, George Washington and Adams had expressed the suspicion that France was conspiring against America. Now the Federalists could point to the Illuminati plot as evidence their political opponents were covertly in league with a foreign foe. But the Illuminati panic was not merely a happy coincidence for the Federalists. Oliver Wolcott Jr., Adams's Treasury secretary, had slipped Morse the supposedly incriminating documents, which were likely phony. The Federalists were not only exploiting the paranoia that had taken hold within the populace; they were goosing it along. This was good politics for them.

The Illuminati scare had concrete consequences. It helped grease the way for the Alien and Sedition Acts, enacted by Adams and the Federalists, which made it a crime to "print, utter, or publish... any false, scandalous, and malicious writing" about the government and allowed the president to deport any alien he suspected was involved in "secret machinations against the government." The political establishment was capitalizing on irrational extremism to undermine the opposition and to limit democratic expression.

The hysteria Morse conjured up did not last. A newspaper revealed a letter from a prominent German scientist to Morse dismissing Robison as a crackpot and reporting that the Illuminati order was both harmless and long gone. (The group had never numbered more than a couple of thousand and had been shut down in 1785.) This correspondence and Morse's unsuccessful efforts to suppress it demolished his credibility. With the chief pitchman of the Illuminati conspiracy theory diminished, this grand idea faded fast—and did so even before it could impact the 1800 presidential election, in which Jefferson defeated his archrival Adams.

Years later, Morse would descend deep into debt and be expelled from his congregation. But with this episode, he had demonstrated that a preposterous and irrational notion that lacked solid proof could be wildly promulgated, accepted by many citizens, and used by politicians to stir up fear and demonize opponents. Soon after Morse's death in 1826, it would happen again—in a much bigger way.

———

On the morning of September 11, 1826, Captain William Morgan—who may or may not have been a military captain—was abducted from his home in Batavia, a town in upstate New York, and imprisoned in a jail fifty miles away for owing a debt of two dollars and sixty-five cents. Oddly, a man Morgan did not know tendered his bail, and Morgan was soon spotted being forced into a carriage while reportedly yelling, "Murder!" What next happened to him was never ascertained. But the rumors and speculation that followed would spark a panic and the creation of a new political party based entirely upon a conspiracy theory.

Earlier, Morgan and a local newspaper publisher had devised a plan to reveal to the world the secrets of the Freemasons, a secretive social order that had been around for several hundred years. George Washington, Benjamin Franklin, and other founders of the nation had been Masons. In the United States, it had become an organization of elites—businessmen, lawyers, doctors—many with political connections. Naturally, this aroused popular suspicion. What went on in Masonic lodges? Did the Masons plot to enhance the fortunes and privileges of one another?

When word got out that Morgan planned to spill Masonic secrets, local Masons feared the coming exposé. Morgan was threatened with prosecution for petty debt. The office of his partner, the newspaper publisher, was torched. Then Morgan was seized and arrested—and disappeared. His case became a cause célèbre. Had the powerful and clandestine Masons kidnapped a fellow to protect their secrets? Had Morgan been murdered?

Investigations were conducted. Several Masons were indicted for kidnapping Morgan, and at a trial three pleaded guilty to conspiring to abduct him, while insisting they had no clue as to his final fate. So there had indeed been a Masonic plot. But the justified public anger over this crime would morph into wider and deeper conspiratorial paranoia—ripe for abuse.

Anti-Masonic sentiment spurred by the Morgan mystery spread rapidly and seeped into the political realm. In upstate New York, public meetings were held to express outrage at Masons. Masonic politicians were denigrated. A printer named Thurlow Weed began recruiting anti-Masonic candidates for local elections. Their agenda had one simple plank: boot Masons out of office. In the 1827 election, Weed's Anti-Masons racked up an impressive accomplishment; this new party elected fifteen comrades to the New York state legislature.

This movement was not just about the vanishing of Morgan. Historians have looked back on anti-Masonry as a popular expression of anxiety over dramatic changes within American society. The nation was starting to shift from an agrarian society to an industrialized one, with immigrants flowing in, the labor market changing, and cities expanding and becoming more influential. At the same time, a debate over the role of religion in America was underway, with religious orthodoxy facing challenges from liberal doctrines, including the idea that laws forbidding work on Sunday improperly imposed religion upon civic life. One hundred and forty years later, political scientists Seymour Martin Lipset and Earl Raab would note that the "key social characteristics" of the Anti-Mason movement were "its appeal to the less privileged, less educated, more ecologically isolated rural population, with its already growing sense of conflict with the urban centers of affluence, culture, change, and immigration." It was a movement of unease and resentment.

Detractors regarded Masonry as an impediment to opportunity, proof of a closed economic order controlled by a covert and powerful elite that traded favors within its ranks and protected its own. The Anti-Mason movement resembled the Illuminati scare, and a secret society could certainly be seen as a threat to republicanism. But its critics condemned it with apocalyptic fervor. A popular anti-Masonic tract called the Masons "an engine of Satan…dark, unfruitful, selfish, demoralizing, blasphemous, murderous, anti-republican, and anti Christian." Anti-Masonic newspapers accused Masons of murdering their foes.

This fire raced across New England and south to Maryland and west to Ohio. In 1828, President John Quincy Adams threw in his lot with this folk movement that had turned into a political powerhouse. He declared, "I am not, never was, and never shall be a Freemason." His opponent that year was Andrew Jackson, a Mason whom Adams had defeated in 1824. Adams's embrace of this new conspiratorial political force, however, did not help him. He lost to Jackson. Yet Anti-Masons captured more seats in state legislatures, and several were elected to the US House of Representatives. The Anti-Masons joined the opposition to Jackson.

As Richard Hofstadter pointed out many years later, anti-Masonic fever "was joined and used by a great many men who did not share its original anti-Masonic feelings. It attracted, for example, the support of several reputable statesmen who had only a mild sympathy with its fundamental bias." That is, cynical politicians were harvesting hyperbolic paranoia for their own ends. An Anti-Mason was elected governor in Vermont. In Massachusetts, the party nabbed almost a third of the seats in the state House of Representatives.

But the new party faced a fundamental problem: Many of its members refused to work with politicians who would not publicly castigate Masonry. That made it tough for the party to function as a productive member of the anti-Jackson coalition. Its 1832 presidential nominee won one state, Vermont, and the party began to wither. Hardcore anti-Masonry slid toward the fringes of political discourse.

Within a few years, remnants of the Anti-Masons would be welcomed within a new party being formed, the Whigs. This marked what would become a common practice in American politics: establishment elites enlisting popular resentments and fears. As Lipset and Raab observed, "This alliance and subsequent merger between the relatively uneducated believers in hidden conspiracies and the privileged, well-educated Whig conservatives, many of whom were or had been Masons, was to be the first of a number of occasions in which extremist bigotry was to find its political home in the conservative Whig or Republican parties."

In the coming decades, political extremism would be driven not only by fanciful conspiracy fantasies but also by outright bigotry against two overlapping groups: Catholics and immigrants. And there was a connection—a family tie—between the earlier paranoia and the religious hatred infusing American politics.

Samuel Morse, the son of Jedidiah Morse and creator of Morse code, followed in his father's footsteps by becoming a virulent conspiracist. In his 1835 book, *Foreign Conspiracy Against the Liberties of the United States*, he warned that Catholicism was "a system of the darkest political intrigue and despotism" determined to seize control of the United States and destroy Protestantism. "A conspiracy exists," he wrote, and "its plans are already in operation…We are attacked in a vulnerable quarter which cannot be defended by our ships, our forts, or our armies." The goal was nothing less than to install a Catholic emperor to reign over the United States. The enemy was within, he claimed: Jesuit missionaries reinforced by the rising population of Catholic immigrants. Waving the universal banner of all devotees of conspiracism, Morse proclaimed, "We must awake, or we are lost."

Anti-Catholicism and nativism, rising in response to swelling immigration, spawned new political parties: the American Republican Party, founded by a secretive nativist order, and the Native American Party, aka the Know-Nothings. (That nickname referred to what members were supposed to tell outsiders who asked about the party.) As they had done in the 1830s with the leftovers of the Anti-Masonic Party, the Whigs formed coalitions with these parties powered by anti-Catholic and nativistic animosity. (In 1844, anti-immigrant riots in Philadelphia led to the deaths of twenty-nine people and the burning of a Catholic church.) When the Whigs disintegrated in the early 1850s, the Northern antislavery wing of the Know-Nothings were welcomed into the new Republican Party. During the 1856 and 1858 elections, the Republicans collaborated closely with these nativistic bigots in several states.

Lincoln privately expressed misgivings about the Know-Nothings. In an 1855 letter to a friend, he had written, "I am not a Know-Nothing. That is certain. How could I be? How can any one who abhors the oppression of negroes, be in favor of degrading classes of white people?" Yet as a presidential candidate in 1860, Lincoln kept mum about his feelings toward the Know-Nothings. His party wanted their votes.

After the Civil War, anti-Catholic extremism remained a potent political force that Republican politicians sought to harness. (A popular conspiracy theory was that Lincoln's assassination had been a Catholic plot.) The Republican state convention of 1875 in Indiana proclaimed it was "incompatible with American citizenship to pay allegiance to any foreign power, civil or ecclesiastical." In other words, Catholics, because they followed the lead of a Pope in Rome, couldn't be US citizens. Rutherford Hayes, while running for Ohio governor that same year, claimed Democrats were conspiring with Catholics to create "sectarian military organizations." And President Grant declared in a speech that if there were to be another civil war, the battle would be between Protestant "patriotism and intelligence" and Catholic "superstition, ambition, and ignorance."

As Hayes pursued the presidency in 1876, Republicans strived to exploit Protestant paranoia over Catholicism. One Republican group openly asserted that should Democrats win, the Catholic Church would "obtain control of our national affairs." Anti-Catholic secret societies proliferated and formed the American Alliance to oppose Catholic political organizations. When the group endorsed Hayes for president, he heartily accepted its support.

Eight years later, the Republicans went perhaps too far with anti-Catholic bigotry. At a New York City rally for presidential nominee James Blaine, a Methodist reverend introduced the candidate and exclaimed, "We are Republicans and don't propose to leave our party and identify ourselves with a party whose antecedents have been 'rum, Romanism, and rebellion.'" The anti-Catholic slur against the Democrats (*drunk, treasonous, Catholics!*) sparked an uproar, especially in the Empire State, which subsequently went for Democratic candidate Grover Cleveland, who won the tight contest by one-half of a percentage point in the popular vote.

———

Throughout the postbellum period, the Democratic Party cultivated its own relationship with hatred. The Ku Klux Klan, formed after the war, was terrorizing—and murdering—freed slaves and Black elected officials (and their white allies) throughout the South. Many Southern Democrats joined its ranks. In 1868, Klan leader Nathan Bedford Forrest—a former Confederate general responsible for a massacre of Union soldiers who were mostly Black—attended the Democratic convention in New York as a delegate. That gathering nominated Horatio Seymour, the former New York state governor who opposed full restoration of civil and political rights for freed slaves. It chose as his running mate Francis Preston Blair Jr., a former Union army general who would campaign as a foe of emancipation, warning that the rule of "a semi-barbarous race of blacks who are worshippers of fetishes and polygamists" would "subject the white women to their unbridled lust." One Democratic slogan that emerged from the convention: "Our Ticket, Our Motto: This is a White Man's Country; Let White Men Rule."

The two parties were each capitalizing on deep-rooted American hatreds. The Republicans championed rights for the new Black citizenry (while arguing among themselves how far to go in this regard), but they calculatingly milked the vicious prejudice within their Protestant base against Catholics and immigrants. The Democrats were more welcoming to these new *white* Americans, while they either accepted or advanced the virulent racism that was developing into the brutal caste system of segregation. Each party was peddling its own poison.

———

World War I yielded new forms of bigotry for politicians to manipulate. Internal subversion waged by foreign foes became a fierce national fear, and anti-German hysteria spread. Thousands of Germans were interned in camps. US government propaganda warned that "German agents are everywhere." The 1918 flu pandemic was blamed on a German company. Moreover, the war led to attacks on elements deemed "un-American"—which had an elastic definition. It could be radicals, Jews, or immigrants, particularly the Irish and the German. Enemies were afoot. Antiwar activists were hounded—and worse. When a band of vigilantes in Butte, Montana, lynched Frank Little, an antiwar union organizer, Vice President Thomas Marshall endorsed the murder, saying the hanging had a "salutary effect." Here was President Woodrow Wilson's number two legitimizing political violence. And within the Justice Department, a young clerk named J. Edgar Hoover was assigned the task of tracking enemy aliens and dissenters, as the prelude to a fresh hysteria: the first Red Scare.

No sooner had the United States and its allies defeated Germany in World War I than a new threat gripped the nation and caused panic: Bolshevism. In the aftermath of the war—and following the Russian Revolution—the United States was undergoing changes unsettling for many. The economy was stalled, with jobs scarce and prices rising. As the nation grew increasingly secular and metropolitan, massive Black immigration from the South was radically altering the demographics of Northern cities. The Nineteenth Amendment provided women the right to vote. Anti-immigration sentiment ran high. The fear of external forces subverting America was not abating but intensifying.

In a postwar speech, Wilson assailed hyphenated Americans—those who identified with the overseas lands of their ancestors—as a threat to the country: "Any man who carries a hyphen about with him carries a dagger that he is ready to plunge into the vitals of this Republic whenever he gets the chance." (A few years earlier, former President Theodore Roosevelt had voiced a similar sentiment: "There is no room in this country for hyphenated Americanism.") The preservation of Americanism had become a national priority, and foreignness was depicted as a danger—and for some Americans, nothing was more foreign than the radical ideas of socialism and communism. Bolsheviks were the new Illuminati.

Labor activism triggered much of the alarm. In early 1919, a general strike in Seattle was widely assailed as Marxist subversion and a troubling sign that the radicalism sweeping through Europe had burrowed into the United States. The *Washington Post* decried the work stoppage as "the stepping stone to a Bolshevized America." The strike failed within days, but a congressional committee later released a report exclaiming it had been an attempted communist revolution and part of a clandestine Bolshevik plot. On May Day, bands of veterans and self-proclaimed patriots attacked labor rallies and socialist parades.

Real events did warrant genuine concern. Moscow announced it intended to spark revolutions around the globe. Anarchists in the United States mounted bombing attacks against US government officials and robber barons such as John D. Rockefeller. One bomb blew up the Georgetown home of Attorney General A. Mitchell Palmer. In response, Palmer declared war on Bolshevism. He instructed the Justice Department to devise a plan to round up and deport alien radicals. The department also started disseminating propaganda that asserted a communist revolution threatened the United States. Palmer tagged Hoover to manage an intelligence unit to gather information on the radicals scheming against the government.

Then came the raids. Under Palmer's orders, federal agents rounded up thousands of suspected radicals. Many were guilty only of having a foreign accent. Most of the subsequent deportation orders were tossed out. These arrests didn't do much to stem the tide of worker protests. But the raids offered Palmer a platform for fomenting paranoia among the citizenry. "The blaze of revolution was sweeping over every American institution of law and order," Palmer proclaimed. He warned that this virus was infecting American workplaces, churches, schools, and "the sacred corners of American homes, seeking to replace marriage vows with libertine laws, burning up the foundations of society." Put simply, he was scaring folks and promoting fanaticism—as he pursued the Democratic presidential nomination (which he would not obtain). Ahead of May Day, 1920, he and Hoover's division predicted a Bolshevik uprising, with widespread riots, bombing, and assassinations. Then...the day passed without incident. Palmer's star began to fall.

In 1924, with nativism and Red fear still active currents, both parties engaged with other strains of extremism. President Coolidge was campaigning for another White House term, and that summer he welcomed Henry Ford as a visitor to his Vermont farm. Ford, with his creation of the Model T and his pioneering of mass production, had become an American folk hero over the previous sixteen years. He was also a raging antisemite and conspiracy theorist—probably the most prominent conspiracist in the nation. Starting in 1919 and continuing for years, the *Dearborn Independent*, a weekly he controlled, ran vicious antisemitic articles that decried an international conspiracy of bankers, Bolsheviks, and Jews. This included reprinting portions of one of the most nefarious hoaxes in modern time: *The Protocols of the Elders of Zion*, an antisemitic tract that originated in Russia in the early 1900s. Ford's newspaper claimed the Jews were behind the Illuminati and the Masons. A collection of the paper's antisemitic work was published as a book titled *The International Jew: The World's Foremost Problem*. In one interview, Ford blamed "Jew financiers" for secretly controlling unions and causing labor unrest.

A few months after the Vermont visit, Ford provided Coolidge his valuable endorsement, and the president accepted it. Ford's vile bigotry was no deal killer.

In the same campaign season, the Ku Klux Klan was involved with both the Republicans and the Democrats. The Klan had withered in the 1870s, but it reconstituted with a broader scope in 1915, following the release of D. W. Griffith's racist film *The Birth of a Nation*, which depicted the Klan as avenging angels protecting white women and white society from vicious emancipated slaves. (The movie was screened at the White House, with President Wilson in attendance.) Now the Klan's enemies list expanded beyond Black Americans and their allies to Catholics, Jews, foreign-born minorities, Bolshevism, and urban political machines, and its focus widened from advocacy of white supremacy to championing fundamentalist Christian values and "pure Americanism." Its members had won political offices in Indiana, Oregon, Texas, Oklahoma, Colorado, and elsewhere. And it was espousing a host of conspiracy theories: A secret Catholic army was preparing to take the country by force; Irish Catholic police officers had a plan to execute Protestants; the Pope was conspiring to seize control of Washington; Harding, who had died of a heart attack, had been assassinated by "hypnotic telepathic thought" from Jesuits; and the Jews had orchestrated World War I *and* the Bolshevik Revolution and possessed a secret plan to impoverish Christians.

This new Klan played significant roles at the Democratic and Republican conventions of 1924. At the GOP gathering in Cleveland, Klan loyalists successfully lobbied the Republicans to prevent any condemnation of the KKK from entering the party platform. Impressed by this demonstration of the group's political clout, *Time* magazine placed Imperial Wizard Hiram

Evans, the head of the Klan, on its cover and dubbed the Republican event the "Kleveland Konvention."

The white supremacist group shaped the Democrats' shindig in New York City's Madison Square Garden more significantly. Prior to the convention, Senator Oscar Underwood of Alabama had run for the party's presidential nomination as a fierce opponent of the Klan. He tarred the group as a "national menace." The Klan had fought back by assailing Underwood as the "Jew, jug, and Jesuit candidate." With the Klan against him, Underwood had fared poorly in Southern primaries and was out of the running by the time of the convention.

As the delegates arrived—hundreds reportedly were Klansmen—the two leading Democratic candidates were the Catholic New York Governor Al Smith and Senator William Gibbs McAdoo, a Southern transplant to California who had been Treasury secretary for Woodrow Wilson, his father-in-law. Delegates from the South and West couldn't stand Smith, the big-city pol who opposed prohibition. They rallied behind McAdoo as their only choice—and so, too, did the Klan delegates, who railed against Smith as a Catholic from "Jew York." McAdoo was no known Klan sympathizer. But all this put him in a bind. If McAdoo renounced the Klan, he would split his devotees and have no chance of beating Smith. So McAdoo and his camp stayed quiet about the KKK—but privately McAdoo pressed his aides to seek support from Klan delegates.

Smith's allies insisted on adding a plank to the party's platform denouncing the Klan. For days, delegates clashed over this. Fistfights erupted, chaos ensued. Eventually, the convention narrowly voted down the anti-Klan measure by three-quarters of one vote. The tumult continued, as the convention in the miserable summer heat battled through 103 ballots to pick a nominee. When McAdoo gave up after the ninetieth ballot, Smith and Underwood remained in the race, both fiercely opposed by the Klan. The delegates eventually settled on a little-known former congressman named John W. Davis. With the tarnish of the Teapot Dome scandal on the Republicans in the White House, 1924 appeared to hold promise for the Democrats. But because of the Klan's influence within the party, the Democrats wound up saddled with a weak nominee.

During the fall campaign, a key question was whether Coolidge or Davis would condemn the Klan. Davis did, but Coolidge refused to say anything. It was an odd situation. The Democrats had torn themselves apart due to the Klan, while the Republicans had reached an accommodation with the racists and bigots. Meanwhile, Coolidge exploited Red fear, telling voters the election was a question of "whether America will allow itself to be degraded into a communistic and socialistic state, or whether it will remain American."

On Election Day, Coolidge defeated Davis in a wipeout. Imperial Wizard Evans declared victory: "We Klansmen may be pardoned for our just pride in the part we have played." The Republicans had outmaneuvered the Democrats on this field of hate.

The next decade was a time of legitimate fear in the United States. The nation was plunged into a severe depression. Up to 13 million Americans were without jobs. Food lines stretched through every city. Fascism was rising overseas. It might have been an opportune moment for political extremism of the right and left. Yet in the 1932 elections, the communists drew only 103,314 votes, and the socialists pulled less than they had in 1920 or 1912. Huey Long, the populist Democratic senator in Louisiana, though, successfully initiated his Share Our Wealth movement that championed wealth redistribution. And hundreds of right-wing extremist groups arose, many of a protofascist bent. Father Charles Coughlin, a populist-minded, conspiracy-theory-pushing Catholic priest with a massive radio audience, created his own movement— the National Union for Social Justice—and he guided it into the ugly shoals of antisemitism and fascism.

These efforts shaped the political atmosphere, and many Republicans (and some conservative Democrats) echoed the sentiments underlying extremist assaults on FDR and his "Jew Deal." When Roosevelt proposed a reorganization of government agencies in 1938, GOP critics compared him to Hitler. Representative Charles Eaton, a New Jersey Republican, accused Roosevelt of imposing fascism in the United States: "You talk about dictatorship. Why...it is here now. The advance guard of totalitarianism has enthroned itself in the Government in Washington." Other Republicans accused FDR of being a Red. Taft huffed that the New Deal would "practically abandon the whole theory of American government and inaugurate what is in fact socialism." At the same time, Coughlin promoted the baseless claim that Roosevelt was scheming to seize all church schools. Extremist and paranoid hyperbole was in vogue.

The armies of Hitler swept across Europe in the spring of 1940, and Roosevelt sought to assist Great Britain. Yet as the Second World War descended upon Europe, isolationists in the United States, led by Robert Wood, the head of Sears, Roebuck and Company, and Jay Hormel, the meat packing magnate, formed the America First Committee. This was a bipartisan effort that included members of FDR's own party, most notably Senator Burton Wheeler of Montana. Some America Firsters sincerely believed that keeping the United States out of the European war was the best policy for the nation. Some were driven by a fear of communism and viewed Nazi Germany as a bulwark against the Bolshevik threat. But conspiratorial paranoia infected the isolationist movement.

Many within the America First movement, historian William Leuchtenburg wrote later, believed that a conspiracy comprised of Jews, Roosevelt, and British capitalists was intriguing to plunge the United States into war. To enhance their political standing, the America Firsters partnered with voices of extremism. Wood and Lulu White Wheeler, the senator's wife, welcomed the followers of Coughlin—now a full-fledged antisemite—into their ranks. A Kansas leader of America First claimed, "Roosevelt and his wife are Jewish and that goes 90 percent for his Administration." Senator Wheeler threatened to investigate "interventionists" in Hollywood for shaping public opinion related to the war—a move widely regarded as a veiled antisemitic assault. Senator Gerald Nye of North Dakota, another America Firster, spread similar slop, accusing Hollywood of pushing prowar propaganda and trying to "drug the reason of the American people" and "rouse war fever."

Charles Lindbergh, the onetime flying ace who in 1938 had accepted a medal presented to him in Germany on behalf of Hitler and who was the most prominent America Firster, made it all too obvious in a September 1941 speech. He lambasted a conspiracy of "war agitators" who "have been pressing this country toward war" and named "the British, the Jewish, and the Roosevelt administration." He added that "a number of capitalists, Anglophiles, and intellectuals" were "behind these groups, but of lesser importance," and that "Communistic groups" were also participants in this anti-American subterfuge.

The antisemitism and bigoted conspiracies of the isolationists came to a sudden halt three months later at Pearl Harbor. What Lindbergh and the other American Firsters had to say no longer mattered.

The United States and its allies, with the Soviet Union, won the war in four years, concluding the hostilities with the deployment of a new source of dread: atomic destruction. In the meantime, conspiracy theories had arisen regarding Pearl Harbor and the dubious allegation that Roosevelt had allowed the attack to happen to provide cause for America's entry into the war. Republicans attempted to mine these suspicions, and toward the war's end in 1945, they used a congressional inquiry of Pearl Harbor to push the idea that FDR had mounted a monstrous plot. One party operative advised

GOP leaders that they desperately needed to take advantage of this issue to regain the White House. If this ploy didn't work, he warned, the Democrats could end up controlling "the entire political and economic system of the country."

This Republican effort to cast Roosevelt, not the Japanese military, as the *real* villain of Pearl Harbor fizzled. The GOP failed to catalyze the sort of frenzy that had been generated in years past by the anti-Illuminati, Anti-Masons, or anti-Reds. Perhaps this was too narrow a conspiracy theory to weave into political gold. It didn't strike deep-rooted fears or resentments.

In a short while, though, the Republicans would engage in much more effective conspiracy-peddling and fearmongering that would shape the political landscape for years to come.

CHAPTER 3

The General and the Scoundrel

It was on a train that Dwight Eisenhower surrendered to Joe McCarthy and allowed the senator's demagoguery of panic and paranoia to roll along. The legendary American general who had overseen the daring Allied invasion at Normandy that led to the vanquishing of Nazi Germany did so because he didn't want to lose any votes.

In early October 1952, Eisenhower was campaigning for president as a Republican. He had entered the race late, and at a GOP convention full of fierce infighting, Eisenhower had snatched the nomination from Senator Robert Taft, the long-suffering hero of the party's conservatives. Once again, embittered Republican right-wingers griped about being outplayed by the Northeastern moderate wing of the party that had pushed through an internationalist who accepted the New Deal social order. Ike was a war hero, but he was currently president of Columbia University. It didn't get more liberal big-city elitist than that.

By this point, much of the party and its voters were enthralled with McCarthy. Ever since the junior senator from Wisconsin had bogusly proclaimed in early 1950 to possess a list of commies in the State Department, he had been on a rampage. His anticommunism had mushroomed into full-fledged conspiracism—with Republican leaders backing his overwrought crusade against the Red Menace and its purported Democratic abettors. During the 1950 midterm election, McCarthy had targeted Senator Millard Tydings, a Maryland Democrat. Tydings chaired a Senate committee that had investigated McCarthy's claim about communists in the State Department and concluded that his charges were "a hoax perpetuated on...the American people" and "perhaps the most nefarious campaign of half-truths and untruth in the history of the Republic." With McCarthy gunning after him, Tydings lost his reelection bid, and Republicans, whether or not they abided by McCarthy's crude and deceptive methods, now viewed McCarthy as a potent weapon to deploy against Democrats. Wisconsin Republican leader Thomas Coleman put it crassly: "It all comes down to this: are we going to win an election or aren't we?"

McCarthy's exploitation of the fears and jitters coursing through America in the postwar years—a time of great prosperity and widespread apprehension—was good politics for a party that had been locked out of the White House for two decades. In their seminal 1970 work, *The Politics of Unreason*, Lipset and Raab noted that with McCarthyism, "vigorous anti-communism" had "replaced anti-Catholicism or anti-immigrant sentiment as the unifying core for mass right-wing extremist action." It had become a movement popular among the business elite of the Midwest and lower-income Americans and recent immigrants. Sociologist Talcott Parsons described it as a "movement supported by certain vested-interest elements and a popular revolt against the upper classes." McCarthyism did not focus on any direct military threat posed by Russia or China; his target was a supposed invisible enemy within, a crafty adversary that resided in the highest levels of American society. Most Republicans, including Taft, would neither block the McCarthy Express nor let pass the opportunity he presented. Many cheered on the unkempt, uncouth senator, as he pummeled the Democrats and inflamed paranoid passions within the public.

McCarthy's conspiracy-mongering reached a new height with a Senate floor speech in June 1951. In this unhinged rant, he accused the Truman administration and Democrats of being traitors to America. The supposed "decline" in American strength from 1945 to 1951, he offered, was no accident; it "was brought about, step by step, by will and intention." The communist victory in China, the stalemate in the Korean War, accommodation with the Soviet Union following the Yalta conference, the Hiss case and other acts of alleged or actual Russian espionage—all of this had occurred for a "deeper reason." McCarthy went on: "How can we account for our present situation unless we believe that men high in this Government are concerting to deliver us to disaster? This must be the product of a great conspiracy, a conspiracy on a scale so immense as to dwarf any previous such venture in the history of man."

McCarthy was mounting a one-man, modern-day Salem witch trial. He had no evidence, only accusations. Demons lurked everywhere. He claimed Secretary of State Dean Acheson "steadfastly serves the interests of nations other than his own." As for President Truman, McCarthy dismissed him as a "captive" of the conspirators and a "satisfactory front" for this black-hearted plot who was "only dimly aware of what is going on."

The true villain, he exclaimed, was George C. Marshall, the present secretary of defense who as secretary of state had helped create the massive postwar recovery program for Europe known as the Marshall Plan. McCarthy ticked off a long list of policies associated with Marshall that he described as "contributing to a strategy of defeat." He charged Marshall with not being merely wrong in his policy decisions but with pursuing a "great conspiracy" to weaken the United States so that it would "fall victim to Soviet intrigue from within and Russian military might from without." With millions of Americans paying attention to his every word, McCarthy asked rhetorically, "Is that farfetched? There have been many examples in history of rich and powerful states which have been corrupted from within, enfeebled and deceived until they were unable to resist aggression."

This was a crazy conspiracy theory designed to prey on and boost fears. Did McCarthy, a drinker, a gambler, and an inveterate liar, really believe Marshall was an evil puppet master purposefully leading the United States to annihilation? For the Republican Party, it didn't matter. McCarthy had struck a chord with a frightened national audience that embraced his baseless bunk. After this display of lunacy, McCarthy was not ostracized. He was cheered on by the party and lionized at its 1952 convention in Chicago, where Republicans enshrined his dangerous folly into their platform. In the fall, McCarthy stumped for many Republicans. He derided Adlai Stevenson, the Democratic nominee, as "Alger." Eisenhower was the presidential candidate of the Republican Party, but McCarthy was its dark soul.

When it came time for Eisenhower to campaign in Wisconsin with McCarthy, the senator's conspiratorial and defamatory assault on Marshall was much on the general's mind. Marshall had served as Army chief of staff during World War II; he and Eisenhower had been comrades in arms. After the defeat of Hitler, they had worked together to forge the postwar order. Marshall was Ike's friend. And now Eisenhower, who was offended by McCarthy and his outsize role in the party, was expected to campaign side by side with this scoundrel who was up for reelection.

On October 2, the day before Eisenhower was supposed to whistle-stop on a train through Wisconsin with McCarthy, he called the senator to a meeting in the Pere Marquette Hotel in Peoria, Illinois. In Eisenhower's suite, the former supreme commander in Europe ripped into McCarthy. "He spoke with white hot anger and just took McCarthy apart," an Eisenhower aide later said. "The air turned blue." McCarthy said little in response.

The next day, the campaign train ferried Eisenhower and McCarthy into Wisconsin. The two men chatted once again. "I'm going to say that I disagree with you," the general said, referring to an upcoming campaign event. McCarthy shot back, "If you say that you'll be booed." Eisenhower replied, "I've been booed before, and being booed doesn't bother me."

In Green Bay, thousands gathered. McCarthy was introduced to the crowd, and only after he was gone did Eisenhower speak from the platform of the rail car. Ike called on voters to support all Republicans. Inside the rear compartment of the train, McCarthy smiled. Ike went on to note that he agreed with McCarthy on "ridding this Government of the incompetent, the dishonest, and, above all, the subversive and disloyal." But he pointed out that he had discussed with McCarthy "the differences" between them, explaining that they only "apply to the method." McCarthy shook his head.

Other stops that day included Appleton, Neenah-Menasha, and Fond du Lac. At each rally, there were no signs of a controversy raging on the train: Should Eisenhower publicly assail McCarthy and separate himself from the conspiracy politics that McCarthy had made a Republican mainstay?

That night, Eisenhower was scheduled to cap off this day of campaigning with a speech before a crowd of thirteen thousand in Milwaukee at Marquette University, McCarthy's alma mater. And he had a plan. Several of his associates in the moderate Republican camp believed Ike ought to distance himself and the party from McCarthy's crude and ugly endeavor. Eisenhower initially agreed. He had instructed a speechwriter to insert an anti-McCarthy riff into his Milwaukee speech. It was a short paragraph: "I know that charges of disloyalty have, in the past, been leveled against General George C. Marshall. I have been privileged for 35 years to know General Marshall personally. I know him as a man and as a soldier, to be dedicated with singular selflessness and the profoundest patriotism to the service of America. And this episode is a sobering lesson in the way freedom must not defend itself."

This was no full-scale fusillade. Yet without mentioning McCarthy by name, Eisenhower was about to slam him before an audience of McCarthy's admirers and supporters. Even if Eisenhower limited his attack to the Marshall accusation, such a declaration—made while McCarthy was on the same stage—would be widely considered a dramatic and clear renunciation of the nation's number one Red-baiter. He would show Americans that the Republican Party of Eisenhower was not one of conspiratorial extremism.

Eisenhower's political advisers on the train had another idea. When Walter Kohler, the Republican governor of Wisconsin, read a draft of the speech, he was horrified. Wisconsin was McCarthy territory—and it had been Taft country. Slapping McCarthy there would threaten Eisenhower's delicate modus vivendi with Taft and the conservative wing, harm his chances in the state, and alienate pro-McCarthy voters across the country, especially those Catholic voters who were cheering McCarthy on and who the GOP now had the chance to move from the Democratic to the Republican column. Kohler advised cutting the paragraph. "When a man calls on the Pope," he told

New Hampshire Governor Sherman Adams, Eisenhower's main political strategist, "he doesn't tell him what a fine fellow Martin Luther was."

Other prominent Republicans on the train agreed. That included Art Summerfield, the chair of the Republican National Committee, Senator Bill Knowland of California, and Adams. Whatever they thought of McCarthy and his reckless accusations, they were driven by something simpler: math. McCarthy had won over the party's base. Eisenhower couldn't afford to take a principled stand without risking millions of votes.

During a meeting with Eisenhower, Adams started to explain the political calculus, reminding Eisenhower of the ill will that remained from the Republican convention. Eisenhower interrupted: "Are you telling me this paragraph should come out?" Adams said yes. "Take it out," Eisenhower ordered. A command decision: Ike would yield to McCarthyism and permit the GOP to continue to exploit this right-wing conniver's treacherous obsession in its pursuit of power. *Are we going to win an election or aren't we?* That's what the man said.

———

During the Milwaukee speech, Eisenhower enthusiastically pounded the anti-communism drum, as if he were the party's chief Red-hunter. He claimed that support of communism—or "economic democracy"—had "partly poisoned two whole decades of our national life. It insulated itself into our schools, our public forums, some of our news channels, some of our labor unions, and, most terrifyingly, into Government itself." This "contamination," he said, had struck "virtually every department, every agency, every bureau, every section of our Government," which meant the government was being run by "men whose very brains were confused by the opiate of this deceit." After the speech, Eisenhower shook McCarthy's hand.

The address was reported in the press as a strident partisan attack on Truman. Eisenhower was mimicking McCarthy's foundational charge: Communism had thoroughly penetrated American life and the US government, and the Truman administration was letting it win. He cited the Hiss case and obliquely referred to the atomic spying case of Julius and Ethel Rosenberg, calling for "the right to call a Red a Red." But he added a vague anti-McCarthy caveat: "We would have nothing left to defend if we allowed ourselves to be swept into any spirit of violent vigilantism. To defend freedom, in short, is—first of all—to respect freedom."

Eisenhower wanted it both ways, as he capitalized on the irrational fear stirred up by the senator and his comrades. He knew communism had *not* penetrated every corner of government and American society. Though Moscow had run several significant espionage rings in past years, federal agencies were not riddled with Soviet spies. Yet as he validated McCarthy's fundamental charge, Eisenhower called for avoiding the excesses of this crusade that could tar people like his friend Marshall. It was a mixed message that tilted heavily in McCarthy's direction. The general may have delivered the junior senator a sharp tongue-lashing in private, but he accepted the basic premise of McCarthyism and was amplifying it in public. As the *Milwaukee Journal* noted, "The general went far toward surrendering ethical and moral principles in a frenzied quest for votes."

Eisenhower would come to regret the decision on the train to cut the anti-McCarthy paragraph. But he had decided not to battle the furies of the day. He went on to decisively defeat Stevenson, winning Wisconsin and thirty-eight other states and leading the Republicans to control of the House and the Senate. In the new Congress, McCarthy became chair of the Permanent Investigations Subcommittee. He now could do more than rant on the Senate floor. He could wield legislative power to chase after his fever dreams of communist subversion, most notably issue subpoenas and hold hearings, and further steer the Republican Party into exploitation of Cold War fear.

With Roy Cohn, a ruthless twenty-five-year-old lawyer recommended by FBI Director J. Edgar Hoover, at his side, McCarthy launched scores of investigations of supposed communist infiltration of the government. (For eight months, Robert Kennedy was an aide on the committee.) Across the nation, state and local officials passed antisubversive laws, police chased after Reds, and private businesses adopted loyalty oaths. Hollywood enforced a blacklist that sought to ban suspected communists and other radicals from the entertainment industry. The Supreme Court ruled that First Amendment protections did not cover communists. At one point, Senator William Jenner, an Indiana Republican and McCarthy ally, hissed on the Senate floor, "This country today is in the hands of a secret inner coterie, which is directed by agents of the Soviet Union. Our only choice is to impeach President Truman and find out who is the secret invisible government." This hysteria was reminiscent of the past wars on the Masons, the Illuminati, and witches.

In reality, there were few communists in the United States. From 1950 to 1951, the number of Communist Party members had fallen from 43,000 to 32,000. Though Russian espionage was a challenge for the national security apparatus, this was a limited threat that had little to do with commies creeping under the beds in American households. Syndicated columnist

Drew Pearson observed the country was being subsumed by a "disease of fear"—and McCarthy was bad medicine.

The Wisconsin senator was an undisciplined demagogue. As chair of this subcommittee, he fired in multiple directions, targeting the Voice of America, the State Department, and other alleged havens of communism. Eisenhower watched in dismay. He told advisers and intimates he loathed McCarthy. Yet when his brother Milton encouraged him to "tear McCarthy to pieces," Eisenhower declined. That would, he fretted, transform McCarthy into a martyr. Perhaps more to the point, the Republicans held a minuscule one-vote majority in the Senate. If Ike went after McCarthy, he would alienate the senator's allies in Congress, and his own legislative agenda would be endangered. The best strategy, Eisenhower resolved, was to ignore the troublemaker, even if that let the flames spread. He would not publicly speak the man's name. At a speech at Dartmouth, Eisenhower advised students, "Don't join the book burners"—a widely perceived poke at McCarthy. He skipped the grand wedding of McCarthy and his secretary. Nixon, Eisenhower's vice president, attended.

Eisenhower probably should have realized that McCarthy would eventually train his fire on him. McCarthy's main targets were not the communists overseas. His enemy was the American establishment, and now the Republicans were the establishment.

It was during a nationwide television and radio broadcast in November 1953 that the senator turned on Eisenhower: "A few days ago, I read that President Eisenhower expressed the hope that by election time in 1954 the subject of communism would be a dead and forgotten issue. The raw, harsh, unpleasant fact is that communism is an issue and will be an issue in 1954... I would...like to remind those very well-meaning people who speak about communism not being an issue that communism is not isolated from other great evils which beset us today." He slammed the Eisenhower administration for not firing a diplomat McCarthy had baselessly accused of "delivering our Chinese friend into Communist hands" and trying to infiltrate communists into the Central Intelligence Agency. He criticized the president for providing foreign aid to countries that traded with communist China, such as England.

One senior Eisenhower aide, C. D. Jackson, wrote Adams, now chief of staff in the White House, that the speech was "an open declaration of war on the Republican President of the United States by a Republican senator." In a diary item a few days later, Jackson observed that McCarthy "had attempted to establish McCarthyism as Republicanism, and anybody who didn't agree was either a fool or a protector of Communism." At a subsequent White

House staff meeting, Jackson warned his colleagues that "this Three Little Monkeys act"—see, hear, speak no evil regarding McCarthy—was not working and that appeasing McCarthy to save a few votes in the Senate was a counterproductive strategy that could yield no legislative program and cause electoral defeats in 1954 and 1956. The first big error, Jackson said, had been retreating in Milwaukee a year earlier.

In a subsequent meeting, Eisenhower declared he would not directly respond to McCarthy. "I will not get in the gutter with that guy," he said. But at a press conference, he took a swing at his antagonist without referring to him by name. Eisenhower observed, "The easiest thing to do with great power is to abuse it." He repeated his "previously expressed conviction that fear of communists actively undermining our government will not be an issue in the 1954 election." Eisenhower touted his administration's "progress in routing them out" and assured the country that communist penetration of the US government "can no longer be considered a serious menace." Still, the White House declined to confront McCarthy directly. A few weeks later, Nixon vacationed with the senator in Key Biscayne, Florida, where the vice president offered the senator a suggestion: Ease up on the administration.

McCarthy was not a fellow to heed advice. His newest target was the US Army, and in his customary reckless fashion he accused the military of harboring communists within various units. This caused havoc within the White House and the Pentagon, as the Eisenhower crowd wrestled over how to handle McCarthy's latest witch hunt. "Pres. very mad and getting fed up," an Eisenhower aide wrote in his diary. "It's his Army and he doesn't like McCarthy's tactics at all." He noted the president had told him: "This guy McCarthy is going to get into trouble over this. I'm not going to take this one lying down... My friends tell me it won't be long in this Army stuff before McCarthy starts using my name... He's ambitious. He wants to be President. He's the last guy in the world who will ever get there, if I have anything to say." In a letter to a friend, Eisenhower attacked the "reactionary fringe of the Republican Party that hates and despises everything for which I stand."

Eisenhower, though, remained determined to stay out of McCarthy's gutter and not distract from his own legislative priorities. When Senator Ralph Flanders, a Vermont Republican, strode on to the Senate floor and denounced McCarthy for donning "war paint" and doing a "war dance" in order to expose a single "pink Army dentist," Eisenhower was pleased and sent Flanders a private note: "American needs to hear from more Republican voices like yours." Yet the Senate Republican leadership stood solidly with McCarthy.

Behind the scenes a related drama was stirring. The Army had drafted David Schine, a subcommittee staffer and close friend of Cohn, and dispatched him as a private to Fort Dix in New Jersey. Cohn was pressing the White House and the Army for a cushy posting for Schine that would allow the young man to be free on evenings and weekends. He reportedly threatened Adams when the White House chief of staff informed him there would be no special treatment for Schine.

As McCarthy barreled ahead, Eisenhower, as disgusted as he was with this rascal's paranoia-driven stampede, gave his antagonist running room. He did chide McCarthy, declaring, "In opposing communism, we are defeating ourselves if either by design or through carelessness we use methods that do not conform to the American sense of justice and fair play." Yet once again, no names were named. The media depicted Eisenhower as yielding to McCarthy.

As the president kept ducking the fight, he wrote a friend: "I by [no] means approve the methods that McCarthy uses...I despise them...Nevertheless, I am quite sure that the people who want me to stand up and publicly label McCarthy with derogatory titles are the most mistaken people that are dealing with this whole problem."

Nixon attempted to signal enough was enough. In a television appearance, he stated, "Men who have in the past done effective work exposing communists in this country have, by reckless talk and questionable methods, made themselves the issue rather than the cause they believe in so deeply." This jab annoyed McCarthy loyalists, while not satisfying Republicans who wanted to de-McCarthyize the party.

———

The shadow feud between McCarthy and Eisenhower came to a head in the spring of 1954 in what would be known as the Army-McCarthy hearings. The Senate investigations subcommittee had been probing a conflicting set of accusations: the charge that McCarthy and Cohn had pressured the Army to provide special consideration to Schine *and* McCarthy's counterclaim that the Army was using this accusation to force him to lay off the military. It was a swirling mess of allegations of blackmail, abuse of power, and communist infiltration of the organization that was supposed to safeguard the nation.

The hearings were televised coast to coast for months, and each day the public could watch the nation's most prominent Red-baiter recklessly hurl baseless accusations, as tales of Cohn's behind-the-scenes maneuvers to assist Schine intermixed with McCarthy's blustery defense and rambling attacks on the Army. The senator, his bullying manner, and his embrace of extremism did not wear well. In the middle of this spectacle, Eisenhower spoke at a dinner at Columbia University and threw a rhetorical brickbat at McCarthy, once more without uttering his name: "Whenever, and for whatever alleged reason, people attempt to crush ideas, to mask their convictions, to view every neighbor as a possible enemy, to seek some kind of divining rod by which to test for conformity, a free society is in danger." The president assailed "demagogues thirsty for personal power and public notice."

The hearings captivated much of the country, and the most dramatic moment arrived when McCarthy accused a young attorney who was associated with the law firm of Joseph Nye Welch, a top Army lawyer, of having once been connected to an organization deemed "subversive" in the 1940s. In response to this cruel sideswiping of a fellow not directly involved in the proceedings, Welch replied to McCarthy in a slow and deliberate manner: "Let us not assassinate this lad further, Senator. You have done enough. Have you no sense of decency, sir, at long last? Have you left no sense of decency?"

Applause erupted in the hearing room. Welch, with this simple and eloquent expression of moral outrage, virtually ended McCarthy's reign of terror. Eisenhower congratulated Welch on a job well done.

––––––––

McCarthy's Red-hunting days were essentially finished, but his party didn't toss out his road map. During the 1954 congressional elections, Nixon assumed the role of the GOP's chief pitchman of paranoia. He claimed the Eisenhower administration had uncovered and fired "thousands" of subversives in the government. (The head of the civil service later said none had been found.) Nixon also shared a terrifying revelation: The administration, upon taking office, had discovered "in the files a blueprint for socializing America." Asked to produce a copy of this bombshell document, Nixon explained he had only been speaking metaphorically. But he cited the existence of a secret Communist Party memo that stated its intention to work through the Democratic Party to advance its underhanded plans.

Nixon's deceit-driven attempt to turn Red fright into votes didn't succeed. The Republicans lost control of both houses of Congress. There would be no more committee chairmanships for McCarthy. A month after the election, the Senate voted to condemn McCarthy on a 67-to-22 vote, with half of the GOP caucus ratifying this political defenestration. The man who had led the Republicans to the extremes of demagoguery and who had been hailed as a hero two years earlier at their convention had become a pariah. Eisenhower snickered that McCarthyism was now "McCarthywasm." McCarthy would die a miserable death in 1957 at the age of forty-eight, most likely of alcoholism.

Eisenhower was wrong. McCarthy was dead, but McCarthyism lived. The Grand Old Party had embedded it in American life. A few months after the 1954 midterm election, J. Bracken Lee, the Republican governor of Utah, delivered a speech in New York City, under the auspices of a right-wing group called Alliance, Inc., which was headed by Archibald Roosevelt (the fifth child of Teddy Roosevelt). Warning that subversives had contaminated schools and churches throughout the land, Lee told the crowd, "We have in Washington today what to my mind amounts to a dictatorship" no different from the Russian government. When someone in the crowd asked how they could fight back, Lee replied, "If you feel that McCarthy's on our side say so." The audience cheered.

For years, Eisenhower had not confronted McCarthy and his perversion of the nation's discourse, and many of McCarthy's party colleagues sought to benefit from his crusade, as he demonstrated how tapping paranoid fear could be politically profitable. This pursuit of subversion was a means for exploiting and exacerbating deep divisions within American society. As Hofstadter observed several years after McCarthy's demise, "The real function of the Great Inquisition of the 1950s was not anything so simply rational as to turn up spies or prevent espionage or even to expose actual Communists, but to discharge resentments and frustrations, to punish, to satisfy enmities whose roots lay elsewhere than in the Communist issue itself." Communism, he pointed out, "was not the target but the weapon" in a tribalistic and unprincipled war against liberals, internationalists, and assorted elites that resonated with millions.

Ultimately, McCarthy's excesses, not his aims, led to his downfall. With the Cold War and nuclear terror now permanent fixtures, there was tremendous terror and worry to manipulate. In 1955, sociologist Daniel Bell keenly noted that McCarthy "was the catalyst, not the explosive force. These forces still remain." There would be plenty of opportunity for other political scare-mongers.

CHAPTER 4

No Good Birchers

Toward the end of 1958, eleven prominent Americans received a letter. Can you come, the note asked, to a secret two-day meeting in Indianapolis in December? The matter to be discussed would be revealed only then.

The mysterious invitation assured its recipients that the attendees would be "all men of well recognized stature, unshakable integrity, proved ability, and fervent patriotism." These patriots included Fred Koch, the founder of what would become Koch Industries; Laurence Bunker, a retired Army colonel who had been aide-de-camp to General Douglas MacArthur; and the palindromic Revilo Oliver, a University of Illinois professor who years later would become an outspoken advocate of antisemitism and white supremacy. Another was T. Coleman Andrews, a former commissioner of the Internal Revenue Service who had run for president in 1956 as the candidate of the States' Rights Party, which advocated keeping the federal government out of such bothersome matters as desegregation and education. Andrews had polled less than two-tenths of a percent of the popular vote.

These four and the others heeded the call and rendezvoused at a brick Tudor house in a residential neighborhood on December 8. Once they were seated in chairs arranged in a semi-circle in the living room, a tall, balding fellow carrying a bundle of notes shuffled into the room. This was Robert H. W. Welch Jr., who had retired as a successful candy manufacturer two years earlier and who could claim credit for the Sugar Daddy, Sugar Babies, and Junior Mints. Welch, who grew up in North Carolina, attended Harvard Law School but did not graduate. A recent board member of the National Association of Manufacturers, he had written a book on how to be a successful salesman and had dabbled in electoral politics, running for lieutenant governor in Massachusetts in the Republican primary and losing. He was also a deranged, paranoid conspiracy theorist.

For two days, Welch outlined the danger at hand. Communist Party membership in the United States had expanded eightfold in the past two decades. (That was unlikely.) The Reds had a secret plan to devalue the dollar to cause economic collapse and societal chaos. The communists were sneaky bastards, he noted. They tended not to use force. They subverted their targets, creeping into political parties, churches, schools, labor unions, other institutions, and governments and taking over from within. Deluding people. Brainwashing them. They were inciting racial conflict in the South to detonate a catastrophic civil war. Most Americans did not realize any of this, Welch said. They were living "in such a fool's paradise." Welch believed that the Russians had launched Sputnik to convince the United States to increase its military spending and lose sight that the true menace to the nation was the internal threat posed by undercover commies at home.

A man of great erudition, Welch sprinkled in references to Oswald Spengler and ancient history, as he decried collectivism and the societal weaknesses of Western civilization that clever communists could slyly exploit. The United States had only a few years to beat back these devious Reds before the nation would fall. But this battle could not be waged according to regular rules and in adherence to the niceties of political debate. To save America, they would have to "fight dirty," just as the commies did— infiltrate other organizations, create front groups, and harass suspected subversives.

Welch had a plan. He and the men in the room would form a "monolithic" organization to engage in a titanic struggle against subversion. It would be controlled from the top because a democratically operated outfit would be too vulnerable to infiltration and disruption from the wily and pernicious enemy. Consequently, Welch would be in charge. He would set policy and issue directives. This would not be a debating society. Welch shared his dream: a force of one million "dedicated supporters" and "sufficient resources." With that, he could conquer the Reds. He would organize his followers into chapters to fight communism at the local level—within schools, libraries, and church groups. This new patriotic legion would be called the John Birch Society, named after an American missionary and military intelligence officer who, while operating in northern China, had been killed by communist troops days after World War II ended. In 1954 Welch had published a hagiographic biography of Birch, claiming he was the first casualty of the Cold War.

Nine of the men in the room—including Koch, Bunker, Oliver, and Andrews—signed up and agreed to join an advisory council for Welch's operation.

Within a few years, the society would have between 20,000 and 100,000 members and an annual income close to $1 million. More important, it would become part of the lifeblood of the Republican Party and conservative movement or, as some would see it, a harmful infection within the right. Historian Jonathan Schoenwald observed years later that the John Birch Society would "move ideas once considered on the fringes of conservative ideology into mainstream politics." Welch's outfit would inhabit a place where right-wing thinking intersected with paranoid extremism, posing the GOP and more sober conservatives a serious challenge.

———

For years, Welch had been—in his mind, at least—revealing the spreading communist danger. In the early 1950s, he published a thirty-thousand-word pamphlet that echoed Joe McCarthy: It is a "certainty" that there are "more Communists and Communist sympathizers in our government today than ever before." In a 1956 speech, Welch accused American leaders of "betrayals" that allowed for the advance of communism around the world. Welch was an early investor in the *National Review*, the magazine founded in 1955 by rising right-wing star William F. Buckley Jr. A grateful Buckley pronounced Welch a national treasure.

Out of his two-day lecture in that Indianapolis living room, Welch fashioned a tract dubbed *The Blue Book*, which became a bible for the John Birch Society. It defined his ambition: The society would "last for hundreds of years, and exert an increasing influence for the temporal good and the spiritual ennoblement of mankind throughout those centuries." As *The Blue Book* showed, Welch saw communists not just under every bed, but behind every door and inside churches, media organizations, schools, courts, and legislatures. US foreign aid to other nations was a scheme cooked up by Stalin. The burgeoning civil rights movement was a Red plot to foster civil disorder that would justify the imposition of a police state. The Federal Reserve banking system was another commie conspiracy. Gun control measures were precursors to the communist-backed seizure of weapons. Housing programs, aid for farmers, the United Nations, the World Health Organization, NATO—all connivances of devilish communists.

Welch had previously penned a manuscript that he constantly revised and shared with intimates and associates and that would later become a book known as *The Politician*. There was no mystery in this volume. Everyone, it turned out, was a communist. Secretary of State John Foster Dulles, CIA director Allen Dulles, and the whole damn elite running the show. This screed revealed the extent of Welch's craziness: Eisenhower was "a dedicated and conscious agent of the Communist conspiracy" and his brother Milton was likely Ike's "superior and boss within the Communist Party." That was,

Welch insisted, the only explanation for US foreign policy setbacks of recent years.

Welch envisioned his counter-conspiracy as a sales operation. He had been a successful entrepreneur peddling candy—an unhealthy product—to millions who craved sweets. Now he was exploiting Cold War dread and a demand for easy answers. He set up John Birch Society bookstores, home-study groups, assorted publications, and a flood of pamphlets, tape recordings, and films. He initiated stealth efforts to win school board and other local elections and mounted assorted advocacy campaigns, such as the call to impeach Chief Justice Earl Warren because of the *Brown v. Board of Education* decision in 1954 that outlawed segregation in public schools.

Welch promulgated a steady flow of bizarre conspiracies, as if they were different product lines. He claimed evil internationalists were plotting to "substitute UN insignia...for conventional Christmas decorations" in department stores. He and the society pronounced the fluoridation of water a communist plot. In a 1960 report to the John Birch Society Council, Welch shared the frightening news that "our federal Government is already, literally in the hands of the Communists." He cited numerous senators—including John F. Kennedy—as "either an actual Communist or so completely a Communist sympathizer or agent that it makes no practical difference." The governors of the two states with the most population—Pat Brown in California and Nelson Rockefeller in New York—were "almost certainly actual Communists." The State Department was "loaded with Communists from top to bottom." The CIA, under Allen Dulles, was "nothing more or less than an agency to promote Communism throughout the world." And "70% to 90% of the responsible personnel in the Department of Health, Education, and Welfare are Communists." He proclaimed that the communist "takeover at the top is, for all practical purposes, virtually complete."

Welch was bonkers, but he found an audience. He provided a way for people to understand the dangerous world that seemed to keep getting more dangerous. (The Russians had sent troops into Hungary in 1956. The following year they launched Sputnik, the first satellite, into space.) In the tradition of the anti-Illuminati panic-mongers of the 1790s and the anti-Masonic hysterics of the 1820s, he was exploiting uncertainty, ignorance, and fear, and he was revving up paranoia in an unsettling era. He was hawking a hyper-conspiratorial version of McCarthyism.

This right-wing movement of anxiety and madness—propelled by a belief in sinister but nonexistent and irrational conspiracies—shaped the environment in which a new conservatism was rising. Hofstadter pegged the John Birch Society as a player in "cultural politics"—conflict detached from "economic discontent" and associated with prosperity that allows for "more luxurious hostilities." He explained: "At times politics becomes an arena into which the wildest fancies are projected, the most paranoid suspicions, the most absurd superstitions, the most bizarre apocalyptic fantasies. From time to time, movements arise that are founded upon the political exploitation of such fancies and fears, and while these movements can hardly aspire to animate more than a small minority of the population, they do exercise, especially in a democratic and populistically oriented political culture like our own, a certain leverage upon practical politics." And within only a few years of Welch's unhinged tutorial in an Indianapolis living room, his Birchers were applying pressure on the GOP.

———

In early spring of 1961, Senator Barry Goldwater was conspiring to protect these promoters of paranoia.

He was concerned about the Birchers. Welch had created a cadre of committed anticommunist conspiracists. What to do about them had become a question for mainstream (and nonderanged) conservatives. This was especially true after Welch's bizarre belief that Ike was a commie asset had become public in the summer of 1960 when the *Chicago Daily News* disclosed the contents of the unpublished manuscript of *The Politician*. This loony nugget about Eisenhower drew great attention and threatened to define Welch and his outfit.

The John Birch Society was a force bringing passion and energetic foot soldiers into a new and revived conservative movement that embraced Goldwater as its leader and preferred contender for the next Republican presidential nomination. And this presented a dilemma for Goldwater. Welch's lunacy could discredit the movement to which Goldwater was tied. But were Goldwater to distance himself from this prominent champion of anticommunism, he could cause a split on the right, alienate thousands of potential campaign recruits, and endanger his own prospects. (The Eisenhower-is-a-commie story did not prompt any mass exodus of society members.) Goldwater confronted a question similar to what Eisenhower had encountered a decade earlier regarding McCarthy. Do you accept— and, thus, encourage—extremism for political gain?

With this on his mind, the senator on March 27 wrote Buckley, the thirty-five-year-old editor of the *National Review*, which had become the lodestar of the conservative cosmos. He needed Buckley's assistance in this sensitive matter.

―――――

Buckley was worried about Welch and his followers, fearing they might taint the entire right. In 1958, Welch had sent him a copy of *The Politician*, and Buckley had asked an associate at the magazine to peruse the manuscript. His colleague's conclusion: "This guy was a nut." Buckley wrote Welch that the problem at hand was not a vast, Eisenhower-led conspiracy but that "the entire nation is diseased as a result of the collapse of our faith." (Buckley himself was not a conspiracist, but he was then a supporter of racial segregation who had recently written that the "white community" should control southern culture because it was the "advanced race.") A year later, in 1959, the *National Review* took a swipe at the Bircher view that the "Communist world" was "monolith perfection...which does not and could not exist outside a fiction *1984*." (Buckley sent Welch a polite note of warning to take the sting out of this slap.) But Buckley and the magazine had not fully confronted "the nut."

Goldwater, too, had long known that Welch was a crackpot. A few years before Welch founded the John Birch Society, he had visited Goldwater at his Phoenix home and handed him a copy of *The Politician*. Goldwater skimmed the manuscript and called Welch the next morning. "I want no part of this," Goldwater told him. "I won't even have it around. If you were smart, you'd burn every copy you have." Welch didn't hold this against Goldwater. He became a major financial donor to Goldwater's 1958 reelection campaign. (H. L. Hunt, a Texas oil billionaire and funder of the John Birch Society, was another.) In 1959, Goldwater joined one of the first Bircher front groups: a committee that opposed summit meetings with leaders of communist nations, particularly the Soviet Union. That same year, Welch joined a band of far-right conservatives encouraging a Goldwater presidential bid in 1960.

In a way, Goldwater owed Welch and the Birchers. In 1960, Goldwater had published *The Conscience of a Conservative*, a slim book of his thoughts on conservativism that had been ghost-written by L. Brent Bozell Jr., Buckley's brother-in-law.* The book had been produced at the suggestion of Clarence Manion, a former dean of Notre Dame Law School who was a member of the national council of the John Birch Society, and Manion's small publishing company put out the volume. It was a cri de coeur from the right, a complete repudiation of government activism and Eisenhower's "modern Republicanism," which Goldwater dismissed as "dime store New

―――――

* Buckley and Bozell cowrote a 1954 book that defended McCarthy and hailed him as a prophet of "American Resistance."

Deal." In the book, Goldwater-Bozell declared, "I do not undertake to promote welfare, for I propose to extend freedom. My aim is not to pass laws,
but to repeal them." It was time to crush communism, not hold it at bay.
And Goldwater extolled "states' rights" as the "cornerstone of the Republic"
and "our chief bulwark against the encroachment of individual freedom by
Big Government"—a from-the-West libertarian sentiment that was music
to the ears of Southern white supremacists who resented federal intervention to advance civil rights for Blacks.

The work was an instant smash. It became Mao's *Little Red Book* for
rightists. At Bozell's urging, the John Birch Society had helped get the book
moving. Fred Koch preordered thousands of copies. Other top Birchers
joined the effort to make it a bestseller. The book was sold in John Birch
Society bookstores throughout the nation, slapped with a sticker on the
front cover announcing it was "approved by" the society.

The Conscience of a Conservative marked a turning point in the latest
struggle for the soul of the Republican Party. Conservatives resented Eisenhower's Modern Republicanism and his abandonment of McCarthy. They
despised his acceptance of New Deal programs. (In 1957, Goldwater had
condemned Eisenhower's budget, huffing that the president had fallen prey
to "the siren song of socialism.") The right recoiled at Ike's pragmatic policy
of containment and coexistence with Russia. Eisenhower and Nixon had
won reelection in 1956, with the Democrats retaining control of Congress,
but two years later, the Republicans were massacred, losing forty-eight seats
in the House and thirteen in the Senate. Not only was I-Like-Ike Republicanism ideologically suspect for conservatives; it was, they believed, damaging the party. Buckley had founded the *National Review* to give voice to this
new generation of demanding far-right conservatives. In 1958, he assailed
the "sonorous vapidities of Mr. Eisenhower."

The Conscience of a Conservative fired up a Goldwater-for-president
movement—though Goldwater himself expected to support Nixon in 1960,
even if the vice president, despite his years of Red-baiting, was ideologically suspect. The John Birch Society jumped on the Goldwater bandwagon,
mailing postcards endorsing Goldwater to Republican politicians throughout the country. Here were committed volunteers a candidate would crave
for a national campaign. Two-thirds of its members, Welch estimated,
volunteered for Goldwater, and Welch proclaimed the senator his choice
for the White House. One of the pro-Goldwater groups—Americans for
Goldwater—was chaired by Manion; another member was Bozell. A Bircher
and a member of the Buckley clan were comrades. Goldwater, historian

John Huntington later observed, "straddled the porous ideological boundary separating the far right from the mainstream."

At the Republican convention in Chicago in July 1960, Nixon was a shoo-in, especially after he had cut a deal with Nelson Rockefeller—the Republican the conservatives despised the most—to insert language into the GOP platform recognizing the need for robust governmental action related to economic growth, education, and civil rights. Conservatives grumbled about a new iteration of an old plot: Eastern liberals conspiring against the heart of the party. Goldwater vilified the Nixon-Rockefeller accord as the "Munich of the Republican Party." (He also claimed the platform of Democratic nominee John Kennedy was a "blueprint for socialism.") Yet he played nice. In a speech to the convention, Goldwater urged all Republicans to "put our shoulders to the wheel of Dick Nixon." He was looking past the election and toward the 1964 presidential contest, and he admonished the faithful: "Let's grow up, conservatives. If we want to take this party back, and I think we can someday, let's get to work."

Three months later, Nixon lost in a squeaker to John Kennedy. With Eisenhower gone and Nixon defeated, there was one job left for the conservatives: *Take this party back.* Goldwater was the man at the center of this storm. For him and other prominent right-wingers, there was a crucial question: Would this be done with or without the extremist fringe?

As he pondered the Bircher matter in early 1961, Goldwater's calculation was straightforward. He wanted to keep the Birchers on his side, and he hoped Bill Buckley would help.

In his letter to the *National Review* editor, Goldwater wrote, "Let's keep together on this John Birch thing and I would suggest as of now that we allow it to go along for awhile before we take any other steps." Mr. Conservative was asking the intellectual godfather of the modern right to abide Welch's conspiratorial nonsense for the time being, even permit it to spread.

There was one big problem with this play-it-down approach: The rest of the world was not cooperating. The controversy over Welch's crazy blast at Eisenhower was still on fire. A few weeks earlier, Senator Milton Young, a North Dakota Republican, denounced Welch and the society on the Senate floor, exclaiming that Welch had made accusations "far beyond anything the late Senator Joe McCarthy even thought of." Senator Thomas Kuchel, the California Republican, also took to the well of the Senate to excoriate Welch and the society. Representative Henry Reuss, a House Democrat, called for a congressional investigation of the group, and a spokesperson for Attorney General Robert Kennedy said the society's actions were "a matter of concern to the Justice Department." In a letter to the *Los Angeles Times* endorsing an editorial criticizing the society, Nixon observed, "One of the most indelible lessons of human history is that those who adopt the doctrine that the end justifies the means inevitably find the means become the end."

In public, Goldwater was supportive of Welch's group. "A lot of people in my hometown have been attracted to the society," he said, "and I am impressed by the type of people in it. They are the kind we need in politics." In a letter to Frank Brophy, an Arizona businessman and conservative activist who was a friend, supporter, and Bircher, Goldwater outlined the goal: "to salvage a very worthwhile organization made up of excellent people from the unfortunate statements and outspoken beliefs" of Welch. The senator stated, "I have nothing but high regard for Bob," but Welch had gone too far with his attack on Eisenhower. The choice was "to either calm Bob down or separate him completely from the society so that we can retain the high interest of this intelligent group of Americans."

Welch had gotten into trouble for his insane comment about Eisenhower. But the fundamental construct of the John Birch Society was fact-free paranoid extremism. The whole thing—commies everywhere!—was lunatic. Yet Goldwater and other conservative Republicans treated the society as a respectable outfit. They desired these voters and volunteers, no matter how batty the group was. Goldwater was looking to protect these extremists and preserve their standing within the conservative world.

In this mission, the senator had allies at the *National Review*. William Rusher, the magazine's publisher, feared an assault on Welch and his group would undermine, as he noted, "*NR's* position *as a leader of conservative opinion* in this country." In an internal memo, he pointed out that "the great bulk of our readership…lies in the more or less organized Right, and large segments of that Right are more simplistic than we are…and also far more closely tied to the John Birch Society than we are." Attacking Welch's brigade would be bad for business. In another memo, Rusher conveyed that point explicitly, stating his concern that a dust-up with the John Birch Society could cause readers to cancel their subscriptions and "thereby jeopardize the journal's financial health." But Buckley worried that the connections between Welch and the magazine could come under attack, and that could be a fatal blow for the publication.

Out of principle or self-protection (or both), in April 1961, Buckley took pen in hand to distance the *National Review* from the society—sort of. Buckley noted that he had "always admired [Welch's] personal courage and devotion to the cause," but he questioned Welch's view that "our government is in the effective control of Communists." If that were the case, the ever-droll Buckley observed, then the "entire educational effort conducted by conservatives...is a sheer waste of time" and rightists should "look instead to one's rifle." Buckley did not take direct aim at the society itself. He only gently jabbed at Welch. This was no unambiguous act of disassociation or denunciation.

Goldwater would not support even Buckley's gentle rap on Welch's knuckles. He refused to alienate his allies. A few months later, on *Meet the Press*, asked about extremists on the right, he retorted, "I am far more concerned, frankly, with the extremists to the left than I am with the extremists to the right." What about Welch? "I speak, as I have said many, many times—only for one [chapter] of the Birch Society, and that is the group I happen to know in my hometown of Phoenix, Arizona." These fellows, Goldwater said, were all right. (The previous year, the *Arizona Republic* had published an editorial commending the John Birch Society for its "boundless energy, unusual dedication and skillful leadership.")

The Bircher question would not go away. President Kennedy identified the far right—including the John Birch Society—as a threat. He urged Americans not to yield to the "counsels of fear and suspicion." Veteran journalist Alan Barth penned a much-noticed "Report on the 'Rampageous Right'" for the *New York Times Magazine*, in which he observed that the nation faced the rise of a right-wing movement of discontent and frustration that offered "no solutions" and that was bounded together by fear, anger, and uncertainty generated by a world of geostrategic stalemate, nuclear threat, and domestic change brought about by greater industrialization and urbanization and "a tremendous transformation in the pattern of...race relations." The rightists, Barth concluded, "will no doubt seek to capture control of the Republican Party but they are unlikely to succeed. Their darling just now is Barry Goldwater. But the Senator will be obliged before very long to choose between the support of the rightists and the support of real Republicans who will not care to forsake the traditions of their party for a forlorn kind of fascism."

Barth was wrong on that last point. Goldwater was not going to choose "real Republicans" over fringe conservatives. He needed the rampageous right.

———

Buckley continued to fret that the John Birch Society was an albatross around the neck of the movement he had helped birth and a threat to the

Holy Grail: a Goldwater presidency. In January 1962, he and other luminaries of the right—including writer Russell Kirk and American Enterprise Institute head William Baroody—met with Goldwater and his top political adviser, Stephen Shadegg, in a suite at the Breakers Hotel in Palm Beach, Florida. Goldwater arrived wearing a cowboy hat, a workman's blue shirt, and denim jeans. A top agenda item was what to do about Welch and the Birchers. Buckley contended that responsible conservatives had to disavow the society. Kirk joked, "Eisenhower isn't a communist, he's a golfer."

Goldwater expressed his hesitancy to throw the society to the curb. He knew Welch was promoting paranoia and conspiracy. He told Buckley and the rest that Welch's outfit contained both "kooks" and decent and diligent conservatives. He thought it would be unwise to publicly slam the society. "Every other person in Phoenix is a member of the John Birch Society," Goldwater said. "I'm not talking about Commie-haunted apple pickers or cactus drunks. I'm talking about the highest cast of men of affairs." When Kirk said it was time to excommunicate the society from the conservative movement, Goldwater groaned: "You just can't do that kind of thing in Arizona."

This group eventually cooked up a compromise: They would denounce Welch but the society as a whole would get a pass.

A month later, Buckley launched the missiles. His magazine published a lengthy editorial disparaging Welch as a man "whose views on current affairs are...far removed from common sense" and who was "damaging the cause of anti-Communism." There was nothing wrong with a society led by this loon; only the founder was flawed. (In a prepublication note to Welch, Buckley spelled this out: "I have been criticizing you, but not the Society.") The magazine hailed the members of the society as "some of the most morally energetic, self-sacrificing, and dedicated anti-Communists in America" and urged them to overthrow their leader.

Two weeks later, the *National Review* published a letter to the editor from Goldwater. "I believe the best thing Mr. Welch could do to serve the cause of anti-Communism in the United States would be to resign," the senator asserted.

Around that time, Goldwater wrote to Robert Love, a leading Bircher in Wichita, Kansas. He pointed out he had known Welch for "a long while" and had "great admiration for him." But it was time for Welch to resign. He recounted that he was delivering about three public speeches a week and "almost without exception" the "question of the Birch Society comes up," often with a focus on Welch's statements. The society, Goldwater told

Love, "has great potential…Remove Welch and the Birch Society cannot be attacked."

This blame-Welch-and-not-the-members stance was disingenuous. Even Nixon knew that. In a statement he released in March 1962, while running for governor of California—a race he would lose—the former vice president assailed Welch's insistence that Ike was an "agent of the Communist conspiracy," and declared, "No responsible candidate, member, or unit of the Republican Party can traffic with this viewpoint." He insisted that "responsible Republicanism abhors demagoguery and totalitarianism, wherever and however it appears." He raised a crucial point: Under its rules, "every individual member of the Birch Society is obliged to approve and support the viewpoints of Robert Welch." That meant there were no good Birchers.

———

The John Birch Society was not just a conveyor belt for noxious political conspiracy theories and baseless allegations; it was a home for racists and antisemites. In a 1970 tell-all book, Gerald Schomp, whom Welch hired as a state coordinator in 1964, reported that the society included "bigots, anti-Semites, and ignorant kooks and degenerates." According to Schomp, the society endured "anti-Semitic and racist members as long as they don't 'spread such views' or publicly embarrass the organization. But by tolerating anti-Semitic and racist views within the membership, Welch practically insures that such views will ultimately be disseminated to more members."

Billy James Hargis, an evangelist who headed the Christian Crusade, which billed itself as "America's largest anti-Communism organization," was an endorser of the society. He held Jews accountable for the "betrayal" of Jesus Christ, declared segregation was "one of nature's universal laws" and "ordained" by God, and derided Martin Luther King Jr. as a Marxist. (Hargis's board of advisers included several Birch officials and members.) The head of the Birchers' New York chapter, Merwin Hart, was an antisemite who directed a group that questioned whether the Holocaust had happened. (In 1962, Welch wrote to an associate that the "Zionist conspiracy…was the father of the International Communist Conspiracy.") A prominent coordinator for the society, Medford Evans, was a fierce segregationist. During a cross-country speaking tour in 1961, Welch was introduced several times by Mississippi congressman John Bell Williams, another fervent segregationist. Willis Carto, a prominent early member and organizer for the group, was a rabid antisemite. Many Birchers had ties to the racist White Citizens' Council, sort of a high-end version of the Klan. A columnist for the society's *American Opinion* magazine, Westbrook Pegler, was an enthusiastic antisemite. The problem was not just Welch. His society was a magnet for—and embraced—world-class haters and fanatics.

Welch was unmoved by Buckley's swipe or Goldwater's call for him to quit the group. Resign he would not. Not willing to denounce the John Birch Society as a whole, Goldwater, the *National Review*, and other conservatives were stuck with Welch and the conspiratorial extremism he marketed to his adherents. All their pussyfooting was empty posturing, for Goldwater and the Republicans would soon welcome the assistance of Welch's paranoid army and its extremist compatriots.

CHAPTER 5

In Your Heart

Madison Square Garden in New York City was bedecked with red-white-and-blue bunting and balloons on the evening of March 7, 1962. A band played patriotic music. The arena was stuffed with young clean-cut conservatives eager to see their champion, Barry Goldwater. Eighteen thousand rightists had flocked to the Garden for an anticommunism rally organized by Young Americans for Freedom, a new outfit of hardcore right-wing activists. When Goldwater hit the stage, the band struck up "The Battle Hymn of the Republic," and the crowd belted out, "Glory, hallelujah!" A banner unfurled: FOR THE FUTURE OF FREEDOM: GOLDWATER IN '64. The adoring crowd afforded the senator a five-and-a-half-minute-long ovation. Conservatism, he proclaimed, was "the wave of the future, come to life after thirty years of apathy."

Other speakers pumped up the audience. Brent Bozell Jr. hailed the conservative cause as promoting and serving the "Christian West." As part of the hoopla, YAF handed out awards to various conservatives, including former President Herbert Hoover (who was not present), actor John Wayne, libertarian economist Ludwig von Mises, and Roger Milliken, a textile manufacturer who was a major financial backer of the *National Review*. Von Mises and Milliken were John Birch Society members.

One of the originally scheduled speakers was not in the house: retired General Edwin Walker. He had become a cause célèbre for the right following his resignation from the Army after he was caught politically indoctrinating his troops. He allegedly had advised his soldiers to follow a voter guide crafted by a fringe far-right group, had urged them to read Welch's *The Life of John Birch*, and had referred to Harry Truman, Eleanor Roosevelt, and Dean Acheson as "definitely pink." In the Senate, Goldwater had defended Walker, a hero to the Birchers. But YAF had decided to bump the controversial Walker and replace him with another kind of extremist: Senator Strom Thurmond, the avowed segregationist.

There was little separation between the conspiratorial right and Goldwaterism; right-wing extremism was melding with conservative Republicanism.

Months earlier, one of the YAF rally speakers, Representative Donald Bruce, an Indiana Republican, declared on the House floor that "misguided arrogants" endangered the nation by pushing for a "centralized, collectivist form of government." And Representative John Ashbrook, a fierce conservative and champion of YAF, had prophesized the country was heading toward "national suicide." Welch wrote a letter to a YAF adviser offering to quietly slip the new group money: "Our only stipulation is that our name does not appear on any list of contributors." Birchers, YAF, Republicans—the lines were blurred.

As the Goldwater-for-president movement grew, its ranks became loaded with Birchers and other ultraconservatives. A reporter who covered a Draft Goldwater rally in July 1963 at the National Guard Armory in Washington, DC, described the nine thousand attendees from forty-four states: "There were little old ladies in tennis shoes, truck drivers with tattoos, professors who read Mises rather than Keynes, right-wingers convinced that Wall Street and the Kremlin were conspiring to run the world, Southern whites who had faith in the Cross and the Flag, retired people on Social Security worried about inflation, Westerners tired of catering to Easterners, anticommunists demanding action against Cuba and Khrushchev, small businessmen fighting a losing battle against government rules and regulations, readers of *The Conscience of a Conservative*, high school and college rebels looking for a cause."

Welch was all in on Goldwater. He sent a message to John Birch Society members calling the senator "a very patriotic American...who is determined to use his political skills to do all he can towards saving our country from the dangers now closing in from every side." Birchers gained control of YAF chapters and GOP organs, including the Young Republicans of California. (About this time, Welch sent out a mailing to his members saying civil rights protests were part of a communist plot to establish a "Soviet Negro Republic.")

Surveying the Republican landscape from his governor's office in Albany, New York, Nelson Rockefeller feared for his party. He issued a statement excoriating the "vociferous and well-drilled extremists boring within the [Republican] party." He noted that the Young Republicans convention recently held had been "dominated by extremist groups" that employed "the tactics of totalitarianism." A few days later, Rocky urged Goldwater to renounce the Birchers and to demonstrate he was not a pawn of the extremists. With his eye on the White House, Rockefeller aimed to cast the upcoming nomination fight as a battle between reasonable Republicans and a wild, out-of-control fringe.

The White House, too, continued to be concerned about far-right extremism. In August 1963, Myer Feldman, deputy special counsel for the president, wrote a memo for Kennedy on the state of right-wing groups. All told, he noted, they spent between $15 million and $25 million a year and aired programs on at least one thousand radio stations. He noted the John Birch Society had between 20,000 and 100,000 members but its "impact derives from the energy, dedication and devotion" of its followers. "The radical right-wing," Feldman concluded, "constitutes a formidable force in American life today."

For his part, Buckley was still treading a careful path, adhering to the misleading stance that there was nothing wrong with the John Birch Society besides a few bad eggs. In a column, he acknowledged some Birchers evinced "the quintessence of intolerance, of a crudeness of spirit, of misanthropy," but these miscreants, he insisted, did not comprise a majority of the group. Moreover, he huffed, liberal Republicans had no cause to denigrate the society. Like many conservatives, he was playing footsie with the Birchers. Months earlier, Buckley had cochaired a testimonial dinner for Charles Edison, a prominent conservative and former New Jersey governor who served on the advisory committee of the John Birch Society's magazine, *American Opinion.*

———

On January 3, 1964, Goldwater officially announced his candidacy, vowing to "offer voters a choice, not an echo." His presidential bid would also offer the extremist right a ticket to the mainstream. Shortly before Goldwater leaped into the race, *Advance* magazine, published by liberal Republicans, warned of what Goldwater was bringing into the party:

The National Draft Goldwater Committee is led by segregationists like Wirt Yerger and James Martin in the South and assigns *National Review* publisher, William Rusher, to the job of "liaison" with the lunatic fringe—keep them working but quiet.

We the People!, a strident right wing action organization, is sending out Goldwater petitions. The Patrick Henry Group, having recently published "Is the Supreme Court Pro-Communist?" is now mass-distributing "Rockefeller Can't Win" in New Hampshire. John Birch leader N.B. Livingston Jr. has taken the helm of Ohioans for Goldwater, while another Society stalwart, Kenneth G. Bentson, is treasurer of the Arizona Goldwater for President Committee. Coloradoans for Goldwater have as their president a leader in a group of far right doctors, led by Birchers, who broke away from the "too liberal" AMA. Birch leader John Rousselot is continually addressing Goldwater meetings in California.

The Republican race was chiefly a contest between Goldwater and Rockefeller, the opposing ideological halves of the party. But there were crucial factors unrelated to ideology—most notably, Rockefeller's personal soap opera. In 1962, he divorced his wife of thirty-one years. The following year he married Happy Murphy, who had worked on his staff and who had divorced her husband and signed away custody of her four children. Now Happy was pregnant. All this drama didn't sit well with the family-first conservatives of the party.

Goldwater faced a different set of problems. He was dogged by the accusation he was an extremist—he had referenced the possibility of using low-yield atomic weapons in Vietnam—and nothing better proved this point than his reluctance to give the kooks who attached themselves to his campaign the heave-ho. As one Goldwater campaign memo pointed out, "Fortunately or unfortunately, the Birchers are contributing a substantial portion of our workers and some of our leaders in important areas... [The] Society does, in fact, harbor some of the soundest conservatives and some of the wildest extremists." (In early 1964, *American Opinion* published an article by Revilo Oliver, a Welch intimate, that asserted Kennedy had been gunned down in Dallas for "becoming a political liability" to his communist overlords.) Goldwater refused to separate himself from the Birchers, going as far as to declare, "I don't consider the John Birch Society as a group to be extremist."

The battle for the GOP nomination came down to the last major primary: California. If Goldwater won there, he would likely rack up enough delegates for a first-ballot victory at the convention and demonstrate to the naysayers that his brand of no-surrender Republicanism could triumph in a large and influential state. And to win, he needed the Birchers, the conspiracists, and the conservative fringe.

Rockefeller flooded California with money, buying up volunteers and blanketing the state with ads and leaflets. He denigrated Goldwater as an extremist revered by the John Birch Society and the Ku Klux Klan who would eagerly initiate nuclear warfare. Moderate Republicans in the state— led by Senator Thomas Kuchel—distributed information showing Goldwater's various ties to the radical right. They exposed a plan cooked up by Birchers to gain control of the state party. The moderates pushed the point that Goldwater donors were connected to the crazy group that believed

Eisenhower was a commie and publicized a list of Goldwater funders who the previous year had sponsored a dinner in Los Angeles honoring Welch.

Goldwater loyalists accused the moderates of engaging in guilt by association. He recruited a battalion of Hollywood celebrities—John Wayne, Rock Hudson, Ronald Reagan, Walter Brennan, Hedda Hopper, and others—and attracted plenty of donations from right-wing moneybags, including movie mogul Jack Warner; Theodore Petersen, the former corporate chief of Standard Oil Company of California; and Justin Dart, the chairman of Rexall Drugs. Goldwater's campaign enlisted thousands of foot soldiers: Birchers, YAFers, and Young Republicans. Goldwater would not turn any kook away. One campaign staffer told a journalist, "The senator is too busy to run a security check. Anybody who wants to carry a leaflet can carry a leaflet."

During the California contest, Goldwater appeared on Steve Allen's television show, and the host played a joke on him. With Goldwater looking on, Allen dialed a far-right hotline and received a recorded message that warned of "an internal takeover of the United States by the Communist conspiracy later during the year." The audience roared with laughter, and Allen asked Goldwater for his thoughts. The senator did not dismiss this absurd paranoia. He gave it a bit of a hug: "Instead of just laughing these people off, I recognize them as people who are concerned, people who recognize that some things in this government are not going the way they like." He stood with the loons who stood with him.

Into the breach entered one of Goldwater's most ardent devotees: Phyllis Schlafly, a twice-unsuccessful Republican congressional candidate who led the Illinois Federation of Republican Women. In May, she self-published a paperback titled A Choice Not an Echo, in which she lauded Goldwater as "the obvious choice" for the Republicans. He was, she gushed, "the man with the courage to give us simple solutions." The book was a sensation, selling three million copies in months. The senator wrote Schlafly to congratulate her on a "very well done" book and informed her of a person who had offered to hand out the book to every delegate at the upcoming Republican convention.

The book was brimming with conspiracy theories—not surprising, for Schlafly had been a secret Bircher.

Schlafly, in the slender work, claimed a claque of "secret kingmakers" had plotted to thwart the will of Main Street Republicans for decades, using their behind-the-scenes sway to compel the party to select presidential nominees who were destined to lose (Landon, Willkie, Dewey) or who could block a true conservative from grabbing the party's nod (Eisenhower). "It wasn't any accident," she wrote. "It was planned that way. In each of their losing presidential years, a small group of secret kingmakers, using hidden persuaders and psychological warfare techniques, manipulated the Republican National Convention." This cabal was so fiendishly clever and foresightful that they had managed to place Eisenhower "in an important non-public job to keep him in the public eye"—that is, the president of Columbia University—so they could later deploy him to defeat Taft at the 1952 convention. And President Lyndon Johnson, who succeeded the slain Kennedy in 1963, was in league with these clandestine "kingmakers" and had covered up the number of Reds and deviants in the government.

Schlafly purported to have "stumbled on clear evidence that very powerful men actually do meet to make plans which are kept secret from American citizens." She recounted that during a visit to Sea Island, Georgia, she "discovered" that a covert meeting had been held on nearby St. Simons Island in 1957 of "many of the top-level kingmakers who exercise financial, political and propaganda control over American citizens and policies." The clique, she revealed, was called the "DeBilderberg group."

This was light Bircherism: clandestine elites scheming against American interests and purposefully assisting the worldwide communist conspiracy. Yet Schlafly's "discovery" of the "DeBilderberg group" was no discovery. Indeed, the *Bilderberg* Group had held a conference on St. Simons Island seven years earlier, and it had publicly issued a thirty-four-page description of the confab, its fifth gathering of prominent businesspeople and government policymakers. (Dewey, Henry Kissinger, and David Rockefeller were among its swells.) The conversation—an assessment of world affairs—had been private, but the organization had put out a press release detailing the discussion.

Though Schlafly would until her death in 2016 deny she had been a member of the John Birch Society, that was a lie. In a 1959 letter to an associate, she had written, "The John Birch Society is doing wonderful work, and my husband and I both joined promptly after the Chicago meeting." But in 1964, she and her allies within the Goldwater operation did not want this bond known, for fear it would taint her work and further affix the Bircher tag to the Goldwater campaign.

In a letter that year to a supporter, Welch spelled this out. At the request of Schlafly—"a good friend of mine for a long time"—the John Birch Society, he reported, did not initiate a "massive exploitation" of *A Choice Not an Echo*. He believed Schlafly's book was "excellent" and would be "very helpful in the campaign." But, Welch explained, Schlafly and "some of the Goldwater higher-ups with whom she was in close association, were extremely fearful...that the usefulness and effectiveness of the book, especially in the

Primary Campaign, could be nullified by the enemy if they could tie it in any way to the John Birch Society; and that any such development might actually damage rather than help the total Goldwater cause." Welch noted that Schlafly "even resigned from the Society when she brought the book out, in order to avoid this possibility."

The fix was in, and the society did not orchestrate a promotional campaign for the book. But as Welch noted in this letter, Birchers "in many areas" bought up *A Choice Not An Echo* in large quantities and helped "mightily" in distributing it. He cited an effort that distributed three hundred thousand copies. Welch the conspiracist was conspiring with Schlafly and the Goldwater campaign.

In the final days of the California primary campaign, Goldwater praised two former Republican congressmen who were Birchers and refused to disavow society members. The reason was clear. Birchers were among the Goldwater enthusiasts blanketing the Golden State with Schlafly's Welch-like work and executing other campaign tasks. The United Republicans of California, an ultraconservative outfit influenced by Birchers, targeted book drops to precincts that favored Rockefeller. Schlafly later recalled that "the guy who distributed *Choice* in California was a man who ran a door business." He had a loading dock, and she would ship books to his facility and sell them at cost—$10 for a box of one hundred books. Goldwater workers would come by, purchase copies, and sell or hand them out in their precincts. A secret Bircher was shaping the race. Years later, Stephen Shadegg, Goldwater's longtime political strategist, would note that Goldwater vote was particularly high in the "book precincts."*

In California, the moderate Republicans kept throwing the extremist charge at Goldwater. But Happy Rockefeller helped the Goldwater camp change the discussion. She gave birth to Nelson Rockefeller Jr. three days before the California primary—reminding Republican voters of the charge that Rocky was a home-wrecker.

On Election Day, Goldwater tallied 68,350 more votes than Rockefeller out of 2.1 million cast. He would arrive at the convention in a few weeks with enough delegate commitments to triumph on the first ballot.

———

At the San Francisco gathering, the moderates did not roll over. The staff of Governor Bill Scranton of Pennsylvania, an establishment Republican,

———
* Denison Kitchel, Goldwater's campaign manager, had been a member of the John Birch Society, but he resigned in 1960 after reading *The Politician*. Shadegg called this the "best-kept secret" of the campaign.

issued a letter castigating Goldwater as a voice of the party's extremists. The missive did nothing to change the dynamics of the convention. But for those watching from home and elsewhere, it emphasized a theme of the week: Goldwaterism was fringe extremism in a cowboy hat. Welch boasted that one hundred of the 1,308 delegates at the convention were Birchers; many others clearly were ultraconservatives. Over 92 percent said they had read *A Choice Not an Echo*.

The media took notice. *Life* magazine observed the GOP had been captured by the "unyielding right wing" and subsumed by a "tide of zealotry." *Time* called the convention the "conquest" of the Republican Party by fanatics. Columnist Drew Pearson observed that the "smell of fascism has been in the air at this convention." A reporter for the *Los Angeles Times* called Goldwater "an intellectual with a keen rationalization of his political position [who] finds himself bedded down with kooks."

It was on the second night that the moderate forces placed extremism on the convention's center stage. Over the jeering of the delegates, Rockefeller spoke in favor of the platform proposal that denounced the John Birch Society, the Ku Klux Klan, and the Communist Party. After the measure was defeated, the riled-up delegates even killed a weaker amendment that merely denounced extremism in general without naming the John Birch Society or any other group.

Rockefeller and his fellow moderates had lost the party, but by triggering a visceral reaction to the anti-extremism planks they might have won a battle. Years later, F. Clifton White, a top Goldwater operative, recounted this moment: "How many votes Barry Goldwater lost on that one night alone could never be calculated. But I would wager they ran into the hundreds of thousands, perhaps millions, when his opponents were done branding him and his supporters by unmistakable implication as extremists, anti-civil rights fanatics and nuclear warmongers." Journalist Theodore White agreed: "As the TV cameras translated [the Goldwater supporters'] wrath and fury to the national audience, they pressed on the viewers the indelible impression of savagery which no Goldwater leader or wordsmith could later erase."

The next night, Goldwater won the nomination on the first ballot. After decades, the conservatives had finally beaten back the Me Too moderates within the party or, as Schlafly would call them, the "kingmakers"—and they had done so by encouraging and accepting the extremist forces of the far right. Goldwater's dalliance with the kooks would remain a problem, one that he exacerbated the next evening in his moment of glory.

On the final night of the convention, Goldwater delivered an acceptance speech that was 3,186 words long. But all anyone would remember were two sentences: "I would remind you that extremism in the defense of liberty is no vice. And let me remind you also that moderation in the pursuit of justice is no virtue." The crowd roared with approval, but the candidate who had been chased by accusations of extremism had just self-identified as an extremist.

Shadegg later observed that Goldwater—especially with his "harsh, almost belligerent delivery"—had given "his enemies new ammunition to use against him." The convention had refused to criticize Birchers and extremists. Then Goldwater—who Democrats were depicting as a scary fellow who might blow up the world in pursuit of his right-wing ideological convictions—embraced the kooks and their extremism. These people had brought him to the ball, and he was still dancing with them.

———

Weeks after the convention, Eisenhower convened a gathering of the party's bigwigs to fashion a truce. Goldwater, Nixon, Rockefeller, and others came. The party's nominee pleaded for unity. He promised to embrace Eisenhower's foreign policy of "peace through strength" and to support Social Security, the United Nations, and the Civil Rights Act of 1964 (which he had voted against). He vowed not to "seek" the support of extremist groups. That was not sufficient for Rockefeller. This would still allow Birchers and other barmy zealots to be part of the campaign. He pressed Goldwater to announce he "completely" rejected any assistance from such groups, particularly those that peddled conspiratorial trash. Obviously, that meant the Birchers. Goldwater would not go that far, and Ike settled the matter: Goldwater's statement was good enough.

For President Johnson and his campaign team, that was just fine. They wanted Goldwater to be defiant in the face of the accusation he palled around with extremists. They were delighted to be running against a revolutionary calling not for a reform here or there but for a reversal of the government activism borne of the New Deal. Goldwater had openly mulled changes in Social Security that would eviscerate the popular program. He had casually mentioned the possible use of nuclear bombs. He had sided with segregationists. His campaign slogan—"In Your Heart, You Know He's Right"—seemed a tacit acknowledgment he harbored positions best not said aloud.

As the final stretch kicked off in September, Jack Valenti, a top aide to LBJ, sent the boss a memo advising they treat Goldwater "not as an equal who has credentials to be President, but as a *radical*, a preposterous candidate who would ruin this country and our future." And the Johnson campaign hit Goldwater with perhaps the most notorious political ad of all time: a spot showing a young girl picking the petals off a daisy as an ominous nuclear countdown plays. A nuclear detonation then occurs, and Johnson, in a voice-over, intones, "These are the stakes." Not too subtle: Don't vote for the crazy man.

Another Johnson ad, titled "Confessions of a Republican," showed a clean-cut fellow in a suit sharing his reservations about Goldwater: "The man scares me...So many men with strange ideas are working for Goldwater...When all these weird groups come out in favor of the candidate of *my* party, either they're not Republicans, or I'm not." The message once more: Goldwater was the candidate of extremism.

The Birchers were hardly the only fringe riders on Goldwater's train. On September 16, segregationist Strom Thurmond left the Democratic Party to join the Goldwater crusade. The next night, he attended a Goldwater rally at the Sugar Bowl Stadium in New Orleans. Also on the stage was Leander Perez, a notoriously racist and antisemitic Democratic political boss in Louisiana who had flipped sides to be on Goldwater's team. He had bankrolled the White Citizens' Council of Greater New Orleans in the 1950s, and in 1962 the Catholic Church had excommunicated him for opposing the desegregation of parochial schools. (Perez compared integration to "hell.") He was now Goldwater's point man in the state, raising money and organizing events. He insisted that communists were backing Johnson and that if LBJ were reelected, "race riots will break out to such an extent that our civilization will be pushed back into the jungle age."

The fringe of the fringe was with Goldwater. Gerald L. K. Smith, a longtime antisemite and onetime Nazi sympathizer, backed Goldwater, exclaiming that the Republican Party was "the white Christian party." Top Klan officials also gave their blessing to his campaign. The Minutemen militia—led by a Bircher—threatened to sabotage Democratic campaign offices to help Goldwater. Allen Zoll, a prominent 1930s fascist (and Christian nationalist and antisemite), was a full-time staffer in Goldwater's campaign headquarters. Dean Burch, Goldwater's man running the Republican National Committee, had a forgiving attitude about all this: "We're not in the business of discouraging votes."

They were, though, in the business of exploiting the anger of extremism. Russ Walton, a Goldwater ad man, described the campaign's strategy for reaching voters: "We want to just make them mad, make their stomach turn, take this latent anger and concern which now exists, build it up, and subtly turn and focus it."

There was plenty of anger. When Lady Bird Johnson, the president's wife, campaigned in Columbia, South Carolina, a collection of Birchers at the front of the crowd waved inflammatory signs: BLACK BIRD GO HOME; JOHNSON IS A COMMUNIST; JOHNSON IS A NIGGER-LOVER. As the assembled booed the First Lady, Representative Hale Boggs, a Louisiana Democrat, grabbed the microphone and exclaimed, "This is reminiscent of Hitler! This is a Democratic gathering, not a Nazi gathering."

———

In the final months of the campaign, Goldwater and the Republicans mined not just bigotry to win over voters but conspiracy theory and paranoia. Across the country, his campaign offices were selling Schlafly's *A Choice Not an Echo* and two other self-published extremist screeds: John Stormer's *None Dare Call It Treason* and J. Evetts Haley's *A Texan Looks at Lyndon: A Study in Illegitimate Power.*

Stormer, the chair of the Missouri Federation of Young Republicans, was peddling classic anti-Red hysteria. Citing FBI Director J. Edgar Hoover's warning that communists had infiltrated every nook and cranny of American life, Stormer asserted the United States government "has been rendered helpless in the struggle with communism" due to purposeful action and inaction on the part of government officials. America, he claimed, was "rapidly losing" the Cold War and stood on the precipice of annihilation, either as the result of a "conspiratorial plan to destroy the United States" (which included disarmament, inflation, and foreign aid) or "the work of well-meaning but misguided idealists." Stormer denied being a member of the John Birch Society but acknowledged his wife was.

Haley was a prominent Texan ultraconservative and a onetime Confederate apologist who had advocated segregation. At a January convention of segregationists in Jackson, Mississippi, he had derided Johnson as "a counterfeit Communist, the Benedict Arnold of the South, a traitor to Texas." Two years earlier, he had called for the lynching of Chief Justice Earl Warren. In his anti-Johnson book, he claimed the National Youth Administration, a New Deal agency for which Johnson had headed its Texas division, was a "disloyal, subversive organization, under the domination of Russia." Haley maintained that Johnson, as a member of Congress, had supported farm programs "conceived by the Communist cell in agriculture." And as president, Haley contended, Johnson had helped to "white wash the Communist conspiracy" behind the assassination of John Kennedy. A. C. Greene of the *Dallas Times Herald* called Haley "a case of unhospitalized paranoia."

These books appealed to irrational and ill-informed fear. They encouraged

Americans to believe conspiratorial nonsense. They undermined the national political debate and demonized Johnson and the Democrats, representing them as anti-American and malignant threats to the nation. And the Goldwater campaign embraced them, every page.

With Goldwater offices, local GOP chapters, and John Birch Society bookstores pushing the attack books, they sold millions of copies. "Never before has such literature been used to such an extent in a Presidential campaign," reported the *New York Times*. Dade County Republicans in Florida alone handed out 172,000 copies of Stormer's book. Goldwater partisans in California convinced chain drugstores to carry these books by providing them free. In a letter to an associate, Welch reported that "we have made an outright purchase of half a million copies of Haley's book" to distribute to Bircher bookstores and members. The society was negotiating the purchase of another half million copies.

Another important component of the Goldwater campaign was overseen by extremists with lots of money in their pockets. The television committee for the Goldwater citizens organization—which was separate from the official campaign run out of the Republican Party—was cochaired by Patrick Frawley Jr. and Walter Knott, well-to-do businessmen with long-standing ties to the fringe right. Frawley was a pioneer in the ballpoint pen business who parlayed his profits into controlling shares of Schick and Technicolor. He was a supporter of Fred C. Schwarz's Christian Anti-Communism Crusade, which staged large rallies denouncing the Reds. (One such event held in 1961 at the Hollywood Bowl featured Roy Rogers, John Wayne, and James Stewart, and prompted one television critic to call it "a monster three-hour concentration of pure venom on television...in which the patriots suggested again and again that the United States was largely peopled by traitors.") Knott, who had transformed a small fruit ranch in southern California into the amusement park Knott's Berry Farm, was the founder and head of the California Free Enterprise Association, which distributed material from the John Birch Society and assorted far-right extremists and fringe conspiracists.

The committee led by Frawley and Knott produced one of the highlights of the Goldwater campaign: a half-hour televised speech on the candidate's behalf delivered by Ronald Reagan a week before Election Day. For years, Reagan, a B-movie actor who became a corporate pitchman for General Electric, had been slinging a right-wing speech extolling freedom, denouncing big government, and decrying accommodation with foreign communist powers, which he now modified to celebrate Goldwater. He read his lines well and deftly presented the hard-right views he shared with Goldwater, yet in a folksy, aw-shucks, good-humored manner—a skill Goldwater never developed. "There is no such thing as left or right," Reagan nearly sang in his infomercial for Goldwater. "There is only an up or down. Up to man's age-old dream, the ultimate in individual freedom consistent with law and order; or down to the ant heap of totalitarianism." He presented a stark choice for the election: either "preserve for our children this, the last best hope of man on earth" or "sentence them to take the last step into a thousand years of darkness." When he finished, the studio audience cheered.

Whether or not this long ad—dubbed "A Time for Choosing"—did much good for the candidate, it established the smooth-talking Reagan as a star in the conservative firmament and got right-wingers talking: *Maybe this guy should run for office.*

———

Throughout the campaign, Goldwater had sent a clear message to the extremists: Join us. A report from the American Jewish Committee noted, "The radical rightists apparently interpreted Goldwater's refusal to repudiate extremist groups and organizations unambiguously as a signal to go ahead. Abusive pamphlets, cartoons, newsletters and flyers with racial and religious overtones cropped up in all parts of the United States." The AJC added, "It was often the Bircher or other extremist zealot who rang doorbells, distributed handbills, heckled the opposition, mounted telephone campaigns, and served as a foot soldier in the army of [Goldwater] campaign volunteers." Goldwater was good for Welch. Each month through the general election campaign, the society set a record number for recruits and new chapters.

The extremists lost on Election Day. It was a bloodbath. Johnson pocketed 61 percent of the popular vote and whomped Goldwater in the Electoral College, 486 to 52. His party gained two Senate and thirty-seven House seats. Goldwater's unspoken alliance with Birchers, bigots, and conspiracists had yielded the largest defeat in a presidential campaign since 1820. George Herbert Walker Bush, a Republican oil executive who had beaten back a Bircher attempt to take control of the Houston GOP, lost the US Senate race in Texas and blamed that year's Republican trouncing on "the so-called 'nut' fringe."

Goldwater had energized, mobilized, and legitimized fanatics and extremists. The top-line election results suggested that had been a dumb political move. James Reston of the *New York Times* harrumphed, "Barry Goldwater not only lost the Presidential election...but the conservative cause as well." And the *Los Angeles Times*' Roscoe Drummond had a blunter verdict: "Thus ends the Republican Party's experiment with extreme conservatism."

Yet to a more discerning eye, the Goldwater campaign demonstrated that the dark forces of American politics were powerful and now, thanks to the senator, more established. Goldwaterism, with its appeal to racists and segregationists, had flipped five Southern states from the Democratic to Republican column—the start of a long-term trend much desired by Republicans. The Arizona senator had led a new generation of conservative political activists into the Republican Party, and they had no intention of leaving. Moreover, the campaign had revealed there was a cadre of hundreds of thousands of Americans who would respond to fearmongering and eagerly toil for and send money to a conservative cause. The campaign raised $5.8 million from 650,000 contributors and fielded close to half a million campaign workers on the day of the election. These were troops that could later be activated.

"Any notion that the Johnson landslide in the 1964 elections had eliminated or even seriously impaired the extremist movement was not warranted," the American Jewish Committee warned. The extremists were beaten, not eradicated. They were only getting started.

CHAPTER 6

Keeping the Kooks Quiet

On an April afternoon in 1965, Ronald Reagan had a lunch date at one of his favorite Hollywood haunts, Cave des Roys, a private club started by several Los Angeles tycoons and movie and television stars, including Paul Newman, Desi Arnaz, and Tony Curtis. Boasting a fifteenth-century French style, the establishment featured suits of armor, a balustrade from Maximilian's palace in Mexico, and leather wallpaper from a Rothschild chateau in Vienna. The waitresses wore scanty mock-medieval costumes. The menu offered an assortment of steaks.

Dining with Reagan were two hot-shot political pros, Stuart Spencer and Bill Roberts. Five years earlier, they had created a consulting firm that quickly became a powerhouse for Republican office seekers. They had a strong preference for moderate Republicans; right-wing ideologues were not their bag. In 1964, the duo ran Rockefeller's losing effort in the California primary against Goldwater. The subsequent November election confirmed their belief: Extremists make lousy candidates.

Reagan was considering entering the 1966 gubernatorial race against Democratic incumbent Pat Brown. His speech for Goldwater the previous fall had turned him into the great hope of the right. A band of conservative California millionaires had embraced Reagan as their guy for what was certain to be a tough battle against Brown, who had defeated Nixon three years earlier. And Reagan had asked Goldwater for advice. "I'd hire those sons of bitches, Spencer-Roberts," Goldwater told him, recommending the team that had waged a fierce fight against him.

On the table that day in addition to the food and drinks were two crucial matters: experience and extremism. Reagan, though a talented pitchman and a seasoned (if not acclaimed) actor, had never run for public office. More troublesome, he had a reputation as a right-wing radical, a Bircheresque ideologue. Spencer and Roberts didn't want another Goldwater on their hands, a contender weighed down by ties to fanatics and kooks.

Spencer and Roberts were far from the only politicos who thought this way. The lingering lesson from the Goldwater debacle, it seemed, was that a

GOP candidate associated with the fringe was doomed. In California, Goldwater had collected only 41 percent of the vote to Johnson's 59 percent. *Time* magazine had pronounced a stern assessment: "The conservative cause whose championship Goldwater assumed suffered a crippling setback... The humiliation of their defeat was so complete that they will not have another shot at party domination for some time to come." An NBC News anchor dismissed Goldwater's fans as "segregationists, Johnson-phobes, desperate conservatives, and radical nuts...the coalition of discontent."

The Goldwater disaster did provide slivers of hope for conservatives: the Republicans' gains in the South, the massive grassroots fundraising effort, the hundreds of thousands of volunteers. But the GOP had to erase—or hide—its bond with extremism. In that regard, Reagan was not the best test case. He had been a fire-breathing anticommunist, warning that "Communism and Capitalism cannot exist side-by-side" and that communists were boring into American institutions and scheming to overthrow the government. Social welfare programs, he proclaimed, had placed the nation on a fast track to totalitarianism. He was shrill and radical. He was not a Bircher. But he talked like one.

Still, Spencer and Roberts were intrigued by Reagan. This guy, they thought, had potential. He was articulate. He had a winning personality. The Republican base loved him. He had a set of core values but also a pragmatic side. Maybe there was a way around his extremism problem.

Reagan had once been a solid New Deal Democrat and FDR fan. After a radio career in the Midwest, he landed an acting gig with the Warner Bros. studio in 1937. His work was hardly stellar, but he became a Hollywood star and a top official of the Screen Actors Guild, the union for actors. After the war, Reagan—reacting to labor agitation and fears of communist infiltration—lurched to the right. He testified before HUAC about supposed communist efforts to take over Hollywood and provided names of left-wing screenwriters, producers, and directors whom he believed were part of this plot. His shifting politics coincided with a decline in his acting fortunes. He was no longer obtaining juicy roles. But General Electric hired him to host a television show it sponsored, sell its products, and deliver inspirational and homespun speeches about individual initiative, self-reliance, and free enterprise to its workers (to help them resist the lure of unions).

Reagan developed a winning schtick that merged tales of his Hollywood days, praise of free enterprise, and criticism of big government programs, the gateway to dreaded socialism. He was an amiable vessel for a message of fear. He often remarked that "by 1970 the world will be all slave or all free." In a 1960 letter to Nixon, Reagan said of John Kennedy, "Under the tousled boyish haircut it is still old Karl Marx," and he compared Kennedy's proposed programs to "the idea of a government being Big Brother to us all," referring to Hitler's "State Socialism." The following year, Reagan was the featured speaker at a fundraising dinner for Representative John Rousselot, a California Republican and John Birch Society member. Reagan supported a group whose members advocated hanging Chief Justice Earl Warren. He claimed new federal health care programs would end freedom in America. He shared stages with segregationists and virulent anticommunists. In 1962, he was campaign chairman for a challenger to Republican Senator Thomas Kuchel who endorsed the John Birch Society and called for war with the Soviet Union.

Though Reagan steered clear of the most bizarre anti-Red conspiracy theories, he was one of them. He was a kook. As historian Matthew Dallek later observed, "If politically aware Californians had been pushed in late 1962 to give their opinion of Ronald Reagan, they would have identified him as an extremist. A pleasant one, perhaps, but nonetheless a man on the edge of the spectrum."

———

In the early months of 1965, Reagan was speaking throughout California, pondering whether he should heed the call of those tycoons egging him on to enter the gubernatorial race. At a convention of conservative Republicans, he was asked what he thought of the John Birch Society. This was a tender topic among Republicans in California. While running for governor in 1962, Nixon had assailed the society and alienated a thick slice of GOP conservatives. And Rockefeller had nearly beaten Goldwater by painting him as a Bircher-friendly radical. What was a Republican candidate to do? Disavow Welch's outfit and tick off right-wingers? Or accept the kooks and be lumped in with them?

Reagan offered a muddled response, referring to a state legislative report that had *not* declared the John Birch Society a "subversive" organization. It looked like a dodge from a guy with his own history of extremism, someone who didn't want to anger the fringe radicals whose votes, money, and bodies he could use in a campaign against Brown. In another statement, Reagan made it clear he wanted the Birchers on his side. He said he did "not agree with everything about the society," but he reiterated there was nothing "subversive" about it.

Right-wing extremism had not abated in California. In July 1965, political reporter Ben Bagdikian surveyed the remains of Goldwater's movement in the Golden State for the *New York Times*. "It is almost a religion governing the lives of its adherents," he reported. "It includes gun-toting psychopaths who think the John Birch Society is a ·club for sissies, Birchites and other white-collar radicals, tax-hating non-joiners and regular Republicans who are simply more conservative than [Pennsylvania Republican Governor] William Scranton or California's liberal Republican Senator, Thomas Kuchel." The John Birch Society claimed to have inherited 30 percent of the Goldwater activists in Los Angeles County and boasted more than fifty members among the two-hundred-person Los Angeles County Republican Central Committee. And, Bagdikian pointed out, the Goldwaterites were giddy about Reagan.

Still testing the waters on a speaking swing through northern and central California in late July, Reagan kept ducking the Bircher question. He denounced critics for "trying to paint me into a corner and suggest I'm a kind of right-wing kook." But he wouldn't break with the Birchers, saying he had "no basis for the blanket indicting of people, or of applying loyalty oaths." As Henry Salvatori, an oil millionaire backing Reagan, later noted, Reagan "had to convince [people] that we weren't a bunch of kooks."

Ever since their lunch with Reagan in April, Spencer and Roberts—who had signed up with the former actor—had pondered what to do about his extremist problem. A full-scale repudiation of the Birchers was not going to happen. That had not helped Nixon. They would have to find a way for Reagan to denounce the *extreme* extremists but not all Birchers and other ultraconservatives. In an interview with *Newsweek* in June, they mentioned they might ask the more radical Republican groups in the state, such as the Young Republicans, not to endorse Reagan, and they conceded that Reagan had to tone down his act and sell himself as someone "who is not the darling of the extremists, a sensible, reasonable guy who leans to the right but who doesn't spout all this nonsense about... fluoridation. Our toughest job is going to be proving that he isn't a right-winger." Reagan told the newsmagazine that the extremist label wouldn't "stick if people will listen to what I've got to say."

Discussing the Bircher issue with his aides, Reagan was adamant. He would not denounce the group: "I see no reason to indict or repudiate an organization of what I am not a member." But Reagan realized he had to do something. The obvious step was to follow the course of Buckley and Goldwater: target Welch but show respect for Birchers.

On September 24, Reagan threaded that needle. In the only official statement on the society that he would issue during the campaign, he declared he had never been a member. He called Welch's smear of Eisenhower and his other conspiracy theories "utterly reprehensible." He urged Birchers to renounce Welch's ideas. But he pointed out that, according to the FBI, there was nothing subversive about the outfit. He said he would not seek assistance from "any blocs or groups"; he would look for support from voters "by persuading them to accept my philosophy, not by my accepting theirs." This was no repudiation, just a gentle brush-back. The *Des Moines Register* observed, "The record now is sufficiently confused so that it is probably difficult to know just what the relationship between Reagan and the Birch Society leaders really is."

Some Birchers were peeved. But there was no outcry from the radical right. After all, Welch had for years told his followers that they had to be sneaky like the commies. If this was what arch-anticommunist Ronald Reagan had to do to win, well they could live with that. In private communications with fellow conservatives, Reagan shared his generous view that most Birchers were fine upstanding citizens. In a letter to one of the original society members, Reagan noted, "I'm going to do my utmost to take this entire subject out of the campaign dialogue."

Reagan's statement came just as the national Republican Party was trying— and failing—to break away from the Bircher extremists.

After a Bircher in South Dakota declared he would challenge incumbent Senator Karl Mundt, a solid conservative, in the Republican primary, Senator Thruston Morton declared, "As a partisan Republican, I am concerned by the fact that the John Birch Society has picked my party...as the vehicle to promulgate its monolithic philosophy." He slapped the group hard: "There are three organizations in this country which give me grave doubts as a citizen: the Communist Party, the Ku Klux Klan, and the John Birch Society." But Morton did not want to scare off all those possible voters and volunteers—no matter how paranoid or misguided they were—and he added, "It's not the Birch membership I'm aiming at. Most of the members would be welcomed into the Republican Party. But the leadership takes over the party at the precinct level. This is a threat to our party." The national Republicans remained hung up on a phony distinction: The society's leadership was a problem, but its members and activists, who fancied the taste of Welch's conspiratorial mush, were perfectly fine.

A few days later, Senator Everett Dirksen of Illinois and Representative Gerald Ford of Michigan, the top Republicans in their respective chambers, held a press conference in which they hoped to bury the Bircher question. Dirksen began: "Let me emphasize this with as much vigor as I can that the John Birch Society is not a part of the Republican Party." Ford pointed out that congressional Republicans had supported the Civil Rights Act of 1964 and the Voting Rights Act of 1965 and the society was opposed to both. A short time later, Ray Bliss, the party chairman, pressed all Republicans to "reject membership in any radical organization which attempts to use the Republican Party." He did not directly refer to the John Birch Society, but he did target Welch: "Honest, patriotic and conscientious conservatives may be misjudged because of irresponsible radicals such as Welch."

In this stretch, William Buckley reappeared as the right's knight bent on ridding his movement of Welch. He again sicced the *National Review* on Welch, and he went further than he had in 1962. He blasted not only Welch's harebrained and conspiratorial notions; he rebuked the entire organization. Buckley assailed the society's core belief that communists covertly controlled critical branches of the government. For years, he and his allies had ignored an inconvenient reality: A lot of their subscribers and supporters were nutters. Now he wondered how the group's members could abide "such paranoid and unpatriotic drivel." Buckley was sidestepping a fundamental truth of the right: The Birchers were Birchers *because* of this drivel.

The Birchers responded predictably to the Republican assault. Welch maintained that Morton, Dirksen, Ford, and other top Republicans were being manipulated by communists. "The Communists have now inspired, initiated, created and unleashed a campaign of attack against the John Birch Society," he wrote to members. Rousselot charged that Ford was part of the left-wing "DeBilderberger Group" that "meets clandestinely." (This was the organization that Phyllis Schlafly had claimed pulled the strings of moderate Republicans.)

When Republican Party leaders gathered in Washington in December for a meeting of the Republican Coordinating Committee, the agenda included considering a resolution repudiating the John Birch Society. But the GOP blinked. Instead, the group passed a watered-down measure that called only for Republicans to say no to joining extremist groups. Media organizations lambasted the GOP for wimping out. The *New York Herald Tribune*, in an editorial headlined, "Sparing the Birch Rod," opined, "The responsibility of political leaders is not merely to denounce sin, but to identify the sinners—or at least specify the sin." The GOP could not bring itself to give the Birchers the boot.

———

Leading national Republicans were endeavoring to swat the society to the side without causing a backlash among its members. Yet in Reagan country, the Republican attitude toward the Birchers was quite different. In California, the party's conservative wing embraced them. Local Republican clubs opened their doors to society speakers. An official of the United Republicans of California estimated that 10 to 15 percent of its members were Birchers or sympathizers. The Los Angeles County Young Republicans approved a resolution expressing "confidence that the John Birch Society is composed of loyal and concerned Americans." The president of the California Republican Assembly defended the society from the criticism of the national GOP. Moderate Republicans complained all this love for the Birchers was political suicide for the state party, but the right was on a roll.

To Reagan's benefit, the question of extremism would not dominate the gubernatorial campaign because of chaos.

In the fall of 1964, protests had exploded at the University of California at Berkeley—over free speech rights, civil rights, and the Vietnam War that Johnson was expanding. Students had occupied school buildings and confronted police. Hundreds were arrested. For Reagan and his team, "Berkeley" became shorthand for what they saw as a winning campaign issue: cultural disorder. This included free love, pot smoking, pornography, dirty, long-haired kids sneering at traditional values and American wholesomeness, and everything else that was part of the social upheaval engulfing the nation. The tumult intensified in August 1965 with the Watts riot, a conflagration triggered by an incident in which white police officers in South Central Los Angeles, a predominantly Black neighborhood, pulled over a young man suspected of drunken driving. The arrest turned into a physical confrontation that led to six days of civil unrest, fueled partly by rage over police abuse, racial segregation, and economic deprivation. Governor Brown, who was vacationing in Greece, called in the National Guard to suppress the uprising. Thirty-four people were killed, as tens of millions of dollars in property damage occurred.

Rebellious students and rioting citizens were shaping the state's tense political climate. There was increasing worry and resentment—particularly among white, middle-class voters—over crime, welfare, and the bulging state ballot. In November 1964, 65 percent of the state's voters had backed a ballot initiative to nullify a civil rights law passed the previous year that banned racial discrimination in house sales and rentals. It was a spasm of white backlash to the calls for increased civil rights. Reagan had opposed the Civil Rights Act of 1964 and the Voting Rights Act of 1965—positions that placed him on the far right. But in California, the main racial political issue was the fair housing measure that two-thirds of the state's voters rejected. What was extreme about being on the side of this majority?

In the face of all the turmoil and commotion, Reagan served up straightforward—or simple—answers. Unruly, elitist ingrates overrunning Berkeley *and* wild lawbreakers in the inner city? Law and order. The budget crisis? Cut 10 percent of state employees and shut down programs. After all, didn't the urban unrest show those antipoverty initiatives just don't work? Obviously, the answer was private initiatives, charity, people helping themselves and each other.

Reagan didn't have to defend extremism, as Goldwater had done. The times had become extreme. For a huge swath of the electorate, the radicals, the rabble-rousers, the long-hairs—not Goldwaterites and Birchers—were now the extremists.

Much of the radical right extremism of recent years had been energized by conspiratorial notions about communism and internal subversion. These were hidden, unseen, abstract threats lurking out of view. Now, for many voters, the enemy to America was in plain sight and could be seen on the evening news: violent mobs in the cities, troublemaking students on campuses, protesters in the street. Free Love, Free Sex, Free Speech, Filthy Speech, drugs, homosexuality, questioning authority, beatniks, anarchists, radicals. A Bircher or McCarthyite could view all this as part of that fiendish communist plot to subvert the United States that he or she had feared for years. But others could look at this ferment with unease and ask, "What is happening to my country?" When Reagan railed against antiwar marches as "the fruit of appeasement," he rang a bell for the traditional anticommunist crowd. But that appeal also resonated for voters who wondered what the hell was going on.

———

Reagan officially entered the race on January 4, 1966. He assailed the disorder and moral rot infecting the Golden State. "Our streets are jungle paths after dark," he bemoaned. He asked whether the state would accept the "neurotic vulgarities" of the Berkeley students or "enforce" decency. But he avoided the trap of Goldwater-ish dourness. It was not the end of days for California, he reassured voters, declaring that the capacity for solving California's problems was "limitless." He melded traditional right-wing scolding with an upbeat sunniness.

His main GOP foe was George Christopher, a businessman and former mayor of San Francisco. He had been Rockefeller's northern California chair in 1964, and like a general fighting the previous war, he had been flaying Reagan for his history of ties to the kooks of the right. "I ask no aid from the extreme right," he said. "If I thought the difference between winning and losing required embracing any extremism, I'd prefer to lose."

The extremist issue was hard for Reagan to shake off entirely. In February, the California Young Republicans elected new officers: Three of the top four new officers were members of the John Birch Society. Weeks later, Brown held a press conference to dismiss Reagan as a "Goldwater Republican" and "an exponent of the far right for the last three or four years at least." But with all the turbulence in California and elsewhere, Reagan's links to extremism were not a liability that kept Spencer, Roberts, and other Reagan advisers up at night.

The greater problem was Reagan's inexperience and lack of basic knowledge about the state he sought to lead. But that was fixable. At the urging of Reagan's moneymen, the campaign imported two eggheads, Kenneth Holden and Stanley Plog, respectively professors at UCLA and San Fernando Valley State, and the proprietors of the Behavior Science Corporation, a consulting firm specializing in research based on behavioral psychology. After huddling with Reagan for a few days at a Malibu beach cottage, they put together a crack team of statisticians, sociologists, psychologists, and other experts who crafted position papers for the candidate and, more important, organized black binders crammed with hundreds of index cards bearing facts, figures, and talking points.

The two would later come to be seen as Reagan's Svengalis. They did help the actor refine his bits on welfare, crime, Berkeley, and all the rest. But they didn't put any words in Reagan's mouth that were not already part of his worldview. The pair deconstructed his opinions and packaged his basic beliefs into a dozen or so research books stuffed with those index cards. The cards were the key. They went everywhere with Reagan. These two psychologists advised Reagan on the most salient arguments. Hit hard on welfare, they recommended. It stirred resentment. This campaign was all about picking at the scabs of populist anger, which included white backlash.

On June 7, Reagan routed George Christopher 65 to 31 percent. In what should have been a wake-up call for Democrats, Reagan collected 1.4 million votes, almost 100,000 more than Pat Brown drew in his primary contest against Los Angeles Mayor Sam Yorty.

The Democrats, though, had hoped for a Reagan win, believing he would be easier to defeat in the November election. But in the past year, the former actor had honed his public speaking skills, developing a stunning talent for deploying sound bites and quips to deliver simple messages at a time when the world seemed increasingly complicated and chaotic. He fared well in

Q&A sessions on the campaign trail. He easily parried attacks from opponents and reporters, firing off zingers with an isn't-this-fun twinkle in his eye. His smile was warm. He displayed down-home good humor and charm but also projected certitude and strength. He had good hair. He knew his lines. His targets were clear: big government, welfare programs, threats to law and order. He was a champion of traditional values, a candidate offering grit, grace, and glamour.

Immediately after the primary victory, Reagan sent a signal to Goldwater, who had offered to hit the campaign trail in California for his pal: Thanks, but no thanks. Instead, Reagan planned a visit to Eisenhower. The message for the general election was obvious: *I'm no extremist*. He was dressing up—or covering up—his far-right views in the garb of a good-natured and upbeat fellow. The Reagan campaign kept Birchers at bay, making certain no prominent positions were held by Welch's acolytes. It also distanced itself from the assorted right-wing GOP outfits that had Birchers within their ranks.

The Reaganites managed to do this without ticking off the right. Four years earlier, Nixon had told the Birchers to get lost and sacrificed right-wing support. Reagan adopted a gentler approach, as if to say, "Hey, fellas, it's best if I do this on my own. Would you mind waiting over there?" The far right was fine with this. Reagan knew maintaining this separation was crucial for victory. In a letter to Senator George Murphy (another actor turned GOP politician in California), he noted, "We do have the party glued together, if only we can keep some of the kooks quiet." Reagan exhibited discipline in saying little when questioned about the John Birch Society. On *Meet the Press*, when asked about the group, he said he rejected "the idea [the society] is a Republican issue."

Meanwhile, Senator Thomas Kuchel was grousing that the GOP in his state had been taken over by "fanatical" and "neo-fascist elements." And the Democrats kept waving the Reagan-is-a-Bircher flag, as if the extremist charge—which undid Goldwater—would undo Reagan. They charged Reagan with pocketing campaign money from the John Birch Society. He denied that. State controller Alan Cranston, a Democrat, confronted Reagan at the Sacramento airport and tried to hand him a report that disclosed there was "growing anti-Semitism" within the Bircher crowd. Reagan told him, "I'm just a private citizen myself, not an investigator."

The Democrats wouldn't let up on this front. In mid-August, they produced a twenty-nine-page report tying Reagan to right-wing extremism. It listed Birchers who were Reagan supporters and noted that his top fundraisers included Walter Knott and Patrick Frawley, who had underwritten numerous extremist causes. Robert Coate, the state Democratic chair, demanded Reagan repudiate the society and reject contributions from its members. Reagan shot back that it was "absolutely not true" that he was influenced by extremist groups. "It never occurred to me to give a saliva test to the people who have supported me," he cracked. He said he was unaware of any extremism among his top supporters.

———

The Democrats tried various angles. They noted Reagan had been part of planning sessions with Rousselot for Project Alert, a militant anticommunist group that included speakers who warned that the Reds infiltrated all levels of government and who called for threatening the Soviet Union with a military attack. One Project Alert activist had urged Chief Justice Warren's execution. They pointed out that Reagan had campaigned for a segregationist candidate for governor in Louisiana in 1964. And Brown sent Reagan a telegram pressing him to denounce the John Birch Society, the Communist Party, and the Ku Klux Klan and to distance himself from Birchers running for the state assembly. "Once you take these steps, I will no longer consider extremism a valid campaign issue," Brown helpfully added.

The blasts continued in the final weeks of the campaign. Brown assailed Reagan for being the "political darling of the right wing," and as proof he cited Reagan's financial supporters, including oil and shipbuilding tycoon J. Howard Pew, who was on the editorial advisory board of *American Opinion*, the society's magazine, and was listed as a major stockholder in Robert Welch Inc., the group's publishing arm. But none of this blew up in Reagan's movie-star face. He kept dismissing these attacks as desperate diversions from Brown and the Democrats.

———

The Brown campaign had one last extremist card to play. Earlier in the campaign, Reagan's camp had been looking for a nifty phrase to sum up his upbeat and forward-looking message that free enterprise and private initiative—not government programs—could efficiently address the nation's woes. Roosevelt had the New Deal; Truman, the Fair Deal; Kennedy, the New Frontier; and Johnson, the Great Society. The Reagan camp wanted its own tagline and hit on the "Creative Society"—a term that had been coined by right-wing extremist W. S. McBirnie, a California pastor with a radio show.

McBirnie had pitched this idea to the Reagan campaign in late 1965. Reagan's people loved it. One campaign memo laid out the reasoning:

"Republicans have sometimes been caricatured as people who want to turn back the clock...But, on the contrary, our eyes are turned to the future... If the socialistic type of government is called the 'Great Society,' which it is mistakenly called, let us propose another, a better idea, a happy and constructive alternative: THE CREATIVE SOCIETY."

Brown attacked Reagan for adopting a catchphrase concocted by a right-wing kook, noting that the pastor had attended John Birch Society meetings. McBirnie countered, "I am not among the critics of the Birch society nor am I a member." He called himself "a responsible conservative and loyal Republican." That was not quite the case. McBirnie had a controversial history. He had been forced in 1959 to resign as pastor of a Texas church after it became known he had been trysting with the wife of a parishioner. In recent years, he had blamed communists for everything he considered wrong in America: antidiscrimination housing laws, pot smoking, pornography. "Communism has infiltrated the civil rights movement," he declared in 1965. In one of the hundreds of pamphlets he wrote and distributed, he chastised parents for giving allowances to their children, contending that led to socialism. He was one of the kooks Reagan had said he needed to eschew.

But the McBirnie controversy went nowhere. The entire line of attack on Reagan's extremism paid few dividends for the Brown campaign. "Instead of sticking, the labels slid off Reagan's slick coating and fell away, impotent," historian Jonathan Schoenwald later observed. "Brown might have been the first to experience what was later known as Reagan's 'Teflon personality.'"

In the final campaign stretch, the Brown camp directed its remaining firepower at Reagan's lack of experience—which reinforced one of the actor's chief selling points. He was an outsider ready and eager to apply old-fashioned common sense to the various crises at hand and a bloated bureaucracy that seemed unable to cope with the state's problems.

On Election Day, a rockslide hit the Democrats. Reagan won 58 to 42 percent, pocketing nearly 1 million more votes than the governor. Two years earlier, Goldwater had lost to Johnson by 1.2 million votes.

Reagan had broken the Democratic Party, robbing it of white working-class voters. His politics were no different from Goldwater's. He had spent years in the far-right realm of Red Scare paranoia and anti-government hysteria, hobnobbing with zealots and crackpots. Yet at a time of riots, protests, civil unrest, and societal upheaval, Reagan's extremist roots didn't matter. He and his team of consultants and behavior psychologists had harnessed the resentments, fears, and grievances of voters upset by the changes and convulsions of the 1960s, and they forged a coalition that combined white blue-collar and union voters—previously stalwart Democrats—with conservatives and far-right voters. If American politics was turning into a cultural clash, Reagan was there to hold back the tide of change and promise a bright future that would look more like the past.

Reagan's victory in California came amid a GOP wave. Without the burdensome weight of Goldwater's extremism, the Republicans gained three seats in the Senate and forty-seven in the House. A big win in gubernatorial contests—adding eight chief state executives to their roster—placed the Republicans in control of half of the nation's statehouses. Goldwater had not killed the GOP.

After the election, Welch chirped that Birchers helped "in large part" to elect Reagan. "The sharp change in the California political climate," he wrote in the bulletin to his members, was due in great measure to the "untiring" work of "thousands of members of the John Birch Society."

In a single campaign, Reagan mainstreamed far-right radicalism and irrational conservative paranoia. He had been guided into the race by millionaires who had funded kooks. He had made his political bones with kooks. He had kooks as contributors and volunteers. His Big Message had been cooked up by a kook. Only a few years earlier, he had declared that enacting programs like Medicare would lead to the end of freedom in the United States—a foundational belief of right-wing kooks. Yet Reagan himself was not perceived by most voters as a kook.

Goldwater had embraced extremism; Reagan had embraced toughness and optimism. He had laundered extremism through his Hollywood stardom and his well-deployed geniality. He severed the bond between the GOP and extremism—at least in terms of the party's public image. "Cutting off the millstone from around their necks amounted to nothing less than a turning point for conservative Republicans," Schoenwald pointed out. "...This *lack* of extremism made conservatism—and Reagan—much more palatable."

With his California success, Reagan pioneered a path to power for extremists who could cloak their extremism.

CHAPTER 7

"Bring Us Together"

R ichard Nixon had a problem. Actually, two: George Wallace and Ronald Reagan.

After losing the California gubernatorial contest in 1962 and telling reporters (and the world), "You don't have Nixon to kick around anymore," the veteran Republican warrior, six years later, had returned to the arena and was again chasing the presidency. He entered the 1968 contest as the odds-on favorite to capture the Republican nomination.

It was a tough time to seek the top job. The nation was undergoing profound unrest: urban riots (or uprisings), civil rights actions, the advent of Black Power, protests against the Vietnam War, campus demonstrations, the burgeoning movement for gender equality, and widespread cultural warfare over...well, just about everything—drugs, sex, free expression, religion, movies, music, television shows, traditional values, and social mores. In the first months of the year, the change and conflict—or, as some saw it, the craziness—appeared to be intensifying. The Tet Offensive—a series of surprise attacks launched at the end of January by the North Vietnamese army and the Viet Cong—stunned the American public, which had been reassured the unpopular war was close to being won. Then President Lyndon Johnson issued the shocking announcement he would not run for reelection. Then Martin Luther King Jr. was gunned down on the balcony of a Memphis motel, and more riots of rage and despair detonated. Then protests erupted at Columbia University and students occupied key buildings—until the police violently ended the siege. Was the nation spinning out of control?

Amid all this discord, Nixon offered the country a "new Nixon." He decried "rampant lawlessness" throughout the land. He promised to "end the war and win the peace"—without saying how he would do that. (Early in the campaign, Nixon told his speechwriters he had "come to the conclusion that there's no way to win the war. But we can't say that of course.") He had written a piece for *Reader's Digest*—"What Has Happened to America?"—that bemoaned, "Far from becoming a great society, ours is becoming a lawless society." He blamed permissive "teachers, preachers, and politicians" who made excuses for rioters, antiwar demonstrators, student radicals, and street criminals. He merged all the troublemakers into one big mass of disruption.

With vague pronouncements and a fuzzy slogan—"Nixon's the One"—he was leading his main contenders: Nelson Rockefeller, who erratically withdrew from the race in mid-March and then rejoined six weeks later, and Ronald Reagan, who was mounting a not-so-secret stealth candidacy, hunting for delegates without declaring an official campaign. And there was George Wallace, the former Alabama governor and fierce segregationist, who was seeking the White House as a third-party candidate, amassing support throughout the South, as well as in the North among working-class white voters who relished his racist, regressive, and angry populism.

Gazing past the primaries, Nixon feared Wallace would be a magnet for conservative voters in the South and deny him the electoral votes Goldwater had picked up in the region. But his more immediate concern was the former General Electric frontman who had accomplished what Nixon could not—beating Pat Brown in California—and who was now the darling of the right wing. Ray Price, a top Nixon aide, had crystalized the threat posed by Reagan in a memo: "Reagan's strength derives from personal charisma, glamor, but primarily the ideological fervor of the Right and the emotional distress of those who fear or resent the Negro, and who expect Reagan somehow to keep him 'in his place'—or at least to echo their own anger and frustration." The implication: Nixon couldn't allow Reagan to best him in exploiting anti-Black backlash among white voters.

Wallace and Reagan—these were interlaced challenges. The Southern leaders of the Republican Party were obsessed with the danger Wallace presented to them. His extremist appeal to *their* voters was an existential threat. Could this fiery white supremacist entice Republican voters to join his racist crusade? And they also wondered if Reagan might be a more attractive option to their flock than Nixon. As Price had pegged it, Reagan, with his libertarian, anti-government temperament, and his embrace of states' rights, was a natural fit for those Americans who weren't Wallace loyalists but still looking to keep the "Negro…in his place." And Reagan knew that. At a Republican fundraiser in New Orleans, he declared, "This nation is totally out of control." He blamed politicians who demanded that welfare and Social Security be expanded, that the Vietnam draft not be honored, and "that Negroes need not obey the law." Reagan was peddling diluted Wallace-ism—with that winning smile.

For his part, Wallace was expanding beyond his racist appeal and stoking political paranoia, decrying the "pointy-headed professors," "intellectual morons," "theoreticians" who had taken over the federal government, "federal judges playing God," the "beatnik mob" in Washington, the "liberal" media, and others conspiring against good Americans. It was classic demagoguery: These think-they-know-best elites were the enemy within, and they were destroying the nation. "Our lives are being taken over by bureaucrats, and most of them have beards," Wallace exclaimed. His solution: law and order.

This won Wallace the devotion of extremists who had backed Goldwater four years prior: Birchers, Klan groups, antisemitic outfits, right-wing paramilitary organizations, and others on the lunatic fringe who were as crazy as ever. (Robert Welch suggested King's assassination was "arranged by the Communists" or the "*Insiders* above them" because King would be "worth infinitely more to them as a dead 'martyr' than as a live stooge.") Unlike Goldwater, Nixon had no claim on the kooks—he had blasted the Birchers in 1962—and he did not have to face the dilemma of disavowing them or not. He would look toward a different set of extremists to buoy his campaign.

––––––

Through the winter and spring, Nixon won most of the primaries and led in delegates. Yet he feared a Southern-led rebellion at the Republican convention, scheduled for the first week of August in Miami Beach—the first GOP national gathering held in a Southern state. Southern conservatives might heed the siren call of that smooth and handsome Reagan.

Nixon was aware he was no favorite of the right. Yes, he had once been the party's most committed anticommunist, pursuing Alger Hiss and ferociously Red-baiting Democratic opponents. But extremists and conservatives questioned his devotion, suspecting that Nixon was overly cunning, opportunistic, and—the biggest sin—ideologically flexible. He had been the moderate Ike's loyal lieutenant. During the 1960 campaign, Nixon had refused to boldly wave the conservative banner in his battle against Kennedy. In fact, he often noted that there were not many policy differences between him and the young Democrat. That enraged many on the right. And while Goldwater and others encouraged Nixon in 1960 to focus on the South—meaning, play the states' rights card to appeal to the racism of the region—Nixon stuck with the conventional calculus: The Party of Lincoln needed to hang on to its loyal Black voters in the North.

Nixon was a man who knew his limitations—and realized his limited appeal. Having not won an election on his own in eighteen years, he justifiably fretted that this nomination could be stolen from him. That was what led him to an Atlanta hotel and into the arms of an unrepentant racist.

On May 31, the Southern state chairs of the Republican Party gathered in the Marriott Motor Hotel to hear from Nixon. The front-runner pandered to the crowd. He told the gang he opposed forcing the pace of integration and was against the busing of schoolchildren to combat segregation. He favored strict constructionists for the Supreme Court—that is, justices not keen on supporting federal initiatives to protect and advance rights for Black Americans. He cited his support of anti-riot legislation. He talked tough on the military but, as he always did, doled out vague statements about Vietnam.

The Southerners had a message for him: Wallace could do serious damage to the party. He would likely steal votes from Nixon, not from the Democratic nominee. What can I do? Nixon asked. The best way to stop Wallace, they said, was to enlist Strom Thurmond. "Well, where is he?" Nixon asked.

A call was made to the segregationist South Carolina senator, who had praised the John Birch Society in 1962 and who would soon release a book blaming crime, riots, the breakdown of traditional values, and "a free rein for communism" on the Supreme Court. Courtesy of a chartered flight, Thurmond arrived in Atlanta the following day.

In front of the party's Southern command, Nixon laid it on thick for Thurmond: "They tell me you are the only man who can defeat Wallace. Will you help us?" He repeated the song-and-dance he had performed the previous day. (No liberal judges!) It was good enough for Thurmond. The godfather of Southern politics afforded Nixon his protection. He would campaign for the former veep against Wallace and, more important in the short run, guarantee that the South Carolina delegation, which was loaded with Reagan lovers, would stick with Nixon.*

In the weeks between the Atlanta meeting and the Republican convention, Nixon and his aides discussed how Nixon could best position himself on racial issues. H. R. Haldeman, Nixon's chief of staff, recorded in his notes the thoughts Nixon expressed during a private dinner on July 3: Nixon "has emotional access to lower middle class white" voters. It was "not fair" to call these voters "racist," but they were "concerned re crime & violence, law and order." And Nixon needed a "stronger" position on this. The goal was to "dry up" the "Wallace vote."

---

* Not until after Thurmond's death in 2003 did the public learn that when he was twenty-two he impregnated a Black woman named Carrie Butler, who worked for his parents and who was fifteen or sixteen when she gave birth to a daughter.

In his notes, Haldeman documented Nixon's belief that he had a "good chance on ethnics—Irish, Ital, Pole, Mex." Kennedy in 1960 had done well with these voters because of his Catholicism, but "they're afraid of Negroes." This was a fear Nixon could exploit. There was "not much mileage for us in talking about ghettoes," Haldeman wrote. He also chronicled another Nixon conversation: "forget Jewish and Negro vote—go for Catholic and Wallace. Drop Negro activity, etc. Do no Jewish things."

Meanwhile, Reagan was courting Southern GOP delegates, touring Southern states and flying delegates to the Golden State to visit with him. And both Reagan and Nixon camps were flirting with voters drawn to the racist Wallace. In a television interview, Reagan remarked, "It's very difficult to disagree with most of things that Mr. Wallace is saying." Then he added that he was compelled to disagree. This was one huge wink at Wallace voters and Southern Republican delegates. Howard "Bo" Callaway, a former Georgia congressman who was a top Nixon strategist for the South, publicly stated that Wallace "belongs" in the Republican Party. He also at one point said, "I think the ideas expressed by George Wallace are the ideas a great many Republicans espouse."

For Nixon, Thurmond was the firewall. If the old racist could hold the line in South Carolina, then a pro-Reagan Southern revolt could be averted.

———

In 1964 Goldwater had enthralled the Birchers and paranoid, conspiratorial kooks with his endorsement of extremism. Two years later, Reagan had carefully distanced himself from the kooks without disavowing them, showing Republicans how to enjoy the benefits of the unhinged far-right radicals (their volunteer muscle, their campaign donations, and their votes) without alienating moderate voters. The party's right wing, though, still teemed with extremists. In California, an archconservative named Max Rafferty, who actively solicited Bircher support, defeated incumbent Senator Thomas Kuchel in the party's primary. (Reagan would support Rafferty's losing effort in the general election.) And on Nixon's economic advisory committee sat Roger Milliken, the South Carolina textiles magnate who had been an early endorser of the John Birch Society. Yet with riots, protests, the war, and tidal waves of social upheaval crashing constantly, the issue of extremism within the GOP no longer stirred up a fuss.

In this time of disruption, Nixon was shuffling the deck of American politics. The man who had declined to exploit the Southern opening in 1960 and who had been featured in *Ebony* magazine in 1962 expounding on "what

Republicans must do to regain the Negro vote" was now relying on racist Southern powerbrokers.

In the past decade, the Democrats and the Republicans had essentially swapped places on civil rights. For a century, the GOP had been the Party of Lincoln and the party most supported by Black voters, while the Democrats had included a Southern contingent tied to slavery, Jim Crow, and segregation. Wallace had been a Democrat. Thurmond had been a Democrat. But in the late 1950s and early 1960s, the tectonic plates shifted.

In 1957, the Republican National Committee initiated Operation Dixie to expand its reach in the South and build upon Eisenhower's gains below the Mason-Dixon line. The initial aim was to focus on moderate, nonracist Republicans. But come 1960, conservative Republicans, including Goldwater, argued that a libertarian-leaning platform—meaning throttling back on civil rights legislation—would pull Southern voters into the party. At the Republican convention that year, when Nixon stuck with the party's more progressive approach, one delegate exclaimed, "We've lost Louisiana." Goldwater believed this move sunk Nixon. With white Southerners resentful of federal intervention against Jim Crow, Goldwater and others thought their small-government, leave-it-to-the-states dogma would be highly attractive in the South. As Goldwater put it during a 1961 meeting of Southern Republican state party leaders, "We're not going to get the Negro vote as a bloc in 1964 and 1968, so we ought to go hunting where the ducks are." So dump Black voters in the North for white voters in the South. That meant forging an alliance with white supremacists.

Across the aisle, the Democrats in Washington were alienating their Southern brethren by supporting the fight against segregation. As president, Kennedy deployed troops to integrate the University of Mississippi and introduced civil rights legislation. After JFK's assassination, Johnson signed the Civil Rights Act of 1964 and supposedly remarked, "There goes the South for a generation."

Two years later, Reagan capitalized on white backlash to send Pat Brown packing. Come 1968, the Democrats were not free of their party's racism. (Lester Maddox, a segregationist, was elected governor of Georgia as a Democrat in 1966.) But they were moving away from this shameful piece of their party's legacy. Though the GOP still contained liberals who championed civil rights, it now galloped toward segregationists and voters fed up with government interventions to help Black Americans. Nixon was at the front of the pack, looking to make a deal with the racists—bolstering them—to gain power.

The night before the Republican convention opened—with rumblings that Southern delegates were considering stampeding toward Reagan—Nixon dispatched John Mitchell, his campaign manager, to meet with Southern party leaders. Haldeman chronicled the message Nixon instructed Mitchell to convey to "cool off the Southerners": In choosing a running mate, Nixon would not "ram someone down your throat," and he "will bring peace" on civil rights and "lay off pro-Negro crap." Nixon had supported the Civil Rights Act of 1964 and the Voting Rights Act of 1965. But now...no more *pro-Negro crap*. That was the deal Nixon was willing to make.

Mitchell delivered that message. But as the convention opened, Nixon had not locked down enough delegates to triumph on the first ballot, and his crew still fretted about a Reagan surge out of the South. Nixon and Mitchell met with Thurmond and Harry Dent, the chair of the South Carolina GOP and a longtime Thurmond ally. Together they crafted a message that would go out to the Southern delegations: On the enforcement of the civil rights laws on the books, Nixon favored an approach that respected states' rights, and he opposed busing. As for his veep, Nixon assured Thurmond that his choice would be "acceptable to all sections of the party," meaning he wouldn't upset the segregationists. Nixon then met privately with delegates from the South and presented the points he had rehearsed with Thurmond and Dent. On busing, he said, "I think you destroy that child." He assured the group he was not keen on trying "to satisfy some professional civil rights group." With Thurmond leaning on the Southern bosses, Reagan's breakthrough never came. Nixon won on the first ballot: 692 votes to 277 for Rockefeller and 182 for Reagan.

As British journalists Lewis Chester, Godfrey Hodgson, and Bruce Page put it in *An American Melodrama*, their history of the 1968 campaign, "without Thurmond as an active proselytizing force among the Dixie delegations, Nixon could not have achieved his first-ballot victory." He kept his promise to Thurmond and the Southerners, picking Spiro Agnew, the governor of Maryland, a border state, to join him on the ticket. Agnew had taken a tough-guy approach to rioting and was no champion of civil rights. Columnist Robert Novak observed, "What appealed most to Nixon was Agnew at his public worst—administering a demagogic public-tongue-lashing to black leaders in Baltimore, after the riots following the death of Martin Luther King." As Nixon biographer John Farrell later put it, the selection of Agnew was "a race-baiting wink."

Minutes after being nominated, Nixon proclaimed, "I won the nomination without paying any price or making any deals." That was false. He had won the battle by kneeling before the segregationists and honoring their racism.

In his acceptance speech, Nixon surveyed the dystopic American landscape—cities "enveloped in smoke and flame," Americans "dying on distant battlefields" and "hating each other; fighting each other; killing each other at home." He promised to "bring an honorable end to the Vietnam War." He celebrated "the forgotten Americans, the non-shouters, the non-demonstrators." The quiet Americans, he said, deserved "rule of law" and "new leadership." "Let us have order in America," he intoned. Nixon confronted the criticism that he was blowing a racist dog whistle: "To those who say that law and order is the code word for racism, here is a reply: Our goal is justice for every American." It was a brilliant rhetorical stroke. After all, the point of using coded language is to deny that it is coded language.

Law and order. It could mean anything. People rioting. Students confronting authority. Black Panthers shouting "Black Power." Street crime. Antiwar marches. It appealed to racists who feared Black protests challenging white privilege—as well as to anyone worried about being mugged. If you believed the communists were behind the civil rights and peace movements, you wanted law and order. If you were upset about rising crime rates, you wanted law and order. It didn't *have to be* about race. But it often was.

As the convention came to an end, Chester Gillespie, a Republican from Cleveland, remarked, "The Republican Party reckons it can do without the Negro. It feels it can win on the white backlash." Gillespie, a longtime civil rights attorney, was one of the few Black delegates.

Law and order was not exclusively Nixon's property. Wallace had been drawling about law and order throughout the campaign. During a campaign flight, Wallace told reporters, "I don't talk about race or segregation anymore. We're talking about law and order, and local control of schools, not those other things."

Nixon's call for law and order—which appealed to white suburbanites and racist extremists—received a tremendous boost when the Democrats gathered in Chicago two weeks later and, in the tragic absence of the murdered Bobby Kennedy, nominated the beleaguered Vice President Hubert Humphrey as their presidential nominee. The nation watched in horror the violent clashes in the street—hippies and protesters versus rioting police officers—and witnessed disorder and rancor within the convention hall, as Democrats tore each other apart over the Vietnam War. The Democrats hadn't been able to win (or end) the war. And after the catastrophe in Chicago, they hardly seemed the party that could bring stability and quiet to a country in a state of tumult.

———

Beyond law and order, Nixon was slinging a new iteration of an old idea: There were good Americans, and there were other Americans. His acceptance speech divided the country into two warring factions: the citizens challenging the established order and the "forgotten" ones. He was no longer the fiery Red-baiter of old. But he still pushed the notion there was an internal anti-American force undermining the foundations of the nation.

Nixon was a maestro at playing both ends. In campaign speeches, he warned of the country becoming "two nations, one black, one white, poised for irrepressible conflict." He bemoaned the "terrible poverty" within the "great cities of America," observing, "This isn't going to be a good country for any of us to live in until it's a good country for all of us to live in."

But that was for show. Nixon placed his bet on a less overt racism than what Wallace was peddling. In early September, when Pennsylvania Republicans urged him to reach out to Blacks in the state—a significant voting bloc—Nixon had no interest. He told aides, "I'm not going to campaign for the black vote at the risk of alienating the suburban vote...If I am president, I am not going to owe anything to the black community." Senator Edward Brooke, a Black Republican from Massachusetts, tried to convince Nixon that "law and order" was code for repressing minority groups. Nixon, perhaps in response, publicly referred to "order with justice"—as if that would make a difference.

Publicly Nixon was insisting that he would not divide the country. But he still exploited the racial (or racist) fears of white voters. About a month before Election Day, Kevin Phillips, a campaign strategist, composed a memo outlining the strategy for the final four weeks. Under the heading "Ideology," he noted the campaign needed to adhere to "the conservative course followed so far," and the centerpiece of that course was race: "The fulcrum of re-alignment is the law and order/Negro socio-economic revolution syndrome, and RN should continue to emphasize crime, decentralization of federal social programing, and law and order." Even when pitching his campaign "to the Negroes," Nixon should keep "the white electorate principally in mind."

Phillips advised that Nixon should not denigrate Wallace, noting that "Wallace's great present strength and plausibility is a plus for RN outside the South because of the number of blue-collar Democrats who have been weaned away from [Humphrey]." He maintained that "Wallace's social stances"—meaning, his racist positions—"should not be attacked" and that Nixon should not join liberal Republicans in derogating Wallace "as a racist or crypto-Fascist." That would turn off conservatives "torn between RN and Wallace." So, Phillips advised, go easy on Wallace's racism. Phillips also recommended Nixon adopt no "articulate or definitive position" on Vietnam and "paint himself as a responsible, experienced peacemaker" who would end the unpopular war.*

Nixon followed Phillips's advice. He did not assault Wallace's racism. Instead, the campaign pounded away on the argument Wallace couldn't win and a vote for him was a wasted vote, while sweet-talking voters who were drawn to Wallace. For this mission, Nixon recruited Goldwater. In speeches and campaign literature, the conservative icon said he had respect for Wallace and noted the Alabaman made important points but that he had no chance. Nixon's crew also dispatched Agnew to the South to win white suburban voters. Agnew resorted to the old playbook, asserting Humphrey was "squishy-soft on Communism" and "soft on law and order." He accused the vice president of coddling people "who condone violence and advocate the overthrow of the government."

Nixon was all in on the Southern strategy. In early October, a reporter visited the office of Fred LaRue, a campaign aide focused on the South, and LaRue explained that the campaign was running ads "very selectively"— that is, only in the South—featuring Thurmond talking about crime and busing. Money for this targeted ad blitz was raised by Roger Milliken, the Bircher-linked textiles tycoon. As part of its Southern effort, the campaign distributed a pamphlet quoting Nixon sounding skeptical about desegregation: "I wouldn't want to see a federal agency punish a local community... I don't believe you should use the South as the whipping boy...There has been too much of a tendency...for both our courts and our federal agencies to use the whole program of school integration for purposes which have very little to do with education." On a campaign swing through South Carolina with Thurmond, Nixon exclaimed, "He has stood up for his country, and I am glad to stand with him today." As Agnew hit the hustings, he explained why he was avoiding urban areas: "You've seen one slum you've seen them all."

Eleven days before the election, Nixon taped his final television ads at a Times Square theater. (His savvy media team included a young Roger

---

* Decades later, evidence would turn up—notes from Haldeman—proving Nixon used a back channel to the South Vietnamese government to sabotage the Vietnam peace talks then underway. Nixon feared a breakthrough in the negotiations would give Humphrey a winning boost. He secretly conveyed a message to Saigon to hang tough and not cooperate, suggesting it would get a better deal during a Nixon presidency. This act of treachery worked. The peace talks foundered, and the war—and the deaths of US troops—continued.

Ailes, who years later would create Fox News.) Each spot focused on law and order. In one, the candidate, citing "riots in three hundred cities" and an increasing crime rate, declared, "One issue on which the greatest difference exists between the two candidates is that of a law and order in the United States." After recording an ad that zeroed in on discipline in classrooms, Nixon remarked to an aide, "This hits it right on the nose...It's all about law and order and the damn Negro-Puerto Rican groups out there."

Nixon barely won the election with 43.4 percent of the vote, seven-tenths of a point ahead of Humphrey. Wallace collected 13.5 percent. The Thurmond deal worked, as had Nixon's Wallace strategy. Five former Confederate states chose Nixon over Wallace: Tennessee, Virginia, Florida, and the Carolinas. Three-fifths of onetime Wallace supporters who ended up voting for one of the two major-party candidates landed in Nixon's column. The law-and-order gambit succeeded: Crime and violence was the issue most voters cited as a presidential priority. (Also high on the list were riots and rising living costs, not the Vietnam War.) After the election, Wallace quipped, "Mr. Nixon said the same thing I said."

When Nixon delivered his victory speech the morning after in the ballroom of the Waldorf-Astoria hotel in New York City, he declared his motto as president would be a message he had spotted on a sign at an Ohio campaign stop: BRING US TOGETHER.

CHAPTER 8

Ratfucking America

B *ring Us Together.* Not exactly.

Nixon attained the presidency by exploiting the paramount divisive force in American society—racism—and the sense of fear and dread spreading through much of the nation. As the country's chief executive, he would chart a centrist course on policy, enacting a mix of liberal and conservative social programs, and he would pursue bold foreign policy initiatives that challenged Cold War conventions, though failing for years to secure an end to the increasingly pointless war in Vietnam. Yet, through it all, Nixon would continue to scratch at America's scars for partisan advantage, seeking to gain from racial resentment and encouraging the tribalism growing within the American polity. Worse for Nixon himself, the politician who had recklessly inflamed the Red Scare of the 1950s would come to reflect and embody the paranoia of the 1960s and 1970s. He would believe his own tale of an America bedeviled by conniving, underhanded, and disloyal internal enemies—and it would drive him to ruin.

Law and order. The Southern strategy. An Us-versus-Them America. As stormy change continued to rock the nation in 1969, Nixon advanced his divisive-by-design themes. Months into his administration, the White House, on the occasion of Law Day (May 1), dispatched top officials to deliver hair-raising speeches bemoaning crime, emphasizing Nixon's commitment to law and order, and drawing sharp battle lines. Deputy Attorney General Richard Kleindienst foresaw a possible need in the future for "concentration camps" for "ideological criminals." William Rehnquist, an assistant attorney general, decried student demonstrators as the "new barbarians" and "a threat to the notion of a government of law which is every bit as serious as the crime wave in our cities."

Most of all, there was the race button to push. Nixon had risen in politics employing anticommunist paranoia as a disruptive force. Now he was exploiting the most basic American form of tribalism. Keeping his bargain with Thurmond and the South, he nominated federal court of appeals Judge Clement Furman Haynsworth Jr. of South Carolina to fill a Supreme Court vacancy. But Democrats accused Haynsworth of rendering decisions that favored segregation and defeated his nomination 55–45. Next up was native Georgian George Harrold Carswell, another federal appeals court judge, who two decades earlier had proclaimed himself a segregationist and a white supremacist, declaring, "I shall always be so governed." Though he had renounced that vow, Carswell, too, was defeated. Nixon decried the rejection of these two men, contending "the real issue" was not racism but "their philosophy of strict construction of the Constitution and the fact that they had the misfortune of being born in the South." He called the repudiations of these nominees "regional discrimination." After these two misses, Nixon nominated Harry Blackmun, a Minnesotan federal appeals judge, who was confirmed on a unanimous vote. (Three years later, Blackmun would write the majority opinion in *Roe v. Wade*, affirming a woman's constitutional right to an abortion.)

Nixon did enact an affirmative action program requiring federal contractors to hire minority workers. And in 1970, compelled by Supreme Court decisions, he created a cabinet committee to implement the desegregation of Southern schools—an effort in which Agnew declined to participate. Yet Nixon was constantly on the lookout for a racial wedge. In August 1969, he proposed an extensive overhaul of the federal welfare program. The reform would more than double the number of welfare recipients and almost triple its cost, but the benefits would shift from Black families headed by single mothers to white working families. The political goal was to appeal to Northern white working-class and middle-class ethnic voters who resented the antipoverty and welfare programs of Lyndon Johnson's Great Society.

Nixon was expanding the Southern strategy by adding blue-collar voters of the North to his coalition of racial grievance. This move was in sync with the grand theory that Kevin Phillips, now working for Attorney General John Mitchell in the Justice Department, was promoting in a new book *The Emerging Republican Majority*: The GOP could construct a national electoral majority of resentment and rage by joining Southern whites opposed to civil rights with middle-class and ethnic Americans, especially Catholics, in the North (and elsewhere) who were enraged by urban rioting, bitter about handouts to low-income Black Americans, and frightened by an increasingly militant civil rights movement. Ultimately, Nixon's welfare ploy failed, when it turned out there was no way in hell that Southern white politicians were going to vote for any expansion of welfare spending, even if the money ended up with white families. But Nixon could still complain about the existing welfare program—an obligatory component of backlash politics.

Nixon never stopped sending positive signals to racists. In a September 1969 press conference, he equated civil rights advocates who desired "instant integration" with extremists who called for "segregation forever." Such a comparison was a phony and loathsome equivalency. A few months later, Lamar Alexander, a young White House aide (and future Tennessee senator), griped in a memo, "There is an unstated attitude (almost a policy) of disregard toward blacks brought about by a political concern for white votes. As a result, we generally think all white, ignore black."

Nixon would back constitutional amendments to prohibit court-ordered busing and "forced" integration of all-white neighborhoods. He enthusiastically ordered his aides to exploit hot-button racial issues. "The political message that was going forth was one...of nods and winks," Sallyanne Payton, a Black lawyer on Nixon's staff, subsequently observed. In his memoir, John Ehrlichman, Nixon's top adviser on domestic affairs, offered the same verdict: "The subliminal appeal to the anti-black voter was always in Nixon's statements and speeches on schools and housing...Nixon said he believed blacks could only marginally benefit from federal programs because blacks were genetically inferior to whites." He added, Nixon "was never as blatant as George Wallace or Lester Maddox, but he delivered a clear message that was hard to miss." John Farrell, an evenhanded biographer of the thirty-seventh president, concluded that Nixon "gave credence to the feelings, shared by millions and fanned by Wallace and his kindred, that blacks were ingrates, offenders, and welfare chiselers handed unfair advantages by dizzy Democrats at the expense of hardworking, law-abiding citizens." Nixon kept racism alive within the GOP.

The Nixon crew looked to exacerbate sharp societal divisions beyond race—to engage in the extreme politics of hate. Throughout the first years of the Nixon presidency, Agnew had the mission to spray the burning social fabric with gasoline. In speeches across the land, the vice president launched demagogic assaults designed to demonize the opposition. Antiwar demonstrators and intellectuals were "an effete corps of impudent snobs." The leaders of the peace movement were "ideological eunuchs" and "parasites of passion." Violence on campus was the fault of "well-born" elitists. The vice president slammed the media time and again as an anti-American force, noting the "views of the majority of this fraternity do not—and I repeat, not—represent the views of America." The racist National States' Rights Party hailed Agnew's assault on the journalistic elite and contended, approvingly, that the vice president was using coded language to target Jews in the media.

Agnew did not hide his lust for Wallace voters in the South. During an October 1969 speech, Agnew made it plain: "In 1968, [Wallace voters] felt they had no place else to go but Wallace. But that's no longer true." Wallace could see his race-baiting populism was being plagiarized. He called Agnew "a copy-cat." During a television appearance, he cracked, "I wish I had copyrighted or patented my speeches. I would be drawing immense royalties from Mr. Nixon and especially Mr. Agnew."

On the circuit, Agnew sounded like an unleashed Bircher. He excoriated liberals for supporting dissidents who wanted to demolish the United States: "Right now, we must decide whether we will take the trouble to stave off a totalitarian state...Will citizens refuse to be led by a series of Judas goats down torturous paths to delusion and self-destruction?" Nixon's critics were nothing but "nattering nabobs of negativism." The vice president proudly proclaimed his love of "polarization": "It is time to rip away the rhetoric and divide on authentic lines." His message was unmistakable: You're either a friend or a foe. Americans were divided, and Team Nixon encouraged its supporters to see political opponents as vile rivals looking to decimate the nation they loved and cherished.

In a memo to Nixon, White House official Pat Buchanan urged the president to pursue "heated political warfare, of not cooling off our supporters but of stirring the fires." As the pugilistic aide saw it, Nixon was in a fundamental struggle of good versus evil: "a contest over the soul of the country" against the liberals, the media, the cultural elites, the protesters, and you-name-it. "It will be their kind of society or ours; we will prevail or they shall prevail," he declared. In this atmosphere, riling passions and widening the rupture was God's work. "Dividing the American people has been my main contribution to the national political scene," Agnew proclaimed. "I not only plead guilty to this charge, but I am somewhat flattered by it."

In a November 3, 1969, speech announcing he had initiated a plan—Vietnamization—that would supposedly end the war, Nixon acknowledged Americans had the right to protest the war. But he implied the dissenters were assisting totalitarians and posed a threat to the country's future: "If a vocal minority, however fervent its cause, prevails over reason and the will of the majority, this nation has no future as a free society." He asked the "great silent majority" for its support—once more suggesting the nation was cleaved into two tribes.

Nixon was always on the search for *his* America, looking to rally its citizens, be it the *forgotten* or the *silent* people—and to encourage them to see the *other* America as the enemy. For this mission, race was a crucial element. Phillips spelled it out for a visiting reporter: "The more Negroes who register as Democrats in the South, the sooner the Negrophobe whites will quit the Democrats and become Republicans. That's where the votes are. Without that prodding from the blacks, the whites will backslide into their old comfortable arrangement with the local Democrats." Nixon and the Republicans needed racial animus to win. As the spring of 1970 showed, they were eager to cash in on hatred and not just in the South.

———

On April 31, 1970, Nixon announced attacks on "enemy sanctuaries" along the Cambodian-Vietnamese border. In straight talk, the United States had invaded another country: Cambodia. This news sparked a fierce round of antiwar demonstrations, with Nixon denigrating student protesters as "bums." On May 4, National Guardsmen clashed with demonstrators on the campus of Kent State University in Ohio. In a burst of violence, they fired into the crowd, killing four and wounding nine others. Shock, rage, anger, and sadness spread throughout the country.

On May 8, New York City Mayor John Lindsay ordered all city flags lowered to commemorate the young Americans slain at Kent State. At noon, about a thousand antiwar students gathered by the statue of George Washington in front of Federal Hall in Manhattan's financial district—the site of the first US Congress—to demand the immediate withdrawal of troops from Vietnam and Cambodia.

The demonstration was peaceful. As clear skies emerged from a light rain, the students were listening to a series of speakers. Suddenly about two hundred construction workers—most wearing overalls and orange and yellow hard hats—pushed through a thin line of police officers. They carried flags and shouted, "All the way, USA!" and "Love it or leave it." They attacked the students, swatting the protesters with their helmets. They chased after youths with long hair, beating, kicking, and pummeling the demonstrators they caught. It was "savage violence," an eyewitness would later say. Blood was flowing. The construction workers screamed at the hippies: "Bums!... Faggot!...Commie!" Antiwar demonstrators were on the ground. Others were trying to flee, shrieking. Some attempted to stand firm against the rampaging hard hats, shouting, "Fascist pigs!" The marauders fought their way on to the steps of Federal Hall, pounding and decking students. They placed their flags on the statue of George Washington and sang "God Bless America."

More hard hats showed up. The workers assaulted businessmen trying to aid the students. At nearby City Hall, a lawyer was beaten and stomped by a group of workers screaming, "Kill the Commie bastards." A gang of hard hats brutalized a teacher. Police officers stood by and watched. Few arrests were made.

The mob, reinforced by additional workers from the construction site of the World Trade Center, descended on City Hall, shouting, "Lindsay's a Red!" Now the violent throng numbered about five hundred, maybe a thousand, and cheered when the flag on the roof that had been lowered to half-mast was raised. Moments later, a Lindsay aide lowered the flag. The workers went wild. They jumped over police barricades and stormed through the cops. They were trying to force their way into City Hall. "This is the Silent Majority, but they are not silent anymore," one worker said.

Police beseeched city officials to raise the flag, and when it went back up, the rampaging workers sang "The Star-Spangled Banner."

While this occurred, a group of hard hats attacked Pace College, across the street from City Hall Park. "Kill those long-haired bastards," one cried. They grabbed a peace banner hanging on the building and burned it on the street. The hard hats broke into the school and chased students, beating young people curled up on the ground to protect themselves. Students were bashed by lead pipes wrapped in American flags.

The riot raged for about two hours before it petered out. Scores of students and bystanders were injured—likely well over one hundred people, including four police officers. At least half a dozen young men had been beaten unconscious. Many victims were treated for bruises, gashes, busted lips, and black eyes at Trinity Church. Others, bloodied and in pain, ended up in a nearby hospital. They suffered concussions, memory loss, fractures.

———

The hard hats had acted like a brownshirt brigade. The Nixon White House sought to embrace and protect them.

Four days after the melee, Tom Huston, a White House aide, wrote a memo to his bosses "strongly" recommending the Justice Department *not* investigate the riot: "While there may have been a lack of zealous law enforcement...it is questionable whether the civil rights of the protesting students were any more violated than those of countless thousands, who have previously been on the receiving end of student demonstrations. We are currently running a very large risk of alienating the Silent Majority." There would be no federal inquiry. Law and order did not apply to violent thugs on Nixon's side.

In the days and weeks following the riot, construction workers returned to the financial district at lunchtime to march and protest the protesters. The crowds reached into the thousands. The assembled expressed support for the Vietnam War and waved signs that read WE LOVE NIXON, AGNEW, MITCHELL, HIS WIFE, AND REAGAN and GOD BLESS THE ESTABLISHMENT. These actions culminated with a march on May 20 sponsored by the Building and Construction Trades Council of Greater New York. About 150,000 people—construction works, Teamsters, longshoremen—formed what the *New York Times* called "a river of yellow, red, and blue hard hats" beneath a blizzard of ticker tape. *Time* magazine dubbed it "Workers' Woodstock."

Following the event, Nixon phoned Peter Brennan, the head of the building and constructions union, and Thomas Gleason, the chief of the longshoremen's union. Haldeman that day noted in his diary that Nixon believed "we're still too timid mobilizing the Silent Majority." Nixon saw an opportunity with the riot and invited Brennan, Gleason, and other union leaders to the White House.

Six days after the parade, the labor chieftains gathered with Nixon in the Oval Office. Nixon told them their demonstrations of support for his Vietnam policy were reassuring and "very meaningful." There was no discussion of the violence that had occurred. Here was another wink from Nixon—this one at the violent workers who smashed those damn hippies. Even the conservative editorial board of the *Wall Street Journal* could see this: "Mr. Nixon's embrace included not only those who attended the [May 20] rally but those who bashed heads as well." It did not approve: "We think this is no time for such ambiguity." The president of the United States was celebrating political violence.

The White House was willing to ignore the violence because it hoped to pull blue-collar workers away from the Democratic Party for Nixon's reelection effort. Months earlier, Nixon had asked Assistant Secretary of Labor Jerome Rosow to study the sociology of blue-collar workers, and Rosow had finished his report three weeks before the hard hat riot in New York City. "People in the blue-collar class are less mobile, less organized, and less capable of using legitimate means to either protect the status quo or secure changes in their favor," Rosow wrote. "To a considerable extent, they feel like 'forgotten people'—those for whom the government and the society have limited, if any, direct concern and little visible action."

This perfectly fit Nixon's plan to create an overpowering electoral majority of silent, forgotten Americans—*white* Americans. He would not align with these workers on bread-and-butter matters (say, union rights or taxes), for that would place him in opposition to the business community Republicans relied upon. But he could exploit their apprehension, bitterness, and grudges and be their champion in a divisive *culture* war, a battle of attitudes, values, and identity. Who was a *real* American? The hard hats and other citizens aghast at the turmoil of the times knew. For Nixon, the enemy of his enemy—all those *anti-American* hippies, freaks, druggies, protesters, Blacks, student radicals, women libbers, gays, liberal intellectuals—were his voters.

Haldeman jotted down in his notes that Nixon "thinks now the college demonstrators have overplayed their hands, evidence is the blue collar group rising up against them, and P can mobilize them." Pat Buchanan agreed. In a strategy memo to Nixon on how best to overcome the White House's opponents, the pugnacious White House adviser included a section on the hard hats: "A group of construction workers came up Wall Street and beat the living hell out of some demonstrators...Whether one condones this kind of violence or not, probably half the living rooms in America were in standing applause at the spectacle." No union man would have marched for Nixon ten years ago. But, Buchanan pointed out, these are *our people now...*if we want them."

A little over a year into his presidency, Nixon was fortifying his relationship with a new band of extremists, while keeping his promise to the segregationists who had helped him attain the White House. And Agnew was maintaining his crusade against the media, liberals, student protesters, Democrats, and other enemies. The vice president accused the *Washington Post*, *Life* magazine, the *New York Times*, and the broadcast networks of working together to "tear our country apart," promoting a Bircher-like paranoia. Even Kevin Phillips acknowledged that Nixon was playing with fire and constructing a coalition with dangerous tendencies: "The popular conservative majority now taking shape like past popular movements, is vulnerable to aberration. With its important component of military, apprehensive bourgeois and law-and-order seeking individuals, there is a proclivity toward authoritarianism." Nixon was manipulating perilous passions.

———

In October 1970, with the midterm elections approaching, White House aide Charles Colson told Nixon that they had "effectively associated the liberals with all that is bad about permissiveness in society." As the campaign came to a close, Nixon—after being targeted by unruly, rock-throwing protesters in San Jose—delivered a harsh speech lambasting "thugs and hoodlums" and decrying the "creeping permissiveness in our legislatures, in our courts, in our family life, and in our colleges and universities." In a Phoenix airport hangar, Nixon declared, "The time has come for the great silent majority of Americans of all ages, of every political persuasion, to stand up and be counted against appeasement of the rock throwers and the obscenity shouters in America." He promised "law and order."

It didn't work. The House Democrats gained twelve seats in the elections. Senate Democrats dropped two seats but remained in the majority. A sluggish economy had countered Nixon's Southern and Northern strategies and his and Agnew's deliberate efforts to polarize Americans.

The disappointing results did not dissuade Nixon and his men from sticking with divide-and-conquer politics for the reelection campaign ahead. Buchanan pointed out to Nixon, "There are more Queens Democrats than there are Harlem Democrats and they are a hell of a lot easier for a Republican to get." This would mean telling "the *New York Times* that, no, we have not done anything for the blacks this week, but we have named a Pole to the Cabinet, and an Italian Catholic to the Supreme Court." It was full speed ahead for Nixon's racism-infused politics of tribalism. Yet the president was heading toward his own demise, for he was about to turn the political culture war he was leading into a covert criminal operation.

———

Paranoia—the currency of the far right—infected the Nixon White House. Nixon, a man motivated by dark suspicions and insecurities, envisioned his foes ceaselessly plotting against him and employing deceitful and unscrupulous means to screw him. Naturally, he had to fight fire with fire. His effort to exploit political divisions ran parallel to the by-any-means-necessary skullduggery emanating from the White House. After all, this was war. The nation was at war overseas, and Nixon was at war with his enemies, real and imagined. Desperate measures were needed. Extremism was no vice in such a situation. Break-ins. Illegal wiretaps. Slush funds. Dirty tricks. Whole books have been filled with all the illegal schemes Nixon and his crew contemplated and implemented. The Watergate burglary in June 1972—in which White House operatives broke into the offices of the Democratic National Committee to reset a bug previously placed on a phone in a search for dirt—and the subsequent coverup were merely slices of the rotten enterprise operated by the White House and Nixon's 1972 reelection campaign.

Nixon himself was the ringleader, often proposing illicit and sleazy operations: use the IRS to audit political foes (including "big Jewish contributors" whom Nixon referred to as "cocksuckers"), break into the liberal Brookings Institution to steal files that he believed would embarrass the Kennedys and other Democrats ("Goddamn it, go in and get those files. Blow the safe"), investigate the "Jewish cabal" he imagined at the Bureau of Labor Statistics (which he thought was releasing information to make his administration look bad). After the New York Times in June 1971 began publishing the Pentagon Papers—a massive trove of Pentagon-commissioned studies that showed previous administrations had brazenly lied to the public about the Vietnam War—an enraged Nixon cooked up various criminal plots to combat the widespread conspiracy he believed was arrayed against him.

One idea Nixon tossed out to his aides: recruit "another Senator McCarthy." That is, someone with congressional immunity who could say anything and hurl accusations at those plotting against Nixon without fear of libel or slander. He didn't mind tapping the fringe for this. Possible names included far-right legislators Representatives John Ashbrook, an Ohio Republican, and Phil Crane, an Illinois Republican and former head of the Young Americans for Freedom, as well as two Birchers who were in the House: John Schmitz and John Rousselot, both California Republicans. Nixon said of Rousselot, "He'll lie, do anything." For Nixon, that was a good thing. At one point, White House operative G. Gordon Liddy proposed assassinating investigative columnist Jack Anderson.

All of this was hidden from the American public—at least for a while. In public, Nixon was an ideological juggler. He proposed universal health insurance and created the Environmental Protection Agency. His historic opening to China enraged many conservatives, as did his engagement with Moscow (and subsequent arms control agreements). So, too, his imposition of wage and price controls. (A John Birch Society publication declared this "fascism.") Policy-minded people on both the right and the left were dissatisfied with Nixon's handling of Vietnam. He wouldn't pull out; he wouldn't escalate as the hawks desired. YAF proclaimed, "We've had it. The Nixon policy is not one of victory."

The president kept the faith with the right on other fronts, vetoing a national child-care system (which conservative opponents had denounced as a communist scheme) and opposing busing. His administration made room for denizens of the far-right world of the Birchers. At the start of Nixon's term, his highest-ranking Black appointee was James Johnson, a member of Ronald Reagan's cabinet in California, a supporter—though not a member—of the John Birch Society. (Nixon placed him on the Civil Service Commission and later promoted him to assistant secretary of the Navy.) Nixon named Otto Otepka, a Red-chasing far-right hero who had been fired from the State Department, to the Subversive Activities Control Board, even though he was tied to the Birchers. J. Howard Pew, the oil tycoon who was a financial backer of the society's publishing company, was invited to dine at the White House. Charles Keating, an anti-porn campaigner whose Citizens for Decent Literature collaborated with Birchers, was placed on the US Commission on Obscenity and Pornography. (Two decades later, he would become known as one of the top savings-and-loan swindlers in the nation.) Mary Cain, an ardent Mississippi segregationist who attended Bircher events, was appointed to a Pentagon advisory committee. Outside of Washington, Birchers were still strong within the GOP ranks, with society members gaining key positions in state parties in Alabama, Oregon, and elsewhere.

———

Nixon's reelection campaign was an orgy of lawlessness: blackmail proposals, forgeries, laundered money, and assorted underhanded operations, with much of this "ratfucking," as the Nixonites called it, waged by veteran ultra-right YAF operatives. (Tom Huston, a former national chair of YAF on the White House staff, had crafted an elaborate plan for ambitious black ops—burglary, surveillance, and more—against domestic radicals.) The goal was to end up with the Democratic nominee that Nixon wanted: Senator George McGovern, a South Dakota liberal and decorated World War II bomber pilot whom Nixon believed could be tarred as outside the American mainstream.

Nixon had learned a lesson from the Goldwater disaster of 1964. The charge of extremism can be tough for a candidate to shake—and it could be lethal. In a memo to Mitchell, he wrote, "One of the factors that brought Goldwater down to such a shattering defeat in 1964 was the success of the media in tying him to ultra-right-wing supporters like [billionaire] H. L. Hunt, the John Birch Society, etc. The fact that [leftwing activists] Abbie Hoffman, Jerry Rubin, Angela Davis, among others, support McGovern, should be widely publicized and used at every point. Keep calling on him to repudiate them daily."

McGovern, partly thanks to Nixon's subterfuge, did become the Democrats' nominee, and the Republicans went to town, portraying him as the extremist in the race. One GOP publication declared, "While South Dakota Sen. George McGovern may give the impression of being a mild-mannered milquetoast...he is in reality a dedicated radical extremist who as President would unilaterally disarm the United States of America and open the White House to riotous street mobs." Senator Hugh Scott, a Pennsylvania Republican, called McGovern "the acid, abortion, and amnesty—the triple-A—candidate."

Nixon, the president who had forged an alliance with racists, who had hailed violent hard hats, and who had enlisted a small army of right-wing fanatics for criminal assaults on his enemies, was fixated on smearing McGovern as a fringe candidate. At the GOP convention in Miami Beach, Goldwater compared the Democrats to coyotes who "just wait... until they can tear something down or destroy part of America." Richard Lugar, the mayor of Indianapolis, exclaimed, "A small group of radicals and extremists has assumed control of the Democratic Party."

In his acceptance speech, Nixon launched the usual attacks on the Democrats: They were too eager to tax and spend, too weak on defense, too quick to turn tail in Vietnam, too keen on welfare programs, and too soft on crime and drugs. He called on voters to join his New Majority: "It has become fashionable in recent years to point up what is wrong with what is called the American system. The critics contend it is so unfair, so corrupt, so unjust, that we should tear it down and substitute something else in its place. I totally disagree. I believe in the American system."

———

Though the Watergate break-in of June 17, 1972, generated headlines (mainly in the *Washington Post*), Nixon and his aides managed to lie their way through the final months of the race, denying wrongdoing and firing back that *they* were the victims of a conspiracy waged by the McGovern team and the *Post* to undermine Nixon with false reports.

It succeeded. The dirty tricks. The division. The denials. The Southern strategy. The courting of blue-collar workers. Nixon overwhelmingly won reelection, collecting 61 percent of the popular vote, triumphing in every state but Massachusetts and the District of Columbia. The Republicans did lose two Senate seats and gained only modestly in the House. But Nixon's vision of America, his celebration of the supposedly silent and forgotten majority and the demonization of liberals, dissenters, elites, and intellectuals, prevailed. On Election Day, as Air Force One carried him from California to Washington, Nixon told journalist Theodore White that he knew people would say he had won the South with racism. At that moment, Southern voters who had sided with Wallace in 1968 were breaking for Nixon three to one. Yet the president insisted his victory had nothing to do with bigotry: "You know what did it? Patriotism, not racism."

———

Nixon's triumph was no salve for the grudges and malice that animated his politics. A few weeks after his triumph, he told his aides, "Never forget, the press is the enemy. The press is the enemy. The press is the enemy. The establishment is the enemy. Professors are the enemy. Write that on the blackboard 100 times and never forget it." He entered his second term propelled by fear and hate, not hope. His landslide victory would turn into a disastrous avalanche. A man with a tormented soul, who had bonded with bigots and bullies, had won the soul of the nation and defined the *real* America. But this man, driven by paranoia and dread, had succeeded by exploiting paranoia and dread among his fellow Americans. He had drunk his own poison.

In his last nineteen months in the White House, Nixon would sign the Paris Peace Accords ending the Vietnam War. (It was not a peace with honor. The United States was bugging out, after losing more than fifty-eight thousand American lives and spending $168 billion.) He would increase the federal minimum wage and Social Security benefits. He would hold two summits with Soviet leader Leonid Brezhnev.

Yet this stretch was a slow descent into a political abyss, as Watergate and adjacent scandals consumed the Nixon presidency. The Senate Watergate hearings began in May 1973, exposing a sordidness the American public had never before witnessed. In July, the public learned Nixon had installed a taping system in the Oval Office. The following month, Agnew resigned to escape prosecution for accepting bribes and kickbacks as Maryland governor and vice president. (So much for law and order!) Months later, Nixon began releasing transcripts of the White House tapes, and the public began to learn of his bigotry and thuggery. As Nixon protested his innocence—"I am not a crook"—the drip-drip-drip of Watergate revelations never ended. Hush money schemes. Illegal plots. His top aides resigned, some destined for prison. A federal grand jury named Nixon as an "unindicted co-conspirator." Finally—after Nixon lost a battle before the Supreme Court to withhold key White House tapes—the "smoking gun" tape became public. It was a recording of Nixon ordering the Watergate coverup six days after the break-in. Two days later, on August 8, 1974, he announced his resignation.

Following Reagan's lead in California, Nixon had built a coalition without directly relying on the far-right extremists who had once been associated with Goldwater. He had practiced a different sort of paranoid politics that wed the Republican Party to racists and encouraged profound polarization. His error was believing that extremism in the defense of Nixon was no vice. That fundamental miscalculation wrecked his presidency.

He was gone, but the dark forces Nixon stirred remained.

CHAPTER 9

"Make Them Angry"

Ronald Reagan was being crushed, and he desperately needed the assistance of the far right in North Carolina.

Not long after ending his eight years as California's governor, Reagan had entered the presidential race in November 1975, daring to challenge the leader of his own party, President Gerald Ford, who had succeeded the fallen Nixon. Ford's truncated term had not been going well. His party was demolished in the 1974 midterms, as post-Watergate reform-minded Democrats capitalized on the Nixon catastrophe. Though Ford was a conservative who was moderate in disposition and approach—and had appointed Nelson Rockefeller, a foe of the far right, as his vice president—he had tried during that election season to resurrect that not-so-old Nixon-Agnew demagogic magic. While campaigning for his party colleagues, he declared that the "election of these extremists of the Democrats Party" would endanger "the survival of the two-party system in the country." The voters didn't buy his hyperbole. Only 18 percent of Americans identified as Republicans, and most of the country, according to one GOP pollster, saw Ford's party as "untrustworthy and incompetent."

Worse for the GOP, though Nixon was out of the White House (and pardoned by Ford), the scandals kept coming: A huge CIA operation spied on antiwar Americans and other political dissidents during the Johnson and Nixon years; the FBI had poked around the private lives of members of Congress, had spied on Martin Luther King Jr., *and* had tried to blackmail him into committing suicide; the CIA had plotted to assassinate foreign leaders and had tested LSD on unwitting subjects. Watergate had been a small part of a massive wave of criminal government conspiracies.

Ford's big idea to combat persistent inflation—encourage Americans to buy less and save more by wearing pins that declared "WIN" (Whip Inflation Now)—was a flop. The US economy contracted in 1974 and 1975. The chaotic collapse of Saigon—an inglorious end to a war fueled by lies—happened on Ford's watch. Contemplating the ugly last chapter of this war he had supported, Reagan observed, "You know, Lenin said the

Communists will take Eastern Europe, they will organize the hordes of Asia, he said they will then move into Latin America, and he said the United States, the last bastion of capitalism will fall into their outstretched hands like overripe fruit." Lenin never said that. This phony quote, long popular on the fringe right, especially among Birchers, had originated in Robert Welch's *Blue Book.*

On top of it all, a stumble here, a fall there had turned Ford—thanks to a new television show called *Saturday Night Live*—into something of a national joke.

Reagan presented a serious challenge to the quasi-incumbent who had never won an election outside the Michigan congressional district he represented before replacing the scandal-struck Agnew as veep. His two terms as California governor, though a political mish-mosh, were generally regarded as successful. He had become a national figure for his opposition to campus radicalism. He sent in National Guard troops to put down a student demonstration, and when a student was shot, he said, "The police didn't kill the young man. He was killed by the first college administration who said some time ago it was all right to break the laws in the name of dissent." Days before the massacre at Kent State, Reagan vowed, "If it's to be a bloodbath, let it be now. No more appeasement."

As governor, Reagan signed a liberal abortion bill and a gun control measure, the latter designed to prevent Black Panthers from mounting armed patrols of Oakland neighborhoods. Working with the Democratic state legislature, he enacted welfare reform that reduced the number of recipients but raised benefits. Despite his anti-government rhetoric, the state budget more than doubled during his two terms as governor. He oversaw $4 billion in property tax relief, but he also signed record-setting state tax increases. He enacted laws to stiffen criminal penalties, yet the state's homicide rate doubled.

After his two terms as governor, Reagan pursued a career as a public figure. He gave public speeches (eventually earning $5,000 a pop). He delivered radio commentaries on hundreds of stations throughout the land. A column he penned appeared in almost as many newspapers. Through all these avenues, he peppered his audiences with scalding denouncements of governmental and bureaucratic folly and folksy anecdotes praising free enterprise and American goodness. The true enemies were those officials and intellectuals who would turn the land of the free into a socialist hellhole and who, of course, were aided and abetted by a liberal media. He laced his commentaries with what he presented as facts—though he had a penchant for putting forward claims that did not check out or were uncheckable (*a recent article said...*). In addition to all his for-profit evangelizing, Reagan had another line of work: running for president.

At the start of Reagan's attempt to land the role of a lifetime, an old problem weighed on his political advisers: Would Reagan be seen as an extremist? "We were trying to establish we were not the candidate of the kooks," one of his aides said. Even after his eight years as a governor, Reagan, still known to many voters as a B-movie actor who had starred with a chimpanzee in *Bedtime for Bonzo*, faced a twinned stereotype: He was a lightweight, and he was a fringe-y ideologue.

It also didn't help that Reagan had a penchant for excess and exaggeration, if not fabulation. He routinely told the story of a woman in Chicago who used multiple names and identities to collect welfare and other low-income assistance, pocketing $150,000 a year. It was his way of denigrating all government assistance. But his account was false. She had been caught and was being prosecuted for $8,000 in fraud. He spoke in absolutes. "Government is not the answer to the problem; government is the problem," he declared, despite his own years of public service. He claimed the National Education Association, a teachers' union, wanted to impose a "federal educational system" and compared that to Nazi Germany. Elliot Richardson, Ford's commerce secretary, dismissed Reagan's supporters as "right-wing ultra conservatives."

But Reagan had demonstrated in California that he could sell a far-right line without coming across as an extremist. Veteran journalist Elizabeth Drew described his secret sauce: "He comes across as a pleasant man who understands why people are angry... He talks to people's grievances, but he doesn't seem mean." Reagan conveyed "a respectful mad, a decent American fedupness." He took aim at the same targets as Wallace and Agnew. But he prosecuted the battle "in a much nicer way."

Reagan lost the opening rounds of the GOP nomination fight to Ford in Iowa and New Hampshire. To juice up his campaign, he turned to a favorite issue of right-wing kooks: the Panama Canal. The State Department had for years been in negotiations aimed at granting Panama more control over the Canal Zone and perhaps ending US dominion of the canal. For conservatives and the John Birch Society, this was close to treason. Maintaining full sovereignty of the Zone had become a holy cause—a fight to preserve American might and influence after Vietnam. Jesse Helms, a rising champion of the right elected senator from North Carolina in 1972, was leading this crusade, and Reagan moved to exploit the right's anger at Ford, whose administration, like that of Nixon, had been pursuing these negotiations. (A goal of the talks was to calm a growing restiveness in Panama that could spark conflict and violence in the Canal Zone and disrupt its operations.) Reagan adopted the simple line Helms had been pushing: *We paid for it. We built it. It's ours.* (Goldwater criticized Reagan for "gross factual errors" and "a surprisingly dangerous state of mind.") For good measure, Reagan blasted Ford's entire foreign policy, which had been inherited from Nixon and Henry Kissinger, who still served as secretary of state. "We are getting out of détente," Reagan exclaimed, referring to the effort to thaw relations between Washington and Moscow.

Promoting the obsessions of the far right wasn't enough for Reagan to shoot past Ford. He fell to the president in Massachusetts, Vermont, Florida, and Illinois. Perhaps GOP voters were less attached to foreign affairs red meat than Reagan and his brain trust assumed.

In North Carolina, conservative extremists came riding to Reagan's rescue.

Working with Helms—who had denounced the civil rights movement as a bastion of communists and "moral degenerates," called Social Security "nothing more than doles and handouts," and excoriated Medicaid as a "step over into the swampy field of socialized medicine"—the American Conservative Union poured tens of thousands of dollars into newspaper and radio ads to boost Reagan. The ACU had been organized by William Buckley and others following the 1964 Goldwater campaign, and, at Buckley's insistence, it had kept Birchers out of its ranks. But it had in its early days developed a film claiming communist agitators orchestrated the urban riots—a fringe position in line with Bircher paranoia and conspiracy theory.

The ACU had recently demonstrated that the line between the supposedly respectable right and the kooky extreme right was faint. At a fundraiser the previous October in Pasadena, California, the ACU had honored Reagan. The attendees included Representative John Rousselot, the Republican who previously was a John Birch Society official. An organizer of the event was Colonel Doner ("Colonel" was his name, not a title), a onetime youth leader of the Christian Crusade, the fundamentalist religious outfit run by Billy James Hargis, the segregationist Bircher supporter. The following month, the California chapter of the ACU held a conference featuring Rousselot and Representative Larry McDonald, an ultraconservative Georgia Democrat on the national council of the John Birch Society and a proponent of the basic fringe-right conspiracy theory: elite internationalists—the Council on Foreign Relations, the Trilateral Commission, the Bilderbergers—were plotting to achieve global dominance.

In North Carolina, the ACU financed thirty-three major newspaper ads and 882 radio spots in favor of Reagan. One radio ad featured a straight-forward message: "Gerald Ford appointed Nelson Rockefeller [vice president]." Helms fired up his mighty political machine as well, with the operation overseen by Tom Ellis, who had fiercely fought school integration in the 1960s. Ellis had managed Helms's successful 1972 Senate campaign and was also a director of the Pioneer Fund, which financed research seeking to prove Black people were genetically inferior to whites. Its recipients included William Shockley and Arthur Jensen, two academic proponents of scientific racism, and Roger Pearson, a racist extremist with ties to former Nazis. Reagan's political fortunes were riding on the endeavors of bigoted extremists of the right.

Under Ellis's command, Helms's operation weaponized racist fear, disseminating a flyer that quoted Ford saying that Senator Edward Brooke, the Black Republican from Massachusetts, "should be considered for vice president." In an unprecedented feat, the Helms machine developed a list of eighty thousand Republican primary voters—about 40 percent of what would be the total GOP electorate—to target with flyers and phone calls.

Nixon had Strom Thurmond in 1968. Reagan had Jesse Helms and the ACU—the far right that overlapped with the kooks who had contended the civil rights movement was a commie plot and Social Security and Medicare were socialist traps.

Reagan's alliance with the anti-Black fanatics was a success. He clobbered Ford 52 to 46 percent in North Carolina. No sitting president had ever lost a primary he had actively contested until this race. Reagan's candidacy had been saved. The day after, the ACU called on Ford to withdraw, citing "an embarrassing repudiation of the President's leadership."

———

The fight was on. Over the next months, Ford and Reagan bitterly slugged it out, each winning a primary here and there, with no knock-out blows. The ACU continued supporting Reagan, raising at least $235,000 for its efforts to assist the former movie star.

In Texas, where Democrats could vote in the Republican primary, the Reagan team tried to win by pulling in voters drawn to Wallace, whose 1972 campaign ended when he was shot by a would-be assassin and paralyzed below the waist and who was now running for the Democratic presidential nomination. Reagan's campaign aired a television spot featuring a voter who said, "I've always been a Democrat. As much as I hate to admit it, George Wallace can't be nominated...So for the first time in my life, I'm gonna vote in the Republican primary. I'm gonna vote for Ronald Reagan."

Attempting to harvest voters sympathetic to a racist, the ACU purchased ads in Texas newspapers encouraging Wallace fans to vote for Reagan. And Reagan, adopting another favorite right-wing cause, called for lifting pressure on Rhodesia and South Africa to end their minority-rule regimes. The United States, he declared "would be well to make sure our own house is in order before we fly off to other lands to attempt to dictate policies to them." It was a new way to play the race card: assail the opposition to racist governments in Africa. Reagan won Texas with two-thirds of the vote.

About now, the Ford gang woke up and realized it was not just battling the campaign of a candidate. It was facing a new conservative movement that would come to be known as the New Right.

For the past twelve years—since Goldwater's crushing defeat—die-hard activists on the right had been constructing a sweeping infrastructure. At its heart was a relatively new and lucrative fundraising device: direct mail. One of the first experts in the use of this tool, an archconservative named Richard Viguerie, had raised $6 million for George Wallace in 1968 and another $7 million for the segregationist in 1972. For the rising organizations of the right—think tanks, political action committees, advocacy groups of all sorts (antiabortion outfits, hawkish foreign policy shops)—Viguerie was the man to see. He kept developing bigger and bigger mailing lists of conservative Americans who could be targeted through the US postal service with dire fundraising appeals. This allowed far-right groups to reach a large audience of conservatives without having to navigate the mainstream media and was the start to what would become an immense right-wing media ecosystem and echo chamber. Moreover, the money poured in, including rich commissions for Viguerie. (A newsletter published by Viguerie would note at the end of the year that a dozen of these New Right organizations raised a total of $7.5 million for 1976 election activity.)

This burgeoning conservative network also found financial angels in a few right-wing tycoons, particularly beer magnate Joseph Coors and Pittsburgh billionaire Richard Mellon Scaife. One of Coors' companies was a frequent advertiser in a John Birch Society magazine—an effective way to support Welch's group. Coors himself made financial contributions to the society, according to the *Washington Post*. And both Ford and Nixon had appointed Coors to the governing board of the Corporation for Public Broadcasting. *People* magazine noted that Coors had spent $1 million on Reagan's 1976 presidential effort before Reagan even announced his candidacy.

The new powerhouses of the right came to include the Heritage Foundation, the Conservative Caucus, and the National Conservative Political Action Committee. One of these new organizations, the Committee for the

Survival of a Free Congress (CSFC), had contributed heavily in 1974 to a Birch leader who ran an unsuccessful campaign for US Senate in Alaska. (Coors was this committee's largest donor.) In 1976, this group mounted a direct-mail appeal—concocted by Viguerie and signed by Senator James McClure, an Idaho Republican—to raise $2 million to influence the out-come of a hundred races throughout the country. The key principal of the CSFC—a hyperactive conservative organizer named Paul Weyrich (who had helped start the Heritage Foundation)—was on the payroll of another Republican senator, Carl Curtis of Nebraska. It was all connected: far-right outfits, campaign money, Republican members of Congress, a multimillionaire Bircher who was a Nixon and Ford appointee. No clear divide existed between fringe extremism and the GOP's right flank.

These New Right organizations enthusiastically cultivated an extreme form of hardball politics, exploiting hot-button social issues and race and advancing the dark arts of negative campaigning. As conservative journal-ist Alan Crawford described it at the time, "Collecting millions of dollars in small contributions from blue-collar workers and housewives, the New Right feeds on discontent, anger, insecurity, and resentment, and flourishes on backlash politics."

Not all rightists, according to Crawford, were enthusiastic about this development: "Its emergence has dismayed many conservatives who fear that a reactionary New Right willing to work with groups like the John Birch Society will lead American conservatism back into what [conservative historian] Richard J. Whalen has called the sandbox. They regard the New Right as anti-intellectual, insensitive to questions of civil liberties, hostile to reforms, more concerned with using political processes for social pro-test than with improving the quality of life in America by informed public policy and ameliorative social programs." These fretting conservatives—Crawford did not name them—believed "New Right dominance could mean the end of a responsible conservatism."

The embrace of stridency and severe tactics by this new breed of con-servative was no secret. Terry Dolan, the founder of the National Conser-vative Political Action Committee (NCPAC), remarked, "The shriller you are, the better it is to raise money." The fundraising letters Viguerie sent out, Dolan noted, were aimed to "make them angry" and "stir up hostili-ties." They advanced the fundamental theme of McCarthyism: Diabolical evil liberals were out to destroy America. These missives might not have been as paranoid and conspiratorial as Bircher disinformation—no, Ike was not part of a global commie plot—but they reinforced the views of those who feared internal subversion and who believed an epic battle was being waged against wily commies aiming to obliterate the American way of life. As Weyrich explained, the New Rightists saw themselves as crusaders dedicated to expelling "elitists" who had usurped power from Middle America and who attacked and weakened the United States from within.

The New Right, Crawford contended, was a direct descendant of Joe McCarthy, more sophisticated, perhaps, but just as dependent on Hofstadter's "paranoid style of politics." For them, the will of the American people was being thwarted by conspirators. "While there continues to exist in right-wing circles," Crawford wrote, "a dread of the Chase Manhattan Bank, the Council of Foreign Relations, and the Trilateral Commission, more up-to-date right-wingers prefer to blame their inability to play successful politics on (to give one example) 'the liberal media.' The major television networks, however, are only one part of the vast conspiracy, which encompasses almost all the major institutions of government. These include the federal bureaucracy, the organized labor movement ('labor bosses'), the courts, the national leadership of the two major political parties, all 'moderate' politicians, the 'special interests,' the public schools and public school administrators, big businessmen who believe in one world government and trade with Communist countries, the major centers of intellectual activities such as the universities, New York City...It is a vast conspiracy."

The intent was to exacerbate division and tribalism, to transform American politics into an all-out cultural civil war. One ACU board member told Crawford, "The Viguerie people address only those concerns which tend to stir up lower middle-class whites, but they never address the more important concerns of Americans of all colors, such as income security and unemployment."

Extreme positions were championed with extreme rhetoric that villainized the other side. Dolan later explained the core strategy for NCPAC: "We could say whatever we want about an opponent of a Senator Smith and the senator wouldn't have to say anything. A group like ours could lie through its teeth and the candidate it helps stays clean." And they would say anything. One direct-mail solicitation sent out by the Conservative Caucus cast "liberal politicians" as evildoers who "force your children to study from school books that are anti-God, anti-American, and filled with most vulgar curse words; give your tax money to communists, anarchists, and other radical organizations; do nothing about sex, adultery and homosexuality and foul language on television." It was signed by GOP New Hampshire Governor Meldrim Thomson Jr., the group's chairman. The New Right was institutionalizing a new delivery system for extremism and bigotry.

The Ford camp got a taste of this during the dirty campaign in North

Carolina. Helms was a key figure in the New Right; his signature on a direct-mail piece did wonders. And slash-and-burn was how they conducted politics in North Carolina. Now those tactics were spreading throughout the conservative world. "Organize discontent. That is our strategy," Howard Phillips, a former Nixon administration official who was now the head of the Conservative Caucus, would later say.

————

After the loss in Texas, a Ford campaign official drafted a memo noting that Reagan's "unexpected" success there and in other states seemed "puzzling." Turnout had been high, and the people coming to vote "have not been involved in the Republican political system before." These folks voted "overwhelmingly" for Reagan. "A clear pattern," the memo noted, "is emerging: these turnouts now do not seem accidental but appear to be the result of skillful organization by extreme right-wing political groups in the Reagan camp operating almost invisibly through direct mail and voter turnout efforts conducted by the organizations themselves." A "loose coalition" of right-wing groups had developed, with many working with Viguerie's direct-mail firm. Others were sponsored by Coors or special interest groups, such as the National Rifle Association. The memo listed the culprits: the American Independence Party (a Wallace-originated outfit that had been infiltrated by Birchers), the ACU, NCPAC, the anti-union National Right to Work Committee, the Committee for the Survival of a Free Congress, the Heritage Foundation, the National Right to Life Committee, and others.

"Many of the members of these groups are not loyal Republicans or Democrats," the memo explained. "They are alienated from both parties because neither takes a sympathetic view toward their issues. Particularly those groups controlled by Viguerie hold a 'rule or ruin' attitude toward the GOP.... They will turn out to vote in larger numbers than party regulars." They could, the memo warned, take over the Republican Party.

This political operation, according to the document, was conducting "independent advertising campaigns on behalf of Reagan." It was raising a bundle through direct mail "using outrageous literature designed to motivate people interested in a right wing cause." And these mailing lists were being used in voter turnout programs: "In a state where the GOP vote is traditionally small such an effort can be devastating." Much of this was occurring surreptitiously, clear of the federal reporting requirements that applied directly to Reagan's campaign.

The memo put it plainly: "We are in real danger of being out-organized by a small number of highly motivated *right wing nuts*, who are using funds outside of the Reagan campaign expenditure limits...He is thus able to operate a relatively moderate campaign to capitalize on his natural support and obtain the winning margin from the right wing supporters."

This report nailed it: Reagan had fired up the fanatics. Ten years earlier, with his campaign for governor, Reagan had mainstreamed far-right extremism, applying charm and Hollywood bonhomie to the Manichean worldview of anti-government, commie-chasing, free-enterprise-worshipping ultra-conservatives. In the meantime, the right-wing zealots who were once on the fringe of Republicanism had built an empire, and Reagan had their troops and treasure (courtesy of direct mail) on his side. He was one of them—which he demonstrated during an interview in which he slammed former Georgia Governor Jimmy Carter, the Democratic front-runner, for having supported a bill calling for full employment: "If ever there was a design for fascism, that's it. Fascism was really the basis for the New Deal."

In the final months of the Republican contest, the Ford and Reagan campaigns engaged in trench warfare, practically hunting one delegate at a time in between the primary contests they were splitting. On the Democratic side, Carter coasted to a victory at the party's convention at Madison Square Garden in New York City. In his acceptance speech, Carter called for a "time of healing." He promised an American government "as decent and as competent as its people" and declared, "We can have an American president who does not govern with negativism and fear of the future."

Fear, though, was the weapon of the New Right. Fear was what raised the money and moved the foot soldiers. And with the help of the New Right, Reagan reached the end of the race slightly trailing Ford in the delegate count. It appeared the Mississippi delegation might determine the nominee. And wouldn't a group of conservative Republicans side with the prince of the right? Then came a shocker.

More than two weeks before the Republicans were to gather in Kansas City for the convention, Reagan announced that were he to be nominated, he would select Senator Richard Schweiker, a Republican with a liberal and prolabor record, to be his running mate. His chief campaign strategist had convinced Reagan this move would broaden his appeal and unite the party. But conservatives were outraged. Harry Dent, the longtime Thurmond ally, proclaimed this the "political boner of the century." The head of the Mississippi delegation declared he was now for Ford.

At the convention, Helms and the New Right fanatics pushing for Reagan won tough platform fights to criminalize abortion, embrace school prayer, and oppose détente, gun control, and busing—but this was just a consolation prize. Ford and the GOP establishment held back the Reagan rebellion. When the roll call vote came, Ford claimed 1,187 delegates; Reagan, 1,070. Afterward, at a gathering of his campaign staff, Reagan quoted an English ballad: "Though I am wounded, I am not slain. I shall rise and fight again."

———

Ford headed toward defeat against Carter and became the first sitting president since Hoover to be tossed out by the voters. The Georgian—winning in the South, splitting the Midwest and Northeast, and losing the West—garnered 297 electoral votes to Ford's 240. There was little shift in Congress; the Democrats maintained large majorities.

Following the 1976 election, pundits practically declared the Republican Party dead. The *New York Times* observed, "Most of its national leaders are either defeated, discredited or too old for any claim on future political influence, the political observers say. The no longer Grand Old Party has lost the White House, barely preserved apparently irreducible minorities in Congress and clings to governorships in 13 of 50 states, many of them small and politically impotent."

Several top Republicans suggested that their party's brand was kaput and the GOP should consider changing its name. Among those Republicans was Ronald Reagan.

CHAPTER 10

Onward Christian Soldiers

I n early 1976, a forty-two-year-old lawyer and Mormon Church ward who possessed no political experience decided to chase a US Senate seat in Utah. A partner in his law firm later said, "He felt like God wanted him to run" and defeat the incumbent, a liberal Democrat named Frank Moss. One of the first steps this novice Republican candidate took was to call on a right-wing conspiracy theorist and John Birch Society supporter—a true kook—and ask for help.

The candidate was Orrin Hatch; the extremist was W. Cleon Skousen, a former FBI clerk and onetime Salt Lake City police chief (fired by the mayor and branded as a liar), who had for years been writing books and peddling Bircheresque paranoia, claiming rampant communist subversion and decrying homosexuality. ("Every boy should know that masturbation may be the first step to homosexuality," he maintained.) Skousen championed a host of nutty beliefs. He asserted that the Founding Fathers were the Lost Tribe of Israel and insisted that criticism of the Mormon Church's opposition to integration was a communist plot against Mormonism.

In his 1958 book, *The Naked Communist*, a favorite in Bircher circles, Skousen stated that Karl Marx had set out "to create a race of human beings conditioned to think like criminals" and that "agents of communism" had "penetrated every echelon of American society—including some of the highest offices of the United States Government." He breathlessly revealed that the goals of the commies and their useful idiots included winning control of schools and infiltrating the press ("get control of book-review assignments"). Their scheme to weaken American culture encompassed degrading artistic expression (substituting "good sculpture" with "shapeless, awkward and meaningless forms"), encouraging divorce and promiscuity, and seizing control of unions *and* big business.

Skousen disclosed that the communists even had a date for ultimate victory: "Total conquest is to be completed by around 1973." In his 1970 book, *The Naked Capitalist*, Skousen unveiled a larger worldwide conspiracy, maintaining that a sinister "secret society of the London–Wall Street axis"—which included the Council on Foreign Relations—controlled the planet and orchestrated global events, financing revolutions and collaborating with communists and "dictatorial forces" to preserve its power.

Skousen was a crackpot. (The Mormon Church in a few years would distance itself from him.) But he had a following, especially in Utah. Before Hatch announced his candidacy, he requested a meeting with Skousen. "I knew he had strongly held beliefs and I was very interested to hear what he had to say," Hatch later recalled.

At their first encounter, the two men found what Hatch subsequently called "many areas of common ground," and the conspiracy theorist agreed to help him. "Throughout the coming months, he became a true champion of my candidacy," the future senator recounted. Skousen had an immensely valuable asset for the greenhorn: a mailing list. He sent a letter to eight thousand people promoting Hatch's campaign, catalyzed early financing for the campaign, and helped recruit volunteers for Hatch. A screwball conspiracist kick-started Hatch's bid. The New Right was merging with—and exploiting—Old Right extremism.

Hatch needed more than Skousen's assistance for his long-shot campaign to succeed. He hooked up with Richard Viguerie, the direct-mail king. With the assistance of Ronald Reagan's pollster, Dick Wirthlin, a Mormon connected to Utah politics, Hatch bagged an endorsement from Reagan and achieved an upset victory in the Republican primary. The many dollars Viguerie raised financed Hatch ads that slammed Moss as an "Eastern Seaboard liberal" against guns and the death penalty. Hatch railed against abortion, the Equal Rights Amendment, and unions. A variety of New Right organizations poured money into his coffers.

Hatch won with 54 percent of the vote. He would go on to spend forty-two years in the Senate and become the longest-serving Republican senator in US history.

Though Jimmy Carter's defeat of Gerry Ford and the Democrats' retention of large majorities in Congress defined the 1976 elections, Hatch's win—to those paying close attention—showed what Republicans could do by harnessing traditional conservative extremism and blending it with the power of the New Right. An appeal to divisiveness, an embrace of hard-edged cultural politics, a cultivation of resentments, an adoption of sharp tactics and rhetoric—here was a winning formula. The New Right was on to something.

———

Reagan joined this bandwagon. After his primary loss to Ford, he had close to $1 million in campaign cash and a mailing list with 183,000 names on it.

He poured all this into a political action committee called Citizens for the Republic and joined the ranks of the New Right. That meant getting in on the shrill-athon being mounted by this expanding collection of outfits hitting up—and pandering to—worried conservative Americans. One fundraising message Reagan's group mailed out played upon anti-government paranoia: "Dear Friend: YOU CAN BET THAT SOMEWHERE IN THE VAST LABYRINTH OF THE FEDERAL BUREAUCRACY THERE'S A FILE ON YOU. It may be a Social Security record, an FHA [Federal Housing Administration] record, or an OSHA [Occupational Safety and Health Administration] record…BIG BROTHER GOVERNMENT WILL GO TO ANY LENGTH TO KEEP A TAB ON YOU." What was wrong with the Social Security Administration keeping track of those who received checks? Or OSHA maintaining records of workplace accidents? But that wasn't the point. Reagan's group was part of the demagogic right-wing choir exploiting legitimate concerns by extolling conspiracism. One central element of the New Right was, to put it simply, grift—raking in the bucks by spreading false or exaggerated messages that spurred and fortified the grievances (real or irrational) held by conservatives.

Establishment Republicans feared the invasion of the New Rightists. In early 1977, Representative John Anderson of Illinois, the third-ranking Republican in the House, observed that "extremist fringe elements who claim membership in our party seek to expel the rest of us from the GOP, using their own, arbitrary philosophical purgative." Republican Michigan Governor William Milliken warned of groups with "interests more in ideology than in the Republican Party." But these moderates, whether they knew it or not, were waging a losing battle. In fact, it wasn't even exactly clear how they were fighting—except by grousing. A Knight-Ridder journalist summed up the conflict: "In legislative battles in Congress, in political fundraising, in mobilizing support on controversial issues throughout the country, in winning key off-year elections, and in sheer intellectual energy and talent, the 'New Right' has overwhelmed the traditional Republican establishment."

As the New Right gained influence by hurling red meat at Republican voters, it encouraged the rise of a new generation of more combative and extreme Republicans. Hatch had been one. Another was a history professor at West Georgia College named Newt Gingrich. He had run for Congress in 1974 and 1976 as a reform-minded, pro-environment Republican against a conservative Democrat and lost each time. On his third attempt in 1978, he fashioned himself as an anti-tax, anti-welfare, anti–Panama Canal treaties Reaganite. He captured the spirit of the New Right with his proselytizing of pugilistic politics. Speaking to a gathering of Georgia Young Republicans, he laid it out: "One of the great problems we have in the Republican Party is that we don't encourage you to be nasty. We encourage you to be neat, obedient, and loyal, and faithful, and all those Boy Scout words, which would be great around a campfire but are lousy in politics... You're fighting a war. A war for power... What we really need are people who are willing to stand up in a slug-fest."

———

Reagan continued spreading his folksy version of the conservative gospel, with his newspaper column, his radio commentaries, and his speaking gigs. Through these avenues, he gave credence to right-wing paranoia. A case in point: At a talk in Palm Beach, he claimed that unnamed experts had concluded that "the Soviet Union now believes that they could absorb a blow from us—a nuclear blow—with fewer casualties than they took in World War II—twenty million dead and wounded, unofficially—and that it could be acceptable to them." Moreover, he told this audience, the Kremlin had recently dispatched 20 million young people to the countryside for an exercise rebuilding Russian society in a post-nuclear world. Reagan noted that "as early as next year and at least by 1981," Moscow would present an ultimatum to the United States: Surrender to the Soviet Union or face a nuclear attack. This was all untrue. It was as if Reagan was reciting a Bircher pamphlet.

He assailed Jimmy Carter's new emphasis on human rights in foreign policy. He warned of Soviet "killer satellites." He claimed there was no reason to worry about radioactive waste created by nuclear power; it could be recycled. (False.) He railed against lenient criminal sentences. He decried the proposed Panama Canal treaties. (In a debate with Bill Buckley, who favored the treaty, Reagan muffed one fact after another.) At one point, Reagan joined a "Panama Truth Squad" that was sponsored by the American Conservative Union, NCPAC, Citizens for the Republic, and other New Right shops and that included Jesse Helms, Orrin Hatch, other senators and representatives, Howard Phillips, retired military officers, and two Birchers in Congress. The treaties would, as one truth squadder put it, "let Cuba and Moscow proceed with their master plan for takeover of the Caribbean." It was a reprise of the-Russians-are-coming scare tactics.

The ongoing tussle over the Panama Canal treaties riled up the crazies. Representative George Hansen, an Idaho Republican known for his ultra-conservatism, stormed into the Senate chamber one day and demanded the House be allowed to vote on any transfer of the Panama Canal. (The House had no such right under the Constitution.) Hansen demonstrated how easy it was to move between the conspiratorial and racist fringe and the new power center of the GOP. He had spoken at a John Birch Society gathering the previous year, and he was also associated with the Liberty Lobby, a far-right organization that promoted antisemitism, racism, and neo-Nazism. (Representative Charles Grassley, an Iowan Republican, at one point received $1,000 for speaking at a Liberty Lobby conference.) At the same time, Hansen also had ties to the more respectable pillars of the New Right. He was on the board of advisers for Weyrich's Committee for the Survival of a Free Congress and served as chairman for STOP OSHA, a project of the American Conservative Union.

During the heated Senate debate on the Panama Canal treaties, which began in February 1978, Senator Thomas McIntyre, a New Hampshire Democrat, assailed the recent shift in conservative politics. "The techniques used to exploit the issue of the canal treaties," he proclaimed from the Senate floor, "are the most compelling evidence to date that an ominous change is taking place in the very character and direction of American politics. I see abundant evidence everywhere that dangerously passionate certainties are being cynically fomented, manipulated, and targeted in ways that threaten amity, unity, and the purposeful course of government in order to advance a radical ideology that is alien to mainstream political thought." He assailed right-wingers for claiming that those who disagreed with them had "something sinister in our motivation" and that this justified "any means, however coarse and brutish." He excoriated "the bully boys of the radical right" and deplored what their "politics of intimidation does to America." He intoned, "If you want to see the fevered exploitation of a handful of highly emotional issues distract the nation from problems of great consequence, stand aside and be silent."

Watching his colleague, Senator Mark Hatfield, a liberal-minded Oregon Republican who as governor had been booed by Goldwaterite delegates at the 1964 convention, decided to speak against the far-right extremists again. He took to the well: "I have seldom received letters that spew forth such a venom of hatred as I have received from within this group called the Radical Right who so violently oppose the Panama Canal treaties." The letters accused him of loving "kike bankers," questioned his Christian faith, and impugned his patriotism. Year later, Hatfield would reflect on this episode and observe that the New Right perverted religion to the point "that opposition to their political agenda proves not only that you are un-American, but that you are ungodly," and he would note that the radical right had spun "legitimate questions" about American life and government into "hysterical fears" to "increase its political power."

McIntyre's and Hatfield's cris de coeur from the Senate floor drew media coverage, but these speeches did not arrest the trend. Hatfield was an outlier within his own party. Days later, Governor Meldrim Thomson Jr. delivered a speech at a John Birch Society gathering in Los Angeles. He blasted foreign-born Henry Kissinger and Zbigniew Brzezinski, Carter's national security adviser, as "appeasers and compromisers with Communism" and "co-conspirators in the establishment of one-world government." In remarks elsewhere, Thomson asserted that any senator who supported the treaties "must be swept from office as though he were a Benedict Arnold." He vowed to ride the "crest of the storm until Carter and all of his one-worlders and international bankers are driven from office in 1980." A sitting Republican governor was talking like a Bircher.

Classic far-right, Bircherish conspiracy theory propelled much of the Republican opposition to the treaties. Letters to senators ginned up by the New Right declaimed "elite bankers" and politicians plotting to hand over the canal. Thomson declared that the canal issue "is the last chance we Americans shall have to preserve our freedom, short of catastrophic war."

In a victory for Carter, the Senate, on April 18, 1978, approved the treaties, which called for handing over the canal in 1999. Sixteen of the thirty-eight Republicans in the chamber joined fifty-two Democrats for a total that was one vote more than the required two-thirds majority. And... the world got on. No catastrophic war, no Soviet takeover of the region—just as many of the direst far-right predictions of the past three decades, including those advanced by leading Republicans, had not come true. They never did. Medicare did not ruin the country. The commies did not gain control of the United States. It was all bunk.

But there were casualties—including McIntyre. Months later, he lost his reelection bid to Republican Gordon Humphrey, a professional pilot who had never held political office and who was head of the state chapter of the Conservative Caucus.

In the 1978 elections, with Viguerie and the New Right once more raising millions with red-meat direct mail and with Reagan hopping across the land in a private jet to campaign with GOP candidates (and bemoaning "the betrayal at home"), the Republicans picked up three Senate seats and fifteen in the House. One of those House seats now belonged to Newt Gingrich. During the campaign, he had distributed a flyer showing his Democratic opponent, state Senator Virginia Shapard, in a photo with state Representative Julian Bond, a civil rights hero, with the message: "If you like welfare cheaters, you'll love Virginia Shapard." The *Atlanta Constitution* opined, "The Gingrich approach seems to have gone beyond vigor and into demagoguery and plain lying." It was an inauspicious but telling start to his political career.

During the Carter years, social issues increasingly dominated the political landscape. Phyllis Schlafly was leading what would be a successful crusade against the Equal Rights Amendment. Backlash movements against abortion rights and gay rights were growing. Proposition 13 in California, which severely limited property taxes and restricted the ability of local governments to raise funds for cities, counties, and schools, was approved by voters in June 1978. It was regarded as a sign of a rising conservative populist tide against government.

Carter negotiated a historic peace accord between Israel and Egypt, but his presidency was rocked by the energy crisis triggered by oil shortages that followed the Iranian revolution in early 1979, when the repressive Shah, long a pal of Washington, was chased out of office by popular protests and eventually replaced by Ayatollah Ruhollah Khomeini and a fundamentalist regime. Gas lines formed and enraged Americans. Inflation, fueled in part by the spike in oil prices, hit 11 percent in 1979, and it would keep rising. Unemployment was stuck between 6 and 7.2 percent through the Carter years, as the country moved into a recession. In a July 15, 1979, speech, Carter outlined his plans to reduce oil imports and improve energy efficiency, but what registered most was his observation that the nation was undergoing a "crisis of confidence." The address was dubbed the "malaise speech," though Carter had not used that word.

In November 1979, Iranian students—angered by decades of US support for the Shah and enraged by Carter's decision to allow him to enter the United States to receive medical treatment—stormed the US embassy in Tehran and seized fifty-two hostages. These Americans would remain in captivity for 444 days, casting a never-lifting shadow upon Carter's presidency.

Fundamentalists abroad were undermining Carter's national standing. That was also the dream of fundamentalists at home, for a new component of the conservative movement was on the march: the religious right. The ERA, gay rights, pornography, drug use, school prayer, abortion—these issues had spurred a new political force of anger and disgust. Its leaders were also galvanized by the Carter administration's decision to continue denying tax-exempt status to Christian schools seen as discriminating against

Blacks. This incensed fundamentalist pastors and their flocks—a sign that latent racism lay at the heart of this up-and-coming movement.

Though the religious right encompassed different churches and evangelical leaders, the man who most came to represent it was Jerry Falwell, a television preacher (and former segregationist) who hosted the popular television show *Old-Time Gospel Hour* and ran Liberty Baptist College, which advertised in publications of the John Birch Society and the racist and antisemitic Liberty Lobby. The 3,500-student school in Lynchburg, Virginia, described itself as a "boot-camp for the Lord."

Falwell had a history of hate and prejudice. In a 1958 sermon, he told his parishioners that the *Brown v. Board of Education* desegregation decision ran counter to "God's Word" and that the "true Negro... does not want integration." Moreover, he added, "we see the hand of Moscow" in the civil rights movement. In 1965, Falwell excoriated Martin Luther King Jr. for turning preaching into politics: "Preachers are called to be soul-winners, not politicians."

Yet in the mid-1970s, Falwell was raring to theologize American politics. In 1976, he held "I Love America" rallies across the country to celebrate the Bicentennial and declared, "The nation was intended to be a Christian nation by our founding fathers." He asserted, "This idea of 'religion and politics don't mix' was invented by the devil to keep Christians from running their own country." The next year, he called for a return to "the McCarthy era, where we register all Communists," adding, "Not only should we register them but we should stamp it on their foreheads and send them back to Russia."

Much of the fervor of the religious right arose from its fierce opposition to gay rights. In this crusade, Falwell deployed the language of loathing and demonized homosexuals, casting them as objects of scorn and derision and a present danger. Gay people, he commented in 1977, would "kill you as quick as look at you." That year, he helped Anita Bryant, a singer and pitchwoman for Florida orange juice, overturn an ordinance in Florida's Dade County that barred employment discrimination against gays and lesbians. The following year, he held a "Christians for God and Decency Rally" in St. Paul, Minnesota, to support an antigay rights initiative there. The audience and the pastors on the stage cheered when a speaker described homosexuality as a "murderous, horrendous, twisted act." (The voters backed the initiative by a two-to-one margin.) During a television interview, Falwell proclaimed, "If we allow homosexuality to be presented as an alternative lifestyle... it will bring the wrath of God down upon our nation."

Falwell spread a strident message: Gay people threatened the existence of the United States and its citizenry. Following the assassination of San Francisco Mayor George Moscone and Harvey Milk, the first openly gay member of the city's board of supervisors, Falwell preached that the "people of San Francisco had better awake to the fact that the judgement, the wrath that is falling upon the city, is of divine origin." Even his fellow Christians—those who did not accept his view of God's will—endangered the country: "The liberal churches are not only the enemy of God but the enemy of the nation."

Falwell did not confine his drumbeating to religious matters. He railed against welfare, claiming "we are developing a socialistic state" and "developing a breed of bums and derelicts who wouldn't work in a pie shop eating the holes out of donuts." In *America Can Be Saved*, a book published in 1979, Falwell wasn't shy about his politics: "If you would like to know where I am politically, I am to the right of wherever you are. I thought Goldwater was too liberal!" As part of his vision for America, he said that year, "I hope to see the day when, as in the early days of our country, we won't have public schools. The churches will have taken them over again and Christians will be running them."

This man was about to become a major player in the Republican world.

With help and encouragement from New Right pooh-bahs Howard Phillips, Paul Weyrich, and Richard Viguerie, Falwell in 1979 formed the Moral Majority, an organization that aimed to activate millions of Christian soldiers for political battle. The New Right was birthing the religious right.

Conservative Digest, a magazine published by Viguerie, noted that the "bedrock" of the Moral Majority would be fundamentalist Protestants, particularly fifteen million or so who tuned in for the *Old-Time Gospel Hour* (which had a mailing list of two million names), and that Falwell intended to persuade conservative Catholics, Mormons, and Jews to join his board. Falwell was the group's president. Its executive director was Robert Billings, who had recently written, "If Christians do not master politics, we will, most certainly, be mastered by those who do."

Falwell and the religious right were pushing a new version of us-versus-them politics. It was now the godly against the ungodly. Politics for them was literally a spiritual battle between good and evil, the Lord's team pitted against the unsaved. (The Jesuit magazine *America* accused the Moral Majority of engaging in "moral fascism.")

As the New Right had done, the religious right preyed on and encouraged fear among its followers. At the annual meeting of the Southern Baptist Convention—as conservatives were mounting a coup against a leadership they judged too liberal—James Robison, a Falwell ally, exclaimed, "If we are a denomination that tolerates liberalism in any form, and continues to support it, we will be guilty of the suicidal death of countless millions of people through the world." Reverend Charles Stanley, a board member for the Moral Majority, assailed "demonic" humanism and liberalism as fronts for "socialism and communism." He offered a warning: "Unless we stand up, we are going to lose this republic." What right-wing extremists once said about communist subversives, Falwell and his brethren now said about liberals—and did so from their pulpits.

The politicians took notice. In September 1979, William Gavin, a Reagan speechwriter, sent a note to Peter Hannaford, a top Reagan adviser, pondering how "we can show the movement we are with them on the social issues without, at the same time, alienating those who might be turned off by the 'style' of the movement's people, which seems to be a bit blunt at times." Hannaford replied: "I agree with you that we need to be careful. Fundamentalists—at least the ones I've run into over the years—tend to be rigid, not very tolerant *and* highly tendentious."

Reagan, though, had no such reservations. On November 5, 1979, he appeared on the show of popular televangelist Jim Bakker. He affirmed Bakker's view that government infringed upon Christians regarding abortion and "sexual standards for the American people" and "telling us that we can or cannot do something that is basically against the Bible." As Bakker conveyed his fundamentalist view—"we feel a nation that turns its standard against the standard of the word of God is a doomed nation"—Reagan listened sympathetically and replied, "It concerns me very much." He contended that the law now favored atheism. He expressed his support for school prayer in public schools and asserted that the Constitution "makes it very clear that this is a nation under God." (The Constitution does not mention God or any divine entity.)

When Bakker excoriated Carter for not governing "like an evangelical Christian," Reagan remarked, "Do you ever get the feeling sometimes that if we don't do it now, if we let this be another Sodom and Gomorrah, maybe we might be the generation that sees Armageddon?" With his reference to what fundamentalists saw as an impending apocalyptic clash between the forces of God and those of Satan, Reagan was speaking their language and endorsing their militant worldview: If Americans don't put an end to gay rights, abortion, and other sins, God will smite the nation. (Reagan long had an interest in end-time theology. Nine years earlier, he told a California Democratic state senator that biblical prophecies regarding the final days were coming true, noting, "Ezekiel says that fire and brimstone will be rained upon the enemies of God's people. That must mean that they'll be destroyed by nuclear weapons.")

Eight days after his chat with Bakker, Reagan, in a nationally televised speech, announced his third bid for the presidency. He embraced the belief that the country was on the road to hell: "I cannot and will not stand by and see this great country destroy itself."

CHAPTER 11

Let's Make America Great Again

At the opening event of his 1980 presidential campaign, Ronald Reagan shared the stage with a homophobic racist.

The candidate was in Dorchester, a blue-collar neighborhood of Boston. That morning, Reagan had held a press conference in Washington—where he blamed the Iranian revolution on Carter and insisted the Soviets were committed to creating a "one-world Communist state"—and then hit the road on a five-day, twelve-city tour. His first stop was South Boston, where a campaign memo told him to lean into "BUSING" and "CRIME AND VIOLENCE."

To underscore that point, the campaign had arranged for longtime local pol Albert "Dapper" O'Neil to stand with Reagan at this rally. He was a conservative Democrat notorious for popping off racist and bigoted comments. After President Ford's secretary of agriculture, Earl Butz, had resigned in 1976 for uttering a racist remark—"I'll tell you what coloreds want. It's three things: first, a tight pussy; second, loose shoes; and third, a warm place to shit. That's all!"—O'Neil told a reporter, "He shouldn't have resigned, he was only telling the truth." But O'Neil was a prominent foe of busing who appealed to conservative blue-collar and union voters. That was who Reagan was courting. As he had done in California and Nixon had done nationally, he was looking to exploit white backlash and again hijack a chunk of the traditional Democratic base. O'Neil made a good prop for this effort. In Dorchester, with O'Neil looking on, Reagan touted his own previous union membership and called the election "a battle of philosophy."

Throughout this opening campaign swing, Reagan hit spots where race-driven polarization could be mined for votes. He campaigned with Representative Henry Hyde, a Republican, in Cicero, Illinois, a city renowned for its racist past. After that came Milwaukee, one of the most segregated cities in the United States, where the "hottest issue," according to Reagan's campaign team, was anger over the reopening of a twenty-five-year-old case in which a cop shot an unarmed Black man.

Reagan entered the Republican nomination contest as the front-runner.

His main opponent was George Herbert Walker Bush, the scion of a prominent Republican family who had served two terms in the House before forging a career in appointed positions (ambassador to the United Nations, chair of the Republican Party, ambassador to China, CIA director). The contrast was sharp. Bush, though he had represented a Texas district, hailed from the preppy, Ivy League world of Yankee Republicanism. In Congress, he had been such a vigorous advocate for family planning funds that he earned the nickname "Rubbers." He was no Goldwaterite and not a natural fit with the New Right or the religious right. To the Bircher right, he was another shady insider who was part of the global conspiracy of bankers and other elites plotting one-world government. He resigned from the Trilateral Commission and the Council on Foreign Relations. But wasn't that what a devious conspirator would do?

The race was a matchup between the Republican establishment and the insurgent far right. Shortly before the Iowa caucuses, Reagan pledged to the National Right to Life Committee that he would appoint only antiabortion justices to the Supreme Court. The group endorsed him. Bush was not wooing such voters. He defeated Reagan by 2,182 votes in Iowa. With hubris, he declared he had the "Big Mo." Not really. Like many others, he didn't understand the tectonic shifts within the Republican electorate.

Reagan did. He was playing to the new extremist forces within the party. There was no need for a dog whistle. He was singing their tune loud and clear. Nine days after the Iowa vote, he appeared at a rally in South Carolina at Bob Jones University, a Christian institution that previously refused to admit Black students. Blacks could now enroll, but the school banned interracial dating and marriage. Reagan praised the university as a "great institution." No wonder Bob Jones III urged his students to pray for a Reagan triumph.

Other religious rightists joined this crusade. Falwell left his pulpit to weaponize his flock for Reagan. He traveled to Alaska to help the Moral Majority herd its followers to the Republican caucuses. They surprised the old GOP hands and seized control of the party, electing delegates to the state convention who backed Reagan.

In New Hampshire, another religious right outfit, Christians for Reagan, an offshoot of Christian Voice, was rounding up voters for the Californian. Christian Voice had been forged several years earlier out of several antipornography and antigay organizations, with the help of New Right godfathers Richard Viguerie and Paul Weyrich. Televangelist Pat Robertson had provided start-up money. (Promoting a springtime "Washington for Jesus" rally, Robertson declared America faced "maximum peril" in the next two or three years and the only alternatives were "Christ or chaos.") Christian Voice had first been based at the Heritage Foundation in Washington, where its main representative was Gary Jarmin, who had previously worked for a group connected to Sun Myung Moon's cultlike Unification Church. Senator Gordon Humphrey, who had defeated Thomas McIntyre, was one of its big boosters, as was freshman Senator Orrin Hatch.

Christian Voice adhered to the New Right's basic strategy: Scare the bejesus out of people. One direct-mail letter it sent out, signed by Reverend Robert Grant, the group's head, declared, "The children in your neighborhood are in danger." The enemy? "Militant gays, Liberal Educators, Cruel Atheists, and Godless Politicians." The note claimed that gay rights, busing, and banning prayer in public schools were "just a fraction of a master plan to destroy everything that is good and moral here in America."

The group's spin-off in the Granite State stuck to the same apocalyptic script. It distributed a flyer asking, "Do you believe America was destined for the avalanche of pornography, abortion, homosexuality, murder, rape and child abuse that has befallen us? Your destiny as a Christian and American calls you to join with me in this great Crusade to Save America. Bring God Back to American leadership and elect Ronald Reagan." The National Rifle Association, the anti–gun control outfit that had become a key player of the New Right, also pitched in for Reagan.

While religious right fanatics were deploying the fear of damnation to aid Reagan, he threw a bone to the loony right. He pointed out that nineteen Carter administration officials were past or present members of the dreaded Trilateral Commission (which the *New York Times* described as an organization criticized "as a kind of secret supergovernment"). This was a not-too-coded message to ultraconservatives and conspiracists on the right—and a dig at Bush, who had recently resigned his membership in the group. The commission had long been a bogeyman for the right-wing fringe (and some on the left), the target of paranoid fantasies of a covert cabal subverting the United States. The previous year, Pat Robertson had assailed "the humanistic/atheistic/hedonistic influence on American government" and blamed it on the Trilateral Commission and the Council on Foreign Relations. This was crazy stuff right out of Robert Welch's *Blue Book*.

Reagan, with New Right *and* religious right assistance, slammed Bush in New Hampshire by more than two to one. At a victory celebration, he stood before a banner with a slogan that had been cooked up by a Madison Avenue advertising agency: Let's Make America Great Again.

The next important contest was South Carolina, and Reagan's crew worried about another candidate in the race, John Connally, the former Democratic

Texas governor who had defected to the GOP. He, too, had been courting the religious right, and the Palmetto State was where he expected to take off. But Reagan had a not-too-secret weapon in his pocket: Lee Atwater. Only twenty-eight years old, Atwater was already a master of political skullduggery, and South Carolina was his home turf. He had helped reelect Strom Thurmond in 1978, and he had developed a surefire race-based strategy for winning elections. A year after the 1980 election, he explained his secret to a political scientist in an off-the-record interview that became public years later: "You start out in 1954 by saying, 'Nigger, nigger, nigger.' By 1968 you can't say 'nigger'—that hurts you, backfires. So you say stuff like, uh, forced busing, states' rights, and all that stuff, and you're getting so abstract. Now, you're talking about cutting taxes, and all these things you're talking about are totally economic things and a byproduct of them is, blacks get hurt worse than whites... 'We want to cut this,' is much more abstract than even the busing thing, uh, and a hell of a lot more abstract than 'nigger, nigger.'"

Atwater's mission was to strangle Connally's campaign in the crib. He imported to South Carolina J. Evetts Haley, the anti-Red ultraconservative who had in 1964 written the paranoia-drenched anti-Johnson tract *A Texan Looks at Lyndon*. Haley claimed Connally was just as bad as LBJ. Atwater got Reid Buckley, who sounded just like his famous conservative brother William Buckley, to record radio ads in which "Mr. Buckley"—no first name given—assailed Bush for being too liberal. Perhaps the dirtiest trick, no surprise, involved race. Atwater got Nancy Thurmond, the senator's wife, to tell a reporter that Connally was doling out money to Black deacons to win the Black vote. The rumor made it into the papers. What could be worse for Connally in South Carolina than voters seeing him as a conniver paying off Black voters to steal the GOP primary? Did it make a difference? Reagan swamped Connally—who subsequently dropped out.

Bush held on to his ghost of a chance for several months. Then he quit the race. When a reporter visited him at his home, he pointed to a copy of the Yale alumni magazine on a coffee table. "That's the first time we've been able to put that out for months." The Republican establishment had been overcome by the new trinity of the GOP: the New Right, the religious right, and Reaganism.

At the Republican convention in Detroit, Reagan, rejecting the pleas of various conservative leaders, including Falwell, Weyrich, and Schlafly, selected Bush as his running mate. They did receive a consolation prize: Robert Billings, the executive director of the Moral Majority, was hired as the Reagan campaign's liaison with the religious groups.

To win his spot on the ticket, Bush, who had previously supported

abortion rights and who had sneered at Reagan's supply-side tax-cut philosophy as "voodoo economics," pledged to support the party's platform, which
had a harsh New Right tone to it, opposing abortion rights, the ERA, and gun
control.

In his acceptance speech, Reagan proclaimed the nation was on the precipice of collapse: "The major issue of this campaign is the direct political,
personal, and moral responsibility of Democratic Party leadership—in the
White House and in Congress—for this unprecedented calamity which has
befallen us.... I will not stand by and watch this great country destroy itself
under mediocre leadership that drifts from one crisis to the next, eroding
our national will and purpose."

———

Carter, who had survived a fierce primary challenge from Senator Ted Kennedy, had given Reagan plenty to work with (not all of it his fault): inflation,
unemployment, an energy crisis, and the Iran hostage crisis (the Americans
were still being held). Yet at Reagan's first postconvention campaign event,
he championed a favorite issue of racist extremists: states' rights.

Standing on the stage at the Neshoba County Fair in Philadelphia, Mississippi, in front of thousands, Reagan exclaimed, "There isn't any place like
this anywhere on earth." He was right. In 1964, six days before the opening of that summer's fair, the bodies of three civil rights workers—James
Chaney, Andrew Goodman, and Michael Schwerner—were found buried a
few miles from the fairgrounds. The three had been registering Black voters
in Mississippi as part of Freedom Summer. They were murdered by the Ku
Klux Klan. Local police had been involved in the assassination. The Mississippi state government refused to prosecute the suspected killers. A federal
trial charging eighteen people with civil rights violations related to the killings resulted in seven convictions and relatively light sentences. These murders were one of the most notable racist crimes of the civil rights era. Sixteen
years later the wound was still raw.

Reagan was the first presidential nominee ever to speak at the fair. A
young Republican activist and lobbyist named Paul Manafort, who was
working on Reagan's campaign in the South, had picked the spot—but not
to honor the sacrifice of Chaney, Goodman, and Schwerner or to heal the
fractured past of the nation Reagan was seeking to lead. Months earlier, a
Mississippi Republican official had contacted the GOP to inform it that this
county fair would be a great location for the Republican presidential nominee to win over "George Wallace inclined voters."

When Reagan addressed the predominantly white crowd at the fair, he issued his customary screed against government before delivering these lines: "I believe in states' rights...And I believe that we've distorted the balance of our government today by giving powers that were never intended in the Constitution to that federal establishment. And if I do get the job I'm looking for, I'm going to devote myself to trying to reorder those priorities and to restore to the states and local communities those functions which properly belong there."

No other phrase sent as clear a message to white supremacists as "states' rights." It was under the banner of states' rights that racists had opposed desegregation and federal civil rights laws. Here was Reagan tossing out the words the Southern racists had long clung to.

The exploitative Southern strategy that Goldwater had encouraged two decades earlier and that Nixon had relied upon during his two successful presidential forays was in full view. To win the South in a contest with a Southerner, Reagan's squad knew what needed doing. They would speak to—validate and encourage—the racial resentments and fears that still permeated the region.

They would also honor the resentments of the religious right. Three weeks after the rally in Philadelphia, Mississippi, Reagan planted his flag solidly on the holy territory of the Moral Majority. The occasion was the Religious Roundtable's National Affairs Briefing, held at the Reunion Arena in Dallas. This gathering of thousands of Christian fundamentalists, including 4,500 pastors, was underwritten partly by Nelson Bunker Hunt, an ardent Bircher who had recently attempted to illegally gain control of the global silver market. The line-up was a who's who of the right: Falwell, Helms, Robertson, Schlafly, Weyrich, Tim LaHaye (a popular evangelist connected to Christian Voice who had been a John Birch Society member years earlier), Dallas Cowboys coach Tom Landry, Amway's Richard DeVos, and others. Christian broadcaster D. James Kennedy warned the assembled that "1980 could be America's last free election."

The Dallas shindig was supposedly a nonpartisan event. But no one bought that fiction. The Reagan campaign had been involved with its conception. Speakers urged pastors to join in a fall voter registration drive, with an obvious goal: elect Reagan.

Reagan advisers Michael Deaver and Edwin Meese worried what the fiery Pastor James Robison, an organizer of the event, would say when it was his turn to speak just prior to Reagan's speech. They urged Reagan to wait offstage. But the candidate strode onto the stage and sat behind Robison. "There is no possible way you can separate God from government and have a successful government," Robison thundered. He blasted liberals, homosexuals, and communists, lumping them all together into one giant threat against the families of America. He shouted, "We'll either have a Hitler-type takeover, or Soviet dominion, or God is going to take over this country." Through it all, Reagan nodded and applauded. He was blessing this intolerant, fundamentalist, extreme divisiveness.

When it was Reagan's turn to speak, he expressed his doubts about the theory of evolution and noted the Bible contained answers to all the world's problems. Reagan, a divorced man with a less-than-traditional family who was no regular churchgoer, threw the crowd one gigantic rhetorical wink, using a line that Robison had earlier suggested to him: "I know this is a non-partisan gathering, and so I know that you can't endorse me, but...I want you to know that I endorse you and what you're doing." The crowd roared with appreciation. A few weeks later, the *Washington Post* reported that evangelical leaders who had been at the event were claiming that Reagan in a meeting had promised, in return for their backing, to name Christians to senior administration positions should he be elected. The Reagan campaign denied this. But Ed McAteer, the president of the Religious Roundtable, said such a deal had been made.

Reagan's speech in Mississippi, his appearance at the religious right jamboree—his efforts to court the bigoted and intolerant right were not center stage during the race. Nor were his past associations with ultraconservatives and extreme stances. (On the campaign trail, Reagan insisted multiple times he had never said Social Security should be voluntary—but he had.) There was much else going on, including the continuing hostage crisis in Iran. When Carter attempted to raise Reagan's dalliances with extremism, it didn't work out for the beleaguered president.

On September 16, Carter spoke at the Ebenezer Baptist Church in Atlanta. Following a speaker who pointed out that the Ku Klux Klan had endorsed Reagan—an endorsement Reagan disavowed—Carter took to the pulpit and remarked, "You've seen in this campaign the stirrings of hate. And the rebirth of code words like states' rights. In a speech in Mississippi... Hatred has no place in this country. Racism has no place in this country." The congregants in the pews cheered.

Immediately, the Carter campaign felt compelled to issue a clarification: Carter was *not* suggesting Reagan was a racist extremist. At a White House press conference two days later, a reporter queried the president, "Do you think that Governor Reagan is running a campaign of hatred and racism? And how do you answer allegations that you are running a mean campaign?" *A mean campaign*—the political pundits had adopted this as a theme: The president was petty and vituperative and eschewing the lofty ideals he had promoted during the 1976 campaign. Carter's tone was more relevant, the political press judged, than the affable Reagan's connection to far-right extremism. "I do not think he's running a campaign of racism or hatred," Carter muttered. "And I think my campaign is very moderate."

The religious right chugged along through the fall campaign, proselytizing for Reagan and social conservative candidates for the House and Senate. The Moral Majority was spending $10 million on radio and television ads branding Carter a traitor to the South and no longer a Christian. Reagan was not pressed on his campaign's relationship with the mean and divisive rhetoric of his rightist allies.

———

A month out, polls indicated the election could be close, and Carter was frustrated. He was in a tight race with a man who had advocated sending troops into various crises around the world, who had welcomed an intensified nuclear arms race with the Soviet Union, who had once said trees caused most air pollution, and whose core economic position—cutting taxes would increase revenues and erase government deficits, even with huge increases in military spending—was scoffed at by respectable economists. Carter was also flummoxed by Reagan's association with religious right leaders who would denigrate anyone's relationship with God—and who denied Carter's own Christianity. At a Chicago fundraiser, he pointed out the election would "determine whether or not this America will be unified, or, if I lose the election, whether Americans might be separated Black from white, Jew from Christian, North from South, rural from urban." The press reaction: Carter was being mean again. The next day Reagan responded: "I'm not asking for an apology from him. I know who I have to account to for my actions. But I think he owes the country an apology."

Reagan's relationship with the haters of the right—and with the divisive politics of the New Right—was not a major part of the narrative. Inflation was high. Carter's leadership was in question. Republican moderate John Anderson's independent campaign for president—which seemed to be drawing more votes from Carter than Reagan—was a distraction. Carter often appeared dour and besieged. The disastrous failed hostage rescue attempt in April that had resulted in the deaths of eight American soldiers had become a metaphor for his presidency.

Reagan was the anti-Carter, shiny and strong, offering simple solutions to the nation's woes (less government!) and promising glorious times ahead.

With his optimistic spirit and upbeat nature—and his talent for quips—once more, he didn't *seem* like an extremist or a divider. At one of the two debates between the two men, when Carter raised Reagan's history of opposing Medicare as the supposed path to evil socialism, Reagan sidestepped the accurate accusation by retorting, "There you go again." Carter also tried subtly—probably too subtly—to remind voters of Reagan's ties to the fringe. "I consider myself in the mainstream," he proclaimed, implying Reagan wasn't. Reagan had a different message: "Are you better off than you were four years ago?" For many Americans, with inflation topping 12 percent and unemployment over 7 percent, the answer was no, and not much else mattered.

———

On Election Day, Reagan won 51 percent of the popular vote but achieved an Electoral College near-sweep, triumphing in forty-four states. In an exit poll, 84 percent of Reagan voters had cited "time for a change" as their reason for siding with him. Though Democrats in House races won 50.5 percent of the overall national vote, they lost thirty-three seats but still managed to retain a sizable majority. In the Senate, nine Democratic incumbents, including liberal stalwarts George McGovern, Birch Bayh, Frank Church, and others—were ousted; many had been targets of sharp negative ads from the Moral Majority and the National Conservative Political Action Committee. All told, the GOP netted twelve seats and grabbed control of the upper chamber for the first time in twenty-eight years.

Reagan succeeded in winning 27 percent of the Democratic vote (with Carter claiming only 11 percent of GOP voters), and he bagged 56 percent of the white vote, five points more than Ford four years earlier. Backlash politics appeared to have paid off for Reagan. Moreover, pollster Lou Harris found that 61 percent of white fundamentalist Protestants—who had supported Carter by a two-to-one margin in 1976—voted for Reagan. This swing accounted for about two-thirds of his winning margin. "Reagan would have lost the election by one percentage point without the help of the Moral Majority," Harris observed.

The Moral Majority and its New Right allies had delivered. They had not only appealed to the fears and resentments of many Americans; with their apocalyptic messaging accusing liberals and Democrats (and "militant homosexuals," educators, unions, the media, and others) of deliberately imperiling children, families, and the entire nation, they had encouraged these grievances and worries. They had ignited anxiety, dread, and suspicion—to raise money, to win elections. In a time of economic hardship, international troubles, and cultural change, there already existed angst and apprehension within the American public. The New Right and the religious right did not create this unease and concern. But together they weaponized it and shaped the electorate. As the likable frontman for the new generation of extremists, Reagan legitimized these political forces, fortified their efforts, and gained mightily from it.

"It was my finest hour," Falwell said of Carter's defeat. The day after the election, when Falwell entered a victory rally held in an auditorium at his Liberty Baptist College, the band struck up "Hail to the Chief."

CHAPTER 12

Reaganland

In the early days of the Reagan era, the Reverend Robert Billings was handed a top government position. As the Reagan campaign's ambassador to the Christian right, Billings, a founder of the Moral Majority, had helped the onetime actor land this starring role. His new job, though, was an indication the conservative movement would not get all it dreamed of from Reagan but also a sign the zealots of the right would find much acceptance and influence within his administration.

Billings had hoped to work in the White House as its chief contact with his fellow religious rightists. Instead, he wound up at the Education Department. That was a disappointment. But many leaders of the New Right and the Christian right were disappointed. Reagan's White House crew and cabinet were mostly men whom the conservatives sneered at as pragmatists and establishment Republicans. The ideologues were being kept out of the Gipper's inner circle. The Reaganauts were conveying a message to the rightists: *We're going to use you more than you will use us.*

Shortly after Reagan's victory, the Viguerie gang began howling about not being awarded enough top slots. The social conservative warriors complained about the lack of a commitment from the Reagan crowd for early and forceful action on their top priorities, such as abortion and school prayer. Where was the crusade to clean up America and return it to godliness? Most aggravating for them, old-school Republicans whom movement conservatives detested were in charge of the new administration. James Baker, who had twice run campaigns in opposition to a Reagan presidential bid (the efforts of Gerald Ford and George Bush), was named Reagan's chief of staff—an affront to the far right.

But plenty of plums were dished out to conservatives.

C. Everett Koop, a leader in the antiabortion movement, was appointed deputy assistant secretary of health and designated the next surgeon general. Morton Blackwell, a onetime Viguerie employee and editor of *The New Right Report*, became a senior White House official. Lyn Nofziger, a longtime Reagan aide, die-hard conservative, and consultant to Weyrich's Committee for the Survival of a Free Congress, joined the White House as assistant to the president for political affairs. Don Devine, a leader of Young Americans for Freedom and the American Conservative Union, was placed in charge of the all-important Office of Personnel Management, which managed the government's civil service. Beer magnate and New Right funder Joseph Coors was put on the Commission on Broadcasting to Cuba, as was Richard Mellon Scaife, another major underwriter of the conservative movement. Edwin Feulner, the head of the Heritage Foundation, was named to the advisory panel for the International Communications Agency. Dozens of members of the Committee on Present Danger, a collection of neoconservatives and hawks skeptical of arms control, frustrated with détente and eager to dump human rights as a priority in foreign policy, would find influential jobs in the administration.

The Reagan team was bestowing legitimacy on the extreme forces that had helped it achieve power. A month into his presidency, Reagan hosted a large group of right-wing leaders at the White House. The gang included Schlafly and representatives of the Committee for the Survival of a Free Congress, the National Rifle Association, the National Conservative Political Action Committee, Viguerie's company, and other conservative shops. Reagan did not intend to let this bunch dictate his policies, but he had something grand to offer them: belonging. They would be mainstreamed as a crucial component of the Republican coalition. Their prejudices, their extremism, their demagoguery—it was all in the family. Billings demonstrated that.

A few months after Billings started toiling at the Education Department, the *Libertarian Review*, a magazine owned by conservative industrialist Charles Koch, reported the account of a minister who had attended a Moral Majority meeting in Pennsylvania where Billings had spoken. "I know what you and I feel about these queers, these fairies," Billings had said. "We wish we could get in our cars and run them down while they march." But gay people, he pointed out, were useful for the crusade to "Christianize" America. "We need an emotionally charged issue," Billings explained, "to stir up people and get them mad enough to get up from watching TV and do something. I believe that the homosexual issue is the issue we should use."

A blatant admission of hate *and* a cynical acknowledgment of demagogic exploitation—Billings had spelled out the ugly agenda of the religious right. He and his coreligionists were using people's fears and prejudices to "Christianize" the country. Yet these words triggered no controversy or scandal. The White House took no action to rebuke or dismiss him. Billings would stay in his Education Department post for six years. The fear and loathing of the Christian right had found a welcoming and nurturing home within Reaganland.

Billings's reported remarks were no aberration for the Reagan-boosting Moral Majority. In March 1981, Greg J. Dixon, a Baptist minister and the group's national secretary, appeared on a Chicago radio show and said that according to "God's Word," homosexuals could be executed. Announcing a multimillion-dollar media campaign in the San Francisco area to oppose homosexuality, Dean Wycoff, a spokesperson for the local Moral Majority, publicly stated, "I agree with capital punishment, and I believe homosexuality is one of those that could be coupled with murder and other sins."

Despite the murderous malice within the ranks of the Moral Majority, the Reagan administration repeatedly granted its approval to Falwell's group. "We want to keep the Moral Majority types so close to us they can't move their arms," one administration official told a reporter. Morton Blackwell tended to the White House's relationship with Falwell and his outfit. He attended Moral Majority events and coordinated a steady flow of encomiums from Reagan praising the organization. In one "Dear Jerry" note, Reagan stated, "By furthering the spiritual strength of the American people, your movement helps fulfill the promise of this great land."

But this relationship had its friction. In a letter to James Baker, Cal Thomas, a top Falwell aide, issued a warning—or a threat: "If a timetable [for action to end abortions] hasn't been developed, it urgently needs to be developed. Without one, without something to share with our people, serious political consequences will develop, I assure you." Though Thomas was griping, Falwell remained a stalwart supporter of Reagan in public. He seemed to have calculated that the glowing seal of approval he and his intolerant movement had from Reagan was a prize not to be traded for political warfare against the White House.

Other New Right leaders and social conservatives were not as forgiving. They grumbled as their champion did not rush to dismantle the New Deal, roll back the Soviet Union, and launch a program to rid the land of abortion, pornography, and homosexuality. Instead, Reagan focused on his conservative economic program: a large tax cut that mostly benefitted the well-heeled and severe budget slashing that eviscerated social welfare programs. He proposed huge increases in military spending. He fired striking air traffic controllers—a move that heartened conservatives and business interests looking to weaken unions. His administration would also initiate a deregulation effort to delight corporate America.

Viguerie, Weyrich, Phillips, and others on the right protested loudly when Reagan, half a year in office, received his first Supreme Court vacancy and selected Arizona judge Sandra Day O'Connor for the opening. She would be the first woman to serve on the court. But O'Connor had supported the Equal Rights Amendment and cast votes as a state legislator against the agenda of antiabortion rights activists. The right roared in anguish—though Falwell accepted the nomination.

Some Republicans, anxious about the spreading influence of the religious right within their party, tried to fight back. Senator Robert Packwood of Oregon bemoaned "a growing spirit of intolerance," and Goldwater—probably under the mistaken impression that Falwell was leading the charge against his friend O'Connor—exclaimed, "Every good American ought to kick Jerry Falwell in the ass." On another occasion, he shared that he was "sick and tired of political preachers...telling me...that if I want to be a moral person, I must believe in A, B, or C."

Packwood, Goldwater, and other Republicans concerned about the ongoing merger between the GOP and forces of intolerance and fundamentalism were on the losing side. Throughout the Reagan presidency, the Old Man and the Republican Party would hobnob with haters, extremists, racists, neo-Nazis (yes, neo-Nazis), and purveyors of noxious and sometimes absurd conspiracy theories. At times, they would even hail some of these miscreants and provide credence to assorted forms of political zealotry and paranoia. The Reagan years would be good ones for a far right that relied on and that whipped up apprehension and anxiety.

———

Two days after Reagan's inauguration, the Reverend Tim LaHaye, billionaire Nelson Bunker Hunt, and Viguerie met at the Dallas home of T. Cullen Davis, an oil tycoon who in the 1970s had been acquitted of murder (his stepdaughter) and attempted murder (his ex-wife) in two high-profile trials before professing to become a born-again Christian.

These were heavy hitters of the conservative movement. LaHaye, a prominent figure of the religious right, had been part of the founding leadership of the Moral Majority. In the early 1960s, he had appeared in a recruitment film for the John Birch Society. ("It wasn't until I had read the John Birch Society material," he said in that spot, "that I saw the parallel between the spiritual liberal takeover of the church and the liberal political takeover of our country.") Like any good Bircher, he was a full-blooded conspiracist, but his black-and-white view of the world had a theological cast: the forces of secular humanism ("the world's greatest evil") aimed to demolish the nuclear family, Christianity, and "the entire world." His 1980 book, *The Battle for the Mind*, was a battle cry of paranoia. "An invisible enemy threatens our society," he asserted. "Its name? Humanism. Its target? Your mind." He claimed humanism was a global plot, with the goal of "a socialist Sodom and Gomorrah" and a "worldwide generation of young people with a completely amoral (or animal) mentality." A "humanist elite," he maintained, was "determined to turn America into an amoral, humanist, socialist state similar to Russia." He declared that God-fearing Christians had only one decade, perhaps two, to prevent this takeover. "All humanists," LaHaye counseled, must be removed from public office.

This was full-throated conspiracy nonsense—a shadowy cabal, a plan for worldwide conquest. LaHaye, the onetime Bircher, had supplanted "communist" with "humanist." His wife, Beverly LaHaye, two years earlier, had founded Concerned Women for America to oppose feminism and speak for evangelical Christian women. For her, feminism, a key component of "humanism," was a lethal weapon aimed at the American family and Christianity.

Hunt, a longtime financial supporter of the John Birch Society and a member of its national council, was another prominent player of the conspiratorial right. In 1979 and 1980, he and his brothers tried to corner the silver market—an act of chicanery that would lead years later to their bankruptcy and more than $10 million in fines. Hunt had contributed $1 million to Falwell's Moral Majority and other large sums to a long list of New Right and social conservative groups.

On the table was an audacious idea: creating an organization that would coordinate the vast world of the right—the New Right, the religious right, the GOP, and other conservative elements. Davis, the host of this get-together, later said that these men shared the fear that communists were close to seizing control of the United States and believed that Christianity in America was imperiled.

This dinner led to a larger gathering a few weeks later at a hotel near the Dallas–Fort Worth airport. Participants included Schlafly, Weyrich, and Feulner. Months later, in May, a group of more than 150 conservative leaders assembled in the backyard of Viguerie's home in McLean, Virginia, where they nibbled on Peking duck, lobster, and sushi and drank piña coladas, at a reception celebrating the creation of what was now called the Council for National Policy. There was a special guest in Viguerie's backyard that night: David Stockman, Reagan's budget director, who was handed an award for his budget-slashing endeavors. The next night the new group held a dinner with Richard Allen, Reagan's national security adviser. The Reagan admin-istration was honoring this new venture.

LaHaye, the conspiracy preacher, was named the group's president.* The council's announced members included the usual suspects of the right: Viguerie, Weyrich, Phillips, Schlafly, Coors, Feulner, and McAteer, the pres-ident of the Religious Roundtable. Also on the roster were Reagan adminis-tration officials: Blackwell and Billings.

The CNP represented a fusion of social conservatives, religious rightists, leading Republicans, and conspiratorial nuts—all under the imprimatur of the Reagan White House. An early list of eighty-two members of its board of governors included elected Republicans (Senators Jesse Helms, John Porter East, Don Nickles, William Armstrong, and James McClure, and Represen-tatives John Ashbrook, Guy Vander Jagt, and Larry McDonald, who chaired the John Birch Society). Other notables were Falwell, Robertson, NCPAC's Terry Dolan, and William Rusher, the *National Review* publisher. Aboard also were R. J. Rushdoony and Gary North, a father-and-son-in-law team that advocated a form of Christian fundamentalism called Reconstruction-ism, which called for a theocracy based on Old Testament law. (Adultery, homosexuality, blasphemy, disrespecting parents could all be punished by death.) Another member of the CNP was W. Cleon Skousen, the Reds-are-everywhere conspiracist who had helped launched Hatch's political career and who still maintained that a villainous plot waged by the Trilateral Com-mission and the Council on Foreign Relations to replace the United States with a one-world government threatened the country.

The membership of the CNP—and the participation of Reagan officials—was a clear measure of how the paranoid and fringe right had become part of the conservative establishment and tied to the Republican Party. Rac-ists, religious extremists, practitioners of divisive politics, Bircher con-spiracy cranks—they were all inside the tent. And for the fundamentalists and fanatics who saw their political foes as heinous—perhaps Satan-controlled—threats to God and country, Reagan and the GOP had rolled out the welcome mat.

Midway into his first term, the president embraced and encouraged the original tune of the conspiratorial right: Red-baiting.

---

* In the coming years, the presidency would shift to Tom Ellis, the Helms political operative who had been a director of the racist Pioneer Fund; Hunt; Pat Robertson; and billionaire Amway founder Richard DeVos.

On the day of Reagan's election, a little-noticed event occurred in western Massachusetts that triggered a national political movement that would pose a political threat to the Reagan administration. In fifty-nine towns, voters approved resolutions calling for a US-Soviet joint agreement to stop the testing, production, and deployment of nuclear weapons. Afterward, the nuclear freeze movement spread through the nation, as freeze resolutions were passed in town meetings, city councils, and state legislatures and adopted by scientific, professional, and public health organizations. All major religious denominations voiced support for a nuclear freeze, except the fundamentalist Christians. Legislation calling for the negotiation of a freeze was introduced in the House and Senate. On June 12, 1982, a million people rallied for the freeze in New York City—then the largest political protest in American history.

The Reagan administration's stance on nuclear war had stoked popular fear that the arms race would yield catastrophe. During the 1980 campaign, Reagan had talked tough about confronting the Soviet Union, suggesting that Russia could survive a nuclear war and was close to threatening a nuclear strike against the United States. His administration, which was pressing for a nuclear weapons buildup, earned the rap that it considered nuclear combat not unthinkable but a winnable proposition. Thomas K. Jones, Reagan's deputy undersecretary of defense for strategic and theater nuclear forces, told a reporter that Americans could survive quite well in a nuclear holocaust: "You can make very good sheltering by taking the doors off your house, digging a trench, stacking the doors about two deep over that, covering it with plastic so that rainwater or something doesn't screw up the glue in the door, then pile dirt over it." The United States should be able to recover from a nuclear attack, he said, in two to four years. Jones added, "If there are enough shovels to go around, everybody's going to make it." *With enough shovels*—that became a dark punchline.

The freeze, as Reagan adviser David Gergen recalled years later, "was a dagger pointed at the heart of the administration's defense program." That could not stand. Hawkish right-wing groups turned to a dusty old playbook and accused the freeze movement of being a Soviet conspiracy to weaken the United States. It was commie subversion—again. The American Security Council, a prominent conservative organization, said this plainly: "It is no coincidence that this [freeze] strategy serves to implement the aims of the Soviet Union. It is clearly an integral part of the massive campaign to disarm the West which the Soviets have conducted over the past five years."

Reagan took the lead in exploiting the anti-Red conspiratorial mindset. In October 1982—with freeze resolutions on the ballot that fall in ten states and thirty-seven cities and counties—he declared the freeze movement "was inspired not by the sincere, honest people who want peace, but by some who want the weakening of America and so are manipulating many honest and sincere people." His paranoia-inciting insinuation was obvious: the evil puppet masters of the Kremlin were misguiding and manipulating millions of Americans. Reagan was recycling the conspiracism of the McCarthy era and the Bircher right. The *Washington Post* editorial page, no fan of the freeze movement, denounced Reagan's swipe as a "smear."

Reagan and fellow Republicans maintained this demagogic assault. At a press conference, the president said, "There is no question about foreign agents that were sent to help instigate and help create and keep such a movement going." Pressed for confirmation of Reagan's scurrilous charge, the White House cited articles that had appeared in a trio of conservative journals—*Reader's Digest, Commentary*, and the *American Spectator*—and that did not prove this point.

Assorted New Right groups and Republican members of Congress joined the blitzkrieg against the freeze movement. After nine states and various localities (covering about one-third of the US population) approved freeze resolutions, Reagan let loose again: "One must look to see whether, well-intentioned though it may be, this movement might be carrying water that they're not aware of, for another purposes. Incidentally, the first man who proposed the nuclear freeze was on February 21, 1981, in Moscow, Leonid Brezhnev." That was untrue. The first votes in the United States for the freeze had been in 1980.

In March, a declassified FBI report undermining Reagan's Red-baiting was released. It stated, "Based on information available to us, we do not believe the Soviets have achieved a dominant role in the U.S. peace and nuclear freeze movements, or that they directly control or manipulate the movement."

Perhaps no conservative peddled the baseless conspiracy theory about the freeze movement as enthusiastically as Jerry Falwell. He claimed that freeze supporters had been "duped" and that the movement had been "spawned in Moscow." On his *Old-Time Gospel Hour*, he presented his audience a simplistic and noxious accusation: "I look at the nuclear freeze today. In the Kremlin, [Soviet leader Yuri] Andropov or somebody decides that we need 300,000 to march in Stockholm or Berlin or New York, and the robots stand up and start marching for the nuclear freeze." In one direct-mail fundraiser, Falwell warned, "There are those forces who are fully determined to make America into another Soviet Union or 'Red' China—or another Cuba."

The White House embraced Falwell's fearmongering and provided him meetings with Reagan and a National Security Council briefing on the freeze. Delegitimizing liberals was perhaps Farewell's top political aim. At a conference of religious conservatives, Falwell called Harvard University a "Godless and Marxist institution" and said, "Not only are they anti-Christ but they are anti-American." (Falwell at this time was also pushing for increased aid to the Reagan-backed El Salvador government, which was locked in a civil war with leftist guerrillas and running a military that regularly massacred civilians.)

The president went so far as to declaim the freeze as a threat to godliness in America. During a March 8, 1983, speech to the National Association of Evangelicals—in which he branded the Soviet Union an "evil empire"—Reagan characterized the freeze as a threat to "our freedom" and "our belief in God." This was an act of profound polarization and demonization. Reagan was accusing millions of Americans of aiding a Kremlin plot to destroy the United States and Christianity.

That spring, the House passed the freeze resolution, but the Republican majority in the Senate blocked it. The movement would fizzle in coming years, but Reagan, much to the chagrin of the hawks, would become more interested in arms control and score several successes on this front, perhaps in response to the popular anxiety over nuclear war that was fueled by the freeze movement.

The middle years of Reagan's initial term proved tough for him. With the country in a recession in 1982—compelling Reagan to scale back his initial tax cuts—the Democrats picked up twenty-six House seats and one Senate seat in the 1982 elections.

At the start of 1983, Reagan's approval rating dropped to 35 percent. His foreign policy was not a popular success. Public opinion polls registered little support for his assistance of brutal anticommunist forces in Central America—most notably, the right-wing military in El Salvador and the contra rebels in Nicaragua combating the leftist Sandinista government. The Soviet shootdown of a civilian Korean airliner—later determined to be an accident—did fortify Reagan's rhetorical war against the Kremlin. (Representative Larry McDonald, the head of the John Birch Society, was one of the 269 people aboard who were all killed. Falwell remarked that "the Soviets may have actually murdered 269 passengers…in order to kill Larry McDonald.") An inconsistent policy in the Middle East led to the horrendous suicide bombing attack on Marines deployed in Beirut that killed 241

American soldiers. Yet Reagan rallied much of the country with a military invasion on the small island nation of Grenada to kick out a communist regime that had seized power in a coup. And throughout the year, the economy improved, partly due to a drop in oil prices, the Federal Reserve slashing interest rates, and the normal vagaries of the business cycle.

The chieftains of the New Right—Weyrich, Phillips, and Viguerie—still griped that Reagan was not governing as a true conservative. "We have seen almost a stampede to the left and we are watching with alarm," an exaggerating Viguerie said. One right-wing complaint: The Reagan administration had vowed to argue in defense of Bob Jones University when its case reached the Supreme Court—the issue being whether a religious school that discriminated could be tax-exempt—but in the face of a public outcry, the administration turned tail. (The Supreme Court ended up ruling against the school in an 8–1 decision.)

Yet appointments that conveyed legitimacy upon extremists kept coming. The White House hired John Rousselot, the onetime senior Bircher official and now a former congressman, as a liaison with special interest groups. Reagan nominated Helen Marie Taylor, a director of Schlafly's Eagle Forum and a prominent financial supporter of Pat Robertson's Christian Broadcasting Network, the Moral Majority, and other conservative groups, to the board of the Public Broadcasting Corporation. (The Senate would not approve her, but in a few years she would end up a representative to the United Nations General Assembly.) The White House rewarded Tom Ellis with a slot on the Board for International Broadcasting that oversaw Radio Liberty and Radio Free Europe.

At a confirmation hearing, Ellis did not fare well. Democratic senators, including Joe Biden, pounded him with questions, as Ellis acknowledged he belonged to an all-white country club, owned extensive holdings in South Africa (and had recently traveled there at the expense of the racist South African government), and had been a director of the racist Pioneer Fund. "I do not believe in my heart that I'm a racist," he testified. But he refused to condemn apartheid in South Africa. It was hard to view the Ellis nomination as something other than a prime position being handed to a known racist political operator (who was a member of the Council for National Policy). Biden and others called for the withdrawal of his nomination. After the confirmation hearing, the nomination was yanked.

The White House and the far right shared several passions, particularly the contra cause. As the administration tried to win support on Capitol Hill for sending weapons and supplies to the contras, it recruited conservatives to help sell the Nicaraguan fighters to the nation. Briefings were held on the contra war and other Central American issues at 1600 Pennsylvania Avenue, and dozens of New Right and Christian right organizations attended.

Toward the end of the year, the Reagan-Bush reelection committee named LaHaye its point man with the Christian right. The onetime Bircher who wanted to drive all "humanists" out of government was now running the Christian show for Reagan. The previous year he had joined the steering committee of the Council on Revival, a far-right theocratic group that called for imposing "biblical law" on America.

All these moves—right-wing appointments and enlisting New Right and fundamentalist Christian outfits to advance administration policies and campaign priorities—signaled complete acceptance by Reagan and the GOP establishment of a right-wing that promoted conspiracy theories, nurtured (and financially exploited) the grievances and fears of its followers, and virulently exacerbated political and social divides. Its dour, dread-driven, and dark vision of the world, though, was not what Reagan and his advisers wanted to sell to American voters for his reelection. Reagan had no problem boosting conservatives who preached that the end was nigh and there was precious little time to thwart the fiendish schemes of liberals, the media, humanists, feminists, gays, and others who were on the verge of decimating the United States of America. But to win another four years in office, Reagan's people would once more have to separate him from the extremists.

The New Right and the Christian right relied on the message that the country was sprinting toward hell. Reagan's team had a different vision for the story they wanted to tell America. It would be a feel-good sales campaign that could compete with Madison Avenue's best pitch for a soft drink or Disney World.

CHAPTER 13

Morning (and Nazis) in America

In June 1984, Richard Darman, a senior White House official who had been a professor at the Harvard Kennedy School, sat down to write a memo to address a problem Reagan's advisers had earlier identified: The president didn't have a specific vision for a second term or a set of compelling issues to run on. Tax cuts, raising military spending—he had done that already. His reelection campaign, they resolved, would not be about issues but tone and feeling. Do you want to return to the discouraging days of the Carter years? With the economy on a tear, who would want to go back? But beyond selling economic good news, they hoped to make the election a referendum on national character: Which candidate better reflected the country's image of itself? It would be a knockdown fight over Americanness.

By now, the Democrats had essentially settled on former Vice President Walter Mondale as their nominee. And Darman had crafted a game plan for a divisive campaign predicated on sentiment, not substance. His memo laid it out: "Paint Mondale as (a) weak, (b) a creature of special interests, (c) old-style, (d) unprincipled, (e), soft in his defense of freedom, patriotic values, American interests, (f) in short, Carter II." As for the boss, "Paint RR as the personification of all that is right with, or heroized by, America. Leave Mondale in a position where an attack on Reagan is tantamount to an attack on America's idealized image of itself—where a vote against Reagan is, in some subliminal sense, a vote against a mythic 'America.'"

Lee Atwater, now a top Reagan strategist, had something to add to this: race. He noted in a campaign memo that if Reagan whipped the Democrat in the South and held the West, it would be a rout. "The Democrats," he wrote, "have cast their lot with blacks in the South, and for them there is no turning back."

Atwater viewed the much-publicized campaign to register Black voters in the South being waged by the Reverend Jesse Jackson, a civil rights leader who had competed in the Democratic presidential primaries, a potential gain for the Reagan campaign. He calculated this drive would alienate conservative white voters. The Reagan campaign and its allies could harness this racist impulse, Atwater pointed out, and mount a counteroffensive that could register two white Republicans for every Black Democrat signed up by Jackson. Others agreed. The head of the Moral Majority in North Carolina called on the group's followers in the state to register their own voters "to keep a political blackmailer like the Reverend Jackson from acquiring the kind of political clout that he needs to implement his racist agenda." (The Reagan gang would go on to register what it claimed to be 4.4 million new Republican voters.)

————

At the Republican convention in Dallas, the right ruled the roost. Falwell delivered a benediction on the night Reagan was renominated. (Weeks earlier, at an antiabortion rights convention in Kansas City, he had proclaimed that if abortion was not outlawed, "then America will not survive...America will not deserve to survive.") Schlafly put on a fashion show. The ultraconservatives dictated the platform. One plank went beyond the party's previous support for a constitutional amendment to ban abortion and declared that only antiabortion jurists were qualified for appointment to the federal judiciary. Another opposed gay rights. Goldwater gave a rip-roaring speech reprising the line that had sunk him two decades earlier: "Let me remind you that extremism in the defense of liberty is no vice." The crowd cheered. Extremism, once a vulnerability for the GOP, was now considered de rigueur.

Terry Dolan's NCPAC held a $1,000-a-plate fundraiser at the ranch of Nelson Bunker Hunt, the silver-cornering Bircher. (Dolan, a closeted gay man, would die of AIDS in 1986.) Bob Hope entertained there, and Falwell had his picture snapped while riding a longhorn steer. In a speech to a prayer breakfast crowd, Reagan declared, "Religion and politics are necessarily related. We need religion as a guide...Our government needs the church." It was another blessing for the fundamentalists. "In a single stroke," political journalists Jack Germond and Jules Witcover wrote, "the President had seemed to give the fundamentalists a legitimacy in the political process far beyond what they had enjoyed in the past." Mondale would make an issue out of this in the coming weeks—much to the delight of Reagan's advisers who didn't mind the amplification of Reagan's much-more-than-a-wink signal to Southern and conservative religious voters. In his acceptance speech, Reagan proclaimed, "America is coming back."

————

During the general election, Reagan and his allies insinuated or outright declared that Mondale and the Democrats were not *real* Americans. Reagan exclaimed that the Democratic Party had moved "so far left they've left America." But his core message was, "It's morning in America." The economy was soaring and, more important, so was a national sense of confidence and pride—so the campaign claimed. The mainstay of this pitch were television ads that featured gauzy and soothing imagery of America. The goal, as Germond and Witcover put it, was "to take voters on a television trip to an imaginary America where everything was as rosy as it was in the Pepsi ads." Reagan was America: upbeat, strong, good-natured, full of purpose, grit, and optimism.

His right-wing allies worked a harsher angle. LaHaye organized the American Coalition for Traditional Values, which included Falwell, Robertson, and televangelist Jimmy Swaggart and aimed to register millions of Christian fundamentalist voters. It claimed to have raised $1 million for this effort by September, and one of its advisers stated a top goal was to "flood the federal bureaucracy with Christians."

In motivating Christian rightists, LaHaye prophesized the end of freedom and Christianity should the Democrats win the election. It was a message of doom. "If the liberals regain control of the Senate and White House in the coming election...it will be all over for free elections by 1988," he claimed. "Oh, we may vote in 1988, but it will be no contest, for by then the liberals will have curtailed our access to the minds of the American people."*

The race didn't seem close, until the first debate between Reagan and Mondale, when the president came across as doddering. That raised the question about his age. At seventy-three years, was he too old to continue as the nation's chief executive? But in the second debate, Reagan confronted this issue with one of his trademark quips: "I will not make age an issue of this campaign. I am not going to exploit, for political purposes, my opponent's youth and inexperience." Reagan's mangling of important facts about national security during that debate didn't matter. The zinger dominated the coverage.

Two weeks later, Reagan routed Mondale, winning 59 percent of the popular vote and every state but Mondale's native Minnesota. His coattails, though, were not long. The Democrats gained two Senate seats and held on to the House, despite losing sixteen seats.

———

* In 1986, *Mother Jones* would reveal that LaHaye had received what he called "generous" financial support from Bo Hi Pak, a top aide to Unification Church leader Sun Myung Moon and the founding chairman of the conservative *Washington Times* newspaper. The Unification Church, which held that Moon, not Jesus, was the real Messiah, had for years been supporting GOP-friendly organizations. In 1984 one of its groups handed $500,000 to Terry Dolan's National Conservative Political Action Committee.

Reagan's "Morning in America" schtick was a PR triumph, but there was a dark and creepy underside to the Reagan world that drew little attention: an almost unbelievable intersection between the GOP and fascist extremists.

A few months before the election, Reagan sent a heartfelt message of support to the five hundred attendees of the seventeenth annual convention of the World Anti-Communist League being held at the Sheraton Harbor Island Hotel in San Diego. He saluted the league—a collection of conservative anti-communist organizations from around the world—for "drawing attention to the gallant struggle now being waged by the true freedom fighters of our day." With these words, the president of the United States endorsed an organization that had included neo-Nazis, death squad leaders, and antisemitic haters.

The World Anti-Communist League was created in 1967 by the Taiwanese and South Korean governments and an organization called the Anti-Bolshevik Bloc of Nations. The ABN was an umbrella group for émigré outfits from Central and East Europe, many of which had fascist and Nazi roots. An ABN booklet published in 1960 noted that "many of us fought on the German side against Russian imperialism and Bolshevism"—a self-justifying way of saying they collaborated with Hitler. The ABN founder, Yaroslav Stesko, had been a Nazi collaborator in Ukraine during World War II, when his Organization of Ukrainian Nationalists slaughtered thousands of Jews. In the years since, Stetsko had transformed himself into a fierce foe of international communism, so much so that he had been invited to the White House in 1983 for a ceremony marking Captive Nations Week and met Reagan and Bush. During the 1984 race, the Reagan campaign worked with the ABN and sent a representative to an ABN conference.

At the time of the San Diego gathering praised by Reagan, the ABN remained a part of the World Anti-Communist League and was "the largest and most important umbrella for Nazi collaborators in the world," according to investigative journalists Scott Anderson and Jon Lee Anderson. Of eleven members of the ABN's central committee in 1980, seven were accused war criminals.

The WACL saluted by Reagan had a horrific history. In 1973, a British member protested the organization was "a collection of fringe ultra-rightists, religious nuts, aging ex-Nazis, emigres and cranks." A 1978 exposé in the *Washington Post* reported that year's annual convention, held at a Washington, DC, hotel, was organized in part by the antisemitic Liberty Lobby and was chockful of racists, fascists, and antisemites from around the globe, including representatives of an Italian neo-fascist party; a Mexican delegation that circulated an article denouncing the *Holocaust* television miniseries as "Jewish propaganda to conceal their objective of world communism"; and former Dutch and Austrian SS officers. The presiding officer was Roger Pearson, the notorious white supremacist who headed the American WACL affiliate. Two Republican senators—Jake Garn of Utah and James McClure of Idaho—gave speeches to the assembled. Republican leaders were rubbing elbows with outright Nazis.

Pearson was given the boot in 1980 and the following year, retired General John Singlaub, who had been forced out of the Army after publicly denouncing President Carter's policies, took control of a new US chapter of WACL. He would later insist that he expelled the unsavory elements from WACL. But not really. WACL, according to Scott and Jon Lee Anderson, still included Latin American groups directly tied to death squads. (A Latin American affiliate of WACL had supported Roberto D'Aubuisson, a far-right politician and death squad leader in El Salvador whose backers in the United States included Weyrich, Helms, and Young Americans for Freedom.)

At the San Diego event, some of the most extreme WACL collaborators were gone. A bevy of New Right leaders were present, and representatives of anticommunist fighters in Angola, Mozambique, Afghanistan, and Cambodia mingled with conservative legislators from around the globe. But the stench of extremism remained. General Alfredo Stroessner, the dictator of Paraguay, sent greetings via a telegram and thanked the League for "defending the world from Marxist tyranny." Mario Sandoval Alarcón, a far-right Guatemalan political leader linked to death squads, was in attendance. And WACL still included Eastern European emigrés who had been Nazi collaborators, such as Yaroslav Stetsko, who was not at this conference only because he was ill. But his wife was there to convey his greetings to his confederates.

The Reagan White House was bolstering the most fanatical fringe, and its support of WACL was not an exception. Weeks after the WACL convention, the *Wall Street Journal* broke the news that two years earlier the White House had sent Roger Pearson a letter of commendation from the president. Reagan extolled him for "promoting and upholding those ideals and principles that we value at home and abroad."

Reagan was likely unaware of the letter. But once informed of this misguided endorsement, the White House declined to disavow it or repudiate Pearson. Though Pearson had been associated with the antisemitic Liberty Lobby, the racist Pioneer Fund, and the extremist WACL, he had long maintained ties to mainstream conservatives, serving on the board of editors for the Heritage Foundation's journal *Policy Review*. He proved that the right—inside and outside the White House—often did not mind sidling up to extremists. The *Wall Street Journal* slyly made that point with a quote from John Reese, a contributing editor of the John Birch Society's magazine:

"Generally, the conservatives are so concerned with conspiracies on the left that they don't realize when they may be part of a conspiracy on the right."

———

White House salutations for racists and death squad apologists were not merely a matter of extending pleasantries. There was a transactional aspect to the relationship. Singlaub and his WACL colleagues were becoming part of a secret White House operation. At the San Diego meeting, Singlaub announced the league was launching an effort to raise funds for the contras. With Congress having cut off aid to the contras, Singlaub and other conservatives—including New Right groups, Robertson's Christian Broadcasting Network, and the Unification Church—had begun to collect money for these insurgents who were linked to the regime of former Nicaraguan dictator Anastasio Somoza and who had been accused of corruption, incompetence, and human rights violations, including the murder of civilians. (Later would come revelations tying some contras to drug trafficking.)

Singlaub quickly became one of the more prolific money rustlers for the contras. Consulting with a National Security Council staffer—Lieutenant Colonel Oliver North—by early 1985, he and his comrades in WACL regularly hauled in, by his own estimate, $500,000 a month for the contras. He hit up wealthy conservatives across the country, including Bircher Nelson Bunker Hunt (who would pony up nearly half a million dollars). The money, Singlaub claimed, was for nonlethal supplies. But in the summer of 1985, with North's approval, he brokered a $5 million weapons deal—ten thousand Soviet bloc AK-47 rifles, ammunition, and grenade launchers from Poland—for the contras.

Singlaub was helping the covert war that North, with the guidance of CIA chief William Casey, was running in Central America for Reagan—in contravention of Congress. Meanwhile, North hooked up with a New Right fundraiser named Carl "Spitz" Channell, who had once been a moneyman for the National Conservative Political Action Committee, to gather contributions for the contras. Together, they would beseech well-heeled right-wing funders and bag almost $2 million in donations. At one point, Casey sent Joseph Coors to see North, who needed $65,000 for an airplane for the contras. Coors wired the money to a Swiss bank account. The administration had not just cozied up to the fanatics of the right. It now used them as operatives to finance an arguably illegal war.

———

On May 17, 1985, Reagan entered the ballroom at the Shoreham hotel in Washington, DC, to the applause of four hundred luncheon guests. Less than two weeks earlier, he had faced a red-hot controversy: On a trip to Germany, he had stopped at a military cemetery where Waffen-SS troops were buried. The visit had provoked much outrage—especially after Reagan said that Nazi soldiers "were victims, just as surely as the victims in the concentration camps." Yet at this gathering of the Republican Heritage Groups Council, there was little ire over the Bitburg stop. That was hardly shocking. The council, a collection of assorted ethnic Republican clubs that operated as an auxiliary of the Republican National Committee, was, like the World Anti-Communist League, loaded with Eastern European emigrés who were antisemites, racists, and Nazi collaborators.

The leadership of the GOP heritage council was actually dominated by genuine fascists. Its founding chair, Laszlo Pasztor, had been an official of the Hungarian pro-Nazi party during World War II. Its executive director, Radi Slavoff, had been part of a Bulgarian fascist group. The head of a Cossack GOP unit in the council, Nikolai Nazarenko, had served in the German SS Cossack division and once declared Jews his "ideological enemy." The leader of the council's Romanian group was accused of being a recruiter for the Iron Guard, another fascist group. The chief of its Slovak GOP chapter was a Nazi sympathizer. And there were others.

The GOP had a Nazi problem, as bizarre as that seemed. A few reporters and researchers knew about it. But for some reason, it had never been big news.

This GOP-Nazi hookup began when Pasztor, who came to the United States in the 1950s, joined the ethnic division of the GOP. He worked on Nixon's 1968 campaign and afterward was asked to organize the Republican Heritage Groups Council. Among his recruits were anticommunist right-wingers from Eastern Europe who had been Nazi collaborators. "In setting up the Council, Pasztor went to various collaborationists and fascist-minded emigré groups and asked them to form GOP federations," wrote Russ Bellant, a researcher who spent years investigating the council. "... [It] wasn't an accident or a fluke that people with Nazi associations were in the Republican Heritage Groups Council. In some cases more mainstream ethnic organizations were passed over in favor of smaller but more extremist groups."

In 1971, investigative columnist Jack Anderson reported on the Nazi pasts of several GOP ethnic advisers, including Pasztor. Yet the Republican Party had taken no steps to bounce anyone from its heritage council. The GOP was accepting assistance from full-fledged and unrepentant Nazis.

At the Shoreham hotel event, Nazarenko, the head of the GOP's Cossack group, told Bellant that he was in touch with various Nazi organizations,

explaining, "They respect me because [I was a] former German army officer. Sometimes when I meet these guys, they say, 'Heil Hitler.'" He also
insisted Jews did not die in German gas chambers. At heritage council meetings, Florian Galdau, a member of the pro-Nazi Romanian Iron Guard and
leader of Romanian-American Republican Clubs, routinely charged that the
KGB controlled the Democratic Party.

During the 1985 luncheon, Frank Fahrenkopf Jr., the GOP chair, gushed
about the heritage council: "All of you in this room...were such a vital, integral part of the great victory we achieved on November 6 last year." Michael
Sotirhos, the chair of the council, told Bellant the group had been "the
linchpin of the Reagan-Bush ethnic campaign" in 1984, recruiting eighty-
six thousand volunteers. Before this crowd that included emigré fascists, a
grateful Reagan said, "The work of all of you has meant a very great deal to
me personally and to our party." He urged them to support the contras.

———

After Reagan's massive victory in 1984, "the Reagan revolution," historian
Sean Wilentz later observed, "often seemed divided and oddly adrift during his second term." Inflation had been tamed. The economy was growing,
though unemployment remained relatively high and deficits continued to
expand. (The red ink would amount to a whopping $2.4 trillion.) Multiple
corruption scandals involving Reagan's top aides (Edwin Meese, Michael
Deaver, and Lyn Nofziger, among them) created a taint of permanent sleaze
for the administration.

Reagan had not gone to war for all the New Right's top priorities. But
the president won accolades from the right for placing the ardently conservative Antonin Scalia on the Supreme Court and elevating Justice William
Rehnquist, another conservative favorite, to the chief justice slot. Reagan
refused at first to acknowledge the AIDS crisis—a move in sync with the
religious right's effort to exploit this tragedy for its vicious crusade against
homosexuality and gay rights. (AIDS, Falwell proclaimed, was "judgment
against homosexuality, which is unhealthy, unclean.") Also in line with
the conservative movement, Reagan opposed sanctions against the racist
regime of South Africa. (He falsely and absurdly claimed South Africa had
"eliminated the segregation that we once had in our own country.") Yet conservatives worried about Reagan's talks with Mikhail Gorbachev, the new
leader of the Soviet Union, fearing the president was being bamboozled by
the Russian who they suspected was pretending to be a reformer as part of
a devilish plot to conquer the West. Though Reagan would visit the Berlin
Wall and demand, "Mr. Gorbachev, tear down this wall," their negotiations

would yield a treaty removing intermediate- and short-range nuclear missiles from the arsenals of these two superpowers. The Wall and the Soviet Union would soon collapse, and historians would spend decades arguing over how much Reagan had to do with that.

Reagan and his right-wing allies kept pushing for contra aid—and resorted to 1950s-like tactics. The ultraconservative White House aide Pat Buchanan declared that if Democrats refused to approve military assistance for the contras they would be standing with "the communists." Reagan compared those opposing the funding to the "fellow travelers" who aided the Soviet Union during the early days of the Cold War. In the summer of 1986, Congress narrowly approved $100 million for the contras.

Through Reagan's second term, Falwell continued to sow hatred—while raising boatloads of money. (He bagged $110 million in 1985 for his Moral Majority and other outfits.) As the AIDS crisis raged, he called for quarantining infected individuals, although the illness could not be transmitted by casual contact. He referred to a gay-oriented church as a "vile and satanic system [that] will one day be utterly annihilated."

Even though Reagan would come around to recognizing AIDS as a crisis meriting government attention, Falwell was unrelenting in his campaign of cruelty. In a fundraising letter, he accused gay people of donating blood at a higher rate because "they know they are going to die—and they are going to take as many people with them as they can." He denounced protests against the racist apartheid regime of South Africa and accused these egalitarian-minded demonstrators of being duped by Moscow. He urged Christians to buy Krugerrands, the South African currency, to support Pretoria, and he called Bishop Desmond Tutu, a courageous anti-apartheid leader who had received the Nobel Peace Prize in 1984, a "phony." He also traveled to the Philippines and offered moral support to dictator Ferdinand Marcos.

At the start of 1986, Falwell folded the Moral Majority into a new organization called the Liberty Federation. Its first national summit featured a special keynote speaker: George H. W. Bush. Falwell's Red-baiting, gay-bashing, and apartheid-defending did not dissuade the vice president from standing with Falwell. Given how Falwell and the New Right had tried to stop Reagan from choosing Bush as veep in 1980, it was not too early for the vice president, looking ahead to the next presidential election, to capture the Falwell shine for himself. (Bush was hitting the conservative circuit, addressing the NRA, the Religious Roundtable, various antiabortion groups, and LaHaye's American Coalition for Traditional Values.) At

Falwell's conference, Bush praised him, proclaiming, "America is in crying need of the moral vision you have brought to our political life."

Bush had what he wanted: Falwell's endorsement for president in 1988. This was especially important because of an odd political development: Pat Robertson was plotting a bid for the Republican nomination.

A Robertson candidacy could be considered a novelty act. He was once a faith healer. He believed in speaking in tongues. In 1982, he said that Israel's invasion of Lebanon was predicted by the Bible and claimed Israel would by the end of that year be fighting the Soviet Union in a war that would put the world "in flames," an apparent reference to nuclear war. How could he be so sure? "God talks to me," he explained. (No such war happened.) Three years later, he asserted that only Christians and Jews should serve in government. He purported to have prayed away a hurricane from striking Virginia Beach. (The storm hit elsewhere.) He claimed that Christians were more patriotic than non-Christians and that presidents and Congress did not have to abide by Supreme Court rulings with which they disagreed. A former producer for Robertson's CBN show, *The 700 Club*, voiced concern about a potential Robertson presidency, noting that Robertson believed "that the second coming of Jesus will coincide with a nuclear holocaust" and that "Jesus is telling him to press that button."

Yet Bush and his advisers had reason to worry. Robertson had a built-in audience, with his Christian Broadcasting Network reaching tens of millions of homes. He had collected 3.3 million signatures on a please-run-Pat petition. Billionaire Bircher Nelson Bunker Hunt was a financial backer. Other prominent evangelists were lining up behind the CBN tycoon, as he put forward his agenda: Remove secular humanists from schools, bounce one-world socialists from the State Department, and cut $100 billion from the federal budget. A holy war on the right was a concern not merely for Bush but for the entire GOP. Could a fundamentalist extremist take over the party?

———

In early 1986, as Reagan's White House advisers prepared for that year's State of the Union address, they were not sure how to define Reagan's message at this point in his presidency. What policies, what agenda, was he now offering the American public? They never found a good answer. In the midterm elections, the country did not rally to Reagan. The Democrats regained control of the Senate with eight new seats, and they picked up five seats in the House.

The day before the election, the Reaganites stumbled—or crashed—into a theme they didn't want: the Iran-contra scandal. A Lebanese publication disclosed a bombshell: Reagan had been covertly selling weapons to the Iranian government. Reagan and his aides had hoped these arms sales would lead to the release of American hostages held in the Middle East. But the deals violated his vow to not negotiate with terrorists. Worse, they had not succeeded in winning the release of all the hostages. Three weeks later came the second punch: the shocking revelation that profits from the weapons transactions had been clandestinely diverted to the contras for arms and supplies. This reeked of criminality that could lead to impeachment.

For the next two years, subsequent investigations and disclosures would dominate Washington and unveil a cesspool of corruption: sleazy arms dealers, Swiss bank accounts, front groups, money laundering, shredding in the White House, and lie upon lie. "We did not—repeat—did not trade weapons or anything else for hostages," Reagan at first insisted. He later backtracked with a bizarre statement: "My heart and my best intentions still tell me that is true, but the facts and evidence tell me it is not."

The White House was in perpetual damage control, as its allies on the right embraced North as a conservative hero. Falwell proclaimed, "All I know about Colonel North and Admiral John Poindexter [the national security adviser] is that they're great Americans." Rocked by the scandal, the Reagan administration would largely limp toward a more-whimper-than-a-bang ending. His last year in office would occur in the shadow of the immense October 1987 stock market crash that eliminated half a trillion dollars in paper wealth and marked a calamitous end to the greed-is-good era.

In the twilight of the Reagan years, it was evident that Reagan had not delivered fully for the New Right and conservative fundamentalists that had helped him reach the White House—not in terms of major legislation that would impose their views on the larger public. But, as historian David John Marley afterward noted, "he gave them legitimacy in the public square, and they gave him their votes and the status of a living saint...The very fact that the president of the United States appeared to agree with the agenda of the Christian Right gave them tremendous power."

George Bush, looking to inherit the presidency from Reagan, wanted that power on his side. The excesses of the New Right and the religious right were now embedded in the Republican DNA. But could this man of solid Yankee stock, an Ivy Leaguer, the son of a senator, a patrician whose family once symbolized noblesse oblige, marshal these forces? What was he willing to do to succeed Reagan? To what extremes would Bush go?

CHAPTER 14

Not Kinder or Gentler

On the evening of February 8, 1988, thousands of Christian fundamen-talists poured into high school gyms, churches, libraries, and living rooms across Iowa to serve the Lord. They had been given a memo with marching orders: "Don't flaunt your Christianity...Don't come across as a one-issue person." It recommended, "Be wise as serpents and innocent as a dove." Their mission, two years in the making, was to infiltrate the Republican Party apparatus and to caucus for Pat Robertson, a televangelist trying to become the president of the United States.

The main attraction of this year's GOP presidential nomination battle was the face-off between George Bush and Bob Dole. It was a fight pitting a sitting vice president with all the accouterments of power against a veteran heavyweight US senator from Kansas. Yet on this night, Robertson stole the thunder when he placed second in the Iowa caucuses, behind Dole. Though he had not prevailed, Robertson delivered an embarrassing blow to Bush, who finished third. "I'm going to be the nominee," Robertson proclaimed. Another prophecy he got wrong—but his surprising second-place finish registered the might of the religious right within the Republican Party. Robertson was a bigoted kook, but a quarter of the GOP caucus-goers in the Hawkeye State wanted this bigoted kook to be president.

Eight days later, Bush fought back to win the New Hampshire primary, with Dole coming in second and Robertson a distant fifth. The vice president was on a path toward the nomination, but he was troubled by the extremism that Robertson was injecting into the party. Soon after, at a campaign stop in Kingsport, Tennessee—Reagan country—Bush met a Robertson supporter who refused to shake his hand. This is just politics, Bush told her, we'll all be on the same side when it's done. The woman was unconvinced, and this encounter disquieted the vice president. He wrote in his diary:

> Still, this staring, glaring ugly—there's something terrible about those who carry it to extremes. They're scary. They're there for spooky, extraordinary right-winged reasons. They don't care about

the Party. They don't care about anything. They're the excesses. They could be Nazis, they could be Communists, they could be whatever. In this case, they're religious fanatics and they're spooky. They will destroy this party if they're permitted to take over. There is not enough of them, in my view, but this woman reminded me of my John Birch days in Houston. The lights go out and they pass out the ugly literature. Guilt by association. Nastiness. Ugliness. Believing the Trilateral Commission, the conspiratorial theories. And I couldn't tell—it may not be fair to that one woman, but that's the problem that Robertson brings to bear on the agenda.

Bush had it pegged: His party was infected. Over two decades earlier, he had run for Houston GOP chair to protect the Republicans from the encroachment of Birchers and extremism. Now he sensed a similar struggle was at hand.

Other Republican regulars saw it the same way. The previous year, a Republican committee member named Rusty DePass attended a closed-door meeting of Robertson supporters in Columbia, South Carolina. On the agenda: How they could overrun precinct meetings and seize control of the Republican Party. They wildly cheered Roberston, who was present. DePass told a local newspaper it reminded him of "what a Nazi pep rally would have been like. The group was whipped into a froth, it was a real mob mentality; they were like sheep." At the state convention, the old hands, who referred to the Robertson people as zealots and compared them to Iran's Revolutionary Guard, barely held on to power. But in other states Robertson's fanatics did successfully annex the party operation.

Two days after his unpleasant encounter with the woman in Tennessee, Bush discussed the matter at lunch with Reagan. The president shared his concern about Robertson and, as Bush told his diary, "some of the extremes that he brings into the party." But would Bush do anything about this? In a close race with the Democratic nominee, wouldn't he want—or need—the Robertson vote? Would he lead his party and the nation toward civil discourse and a politics focused on policy substance or bend to the usual political imperative of whatever-it-takes?

Days later, Bush vanquished Dole and Robertson in the all-important South Carolina contest. Three days after that, Bush won every Super Tuesday race, except the caucus in Washington, where Robertson's troops again flooded a small-scale event and delivered him a minor win. Still, neither the preacher nor the senator had much of a chance now.

Through his months of campaigning, Robertson had embraced and promoted paranoia and conspiratorial notions. He claimed the Soviets had stationed missiles in Cuba. (They hadn't.) He accused the Bush campaign of having leaked the news of Jimmy Swaggart's sex scandal, which erupted just ahead of the South Carolina primary, to harm Robertson. (He had no proof of that.) While campaigning in that state, he suggested Bush was allied with the international cabal of bankers who were scheming against Americans.

Robertson dropped out of the race in May and endorsed Bush. He was somehow able to overlook Bush's ties to a global plot. But this was not the end of electoral politics for Robertson. His followers had bored into state Republican parties and taken control of the GOP machinery in Nevada, Washington, Alaska, and Hawaii, and they had gained strong positions in Virginia, Georgia, Texas, Louisiana, and the Carolinas. Robertson, a preacher of division, intolerance, and extremism, had become a minority shareholder of the Grand Old Party, and he still harbored ambitions.

———

In late spring, Bush's prospects were not sunny. He trailed Massachusetts Governor Michael Dukakis, the presumptive Democratic nominee, by sixteen or so points in public opinion polls. Bush had not offered much of a case for himself other than a stale stay-the-course message that relied heavily on keeping the Reagan flame lit. Dukakis, no dynamic figure either, presented himself to voters as a dependable, knowledgeable, and experienced practitioner of government who could devise and oversee policies necessary for the nation's betterment. One fellow had a pedigree, the other had a flowchart. One saw the election as the passing of an old torch, the other as a straightforward job interview. There was not a lot of passion in the race, until the opposition research came in.

Lee Atwater, Bush's devious campaign manager, had tasked the research diggers on his staff to excavate all they could on Dukakis. The Massachusetts governor came across well, a smart and competent man. But he remained largely unknown to most voters—generally undefined. In politics, Atwater knew, if a candidate was not well established, there was an opportunity for his or her opponent to do the defining. A band of researchers trekked to the Bay State to pore over twenty-five years of newspaper and magazine clippings—in search of ammunition.

The squad returned and produced a 312-page bible of opposition research, full of quotes and references to legislation Dukakis had or had not supported over his long years in Massachusetts politics, all purportedly showing that Dukakis was a crazy liberal. It's title: *The Hazards of Duke*. But Atwater wanted it simple, boiled down. A slam-dunk case against Dukakis that could fit on a three-by-five index card. And soon he had that card. It listed the main lines of attack: Dukakis in 1974 had raised taxes after ruling out a tax hike; he opposed many new weapons programs and aid to the contras; he was a self-proclaimed "card-carrying member of the ACLU"; he opposed the death penalty and favored gun control; he once vetoed a bill mandating the Pledge of Allegiance in schools (citing legalistic reasons); and he had supported a prison furlough program.

The prison furlough issue came with a gruesome tale: Willie Horton, after serving ten years for having stabbed a gas station attendant to death during a robbery, had been granted a weekend pass from a Massachusetts state prison in 1986. He did not return, and ten months later he broke into a Maryland home and raped a woman. The furlough program had been enacted under a Republican governor, but it had continued under Dukakis.

Atwater had his ammo. Best of all, it played like a dream in front of focus groups. Tell voters leaning toward Dukakis that he furloughed killers and hated pledging allegiance to the flag—and they recoiled. But Atwater and his allies on the campaign, including Roger Ailes, had to convince Bush that his best chance—probably his only chance—of reaching the White House was to unleash a fusillade of liberal-bashing demagoguery upon Dukakis and that these furies had to be set loose immediately. The campaign couldn't wait until after the conventions. Perhaps out of a sense of honor that still resided in a corner of his political soul, Bush initially resisted. He didn't want to get personal and use the hot-attack rhetoric that had become a fixture of the New Right and other extremists now fully in league with the GOP. He was a high-road kind of guy. But no one had ever hired Atwater to guide them on the moral path. Bush relented: "Well, you guys are the experts," he told Atwater and the others.

And so it began, one of the meanest and emptiest elections in modern US history. The Republicans had slammed McGovern in 1972 as the candidate of abortion, acid, and amnesty. They had depicted Mondale as insufficiently American compared to the heroic Reagan. Now the Bush campaign was hell-bent, as *Newsweek*'s Peter Goldman and Tom Mathews put it, on a strategy not to sell the strengths and assets of the experienced vice president but to achieve the "un-Americanization" of Dukakis. This was a full embrace of the decades-old far-right cry: Liberals were not true Americans and threatened the American way of life.

Atwater thought that for this strategy to succeed, the attacks had to come from the top. Nixon and Reagan had left much of the hatchet work to underlings and surrogates. In the demonization of Michael Dukakis, George Bush would take the lead.

On June 9, Bush hit the stage of the Houston convention center to address the Republican state gathering, and the operation began. Shouting at the assembled, Bush declared Dukakis had imposed the "biggest tax increase" in Massachusetts history. He was a fan of the United Nations. His foreign policy views were born in "Harvard Yard's boutique." He was an adherent of "sixties liberalism" who "opposed the death penalty" and furloughed "first-degree murderers." As Bush yelled out each point, the crowd chanted, "Bush! Bush! Bush!" The next day, he told his son Neil, "I can sort of see the target. I think we're going to win."

Guided by Atwater and Ailes, Bush adopted the direct-mail tactic that had won money and influence for the New Right and the Christian right: hyperbolic, alarmist, and shrill attacks. Over and over. For the next five months, the campaign from the Bush side would be largely a broken record: the flag, the ACLU, the death penalty, and Willie Horton, Willie Horton, Willie Horton. At one point, Atwater publicly kidded that Horton would be Dukakis's running mate.

When the Democrats gathered in Atlanta for their convention, speakers derided Bush for his privilege and lack of vision. (Democratic Texas Governor Ann Richards quipped, "Poor George, he can't help it. He was born with a silver foot in his mouth.") The event celebrated Dukakis as a coming-to-America immigrant success story, and he promised an economy that would produce "good jobs at good wages." This election, he insisted, "is not about ideology. It's about competence."

A week before the GOP convention, Roger Ailes drafted a memo for the Bush campaign with a different view: "On Election Day, the voter must know three things about Michael Dukakis. He will raise their taxes. He is opposed to the death penalty, even for drug kingpins and murderers. And he is an extreme liberal, even a pacifist on the subject of national defense... We must force this election into a very narrow framework."

At the Republican convention in New Orleans, Pat Robertson was embraced by the party—despite his bigotry, conspiracism, and fierce attacks on Bush. Months earlier, he had accused the Bush campaign of "unreal religious bigotry" and committing "every kind of dirty trick known to mankind," and he had mused that the reason the Bushies were "sleazy" was that Bush had been the Republican national chairman during Watergate. Still, the Bush camp needed his voters, and they offered this unhinged extremist a prime-time speaking slot. Bush's concern about the damaging influence of the far right within the party—which he had shared with Reagan months earlier—was easy to put aside. Votes counted more.

In a recent fundraising letter, Robertson had asserted, "God does not want us to turn America over to radical feminists, drug dealers, militant homosexuals, profligate spenders, humanists or world communists." Yet for the sake of the Bush campaign, he dialed back during his convention speech. He assailed the Democrats as a party of "defeat, division, and despair" and called for Republican unity, signaling to social conservatives that, for the time being, Bush was all right with him. By then, many evangelical leaders were already persuaded that the Falwell-endorsed Bush was their man, and the party platform was once again largely shaped by the religious right. And prominent conservatives at the convention—Schlafly, Weyrich, Nelson Bunker Hunt, Falwell—were gushing over Bush's controversial veep selection: the little-known Senator Dan Quayle of Indiana.

During his acceptance speech, Bush, using the now-familiar script, denigrated Dukakis for opposing the death penalty, school prayer, and mandatory recital of the Pledge in schools and for supporting prison furloughs and abortion rights. He vowed to not raise taxes ("Read my lips: no new taxes"). But as he vilified his opponent, Bush also tried to strike a softer tone. He promised to work for a "kinder and gentler nation."

There was nothing gentle about the following three months. Bush stuck to the flag and Willie Horton and other attacks. Lather, rinse, repeat—but without the rinse. For years afterward, the argument would rage: Had the Willie Horton drumbeat been a racist attack? Atwater and the Bush crowd would claim it was only about crime. But when Citizens United, an independent right-wing group, ran an ad featuring a frightening image of Horton, a Black man, it was reasonably accused of exploiting racial fears—and the Bush campaign went three weeks before perfunctorily asking that group to take down the ad.

Bush's constant harping about the flag and the Pledge of Allegiance had a nativist resonance. Reporters noted they had never seen as many flags at a political event than at a Bush rally. He even held a campaign event at a flag factory in New Jersey. The Bush campaign produced a derisive ad with footage of Dukakis in a tank, wearing a helmet, that made it look as if the Democratic nominee was a kid on a ride at an amusement park. (In 1987, *Newsweek*, on its cover, had referred to Bush as a possible "wimp," and now his campaign was attempting to wimpify Dukakis.) And an unfounded rumor—reported on the front page of the Unification Church–owned

Washington Times—spread that Dukakis had been treated for depression. No one could determine its origin. But there was a consensus in the political-media world: This looked like the handiwork of Lee Atwater.

Pundits scolded the Bush team for mounting a hollow campaign that flirted with racism and nativism. "Tell George to start talking about the issues," Barry Goldwater huffed. But through it all, Dukakis, to the chagrin of his aides, never got a handle on how to respond to the pummeling. The Pledge, the ACLU—these were not serious issues, Dukakis believed. He wanted to talk about policy: *good jobs at good wages.* He never comprehended that the Bush campaign had made the contest about values.

This was the game the New Right and the Christian right had been playing for almost two decades. They had weaponized cultural and religious grievance and resentments. Bush, the elitist from Kennebunkport, Maine, had never been part of that crowd. He had often moaned when dragged out to talk to far-right groups. But in pursuit of the White House, he had adopted their tribalistic scare-and-demonize tactics. He was equating liberalism with un-Americanism and trying to depict Dukakis as an outsider unfit to lead Americans.

At the same time, Bush managed to sidestep all scandals. He was not hindered by the Iran-contra affair. He claimed he had been "out of the loop." It would be years before the public would learn he had kept a diary—which he had not turned over to investigators—in which he had written after the disclosure of the Iran arms-for-hostages deal, "I'm one of the few people that know fully the details." Nor was Bush unduly inconvenienced when media reports in early September revealed that his campaign's ethnic advisory board included known antisemites and neo-fascists. Among those cited were prominent members of the Republican Heritage Groups Council, such as Laszlo Pasztor and Florian Galdau. A report by researcher Russ Bellant was released showing Bush at a July event cosponsored by the Nazi-sympathizing Anti-Bolshevik Bloc of Nations. The Bush campaign dismissed the matter as "little more than politically inspired garbage" and called it a dirty trick.

Bush's down-and-dirty strategy triumphed. He won forty states with a seven-million-vote edge in the tally. It had long been an accepted notion within the political world that negative ads and divisive politicking worked. The New Right and the Christian right had employed that approach to amass influence within the GOP. The Bush campaign demonstrated just how base and vacuous American politics could be—and how effective slash-and-burn tactics could be on a national level.

Bush had set a new bottom for the Republican Party. But there were lower depths ahead. After this campaign, America would be neither a kinder nor a gentler place.

CHAPTER 15

Spiritual Warfare

On the Fourth of July, 1988, WABC Radio in New York City launched a new show. Its host, who had previously been fired from on-air jobs at four radio stations in Pittsburgh and Kansas City, most recently had a successful stint as a shock jock in Sacramento. There he had inveighed against environmentalists ("whackos!") and feminists ("feminazis!"). He derided AIDS as "Rock Hudson's disease." He made fun of the homeless. He bashed the American left as "commie pinko liberals." His deep and mellifluous voice conveyed authority and confidence. His schtick was a combination of right-wing views and sophomoric and often cruel satire. He was wry and bombastic, turning his overinflated ego into part of the show. A radio executive thought he could do well on the national stage and brought him to a premier station in the Big Apple.

On this first live broadcast—which occurred the day after a US Navy cruiser had shot down an Iranian passenger jet carrying 290 people—he slammed "the anti-America crowd" that dared to raise questions about the tragedy. "Do we really care about the Iranian families?" he asked. He mocked liberals "[who] just sit around wringing our hands, 'Oh, this is terrible, oh, that's terrible.'" In a month, his show would be syndicated to fifty-three mostly midmarket stations across the country, and within a year, three hundred stations. Rush Limbaugh was a hit.

WABC knew what it was getting. A press release issued to announce Limbaugh's show offered examples of his customary rhetoric: "The feminist movement was created to allow ugly women access to the mainstream of society...There's only one way to get rid of nuclear weapons—use 'em." During his first months at WABC, Limbaugh contended that Americans who don't go to college end up being better informed about foreign policy than students exposed to classroom liberalism. He used the word "faggot" on the air. (He eventually would apologize for cracking jokes about AIDS.) If a listener challenged him, he conducted a "caller abortion" by playing a tape of a loud vacuum followed by a long scream.

Limbaugh's hours-long performances of coarse conservative politics had been made possible by Ronald Reagan. A year earlier, his administration had killed the Fairness Doctrine, which compelled holders of radio and television licenses to present contrasting views on matters of public interest. Freed of this burden, radio stations could sign up Limbaugh's one-man right-wing jamboree without fretting about providing equal time to a liberal perspective.

At first, the thirty-seven-year-old host did not draw much notice from the national media. But one person paying attention was William Buckley.

About two or so months after he began at WABC, Limbaugh received an invitation to attend a *National Review* editorial meeting at Buckley's Park Avenue apartment. During dinner, Buckley and his colleagues questioned Limbaugh about his opinions and broadcasting tactics. "They were fans," Limbaugh later exclaimed. "... That night I was made to feel welcome in the conservative movement."

In short time, Limbaugh would profoundly warp the conservative movement and the Republican Party. He was peddling hate and division—albeit with a boisterous guffaw. Animus cloaked with rough-and-tumble humor and shrouded in the smoke of a good cigar was the stock he was selling to aggrieved conservatives across the country and the base of the GOP. His highest aim—other than amassing fame and fortune—was to belittle liberals and portray them as dishonest and hysterical lowlifes not worthy of the United States' rewards. To achieve this, he deployed fabricated or mischaracterized information that he represented as the ultimate truth.

Limbaugh soon became a one-man permission-granting machine, empowering millions to justify and express politically incorrect—that is, misogynistic, homophobic, racist, or otherwise intolerant and hate-driven—opinions. He made obnoxiousness cool—even compulsory for Republicans. In the era of Limbaugh, derision, not debate, would power a politics of resentment and rancor.

———

In Congress, a new member of the Republican leadership echoed Limbaugh's efforts to delegitimize liberals and Democrats. Newt Gingrich, a vituperative, ambitious, and arrogant congressman from Georgia, who considered himself a bold visionary across the fields of politics, history, and public policy, became House minority whip in 1989, the number two position in the GOP caucus. Since his election to the House in 1978, he had been a bomb thrower, viciously assailing Democrats for ethics lapses (while sidestepping his own ethics troubles and personal scandals) and urging fellow

Republicans, who had languished in the minority since 1954, to be meaner and more aggressive. In his first months in the GOP leadership, Gingrich succeeded enormously by waging an unrelenting and bitter campaign against Democratic House Speaker Jim Wright, who had violated assorted ethics rules, which culminated in Wright's resignation.

Gingrich's goal was to tar the Democrats as the party of corruption. In 1984, one of his advisers wrote a strategy memo saying that Gingrich and his allies should view themselves as the Viet Cong fighting the South Vietnamese government (the Democrats) while accepting support from the North Vietnamese (the Republican establishment). Both, he stated, were the "enemies." The Democrats, he noted, "we must destroy" and the Republicans "we must take advantage of, lie to, sidetrack, confound, and possess by recruitment and propaganda." The goal was to cast Democrats as "the oppressor," a tyrannical enemy warranting the utmost despisal. This memo, as Gingrich's biographer Julian Zelizer later said, was his "road map."

When Gingrich became minority whip, President Bush noted his concerns in his diary: "Will he be confrontational; will he raise hell with the establishment; will he be difficult for me to work with?" Bush answered himself, "I don't think so...He's going to have to get along to some degree, moderate his flamboyance." Bush was wrong. Gingrich was addicted to attack politics. In a speech to the Heritage Foundation, he proclaimed that the assault on Democrats "has to be fought with a scale and a duration and a savagery that is only true of civil wars."

As part of his project to turn American politics into a more brutal place, Gingrich headed a political action committee called GOPAC that trained Republican candidates to fight tougher. About the time Gingrich joined the GOP leadership, his GOPAC was distributing to Republicans a pamphlet called *Language: A Key Mechanism Control*. It noted, "As we mail [instructional] tapes to candidates, and use them in training sessions across the county, we hear a plaintive plea: 'I wish I could speak like Newt.' That takes years of practice. But we believe that you can have a significant impact on your campaign if we help a little."

The "help" was a list of words to be used in campaign speeches and literature.

The words were not subtle. On the list of Gingrich's thirty "optimistic positive governing words": *freedom, family, courage, moral, liberty, reform, pioneer, prosperity, truth*. Use these words, GOPAC suggested, when "defining your campaign and your vision of public service." A longer list contained "contrasting words" to be employed "to define our opponents." It included: *traitors, liberal, radical, sick, anti-child, anti-flag, betray, bizarre, incompetent, pathetic, self-serving, lie, steal, disgrace,* and *they/them.* This was a list that could have come from one of those hair-on-fire New Right direct-mail pieces of the 1970s. Yet now it was advice from a top Republican leader who had eyes on the House speakership. He was instructing his party-mates to brand Democrats and liberals as sick, radical, malevolent, and dishonest traitors who were against children.

This attempt to weld demonization into the Republican infrastructure surpassed what Atwater had devised for George Bush's assault on Michael Dukakis. No prominent elected official in decades had openly pressed such brazen and extreme tribalism. But Gingrich had for years called for a more bellicose Republican Party. This was what he was now building.

———

The Reverend Billy McCormack was an influential man in Louisiana. A prominent Southern Baptist pastor for decades, he became the state coordinator for Pat Robertson's presidential campaign in 1987. Bush won that state's contest with 58 percent; Robertson and Dole evenly split the rest. But the Robertson forces, led by McCormack, joined with other conservatives to assume control of the state Republican committee. He was said to have in his pocket at least sixty of the committee's 140 seats. This soon placed McCormack in the spotlight.

In early 1989, David Duke, a grand wizard of the Ku Klux Klan who left the group in 1980 to create another racist entity called the National Association for the Advancement of White People, entered a special election for a Louisiana state House seat, running as a Republican. His main opponent, another Republican, publicized Duke's past, disseminating a photograph of Duke in Nazi regalia and circulating Duke's endorsement of Hitler's *Mein Kampf* as the greatest piece of literature in the twentieth century. Duke won by 227 votes. He was censured after his victory by Lee Atwater, who had become chair of the Republican National Committee. But local Republicans were far more accepting of the racist antisemite.

Soon after Duke took office, a Republican state committee member named Elizabeth Rickey trailed him to a Chicago gathering of the antisemitic Populist Party and taped him as he gleefully addressed a roomful of neo-Nazis and other extremists. ("My victory in Louisiana was a victory for the white majority movement in this country!") She subsequently discovered he was selling Nazi, antisemitic, and racist literature (including *Mein Kampf*) out of his legislative office.

Rickey insisted the state GOP party censure Duke. When she introduced a resolution to do so at a party gathering, McCormack deployed his bloc of evangelicals to table the motion—that is, to protect Duke. McCormack subsequently defended his action with antisemitism, stating that Duke was no worse than "the Jewish element in the ACLU which is trying to drive Christianity out of the public place" and noting that "Jewish attorneys" in the ACLU "can be just as prejudiced and just as mean as what Duke does." He remarked that Duke was "saying some things that are very true, and that's the reason he's getting as many good marks as he's getting."

About the time he was safeguarding the position of a neo-Nazi in the Louisiana GOP, McCormack became one of the four directors of a new group founded by Pat Robertson called the Christian Coalition. (Another leader was Beverly LaHaye.) In fact, McCormack had come up with the idea for this organization. After Robertson's failed presidential crusade, McCormack had urged the televangelist to launch a group for the hundreds of thousands of people who had worked and voted for him. Robertson told McCormack he would pray on it, and soon McCormack had his wish.

———

Robertson announced the formation of the Christian Coalition in early 1990. Half a year earlier, Falwell had shuttered the Moral Majority. Its funding had fallen by almost three-quarters—and many in the evangelical community remained frustrated by their inability to achieve through politics an end to abortion, pornography, and homosexuality. But Falwell cheerily declared its main mission had been accomplished: "The religious right is solidly in place." (He had been a special guest at Bush's inauguration and had claimed some credit for Bush's victory.) With the Moral Majority kaput, Robertson, who had for years had run a profitable broadcasting empire, saw an opportunity.

Robertson's new group sent out a brochure seeking members to 250,000 homes, proclaiming, "Christian Americans are tired of getting stepped on." Its executive director, the twenty-nine-year-old baby-faced Ralph Reed, who had once been the head of the College Republicans and a campaign staffer for Gingrich and Helms, explained its mission: "What Christians have got to do is take back this country, one precinct at a time, one neighborhood at a time, and one state at a time. I honestly believe that in my lifetime we will see a country once again governed by Christians." The coalition sought to expand on what Robertson's forces had been doing for the past few years: gaining control of local Republican Party machinery.

Political pundits widely regarded the formation of the Christian Coalition as a sign Robertson was readying another presidential run. But the group posed a more immediate threat to the GOP establishment. In the fall of 1990, in sixty of eighty-eight local races in San Diego County, it mounted a sneak attack and elected Christian rightists to office. In these school board, city council, and other low-profile contests, coalition-backed candidates made no appearances, filled out no questionnaires, and conducted no public outreach other than contacting churchgoers. Given the usual low turnout, the fundamentalists were able to win by flooding the polls with fellow coreligionists. It shocked Republican regulars, caught off guard by what they considered an underhanded scheme. This tactic became known as the "San Diego model," and Reed fully owned it. "Stealth was a big factor," he said afterward. "But that's just a good strategy. It's like guerrilla warfare. If you reveal your location all it does is allow your opponent to improve his artillery bearings."

Nothing in the Bible says thou shall not be sneaky. And sneakiness was to be part of Robertson's crusade. The GOP certainly welcomed this when it worked to its benefit. That same election season, polls in the closing stretch of a bitterly fought contest indicated Senator Jesse Helms trailed his Democratic opponent, Harvey Gantt, who had been the first Black mayor of Charlotte, North Carolina. Robertson called Reed and told him to "kick into action."

Five days later, the Christian Coalition disseminated through churches across the state 750,000 voter guides—campaign literature that purported to present neutral descriptions of the candidates' positions on abortion, school prayer, and gay rights but that tilted heavily toward the social conservative view and essentially endorsed Helms. The coalition also made tens of thousands of phone calls in the final week. Overall, the coalition handed out four million of its loaded voter guides in seven states and ran ads targeting members of Congress who supported the National Endowment for the Arts, which was vilified by religious right groups for supporting purportedly obscene and anti-Christian art. "There may be more homosexuals and pedophiles in your district than there are Roman Catholics and Baptists," one ad read. "...But maybe not."

Jesse Helms won by a little more than one hundred thousand votes. The coalition's southern regional director noted, "The press had no idea what we were doing, and they still don't know what we did. But it worked."

Swiping elections from GOP regulars in San Diego, helping an incumbent Republican senator hold on to his seat—the Republican Party took notice of the power of the Christian Coalition. The National Republican Senatorial Committee donated $64,000 to the group.

The rightists had seen Reagan as one of their own, even as he disappointed them on critical battlefronts. They had no illusion about Poppy Bush. He was not of their tribe. He had never been. As president, he reneged on his read-my-lips pledge to not raise taxes, increasing taxes by $140 billion to deal with the yawning deficits Reagan had bequeathed the nation. This enraged conservatives. Bush also reversed his opposition on gun restrictions and imposed a temporary ban on the importation of semiautomatic rifles. He condemned the right-wing assault on the NEA as censorship. In October 1990, a delegation of Christian right activists met with Bush and told him they felt betrayed, citing his failure to take forceful steps to end abortion, his inclusion of gay-rights activists at bill-signing ceremonies, and his opposition to restricting the NEA.

Bush had continued Reagan's discussions with Gorbachev and worked out an arms reduction agreement with deep cuts in the two superpowers' nuclear arsenals. And with the fall of the Berlin Wall in November 1989, the anticommunism crusade of the right disintegrated. Yet hawks were reassured that Bush was still flexing US military muscle. He ordered American forces into Panama to capture its dictator, Manuel Antonio Noriega, who had been indicted in the United States for drug trafficking. After Iraqi leader Saddam Hussein invaded Kuwait, Bush condemned the action and boosted the number of US troops in Saudi Arabia to four hundred thousand—setting the stage for military action against Iraq. Bush declared that out of this crisis in the Persian Gulf "a new world order can emerge."

With the economy in a recession, the voting public stuck to historical trends: In the 1990 midterms, the Democrats gained one Senate and seven House seats. New Right leaders blamed Bush. Viguerie declared, "We have been lied to so much by Bush. He spent the entire Reagan years promising he would continue the Reagan revolution. He just flat-out lied." Conservatives began eyeing candidates to run against Bush in 1992, including Pat Buchanan, now a paleoconservative pundit.

———

The Republican Party—despite concerns among some regulars about social conservative guerrillas—embraced the Christian Coalition as an ally. The group's first annual Road to Victory conference, held at its headquarters in Virginia Beach, Virginia, in November 1991, drew luminaries of the far right—such as Phyllis Schlafly and Gary Bauer of the Family Research Council—as well as a grateful Jesse Helms, several House Republicans, and Vice President Dan Quayle. Robertson, addressing the eight hundred delegates, spelled out the goal: "We want to see a working majority in the hands of pro-family Christians by 1996." Two weeks earlier, its stealth tactics had helped conservative Republicans unexpectedly triumph in state legislative races in Virginia.

At the conference, Robertson shared a conspiratorial critique of the political status quo. "The elites," he told the crowd, "have turned against themselves and have tried to destroy the very society from which they drew their nurture. The academic elites, the money elites, and the government elites, turned on their own society...It's going to be a spiritual battle. There will be Satanic forces...We are not coming up just against human beings to beat them in elections. We're going to be coming against spiritual warfare."

Spiritual warfare—that's the idea that all that happens in the world is a manifestation of the epic clash between God and Satan. This view held that the political foes of Robertson, the Christian Coalition, and the Republicans were literally in partnership with the devil. They were Beelzebub's soldiers, wittingly or not. It doesn't get more fundamental than that. One goal of this grandest plot of all time, Robertson noted, was for the United Nations "to rule the world...One world currency. One world army. One world court system, very possibly. And it can happen overnight."

Quayle and other Republican officials, whose presence at the conference afforded respectability to Robertson's crazy conspiracism, might not have realized that this evil, anti-Christian conspiracy was being aided and abetted by President George Bush.

Two months earlier, Robertson had published a book called *The New World Order*, a pile of paranoia that compiled the various conspiracy theories of the ages. He revived the unfounded tales of secret societies, such as the Illuminati and the Masons, and claimed they and their colluders—occultists, communists, and elites—had for centuries conspired to lock the world in a godless, collectivist dictatorship. The Federal Reserve, the J.P. Morgan bank, the Rockefellers, the Council on Foreign Relations, the Ford Foundation, the United Nations, Henry Kissinger, the Trilateral Commission—they were all in on it. So, too, were "European bankers" and the Rothschild family (long a target of the antisemitic conspiracy theories Robertson echoed). The televangelist called the Rothschilds possibly "the missing link between the occult and the world of high finance." Woodrow Wilson, Jimmy Carter, and George Bush—these presidents, he asserted, had "unwittingly" carried out "the mission" and mouthed "the phrases of a tightly knit cabal whose goal is nothing less than a new order for the human race under the domination of Lucifer and his follows."

George Bush, Satanic dupe—that was Robertson's claim. His evidence: Bush had repeatedly in speeches referred to the "new world order." The preacher presented an apocalyptic view of the future. Looking at the US military action Bush had launched earlier in the year that repelled Iraqi forces from Kuwait and interpreting it according to the Book of Revelation, Robertson maintained that the Persian Gulf War was a sign that "demonic spirits" would soon unleash a "world horror" that would kill two billion people.

With this book, which sold hundreds of thousands of copies and became a bestseller, Robertson transmitted classic antisemitic garbage and the slop of conspiracism, within an end-is-near Biblical narrative. The *Wall Street Journal* called the work a "compendium of the lunatic fringe's greatest hits." The magazine of the John Birch Society complained that it didn't go far enough and that Robertson remained a Bush supporter.

Yet Bush, who had once fretted about extremism within Robertson's ranks, and the GOP welcomed Robertson into their tent. Or, in the case of this conference, top Republicans had trekked to his home base to kiss his ring. In search of votes, they validated an antisemitic and paranoid zealot and signaled to his followers and the world that he was worth heeding.

As 1992 approached, conservatives were generally unenthused about Bush's reelection campaign. His appointment of Clarence Thomas, a die-hard rightist, to the Supreme Court had heartened the right wing (though the confirmation process was upended when Anita Hill, who had worked for Thomas at the Equal Employment Opportunity Commission, accused him of sexual harassment). But there was no getting over Bush's read-my-lips betrayal. Feulner fumed, "By frequently talking conservative—while pursuing or acquiescing to damaging policies that are anything but conservative—the administration has given the conservative cause a black eye."

Pat Buchanan was hoping to take advantage of this discontent and reshape the GOP. On December 10, 1991, in a New Hampshire conference room, the combative right-winger who had loyally served Nixon and Reagan announced his challenge to Bush for the Republican presidential nomination. One factor that had motivated him to run was the performance of David Duke in the Louisiana gubernatorial race the month before. The former Klan wizard, who pitched a populist message targeted at alienated white voters, placed second with a surprising 39 percent of the vote. A majority of Republicans had voted for him.

A man of the old right (for whom Joe McCarthy was a hero), an ally of the religious right, a foe of immigration, a fan of isolationism and protectionism, Buchanan assailed Bush for violating his no-new-taxes vow. He dog-whistled to the conspiratorial fringe right and decried the president for putting "America's wealth and power at the service of some vague new world order." He proposed shrinking the welfare state and for "phasing out" foreign aid, saying it was time to start looking out for "forgotten Americans." He called for a "new patriotism" *and* a "new nationalism." He bemoaned a cultural decline and a "moral sickness" that pervaded American life, pledging to preserve the nation's "Judeo-Christian values" and "our Western heritage." This was an announcement of anger and defiance—a mix of the old-school conservatism of limited government and xenophobia and cultural resentment. Buchanan pounded Bush for not addressing the recession that had hit the Granite State hard. "He is a globalist and we are nationalists." He thundered, "We must take America back."

Two days later, William Buckley dropped a bomb on Buchanan. In the *National Review*, he unleashed a forty-thousand-word article examining the long-standing charge that Buchanan was antisemitic. Before the Persian Gulf War, Buchanan had written, "There are only two groups beating the drums for war in the Middle East—the Israeli defense ministry and its amen corner in the United States." To some, this was an accusation that the Jewish neoconservatives then advocating for war were more loyal to Israel than the United States. Other statements in Buchanan's long career of pontificating also had raised red flags. Moreover, Buchanan's advocacy for John Demjanjuk, an accused Nazi war criminal, was, at best, curious. Poring over Buchanan's record, Buckley concluded that many of his remarks about Jews "could not reasonably be interpreted as other than anti-Semitic in tone and substance."

This never became an issue in the campaign. As Buchanan spent weeks in New Hampshire, he knocked Bush for not addressing rising unemployment. He railed against the president's trade policies, Japanese exports, multinational agencies, loan guaranties to Israel, and the two wars Bush had waged. He revived the old "America First" slogan of the isolationists of the 1930s, tapping into populist anger in an effort to hijack the Republican Party.

Buchanan's language, as always, was extreme and tinged with violence. He denounced the president as "King George" and called for a "Pitchfork Brigade" to rebel against him. "Ride to the sound of the guns," he joyfully told large and enthusiastic crowds. For his part, Bush offered little more than an unexciting economic package and no emotional connection to the ongoing suffering. Polls indicated that 75 percent of the country believed the United States was on the wrong track, and Bush had little to say in response. He did win New Hampshire with an unimpressive 53 percent, but Buchanan, with his politics of discord, pulled 38 percent. Gingrich called Buchanan's finish a "primal scream" of populist anger.

Through the rest of the primary season, Bush continued to place first in each contest, with Buchanan collecting between 8 and 35 percent. The insurgent never presented an existential threat to Bush and the GOP establishment, but he demonstrated that about a quarter of the party's voters were drawn to his brand of combative, jingoistic, and tribalistic conservatism and to his savage rhetoric. A chunk of the Republican base was feeding on rage.

Rush Limbaugh and his gospel of derision and division was spreading widely. By 1991, he could be heard on 350 stations, with a total audience of 7.1 million listeners a week. The money was pouring in—millions of dollars a year. His M.O. had not changed: blasting the liberals, targeting gays and lesbians, ridiculing the homeless, bragging of his own wonderfulness. He launched a syndicated television show; its executive producer was Roger Ailes. (The show would end in 1996, but it gave Ailes a few ideas; that same year, he created Fox News for conservative media mogul Rupert Murdoch.) Limbaugh started a newsletter that quickly attracted hundreds of thousands of subscribers.

The belligerent broadcaster published his first book in 1992, in which he elevated one of his favorite noxious and dangerous ideas: Climate change was a hoax. He claimed that concern about the warming planet was the product of a sinister conspiracy and contended that environmentalism overall was a scam, an issue that communists—he always called liberals "communists"—exploited to redistribute wealth. "Despite the hysterics of a few pseudo scientists, there is no reason to believe in global warming," he insisted. Environmentalists' true goal, he asserted, was to spread "terror, dread and apprehension about the future." With his assorted media platforms, Limbaugh had become the top pusher of this disinformation to millions of conservatives and Republicans.

In June 1992, Ailes engineered an important meeting for George Bush: a trip to the Kennedy Center to see a show with Limbaugh and then a chat with him at the White House, where Limbaugh would spend the night. Bush even carried Limbaugh's suitcase up to the Lincoln Bedroom. Limbaugh had supported Buchanan at the start of the primaries. Now with Buchanan out of the race, he showed an interest in H. Ross Perot, the feisty and erratic Texas billionaire running as an independent.

Republican officials worried about a potential Limbaugh endorsement of Perot. Bush wanted the radio man, now the most influential voice on the right, on his side. No hard feelings, of course. The two spent the evening conversing about sports, politics, and the campaign. Following his visit with Bush, Limbaugh appeared on the *Today* show and enthused about the president. When weeks later Perot withdrew from the race and made it a two-man contest between Bush and Arkansas Governor Bill Clinton, the Democratic nominee, Limbaugh exclaimed that the election now boiled down to "socialism versus America." He was on Team Bush.

A few days after giving the White House seal of approval to the top climate change denialist in the nation, Bush jetted off to Rio de Janeiro for a global Earth Summit, where he signed the first major international agreement that recognized climate change and that called for remedial action.

At the Democratic convention in July in Madison Square Garden, Clinton, the centrist who had weathered numerous controversies and scandals (accusations of extramarital affairs, his escape from the Vietnam draft, and an unusual business deal in Arkansas), positioned himself as a new-generation leader, laser-focused on economic progress and change. During his acceptance speech, he said, "I am a product of the middle class and when I am president, you will be forgotten no more." In the convention's aftermath, Clinton led Bush by twenty-five points in the polls.

The Republican convention in Houston would not be defined by anything George Bush would say. He was the nominee but not the star.

Forty percent of the 2,200 delegates who trekked to the Astrodome identified as evangelical Christians, with three hundred or so of them Christian Coalition activists. Religious right advocates easily beat back the attempt of moderates to soften the stark antiabortion plank in the party's platform. The platform embodied the anger of cultural conservatives who were irate that a Baby Boomer libertine who had tried marijuana (without inhaling, he said), skipped the draft, protested the Vietnam War, once looked like a hippie, supported abortion rights, and was not opposed to gay rights could possibly be president. Clinton and his wife were part of the liberal, Hollywoodish, tolerant, traditions-challenging culture that came of age in the 1960s. Hillary Clinton symbolized the feminism that conservatives believed undermined family values. Bill Clinton was not fit to be the leader of *their* America built upon *their* ideas of Christianity and patriotism. One delegate accosted a reporter and declared, "You can't be a Christian and be

a Democrat." The platform accused "elements within the media, the entertainment industry, academics and the Democratic Party" of "waging a guerrilla war against American values."

This crowd wanted a war. When Limbaugh appeared in the hall, they
chanted, "Rush, Rush, Rush!" Rich Bond, the chair of the GOP, gave a
speech harshly attacking Hillary Clinton. (An assault on a potential First
Lady was probably a first for a political convention.) Afforded a speaking
gig by the Bush campaign, Robertson, the antisemitic conspiracy theorist
who claimed the president was a tool of Satan, told cheering delegates,
"When Bill and Hillary talk about family values, they are not talking
about either families or values. They are talking about a radical plan to
destroy the traditional family and transfer its functions to the federal government." Clinton, he exclaimed, wants to "appoint homosexuals to his
administration."

But it was Buchanan who shook the rafters and defined the convention.
On the campaign trail, he had engaged in violent rhetoric, and he stood
credibly accused of antisemitism by Buckley, the godfather of the conservative movement. Still, the Republican National Committee handed him a
prize: a prime-time slot. Buchanan, a natural showman, made the most of
it. "My friends," he roared, "this election is about more than who gets what.
It is about who we are. It is about what we believe and what we stand for as
Americans. There is a religious war going on in this country for the soul of
America. It is a cultural war as critical to the kind of the nation we shall be
as the Cold War itself. And in that struggle for the soul of America, Clinton
and Clinton are on the other side, and George Bush is on our side." The delegates applauded wildly and stomped their feet.

Bush's acceptance speech was utterly unmemorable. He talked about
his warmed-over economic proposals. It was Buchanan's declaration of war
that would resonate deeper and ring longer. His performance summed up
the convention: The GOP was more obsessed with divisive cultural battles
than the economic problems the nation faced. Interviewing Buchanan,
NBC News anchor Tom Brokaw noted the failed candidate had delivered
the message that "if you're not white, heterosexual, Christian, antiabortion,
anti-environment, you're somehow not welcome in the Republican Party."
Columnist Molly Ivins quipped that Buchanan's speech "probably sounded
better in the original German."

The extremists were wagging the dog. In his diary, Bush observed that
Buchanan "made it a polarizing event." The Christian right was indeed riled
up for the election—if not to advance Bush, then to block Clinton. At the

convention, Ralph Reed pledged that the Christian Coalition would spend $7 million on the fall campaign. "This is the year of the Lord," he said.

———

At a large gathering of evangelicals in Dallas a week following the Republican convention, numerous heroes of the social conservatives—Falwell, Schlafly, Oliver North—prosecuted the battle Buchanan had outlined. Though this was supposedly a nonpartisan event, one speaker after another denounced Clinton and urged the thousands of attendees to vote for the Bush-Quayle ticket and to organize their congregations to do likewise

Speaking at the convention, the Reverend Donald Wildmon, president of the American Family Association, warned, "If Bill Clinton goes to the White House, he'll take his friends the homosexuals, the abortionists, and the pornographers." The Reverend Gene Antonio falsely claimed that AIDS could be transmitted through breathing and called gay rights advocates "a Gestapo who will break the back of all of our churches." He described the Democratic convention as "a sea of homosexuals and lesbians, and this is the White House we will be facing in a few months if we do not put in a lot of shoe leather." Linking a supposed decline in American culture to programs to assist low-income Americans, Buchanan exclaimed, "The Vandals and Visigoths are pillaging your cities by expanding the Head Start and food stamp programs." This sounded like racism.

As Reagan had endorsed a similar event a dozen years earlier, Bush did the same when he showed up on the second night. "I was struck," he said, "by the fact that the other party took [thousands of] words to put together their platform, but left out three simple letters, G-O-D." He was affirming the hatred and extremism that had spewed forth and playing to fundamentalists who fervently believed politics was spiritual warfare.

While it continued its efforts to win local elections, the Christian Coalition also focused on the presidential race. Cochairs of the Bush reelection campaign in thirty-nine states were coalition members, including Billy McCormack, the Republican leader in Louisiana who had defended David Duke with antisemitic comments. Coalition officials peppered Bush aides with memos providing campaign advice. One such memo suggested that Bush stop using the phrase "New World Order."

The Christian Coalition and its allies had assumed majority or near-majority positions in state Republican committees across the country. In Washington state, they pushed through a party platform that called for the teaching of creationism, barring gays and lesbians from classroom positions, the withdrawal of the United States from the UN, a return to the gold standard, and banning the occult, witchcraft, and abortion. In Iowa, Robertson sent out a fundraising letter to supporters opposing a proposed equal rights amendment to the state constitution. The over-the-top missive assailed the state ERA as the work of "a socialist, anti-family political movement that encourages women to leave their husbands, kill their children, practice witchcraft, destroy capitalism and become lesbians."

Robertson was peddling extreme hate and encouraging his followers to view political opponents as godless enemies—murderers, witches, and lesbians! But none of this caused the GOP to disassociate itself from him. After all, the coalition was working that fall through thousands of churches to distribute 10 million congressional scorecards and 40 million presidential scorecards. It set up computer-assisted telephone banks to help GOP candidates. All this represented a possible tax code violation, given the coalition had been established as a nonprofit that did not engage in partisan politics as its "primary" activity. But Reed assured reporters everything was kosher.

After the GOP convention, the *Los Angeles Times* reported that Richard Nixon, believing Bush's campaign was flailing, had conveyed unsolicited advice to the president: Dump "fanatics" like Robertson and Falwell; they were damaging the Republican Party. The convention, dominated by the religious right, he noted, was "worse than the Goldwater Republicans" of 1964. Bush needed a positive message. This was a recommendation Bush did not take.

On September 11, 1992, the president addressed the Christian Coalition's second annual Road to Victory Conference. Also present were Secretary of Education Lamar Alexander and William Bennett, who had recently been Bush's drug czar. Alexander praised Robertson and told the crowd of one thousand–plus delegates, "I'm glad to be on his side." Bush lauded Robertson for "all the work you're doing to restore the spiritual foundation of this nation." He then attended a private reception with major contributors to the coalition in the rose garden of Robertson's estate. Black swans swam in a pond, a harpist played, and Bush warmly greeted members of the televangelist's inner circle. Presumably, Bush's alliance with Satan was not mentioned.

The base of the Republican Party considered the election a culture war, but Bush was not leading such a full-throated fight. On the campaign trail, he often came across as a lackadaisical candidate. His debate performances were flat. He poked at the so-called character question about Clinton and suggested the Democrat could not be trusted. Behind the scenes,

Republicans and right-wing operatives tried to gin up various Clinton scandals regarding his sexual conduct and the failed Whitewater land deal in which he and his wife had invested with an Arkansas businessman named James McDougal, who later headed an S&L that went bust. But these efforts did not gain traction.

In September, Bush dropped by Limbaugh's studio. Together, they reiterated the Bush campaign's favorite anti-Clinton talking points: Clinton had evaded the Vietnam draft and had once called the US military "immoral." (The latter allegation was untrue; Clinton, as a young man, had referred to the Vietnam draft as "illegitimate.") During a CNN interview, Bush echoed right-wing suspicions—which had brewed conspiracy theories—about a trip Clinton had taken to Moscow when he was a Rhodes scholar at Oxford.

The Clinton campaign was obsessed with two things: parrying any attacks on its candidate and staying on message. It would not allow the Bushies this time to turn the Democratic nominee into a pitiful caricature. (Atwater had died of brain cancer in 1991, and the Bush reelection campaign did seem to miss his unprincipled killer instinct.) With 78 percent of the nation believing the country was on the wrong track, the Clinton camp remained fixated on his paramount theme: reviving the sluggish economy. James Carville, one of Clinton's lead strategists, posted a simple, three-line reminder for all in the campaign's war room: "Change vs. more of the same. The economy, stupid. Don't forget health care."

The day before Election Day, Limbaugh introduced Bush at a rally in New Jersey. A few hours later, Bush phoned into Limbaugh's show from Air Force One. "Rush," the president said, "I have never wavered in my conviction that we're gonna win because I think the people are gonna say, 'Truth, character—they count.'"

Clinton smoked Bush, winning thirty-two states and 370 electoral votes. In the popular vote, he triumphed 43 to 37 percent, with Ross Perot, who had reentered the race in October, pulling 18 percent. The Democrats dropped nine House seats but still held the majority. The Christian right effort—exhorted by intolerant and bigoted extremists within its ranks— had failed to reach beyond its own faithful. Bush won a majority in only two demographic groups: rich folks (voters who annually earned over $100,000) and white evangelical Christians. Arguably, his party's flirtation with the cultural warriors of the right had turned off voters in other categories.

Robertson's Christian soldiers did better on other fronts. People for the American Way, a liberal group, found that 40 percent of five hundred races it had tracked nationally were won by fundamentalist Christians. Ralph

Reed boasted, "We focused on where the real power is: in the states and in the precincts and in the neighborhoods where people live and work."

With Bush's defeat, moderate squishy Republicanism looked forsaken. Still standing were Buchanan's angry, tribalistic populism, Limbaugh's hostility-driven infotainment, Gingrich's brutal assault on Democrats, and Robertson's literal demonization of government officials, educators, journalists, financiers, and anyone not striving to create a "Christian nation."

The day after the election, Limbaugh, who had predicted a Bush win by four to six points, insisted, "I was not wrong." But there was good news for him. With Clinton as president, he would not lack material. "This show," he declared, "becomes the focus now of the loyal, honest and good-intentioned, well-intentioned opposition to the monolithic power which will descend upon Washington, DC."

A month after the election, Reagan sent Limbaugh a handwritten note calling him "the Number One" voice of conservatism in the United States.

CHAPTER 16

The Clinton Chronicles

O n the afternoon of July 20, 1993—six months into the Clinton administration—deputy White House counsel Vince Foster ate a hamburger for lunch at his desk in his West Wing office. He chased it with a few M&Ms. He told his secretary he'd be back later and drove his 1989 gray Honda Accord to Fort Marcy Park in northern Virginia. He walked about 250 yards to a grove, sat on the ground, placed the barrel of a 1913 Colt revolver in his mouth, and fired a shot.

The suicide of the number two lawyer in the Clinton White House—a lifelong pal of Bill and a former law partner of Hillary—unleashed waves of suspicion and scandal that would envelop the White House and be utilized by the Clintons' foes. Exploiting a blend of paranoia and political opportunism, conservatives and Republican officials would flog outrageously false tales and conspiracy theories about the Clintons in a relentless campaign to delegitimize them and the entire Democratic Party—even as well-founded questions did linger about *some* Clinton actions and associations. All this would cascade into a bona fide sex scandal and an impeachment of Bill Clinton orchestrated by a small cabal of anti-Clinton fanatics.

In the Clinton years, the right and the GOP would weaponize conspiracism for use against an American president. It was to be an era of rabid political warfare propelled by GOP-abetted lunacy and extremism.

———

Foster's suicide reasonably sparked queries. He had been involved in one of the mini-scandals that had struck the fresh administration: Travelgate, the abrupt and mishandled firing of employees in the White House travel office. It was a minor matter, but fodder for reporters and the *Wall Street Journal*'s right-wing editorial page. Foster had also worked on the Whitewater land deal and with Hillary Clinton's task force that was devising a comprehensive health care plan.

He left no suicide message. But a ripped-up note found days later in his briefcase offered insight into his state of mind. Referring to Travelgate, he had written, "The GOP has lied and misrepresented its knowledge and role and covered up a prior investigation...The [*Wall Street Journal*] editors lie without consequences. I was not meant for the job or the spotlight of public life in Washington. Here ruining people is considered sport." Foster suffered from depression—as multiple investigations later concluded.

Soon after Foster's death, questions arose about how the White House staff had handled the torn-up note and access to his office for investigators. The *Wall Street Journal* editorial board called for the appointment of a "special counsel" to investigate the activities of Foster, the Clintons, and others in the administration. It observed with suspicion, "Those who knew [Foster] consider him an unlikely suicide."

Months later, the Foster suicide story took a twist, with media reports revealing that he had handled the Whitewater matter and that files related to that venture—which lost the Clintons money—had been moved out of Foster's office after his death. Now the suicide was connected to Whitewater. "Release the Whitewater Files," the *New York Times* demanded.

There was no evidence Foster's death was related to Whitewater. Still, conspiracy theories spread like wildfire. Accuracy in the Media, a far-right group run by Reed Irvine and financially supported by ultraconservative banking heir Richard Mellon Scaife, published an op-ed in the *Washington Times*, the right-wing Unification Church–owned newspaper, questioning the official finding that Foster had committed suicide. Irvine encouraged Christopher Ruddy, a reporter at Rupert Murdoch's *New York Post*, to write about the case. Top Republicans—including Dole and Gingrich—called for the appointment of a special counsel. William Safire, the old Nixon speechwriter turned *New York Times* columnist, hypothesized (with not a whit of evidence) that Foster killed himself because he dreaded the eruption of a Whitewater scandal. With a frenzy underway, Attorney General Janet Reno in early January 1994 appointed as special counsel Robert Fiske, a Republican Wall Street attorney and former US attorney.

About this time, the right's Clinton attack machine landed a blow. In August 1993, Peter W. Smith, a wealthy GOP donor obsessed with destroying Clinton with a scandal, told David Brock, a reporter for the right-wing *American Spectator* (a magazine supported by Scaife), that he would provide funds to underwrite an article depicting Clinton as a sex fiend based on allegations from Arkansas state troopers who had served as his bodyguards. Brock went to work, and in the meantime the magazine developed what came to be called "the Arkansas Project," subsidized by Scaife, which would spend $2.4

million over the following four years to dig up dirt on the president. Brock's piece appeared in late December, full of sleazy scuttlebutt about Clinton and containing some stories challengeable by known facts and some that were perhaps true. Another Clinton scandal was born: Troopergate.

Troopergate might have faded quickly but for one paragraph recounting the claim that Clinton, while attending an event in a Little Rock hotel, had asked a trooper to bring to a hotel room a woman named Paula. As the story went, after her encounter with Clinton, Paula told the trooper she was available to be the governor's girlfriend.

On February 11, 1994, two of the troopers and a woman named Paula Jones held a press conference in Washington. Jones said she was there to "clear her name" and offered her side of the story: In 1991, she had been a clerical worker for a state commission and was helping to staff a conference at the hotel. A trooper told her the governor wanted to meet her in a suite. She went to the room, believing a contact with the governor could help her career, but Clinton made unwanted sexual advances and asked for a "type of sex." She wouldn't answer specific questions from reporters.

Three months later Jones sued the president of the United States for sexual harassment, seeking $750,000 in damages from Clinton. This seemed a separate mess for Clinton from the never-ending Whitewater controversy. It wouldn't stay that way.

On the Whitewater front, Fiske's appointment did nothing to impede the Clinton conspiracy theory industry. Ruddy published a series of articles in the New York Post suggesting Foster had not committed suicide. The Wall Street Journal editorial page amplified Ruddy's reckless reporting. The Washington Times published its own reports. (It ran a column by Martin Anderson, a senior economic adviser for President Reagan who now worked at the conservative Hoover Institution, suggesting Foster had been murdered.) Meanwhile, journalists for mainstream media outlets were pursuing Whitewater and Foster stories, thinking this could be Washington's next big scandal.

Then came Limbaugh. In the first year of the Clinton administration, he had grown more influential among conservatives. His daily radio show reached about 20 million people. And he had not changed his ways, tossing out false claims, inciting division, and promoting nastiness as a virtue. (After the 1992 election, he compared Chelsea Clinton, the twelve-year-old daughter of the Clintons, to a dog.) In September 1993, the National Review hailed Limbaugh as "the Leader of the Opposition," with an article quoting multiple Republicans swooning over the malicious host. "When Rush Limbaugh talks, you know you're listening to the real world," Dole said.

Republican officeholders these days eagerly sought out the crass and mean-spirited Limbaugh for endorsements and positive coverage. He was leading the conservative assault on the Clinton administration's comprehensive health care plan, mocking Hillary Clinton's role in developing the proposal, and falsely asserting it would end all consumer choice.

Now Limbaugh leaped to the front of the line in Foster conspiracy land. On March 10, 1994, he told his listeners, "Brace yourself." He had a fax that "contains information that…will appear in a newsletter to Morgan Stanley sales personnel this afternoon…What it is is a bit of news which says… there's a Washington consulting firm that has scheduled the release of a report that will appear, it will be published, that claims that Vince Foster was murdered in an apartment owned by Hillary Clinton, and the body was then taken to Fort Marcy Park."

Limbaugh didn't say who had done the killing. The implication was the Clintons were in on the murder or, at least, the cover-up. The nation's top conservative, who Republicans worshipped, was perpetuating a hoax, convincing millions of Americans—perhaps tens of millions—that the Clintons were corrupt operators deserving of utter scorn and unworthy of residing in the White House. This potent dose of poison for the national discourse reaffirmed the worst suspicions and prejudices of the GOP's anti-Clinton base.

Other prominent conservatives and Republicans got into the act. Roger Ailes, who was now running the CNBC cable network, seconded the speculation that Foster might have been murdered. Pat Robertson hinted the death might have been a killing. Citizens United's Floyd Brown, a prominent conservative activist looking for Clinton dirt in Arkansas and passing out so-called leads to reporters, publicly declared he had "new clues that suggest Foster did not commit suicide." It was all bullshit.

Jerry Falwell sought to profit financially off the Clinton conspiracy rush. He despised the Clintons. After Clinton's victory, he had considered resurrecting the Moral Majority. He denounced Clinton's proposal to allow gay people to serve in the military. In early 1993, he sent out a fundraising letter asking, "Are we about to become a hedonistic nation of unrestrained homosexuality, abortion, immorality, and lawlessness?" Falwell ranted that Clinton wanted "perverts in key places," and he insinuated that Hillary Clinton was jamming the new administration with lesbians, "her old friends."

Targeting the anti-Clinton paranoia on the right, Falwell promoted a low-budget video called *Bill and Hillary Clinton's Circle of Power* that claimed "countless people" had "mysteriously died" because of "some connection" to Clinton. It mimicked a bogus list on a conspiracy theory website called "The Clinton Body Count," which presented a roster of dozens of supposedly suspicious deaths related to the Clintons. The video featured Larry Nichols, a longtime Clinton hater in Arkansas who had been spreading unfounded stories about Clinton for years. The video asserted that Foster and Hillary Clinton were having an affair and that Foster did not kill himself. Nichols alleged in the film that Bill Clinton had connections to a drug smuggling operation run out of an airfield in Mena, Arkansas. The video included Bill Dannemeyer, a former far-right Republican congressman, denouncing Clinton as a "draft dodging womanizer who is a pathological liar" and calling for his impeachment.

The film ended with Falwell questioning Foster's suicide and pitching copies of the video for $40. He asked viewers to call a 900 telephone number to join him in demanding a congressional investigation of "murder, witness intimidation, and [the] subsequent cover-up of Whitewater facts." The cost of the call: $1.95 a minute.

This sketchy and libelous video was followed by a longer one called *The Clinton Chronicles*. It regurgitated the allegations from the state troopers and others about Clinton's sexual escapades, the accusation he was a murderous psychopath, and more elaborate charges about Mena, claiming Clinton "was part of a system laundering millions of cocaine dollars." The film maintained that people with information about Clinton's crimes had died mysteriously. A plane crash. A suicide. It concluded with this warning: "If any additional harm comes to anyone connected with this film or their families, the people of America will hold Bill Clinton personally responsible."

Falwell promoted both films on his *Old-Time Gospel Hour*. He taped an infomercial for the videos in which an investigative journalist hidden from full view informed Falwell that Clinton had arranged many murders and that he feared for his own life. The man, though, was no journalist; he was the producer of *The Clinton Chronicles*, Patrick Matrisciana. His previous films had declared evolution a hoax and Halloween a plot to entice children into "Pagan Occultism." Matrisciana also was associated with the Council for National Policy, the secretive group of conservative elites that included leaders of the right (Ralph Reed, Pat Robertson, Oliver North, Phyllis Schlafly, and Paul Weyrich) and prominent Republicans (Senators Jesse Helms, Lauch Faircloth, and Don Nickles, and Representatives Dan Burton, Tom DeLay, Jon Kyl, and Dick Armey).

The CNP and its members were complicit in the effort to portray Clinton as a murderous criminal kingpin. It bulk-ordered copies of *The Clinton Chronicles* and sent tapes to its members. Burton invited Nichols to Washington to brief Republican House members. (Burton at one point tried to re-create Foster's death in his backyard by shooting a watermelon—or a pumpkin or a cantaloupe, whatever it was—to see how far away the gunshot could be heard.) Nichols became a fixture on right-wing talk radio. Of course, Limbaugh echoed the scurrilous nonsense, insisting that "journalists and others working on or involved in Whitewater" had mysteriously died.

Falwell was running a con. But the CNP connection, the meetings with Republican officeholders—this all provided a degree of legitimacy to the sleazy endeavor and the baseless and paranoid-driven speculation. He sold about 150,000 copies of the videos and made millions.

It had been a productive first year for Clinton. He signed into law a family medical leave act and legislation requiring background checks and a five-day waiting period for handgun purchases, and he enacted a mammoth deficit-reduction budget bill. He appointed the first woman to serve as attorney general (Janet Reno) and the second woman (Ruth Bader Ginsburg) to sit on the Supreme Court. He implemented the "don't ask, don't tell" policy that allowed gays to serve in the military (if they didn't publicly profess their orientation). He signed the North American Free Trade Agreement, attended a NATO summit, and lifted the trade embargo on Vietnam. He launched two controversial legislative initiatives: health care reform and revamping welfare. And he confronted several crises: a shoot-out at a cult compound in Waco, Texas, that resulted in the deaths of seventy-six people; a terrorist bombing at the World Trade Center that killed six people and injured more than a thousand; and a horrific firefight in Mogadishu, in which eighteen American GIs died.

Yet Clinton was worried about right-wing extremism.

In an interview, he rued, "There's something that those of us who are Democrats have to contend with. The radical right have their own set of press organs. They make their own news and then try to force it into the mainstream media. We don't have anything like that. We don't have a *Washington Times*, or a Christian Broadcasting Network, or a Rush Limbaugh, any of that stuff." Talking to a St. Louis radio station, he cited Falwell and the Clinton-conspiracy videos as part of the "constant, unremitting drumbeat of negativism." He added, "We don't need a cultural war in this country." Falwell responded that Clinton should direct his ire not at him but at those making these allegations.

———

On June 30, 1994, Robert Fiske, the special counsel, released his report on the death of Vince Foster. The conclusion: He shot himself. There was no indication the suicide was tied to Whitewater or any personal legal matter related to the Clintons. Case closed. But not for the get-Clinton crowd. Senator Alfonse D'Amato, a New York Republican, claimed there were "many questions left unanswered." The Washington Times maintained Foster's body might have been moved to Fort Marcy Park. Reed Irvine said the same. On the House floor, Burton the watermelon shooter declared, "I believe his body was moved to that location."

Fiske was soon off the Whitewater case. Clinton had recently signed into law legislation reviving the independent counsel act, and a panel of three federal appellate judges would select someone to fill that role for the ongoing Whitewater probe. Fiske was the logical choice. But right-wing groups and Republican legislators viewed Fiske as part of the conspiracy. They kept pumping out information to challenge Fiske's conclusions, often basing assertions on unconfirmed or questionable evidence.

The judges, perhaps influenced by all this noise, removed Fiske and appointed Kenneth Starr, a Washington power lawyer who had served as President Bush's solicitor general, as Whitewater independent counsel. He was a prominent figure in conservative legal circles, an influential member of the rightist Federalist Society. But the New York Times editorial page opined that with this pick "the court has enhanced the appearance of an evenhanded investigation." The fate of the Whitewater investigation—and perhaps more—now rested with Starr.

———

While Jerry Falwell obsessed over the Clinton conspiracy theories, Pat Robertson's Christian Coalition burrowed deeper into the Republican Party. In the months after the 1992 election, Ralph Reed claimed the group was signing up ten thousand new members each week. It boasted an annual budget of up to $10 million, full-time staff in fifteen states, and 750 local chapters. In early 1993, it hooked up with John Cardinal O'Connor in New York and elected a slate of Christian Coalition–trained candidates to a majority of school board positions in the city. Similar operations were being mounted in other parts of the country. Under Reed's savvy guidance, the coalition broadened its list of policy concerns, adding tax cuts, crime, spending cuts, and health care, syncing up even more with the Republican Party. Yet Robertson, the theocratic conspiracy-monger, continued to preach paranoia and division. In a six-page fundraising letter, he declared the United States "has become a largely anti-Christian pagan nation—and our government has become a weapon the anti-Christian forces now use against Christians and religious people." The spiritual war was still on.

Robertson's third annual Road to Victory conference in September of that year, held in Washington, demonstrated the coalition's growing clout within the GOP. A host of Republicans, including possible 1996 contenders, made the pilgrimage: former housing secretary Jack Kemp, Senators Dole, Helms, and Phil Gramm, and Representatives Gingrich, Hyde, and Robert Dornan. The mood was combative. Demonization ran rampant. The crowd booed David Wilhelm, the chair of the Democratic Party whom Reed had invited to speak. Keith Fournier, the executive director of Robertson's American Center for Law and Justice, accused the Clintons of engaging in "religious cleansing in the American republic." Don Feder, a Jewish social conservative activist, claimed their political foes were "neo-pagans" and slammed the gay rights movement as a "mortal assault on the soul of our society."

In addressing the assembly, Pat Buchanan went further than he had at the Republican convention. He railed against multiculturalism and proclaimed, "Our culture is superior because our religion is Christianity." The audience cheered.

On a television broadcast, Robertson had a darker message for his followers: "Just like what Nazi Germany did to the Jews, so liberal America is doing to evangelical Christians. It's no different... It is the Democratic Congress, the liberal-biased media, and the homosexuals who want to destroy all Christians." This was a foul and hysterical comparison: Democrats were the equivalent of Hitler and committing genocide against Christians. Robertson beseeched viewers to donate twenty dollars a month: "Send me money today or these liberals will be putting Christians like you and me in concentration camps." The GOP, with its warm relationship with Robertson, was endorsing this absurd and profound paranoia he served up to a large audience of Americans willing to believe his dangerous propaganda.

As the White House and congressional Democrats sought support for Clinton's health care reform package, the Christian Coalition in early 1994 vowed to spend $1.4 million on a nationwide effort in forty congressional districts to defeat the initiative, targeting the sort of voters who Robertson had scared with his concentration-camp pitch. And it revved up its

electoral machine, backing far-right social conservatives in GOP primaries and assisting thousands of Christian rightists in becoming delegates
to state Republican conventions. *Campaigns & Elections* magazine found
the Christian Coalition was "dominant" in the GOP in eighteen states and
maintained "substantial" influence in thirteen others. One major effort
targeted Virginia, where the coalition helped Oliver North—who had been
convicted of several Iran-contra-related crimes and then cleared on legal
technicalities—win the GOP nomination in the US Senate race. The coalition and other Christian right organizations claimed to control two thousand school boards across the nation.

Republican moderates were aghast at the swelling influence of the
Christian right within their party. "Part of the problem," Senator Nancy
Kassebaum, a Kansas Republican, told a reporter, "is that moderates aren't
willing to work in the trenches, while the Christian conservatives have gone
door to door and worked hard and won control fair and square." When
GOP Senator Arlen Specter, a moderate from Pennsylvania, appeared at the
Texas state convention—where attendees waved signs saying A VOTE FOR
OUR CANDIDATE IS A VOTE FOR GOD—he called for church-state separation
and was booed. There were more jeers for a Houston businesswoman who
declared, "There are people in this audience who want the Republican Party
to be a church." The moderates looked on with disappointment, as Dole, the
presumed 1996 front-runner, bowed to pressure from the religious right to
endorse North.

At its 1994 Road to Victory conference, where potential GOP presidential
candidates wooed thousands of delegates, Robertson boasted, "We are seeing the Christian Coalition rise to where God intends it to be in this nation,
as one of the most powerful political forces that's ever been in the history
of America." Clinton, naturally, was pilloried, with much scorn directed at
the health care plan that he had shelved due to intense political opposition.
The coalition announced it would be distributing fifty-seven million voter
guides in all fifty states ahead of the midterm congressional elections and
aimed to register two million new voters at sixty thousand churches. The
intent was clear: to help Republicans win the Congress. Senator Trent Lott,
a Mississippi Republican, exclaimed to the audience, "I'm here to tell you:
Welcome to the Republican Party. We're glad we have you."

———

Eleven days later, Newt Gingrich, who was in line to be House speaker
should the Republicans prevail, gathered House GOP candidates on the
steps of the US Capitol to unveil ten initiatives they promised to pass if they

reached the majority. Dubbed the Contract with America, the plan called for tax cuts, term limits for members of Congress, a constitutional amendment requiring a balanced budget, a three-fifths vote in Congress to raise taxes, expanded applications of the death penalty, and more. It had been drawn up with key GOP-friendly interest groups in mind, particularly the National Federation of Independent Business, the National Rifle Association, and the Christian Coalition.

Gingrich's scheme did not address the social conservatives' most desired policy goals, such as an abortion ban or the reintroduction of prayer into public schools. But the proposed cut in welfare spending and the $500-per-child tax credit were regarded as tribute for the influential Christian Coalition. Surrounded by American flags, Gingrich claimed the contract would "help every human across the planet." Gingrich had another idea, as well. In a meeting with a group of lobbyists, he shared his messaging plan for the final weeks of the election: to portray Clinton as "the enemy of normal Americans."

The day before the election, Rush Limbaugh, who had been beating the drum all season long for the Contract with America and trashing Democrats, told his audience "be ready at dawn tomorrow" to gain Republican control of Congress. He was right. On Election Day, Clinton and the Democrats were swamped. The Republicans netted fifty-four House and eight Senate seats to gain full control of Congress for the first time in four decades.

Not a single Republican incumbent was defeated. A majority of governorships were now in the party's hands. Ten state legislative chambers flipped to the Republicans. The NRA won nineteen of its twenty-four priority races. The Christian Coalition boasted that forty-four of the House GOP victories were candidates backed by the religious right and claimed credit for helping to elect the eight new senators. (Coalition favorite Oliver North did not win.) Ralph Reed pointed out that one-third of the voters in these elections identified as evangelical born-again Christians. These voters, he declared, were now the "core base" for the GOP and in many races "the margin of victory." True or not, the Christian Coalition, led by an unhinged conspiracy theorist, had earned the reputation as a kingmaker within GOP politics.

In midterm elections, the historical tide flows against the party in the White House. The Clintons had botched health care reform, and the various Clinton controversies—actual or exaggerated—had provided ammo to Republicans. But there was little doubt that Limbaugh's abuse, Gingrich's scorched-earth tactics, Robertson's attempts to foment a religious war, and Falwell's conspiracy hucksterism had merged into a powerful assault on the Clintons that encouraged conservative Americans—and maybe some independents—to see the First Couple and the Democrats as a malign force that had to be eradicated to save the nation. The politics of extremism had triumphed; Republicans were overjoyed.

A month after the rout, at the end of a three-day orientation, the seventy-three incoming House Republican freshmen assembled for a dinner with Limbaugh as the featured speaker. Vin Weber, a former House member, exclaimed, "Rush is as responsible for what happened here as much as any individual in America." He noted that voters who listened to ten hours or more a week of talk radio had supported Republicans by a three-to-one margin.

These new House Republicans declared Limbaugh an honorary member of their congressional class. In a speech to the group, Limbaugh advised, "This is not the time to get moderate. This is not the time to start trying to be liked." He added, "Say what you believe, with passion and bravado, and you're going to offend half the people who hear it." That, he said, is a sign of success.

CHAPTER 17

A Vast Right-Wing Conspiracy

B lack helicopters. Mysterious black helicopters rumored to be part of a world-government takeover. That was on the mind of Helen Chenoweth.

On March 17, 1995, Chenoweth, one of Gingrich's new Republican House members, convened a hearing in her Idaho district at Boise City Hall. The agenda was the "excessive use of government force." Next to her sat the lieutenant governor and the secretary of state, each a Republican. She opened the session saying that for democracy to succeed the government must be "afraid of the people."

The first witness was a lawyer who represented Randy Weaver, a hero of far-right anti-government extremists. In 1992, Weaver, an adherent of Christian Identity (a mix of fundamentalist, anti-government, and racist notions), had refused to appear in court on minor firearms charges, and during a subsequent shoot-out with federal agents at his Ruby Ridge compound in Idaho, his wife, his fourteen-year-old son, and a US marshal were killed. The lawyer called for limiting the government's use of force.

Other speakers at Chenoweth's hearing decried government tyranny and demanded that federal agents not be allowed to investigate crimes on nonfederal land. Chenoweth referred to "black helicopters"—a mythical symbol of a nefarious plot to render the United States the subservient ward of that much-dreaded New World Order. She invited Samuel Sherwood, the head of the United States Militia Association, who two weeks earlier had said some lawmakers might have to be killed in a coming civil war, to give a statement. Gary DeMott, the founder of the Idaho Sovereignty Association, which claimed county and state law trumped federal authority, assailed the US government, exclaiming, "What we're talking about here is that Hitler's SS never had it so good."

For several years, an extremist, anti-government movement—called the militia movement or the Patriots movement—had been brewing. It trafficked the most paranoid notions: UN helicopters were conducting operations in the United States, the US government planned to confiscate all guns, federal concentration camps were under construction. White supremacists, antisemites, and neo-Nazis populated the ranks, though not all members fell into those categories. The common denominator was the belief that the government was the enemy, and this was especially true for these people now that the Clintons were in the White House. Ruby Ridge and the deadly clash between Bureau of Alcohol, Tobacco and Firearms agents and the Branch Davidian cult at its compound in Waco, Texas, had been defining moments for the movement. The Clinton administration's enactment of modest gun control measures, these paranoid right-wingers believed, was another warning sign. John Trochmann, a white supremacist Montanan with ties to the antisemitic Aryan Nations, formed one of the first militias. A gun shop owner did the same in Michigan and recruited thousands. Two militia activists in Minnesota were arrested for manufacturing the deadly toxin ricin to use to poison federal agents. Militia groups were spawning in other states.

In Boise, a Republican congresswoman—who won her election with support from Birchers, militia advocates, religious right activists, the home school movement, anti-environmentalists, and remnants of the local Ross Perot outfit—was handing a bullhorn to this rising force of hatred and fear.

A month later, a homemade bomb exploded at the Alfred P. Murrah Federal Building in downtown Oklahoma City, the site of the local BATF office and other government agencies. One hundred sixty-eight people, including nineteen children, were killed. Two days later, the FBI had in custody the bomber, Timothy McVeigh, and his accomplice, Terry Nichols. Both were reported to be white supremacists and anti-government extremists. A government affidavit linked Nichols to the Michigan militia, and media reports noted McVeigh, too, had been part of the militia movement.

Less than a week after the tragedy, Clinton, speaking in Minneapolis, drew a line from the toxic political culture to the bombing. "We hear so many loud and angry voices in America today whose sole goal seems to be to try to keep some people as paranoid as possible and the rest of us all torn up and upset with each other. They spread hate. They leave the impression that, by their very words, that violence is acceptable." The president added, "People like that who want to share our freedoms must know that their bitter words can have consequences."

Conservatives and Republicans cried foul and assailed Clinton for insinuating that tough talk from Limbaugh and others had led to the Oklahoma City massacre. Limbaugh himself called it "irresponsible and vacuous" to associate talk radio with the bombing and accused liberals of exploiting this nightmare "for their own gain." The next day, Clinton softened his approach, saying "reckless speech" from the left or the right "on radio, television or in the movies" can "undermine the fabric of the country."

Yet Clinton had it right the first time. One side of the political spectrum and one of the two national parties had embraced and amplified voices that called for a culture war, compared Democrats to Nazis, fueled conspiracy theories, and excoriated liberals and the government as evildoers bent on destroying the American family, the nation, and Christianity. Limbaugh, Gingrich, Robertson, Falwell, Buchanan, Chenoweth, the NRA, and others were harvesting paranoia and fear among a large slice of the American public. Kevin Phillips, the former Republican strategist who had helped develop the Southern strategy for Nixon, saw the bombing as a problem for the Republicans: "The 'wacko factor' is intensifying...The GOP is failing an old but critical test of U.S. politics: the need for a would-be majority to keep firm control of its fringe groups and radicals."

Republicans showed little interest in reining in the extremists or calming unfounded passions and fears. One only had to look at the NRA, a major player in the GOP's coalition. Days before the bombing, it had sent out a fundraising letter denouncing gun control efforts and decrying federal law enforcement agents as "jack-booted government thugs" who wear "Nazi bucket helmets and black storm trooper uniforms." On the NRA's bulletin board, members posted bomb-making instructions, hurled venom at the BATF, and cited the need to prepare for armed conflict. The NRA, which had funded many of the GOP candidates who had helped flip Congress the previous year, was a haven for the extremist sentiment undergirding the militia movement. At its annual meeting a month after the Oklahoma City attack, a top NRA official felt compelled to tell attendees there were no UN black helicopters flying in the United States.

The bombing shined a spotlight on interactions between the extremist far right and Republicans. Media reports noted that earlier in the year GOP House and Senate members had been advocates for the militias and had expressed concern to the Justice Department about rumors that federal agents were planning a crackdown on the militias. Chenoweth even suggested that government overreach was responsible for McVeigh's dastardly attack: "While we can never condone this, we still must begin to look at the public policies that may be pushing people too far."* She insisted on moving forward with a bill sought by the militia movement that would require federal agents to receive permission from state or local officials before engaging

---

* At his trial, McVeigh would claim that he committed his crimes to "avenge" the Branch Davidians, whom he saw as unjustly killed due to excessive government power.

in law enforcement actions. The *Idaho Statesman* editorial page noted she was bolstering "fringe groups" and was "quickly becoming the poster child for such groups."

When the Clinton administration and the FBI moved to monitor the militias more closely, Dole said they should slow down, and Gingrich warned the nation might be returning to the FBI excesses of the 1960s. Neither criticized the militias. Gingrich even expressed sympathy for those expressing virulent anti-government notions: "There is in rural America... a genuine fear of the federal government and of Washington, DC." Chenoweth chimed in: Americans "have a reason to be afraid of their government." Representative Steve Stockman, a Texas Republican, wrote an article for *Guns & Ammo* endorsing a favorite conspiracy theory of the militia gang: The Clinton administration had mounted the Waco raid to bolster public support for gun control. In protest of the NRA's inflammatory anti-government rhetoric, former President George Bush renounced his membership in the group. No other prominent Republican followed.

Two months after the bombing, Senator Specter held a hearing with militia leaders. It turned into a circus, as these men—one arrived wearing a paramilitary camouflage outfit—defended themselves and propounded one conspiracy theory after another: Japan and the United States had jointly bombed the federal building in Oklahoma; the US government used a weather machine to stir up tornadoes to destabilize the citizenry; Attorney General Reno had hired 2,500 "hit men"; the UN conducted secret military maneuvers in the United States. One witness, John Trochmann, the racist Montana militia leader, issued a statement asserting "the presidency has been turned into a position of dictatorial oppression." Government officials who testified reported that about one-fifth of the nation's approximately 224 militias had connections to neo-Nazi or white supremacist groups, and several Democratic senators denounced the movement. But Specter had handed the conspiracy peddlers what they desired: a high-profile platform.

———

The conspiracism of the right-wing militias soon faded from public attention. But Beltway-focused conspiracy pushers, such as Reed Irvine, the *Washington Times*, Chris Ruddy (now working for the Scaife-owned *Pittsburgh Tribune-Review*), and others continued to concoct and advance groundless Foster theories. The Senate, under GOP control, established a special committee to investigate Whitewater and the handling of Foster's papers. New information trickled out—mainly about what happened in

Foster's office—and none of it challenged the main conclusions of previous investigations. But these leaks kept the fire burning.

Gingrich told one radio interviewer he had asked "several of our congressional chairmen" to "look into" Foster's death. At a July 25, 1995, breakfast meeting with reporters, he remarked, "I'm just not convinced he did [commit suicide]...I believe there are plausible grounds to wonder what happened. There is plausible reason to question whether or not it was a suicide." D'Amato, who was leading the Senate Whitewater investigation, voiced a similar sentiment. A *Time/CNN* poll showed that 35 percent of those surveyed believed Foster committed suicide, 45 percent were uncertain, and 20 percent thought he was murdered. The purveyors of disinformation were finding an audience.

The crazy theories about Foster mutated and expanded. Ambrose Evans-Pritchard, a reporter for the British tabloid *Sunday Telegraph* and a persistent promoter of baseless allegations about Foster, suggested that the deputy White House counsel had been a US intelligence operative. The *New York Post* ran a spurious article—based on allegations by the Scaife-supported troopers—under the headline "Did Foster kill himself in White House parking lot?" After reading the article, Hickman Ewing, Starr's chief deputy, penned a memo positing a speculative scenario in which Foster was killed or shot himself there. The *Washington Post* noted the endless stream of Foster stories "have kept the pressure on independent counsel Kenneth W. Starr to painstakingly reinvestigate Foster's death."

The frustrated Clinton White House composed a 332-page memo outlining what it called the "communication stream of conspiracy commerce." The document noted that "a close connection...exists between Republican elected officials and the right wing conspiracy industry," and it pointed to Gingrich's comments as an example. The memo detailed how conservative operators, such as Floyd Brown, used far-right media outlets, including the *American Spectator*, the *Pittsburgh Tribune-Review*, and the Western Journalism Center (a think tank that bought ads in establishment papers promoting the conspiracy stories), as transmission belts. Allegations planted with these organizations would then receive coverage by more respectable conservative publications—the *Washington Times*, the *Wall Street Journal*, and the *New York Post*—and bounce across the new world of the internet. Then GOP-led congressional committees would announce they were examining the latest twist, and mainstream media would cover this "real" story. "The right wing," the report stated, "has seized upon the internet as a means of communicating its ideas to people. Moreover, evidence exists that Republican [congressional] staffers surf the internet, interacting with extremists in order to exchange ideas and information."

The White House memo characterized Scaife as "the Wizard of Oz behind the Foster Conspiracy Industry," noting he was the major funder of the pillars of this disinformation operation: the *American Spectator*, the *Pittsburgh Tribune-Review*, Accuracy in Media, and the Western Journalism Center. He had recently donated $25,000 to Gingrich's political action committee.

The White House quietly distributed the memo to a few Washington reporters, but this did nothing to change the dynamics it described. Two years later, when the document's existence became publicly known, White House critics would accuse the Clintonites of being paranoid themselves and pushing their own conspiracy theory about conservatives. But the memo had it correct: An anti-Clinton conspiracy machine was working nonstop to create a frenzy of fear and suspicion.

———

As congressional inquiries and Starr's probe of Whitewater ground on, Clinton and Gingrich hurtled toward a dramatic budget showdown. The new House speaker had been busy through much of the year passing most of the Contract with America, though key elements died in the Senate. As for the budget, Gingrich demanded Clinton accept deep spending cuts, including reductions in Medicare and Medicaid, cutbacks in environmental safeguards, and a repeal of Clinton's 1993 tax increase on the wealthy. The speaker threatened a government shutdown if Clinton did not yield. The president professed he shared the GOP desire for a balanced budget, but he insisted on protecting Medicare, Medicaid, education spending, and environmental protections, and Democrats slammed Gingrich and the Republicans for threatening these programs.

No budget measure was passed, and portions of the US government shut down for a week in November—just as Clinton was negotiating a peace deal to end the four-year war in the Balkans.

Gingrich bet that the public would blame Clinton for this dysfunction. But he did not help his case when he publicly stated that one reason why he had shuttered the government was that Clinton had snubbed him during a flight on Air Force One and that he had been forced to exit the plane from the back.

A temporary spending bill was enacted, but another shutdown occurred for three weeks starting in December, until both sides agreed to a budget with modest spending cuts and moderate tax hikes. Clinton was widely seen as the winner of this duel, the reasonable protector of *good* government spending who bested the brash, impetuous, and Grinch-like Gingrich—who had at one point said of Medicare, "We believe it's going to wither on the vine." The speaker looked like an anti-government extremist.

For Clinton, though, trouble loomed. During the first shutdown, he began an extramarital affair with a twenty-two-year-old White House intern named Monica Lewinsky.

―――

On January 23, 1996, Clinton, in the House chamber for the annual State of the Union address, declared, "The era of big government is over." Republicans and Democrats clapped. The president was trying to undercut the standard GOP ploy of vilifying Democrats as out-of-control leftists. Looking ahead to that year's election, Clinton had a plan to use the recent budget battle to sell himself as a centrist who cared about responsible budgeting *and* popular social programs. This was a continuation of his post-1994 strategy of "triangulation"—distancing himself from liberal Democrats, claiming the "dynamic center" (with proposals to reform welfare and support punitive criminal justice policies), and opposing the extremism of Gingrich Republicans.

In his response to Clinton's speech, Bob Dole, still the presumed Republican front-runner, embraced the demonize-the-Democrats strategy that had worked well in past Republican campaigns. He ominously intoned that the president shared "a view of America held by our country's elites," and "the elites in charge don't believe in what the people believe in." He decried Clinton as part of a liberal force that was foreign to real America: "It's as if we went to sleep in one America and woke up in another. It's as though our government, our institutions, and our culture have been hijacked by liberals and are careening dangerously off course." The reviews were awful. Republicans complained the seventy-three-year-old Kansan looked terrible and had come across as passionless and enervated.

Three weeks later, Dole won the Iowa caucuses, but he lost the New Hampshire primary to Pat Buchanan, who had returned to the campaign trail with his far-right, angry-man populist pitch. (Buchanan had to dump six campaign aides when their connections to white supremacist and anti-semitic groups were revealed.) In Delaware and Arizona, Dole came in second behind millionaire publishing executive and flat-tax crusader Steve Forbes, but—with the help of Ralph Reed and the Christian Coalition—he triumphed in South Carolina and cruised to victories in the rest of the primaries.

Dole's candidacy was burdened with multiple problems. He lacked a coherent message. He was a mediocre communicator, often tired. His relationship with the Gingrichian chunk of the party was uneasy at best. He did not excite the NRAers or the Christian Coalition. He had declared his support for repealing Clinton's ban on certain assault weapons, but hardly appeared enthusiastic about it. The same applied to his decision to sign a pledge to not raise taxes. He gave a speech attacking Hollywood for debasing the nation's culture, but he wasn't jazzed to do so. He never seemed to know how far to the right he should go. On an appearance on *Meet the Press*, he insisted, "Bob Dole is not an extremist." A legislator for thirty-five years, Dole couldn't (or wouldn't) wholeheartedly harness the dark energy generated by anger and grievance—and bolstered by the extreme rhetoric of Limbaugh and others—that had won the Republicans control of Congress.

The previous two GOP conventions had been hate-fests. This time, the Republican elders were dead set on distancing themselves from the party's extremists and *not* reviving the 1992 culture war cry.

At the San Diego convention, where the Christian Coalition claimed 25 percent of the delegates were members, the ultrarightists controlled the party platform. They beat back language calling for "tolerance" of those who did not abide by the party's strict antiabortion stance, and they pushed through conservative planks on affirmative action and immigration. Dole, who wanted a more open-minded platform, was furious. He didn't realize that many of the Christian right activists who had pushed their way into the GOP had maneuvered to become Dole delegates. They were committed to vote for him as nominee but not bound to follow his wishes on anything else. Looking to avoid an unruly floor fight, Dole caved to the social conservatives on the assorted platform skirmishes. But the irascible Dole got in one last swing. He remarked he hadn't bothered to read the platform and did not feel "bound" by it.

On a more important front, his team handed prime speaking slots to pro-choice Republican women and prominent Black Republicans. Gingrich was not offered meaningful stage time. In his speech, retired General Colin Powell proclaimed the GOP the "party of inclusion"—more a wish than a fact—and cited his own support for affirmative action and "a woman's right to choose." An AIDS activist spoke. On the third night, Falwell, the promoter of demented crap, presented the closing benediction—a sign the party had not cut off its conspiratorial, intolerant, paranoia-pushing partners on the far right.

During his big speech, Dole attacked Clinton as a tax-and-spender and a lousy choice for leading the military. But he noted Clinton was his "opponent," not his "enemy"—which was not the perspective of much of the party faithful. Dole said, "Let me be the bridge" to the America once known as "a time of tranquility, faith and confidence in action." That is, a bridge to the past.

Two weeks later, Bill Clinton, accepting his party's nomination, slam-dunked Dole on this point: "We do not need to build a bridge to the past; we need to build a bridge to the future." A CNN/*USA Today*/Gallup poll taken after the conventions showed Clinton ahead of Dole, 53 to 36 percent, with Ross Perot, who was running again, at 5 percent.

In the home stretch of the campaign, Dole showed little interest in mobilizing the far right on his behalf. He turned down an invitation to speak at the Christian Coalition's annual conference and sent his running mate, former Representative Jack Kemp. But Dole couldn't escape the Republican necessity of honoring an organization run by the antisemitic conspiracy kook. He dropped by the gathering for an unscheduled appearance and voiced his support for legislation to ban a certain form of late-term abortions.

At the conference, Robertson told the four thousand or so delegates it would take a "miracle from Almighty God" for Dole to win. Still, the coalition planned to hand out tens of millions of its voter guides that would serve as functional endorsements of Dole and GOP congressional candidates. Even less enthusiastic about Dole than the coalition was the NRA. Dole had reversed himself and said that if elected he would let Clinton's ban on assault weapons stand. An enraged NRA decided to not endorse him. But it poured millions of dollars into House and Senate contests to help Republicans.

On the hustings, the dour Dole repeatedly exclaimed, "Where's the outrage?"—a reference to allegations of improper fundraising conducted by the Clintonites and everything else the right despised about the president. It sounded like a get-off-my-lawn cry. But this line hardly matched the anti-Clinton fury that had been whipped up by the far right, its allies within the GOP, and the conservative media.

On Election Day, Clinton won resoundingly, 49 to 41 percent, with the Republicans retaining their majorities on each side of Capitol Hill.

That night, Hillary called Sidney Blumenthal, a friend and reporter who soon would become a senior adviser to the president. "She told me," Blumenthal later recounted, "that with this triumph she believed the pseudo-scandals would recede and the business of governing would be conducted on a more rational basis." The First Lady put aside her customary pessimism. "It's going to be all right," she said.

The convoluted developments of Whitewater never became a defining campaign issue. But the scandal had not gone away—and, with the help of right-wing operators, it would morph into something much worse.

Through the presidential election, the Whitewater hearings had continued, as had headlines. News outlets reported the latest dollops of information—and kept waiting for a smoking gun. Bob Woodward, the dean of Washington investigative reporters, summed up the general media take: "Whitewater and the Clintons' response to it made them look sleazy. Their values were being increasingly called into question."

Early in the year, lost billing records from the Rose Law Firm, where Hillary Clinton and Vince Foster had been partners, mysteriously turned up at the White House. A-ha, Clinton chasers exclaimed. Yet it was unclear what this meant. On the hunt for a Clinton crime he could never find, Starr subpoenaed Hillary Clinton to appear before his Whitewater grand jury. In June 1996, the Senate Whitewater committee released a 673-page final report. It alleged "a pattern of obstruction" and claimed senior White House officials—directed by Hillary Clinton—tried "to block career law enforcement investigators from conducting a thorough investigation of a unique and disturbing event—the first suicide of a very senior U.S. official in almost fifty years." But the report unveiled no firm evidence of illegality. Senate Democrats said errors were made but nothing sinister or criminal occurred.

After the 1996 election, as Whitewater sputtered along, the Clinton administration had to contend with another controversy, this one triggered by the prodigious—and, at times, improper—fundraising the Democratic Party had engaged in during the presidential campaign. Senate hearings revealed sordid campaign-finance abuses (including those of the GOP), but they did not yield evidence to back up yet another right-wing Clinton conspiracy theory: that China had used illicit contributions to buy influence in the Clinton White House.

As Clinton's second term proceeded—he negotiated a new nuclear treaty with Russia and worked out a budget agreement with GOP legislators—the president could not break free of the scandals. A historic Supreme Court decision in May 1997 ruled the Paula Jones civil lawsuit against Clinton could move ahead. (That meant Jones's attorneys could seek out women who might have been harassed by Clinton to try to prove a pattern of misconduct.) In June, the *Washington Post* revealed Starr was investigating Clinton's alleged extramarital activity. The independent counsel's office justified this by asserting it was pursuing possible witnesses who might have learned of information related to Whitewater.

Behind the scenes, the Council for National Policy, that collection of right-wing leaders, Republican officials, and extremists, schemed to orchestrate an impeachment of Clinton. In the group now were key players pushing the Foster conspiracy and other extreme anti-Clinton allegations: Reed Irvine, former congressman Bill Dannemeyer, and Joseph Farah, who ran the Western Journalism Center. Republican establishment bigwigs on the council included Jack Kemp, former Attorney General Edwin Meese, and Bush White House chief of staff John Sununu. The CNP remained plugged into the Republican congressional caucus through the memberships of Representative Tom DeLay, the powerful, Clinton-despising House majority whip, and a dozen other GOP representatives and senators.

At a private meeting in Montreal, CNP members pondered how to grease the way toward impeachment—and even drew up resolutions of impeachment. Two months later, John Whitehead, a CNP member, took over as Paula Jones's attorney. He had founded the Rutherford Institute, a right-wing legal shop that defended religious freedom cases, and was an advocate of Christian Reconstructionism, having once written that Christians should take control of political parties and that "all of civil affairs and government, including law, should be based upon principles found in the Bible," as interpreted by fundamentalist theologians.

Meanwhile, a small coterie of young conservative lawyers connected to the right-wing Federalist Society, a band that would come to be called "the elves," was providing advice to Jones's legal team. They hoped her lawsuit could set a perjury trap for Clinton by forcing the president into a deposition in which he would falsely deny extramarital sexual activity and become vulnerable to a criminal perjury charge. At the same time, a Christian telemarketing firm, in an operation encouraged by the CNP, was calling people who had purchased the scurrilous *Clinton Chronicles* video Falwell had hawked and was asking them to support impeachment—and to send money.

It was a tangle of anti-Clinton initiatives: Republican-run hearings, the Falwell video, the CNP scheming, the elves—all conniving to bring down Clinton through a combination of justifiable criticism, baseless accusations, assorted conspiracy theories, and shadowy legal machinations. The cause was not helped when Starr in October released his report on Foster's death. Its conclusion was the same as previous investigations: suicide in Fort Marcy Park. Anti-Clintonistas feared that Starr's inquiry had stalled and that the Clintons were off the hook.

The internet lit up on January 17, 1998, when the *Drudge Report*, a gossipy, right-leaning, loose-with-the-facts website, reported that *Newsweek* had "killed" a "blockbuster report" on Clinton's "sex relationship" with a White House intern. The following day it revealed Monica Lewinsky's name. The site next reported federal investigators—meaning Starr's team—possessed taped conversations of Lewinsky discussing intimate details of this affair. On January 21, the *Washington Post* disclosed Starr had expanded his investigation to cover the Lewinsky matter and the question of whether Clinton had encouraged Lewinsky to falsely deny their relationship in an affidavit filed in the Paula Jones case. In a television interview, Clinton insisted, "There is no improper relationship" with Lewinsky.

This bombshell—engineered by the elves and Linda Tripp, a frustrated and angry busybody who had worked at the White House—would dominate American politics for the following year. The political culture war that right-wingers and Republicans had waged for decades became distilled in the battle over the Clinton affair. Here was evidence—illicit sex in the Oval Office—that relativistic liberalism was corrupt and anathema to the fundamental values of America. It was proof to support their contention that Clinton was dishonest and not a legitimate leader for the nation—and that he and his tribe did not deserve power.

The seedy drama gripped the nation and dominated the media. The nascent conservative Fox News gorged itself on this salacious story and was rewarded with soaring ratings. Clinton denied the affair for months before acknowledging it in grand jury testimony. From the start, there was talk of impeachment. Republicans claimed the issue was lying and the rule of law—not sex—but many Americans found that difficult to believe and saw the scandal as a brazen Republican power play to overthrow a Democratic administration. Sidney Blumenthal, now a senior Clinton adviser, captured this sentiment a few years later, writing that the episode was "triggered by an Italianate conspiracy—an intricate, covert, amoral operation bent on power. The plotters brandished the law as a stiletto to try to destroy a president they considered illegitimate."

A week into the scandal, Hillary Clinton—falsely assured by her husband the allegation was not true—declared the president was the victim of a "politically motivated" prosecutor allied with a "vast right-wing conspiracy." She was widely mocked for being paranoid. But she was largely correct: A crew of right-wing lawyers and activists had plotted against her husband and collaborated secretly with a zealous and conservative independent counsel, and they had succeeded in turning a significant personal misdeed into a legal issue that threatened Clinton's presidency. Over a year later, conservative columnist Ann Coulter, one of the elves, would acknowledge she had been part of "a small, intricately knit right-wing conspiracy" to bring down the president.

For years, the right's Clinton attack machine had not succeeded. The preachers playing to paranoia. The Clinton crazies marketing conspiracy theories about Foster's death, drug dealing in Arkansas, a string of murders. The Whitewater and campaign finance investigations. Gingrich's endeavors to depict Clinton and the Democrats as "the enemy of normal Americans." Limbaugh's relentless bashing. After all that, Clinton was still president—and popular. But the relentless Whitewater drumbeat had begat the Lewinsky probe. Now the get-Clinton task was up to Starr and his lawyers.

———

In September, Starr sent his final report on the Clinton-Lewinsky matter—445 pages full of lurid and mostly unnecessary details—to the House of Representatives. It listed eleven possible grounds for impeachment. (Brett Kavanaugh, an associate counsel for Starr and future Supreme Court justice, helped draft the report.) Republicans rushed to make the document public and moved forward with impeachment. In the midterm elections, the GOP spent $37 million on ads related to the scandal. One spot featured upset mothers saying, "What did you tell your kids?"

The public didn't care. Since the start of the scandal, Clinton consistently scored high in public opinion polls that indicated Americans overall did not fancy impeachment. The 1998 midterm elections demonstrated this: The House Democrats gained five seats, the Senate balance stayed the same. House Republicans disappointed with the results moved against Gingrich, who had been fined $300,000 for his own ethics violation and who, it was widely known on Capitol Hill, was engaging in an extramarital liaison with a House staffer. He quickly resigned the speakership. Soon after, Representative Robert Livingston, presumably the next House speaker, announced his resignation, as allegations that he had been in an extramarital tryst circulated.

The election results were a clear sign the public did not support the political prosecution (or persecution) of Clinton, who had settled his case with Paula Jones for an $850,000 payment with no admission of wrongdoing.

Yet House Republicans pressed ahead. Blumenthal later observed that this fight "was, ultimately, a struggle about the identity of the country." He saw it as "the climax" of the "conservatives' culture war." Die-hard Republicans shared that view. During House impeachment hearings, Representative Bob Barr, a fierce right-wing Republican from Georgia, raised the evergreen GOP talking point that Democrats were not *real* Americans, declaring, "I realize there are two Americas out there...Real Americans know that perjury amounts to impeachment."

In response to Barr's remarks, well-known attorney Alan Dershowitz, an opponent of Clinton's impeachment, sent a letter to Congress noting that Barr had been involved with the Council of Conservative Citizens, a Confederacy-celebrating, white supremacist group in the South that had evolved from the segregationist White Citizens' Council. Soon news stories would show that Senate Majority Leader Trent Lott and other Republicans had also been supporters of this racist organization. In 1992, Lott had delivered the keynote speech at its national board meeting and said, "The people in this room stand for the right principles and the right philosophy." No Republican proposed Barr and Lott be booted out of office for supporting racist extremists.*

At one point during the impeachment fight, Representative Tom DeLay, the conservative from Texas, described the overarching battle as "relativism versus absolute truth"—a core component of the far right's culture war. A few years later, he told a church gathering that God used him to promote "a biblical world view" in politics and that he had championed impeachment because Clinton advocated "the wrong world view."

This was not about sex or lies. The Clinton impeachment was the culmination of decades of Republican efforts to portray Democrats and liberals as un-Americans and a fundamental threat to the nation and its *true* citizens—to divide the nation into two camps, one righteous and deserving to hold the reins of power, the other dangerously misguided and wicked. This mission depended on generating and appealing to apprehension, division, and tribalism among voters. For the conservatives of the 1990s, Clinton was the enemy within. He was no Red (or maybe he was), but, more important, he had befouled the nation; his odious personal behavior and his political liberalism were one and the same. Both were absolute offenses

---

* Three years later, Lott, celebrating Strom Thurmond's one hundredth birthday, would say of Thurmond's 1948 presidential bid as a segregationist Dixiecrat, "We voted for him. We're proud of it. And if the rest of the country had followed our lead, we wouldn't have had all these problems over all these years."

against the right's idea of America. For the conservatives to win their culture war, he had to be expelled.

On December 19, the House impeached Clinton, mainly along partisan lines. Two days later, a *Washington Post*/ABC News poll charted his popularity at 67 percent. The subsequent Senate trial was a dreary affair, with many Republican senators, let alone the Democrats, unhappy to have been forced to conduct this proceeding. After a month of speeches and presentations, the Senate acquitted Clinton.

Was the right's culture war finally done? Had the conservatives—the preachers, the New Rightists, the conspiracy shoppers, the right-wing talkers, and their pals in the GOP—lost? As the impeachment battle was coming to an end, prominent conservative William Bennett published a book that captured the frustration of the far right: *The Death of Outrage: Bill Clinton and the Assault on American Ideals.*

Four days after the trial, Paul Weyrich, a founder of the New Right, one of the instigators of the Moral Majority, and a CNP member, gave up. In an "open letter to conservatives," he proclaimed his side had been defeated: "I no longer believe that there is a moral majority. I do not believe that a majority of Americans actually share our values...I believe that we probably have lost the culture war."

Weyrich lamented that "if there really were a moral majority out there, Bill Clinton would have been driven out of office months ago." He advised his fellow social conservatives to keep voting but to withdraw from the world of perverted values: "I think we are caught up in a cultural collapse of historic proportions, a collapse so great it simply overwhelms politics." Even though far-rightists had won elections, fought their way to a seat at the table of the powerful by exploiting grievances, resentments, biases, and unfounded notions held by many Americans, and now possessed tremendous influence over the Republican Party, they still had not seen their agenda adopted on the issues they most cared about: abortion, gay rights, school prayer, pornography, and sex and violence in the media. "In terms of society," Weyrich bemoaned, "in general, we have lost."

His verdict was stark: "Politics itself has failed."

CHAPTER 18

Fortunate Son

George W. Bush had them right where he wanted them. He stood before 3,500 of Pat Robertson's troops on the first day of October in 1999 and showed them who was boss.

For months, the Republican Texas governor, the oldest of former President Bush's four sons, had been campaigning for president and selling himself as a champion of "compassionate conservatism." Some conservatives frowned at his catchphrase, grousing it implied that good, old-fashioned conservatism was not compassionate. But Bush and his strategist Karl Rove figured they needed to rebrand conservatism to distance Bush from the harshness of the Gingrich years and the viciousness of the Clinton wars. This meant recalibrating the relationship between the Republican Party and the extremists of the right, particularly the Christian Coalition.

Not all Republicans felt that way. Most of the declared GOP presidential wannabes who showed up at the Washington Hilton Hotel for the coalition's tenth annual Road to Victory conference eagerly tossed red meat to the assembled. The party was still happy to suck up to Robertson and his minions, no matter his well-established pattern of deploying hateful rhetoric and nutty and antisemitic conspiracy theories. The previous year Robertson had decried Disney World in Orlando for holding a gay pride day and warned God would seek revenge by visiting a hurricane upon those heathens. He prophesized: "It'll bring about terrorist bombs; it'll bring earthquakes, tornadoes and possibly a meteor." No meteors struck the Magic Kingdom.

At this gathering, millionaire publisher Steve Forbes promised, if elected president, he would appoint only antiabortion judges. Elizabeth Dole, the wife of Bob Dole who had served in the cabinets of Presidents Bush and Reagan, called for school prayer. Gary Bauer, a prominent social conservative, railed against gay marriage.

Bush the Younger joined the parade of GOP contenders legitimizing Robertson. But in his speech he did not refer to gay rights, school prayer, and other dear-to-the-heart matters for this crowd. He dutifully voiced his opposition to abortion but only in passing. That was unlikely to appease antiabortion advocates appalled by Bush's statement earlier in the year— which was nothing more than an acknowledgment of political reality— that "America is not ready to ban abortion." They also were troubled by his refusal to make opposition to abortion a litmus test for judicial appointments. Yet Bush hadn't come to Robertson's event to whip up the fundamentalist base of the GOP. Quite the opposite. His message to the man who had once called his father a useful idiot for Satan was straightforward: You are not the tail that's going to wag this dog.

Bush was running as a conservative who was moderate in tone. He shared the right's opposition to abortion, its demand for limited government and, of course, its passion for tax cuts and deregulation. But he aimed to signal to voters he was no hater, no bosom buddy of extremists or fringe fanatics, no crusader in a brutal culture war.

With the ultimate in political name recognition, polls showing him fifty points ahead of his nearest GOP rival, tons of campaign cash from corporate funders and special interests, and endorsements from scores of Republican governors and members of Congress, Bush was the front-runner by a Texas mile. Some old-guard conservatives feared he was a closeted moderate like his daddy. They were wrong. But whatever his internal ideological proclivity, political insiders believed Bush represented the party's best chance of recapturing the White House from the Democrats. His path to victory was to campaign as a centrist and to nudge his party a step—maybe half a step—away from the zealots of the right. Looking to reel in independents and moderate Democrats, he wouldn't kowtow to the extremists, the racists, the haters. At least, that was the plan.

Robertson didn't seem to mind. After two terms of Clinton, the wild-eyed conspiracy theorist had adopted a pragmatic mindset. He was willing to make allowances and provide dispensation to Bush for eschewing the purist rhetoric of the fundamentalists. After all, his own Christian Coalition had been through a tough stretch. Membership and fundraising had dropped in recent years. Pundits openly wondered if it still had any juice. The Bush campaign, with its fat bank account and establishment support, looked like a locomotive that would roll over the other GOP candidates. Bush was selling inevitability; Robertson was buying.

The televangelist told one reporter he believed Bush, who had hired Ralph Reed, the former Christian Coalition executive director, as a top adviser, was "committed to the [social conservative] agenda" but was "aware that he needs to be portrayed as a centrist candidate." At a press conference, he called Bush "worthy of the support" of the Christian Coalition. It appeared that an *understanding* had been reached that would allow Bush and the GOP to sidestep that ever-tricky issue of the party's relationship with the intolerant and fringe-ish far right and escape the taint of extremism.

Yet Bush would soon need the extremists.

———

In these pre-primary days, Bush played both sides. In a speech to a conservative think tank, he jabbed at social conservatives and their apocalyptic warnings, saying, "On social issues, my party has painted an image of America slouching toward Gomorrah." He also took a poke at Republicans who professed "a disdain for government" and fixated on economics "to the exclusion of all else." He was blunt: His party didn't care enough about the needy. He criticized congressional Republicans for trying to "balance the budget on the backs of the poor." Conservatives howled. Maybe Bush was a dreaded moderate. Rush Limbaugh huffed, "No conservative running for president would leave his philosophical brothers and sisters dying on the congressional battlefield the way Bush did." He added, "Who wants a Republican moderate for president?" Weyrich popped off: "People will now see that he is a moderate and I believe they will begin to move away from him."

Yet days after lambasting social conservatives for being overwrought and Republicans for being Scrooge-like, Bush jetted to his home state to attend an important event: a meeting in San Antonio with the Council for National Policy, where he delivered a speech behind closed doors, no press allowed. Rumors, though, abounded. According to one, Bush had vowed before the group of far-rightists that no matter what he stated publicly he would indeed only select antiabortion-rights judges for the Supreme Court. Months later, when it was revealed that Bush's remarks had been recorded, journalists and the Democratic Party demanded the audiotape be released. The Bush campaign and the CNP refused. What Bush told the movers and shakers of the right would never be disclosed.

In the weeks after his CNP chat, Bush tossed a few delicious bones to the Christian right. He declared he would "probably not" meet with a group of gay Republicans. During a debate, when asked to name his favorite "political philosopher or thinker," Bush, who routinely talked about the "born-again" experience he had when he was forty, replied, "Christ, because he changed my heart."

Campaigning in Iowa ahead of the GOP caucuses—where an estimated

40 percent of the participants would be Christian conservatives—Bush steered clear of policy pronouncements regarding abortion, but he repeatedly referred to his own personal faith and praised Christian charities. He noted he read the Bible every day and it "influenced me a lot." Asked about evolution, he neither affirmed nor refuted it, saying, "The verdict is still out on how God created the earth."

Pitching his piety, Bush placed first in the January 24 Iowa caucuses with 41 percent of the vote; Forbes was a distant second. Bush's tightrope walk was succeeding. He could attract social conservatives without slinging far-right rhetoric that would turn off moderate voters. But a week later, Arizona Senator John McCain, who was running as a straight-talking, reform-minded maverick, thrashed Bush in New Hampshire, 49 to 30 percent, drawing overwhelming support from independents, who were permitted to vote in that state's GOP primary. Now it looked as if the South Carolina contest in eighteen days would be the make-or-break moment for each man. Bush could no longer merely play footsie with social conservatives. To conquer the Palmetto State, he would have to rely on the right's racists, bigots, and conspiracy-theory-pushing dirty tricksters.

———

The day after being walloped in New Hampshire, Bush hurried to South Carolina to give a speech at Bob Jones University, the citadel of extremist fundamentalism. This was a plea to evangelical Christians for help. In his hour of political need, Bush was wrapping his arms around a racist institution that still banned interracial dating and marriage and that regarded Catholicism as Lucifer's cult. Bob Jones Jr. had once called the Pope an "archpriest of Satan, a deceiver and an anti-christ." And Bob Jones III, the current president, had excoriated Reagan as "a traitor to God's people" for picking George H. W. Bush—whom he assailed as a "devil"—as his running mate. This was hardly the spot for a candidate who preached compassionate conservativism and who sold himself as "a uniter not a divider." In his remarks, Bush said nary a word in opposition to the school's racist policy and anti-Catholic bigotry.

Afterward, a Bush campaign spokesperson defended Bush's visit in the cynical fashion of a political operative: "This is a school that has a lot of conservative voters, and it's a common stop on the campaign trail." Veteran GOP strategist Bill Kristol had a different take: "It's one thing to lurch to the right. It's another thing to lurch back 60 years. You could make the case that 'compassionate conservatism' died Feb. 2 when Bush appeared at Bob Jones U." (For weeks, Bush would refuse to express regret for the visit, and he declared, "I don't make any apologies for what I do on the campaign trail." He later reversed himself and apologized for not "disassociating myself from [the] anti-Catholic sentiments and racial prejudice" of the school.)

Bush, who had sought to separate himself from the hardcore Christian right, now needed Robertson's forces to beat back McCain. Robertson, Reed, and Roberta Combs, the executive director of the Christian Coalition, worked the phones, calling social conservatives throughout South Carolina and urging them to support Bush. It was repeatedly pointed out to Christian rightists that McCain had dared to say that he would let his fifteen-year-old daughter have the final say about an abortion in the case of an unwanted pregnancy and that he had once noted he was not in favor of overturning the Roe v. Wade decision.

The coalition fired off a mailing proclaiming "disturbing facts" about McCain, including that he was supposedly liberal on abortion. (He wasn't.) Falwell and James Dobson, the head of Focus on the Family, released statements blasting McCain. Falwell said McCain had "sold out to the liberal element of the party." Dobson accused McCain of committing adultery and assailed him for his involvement in the Keating Five campaign finance scandal of the late 1980s.

The candidate who liked to talk about his good heart was depending on homophobic religious fanatics and a full-fledged conspiracist to keep his presidential hopes alive. Bush also recruited Senator Strom Thurmond, the onetime segregationist, to assist his cause, and he stated he had no problem with the Confederate flag flying over the statehouse. (McCain went back and forth on this issue, landing in the same spot as Bush. Two months later—*after* the primary—he would apologize for not sharing his true opinion: The flag should come down.)

The South Carolina fight would become legendary in political circles as one of the sleaziest contests in modern American politics. A professor of Bible studies at Bob Jones University zapped out an email claiming McCain "chose to sire children without marriage." A letter assailing McCain for having once called the Confederate flag "a symbol of racism and slavery" was mass-mailed to tens of thousands of conservatives from an unknown political action committee. (Much later it was revealed that the person behind this PAC was a Bush ally.) A flyer went around that accused McCain of having a Black child. Another featured a McCain family photograph that showed a brown-skinned young girl. (She was an orphan from Bangladesh whom McCain and his wife, Cindy, had adopted.) A rumor was spread that Cindy was a drug addict. There was more: *McCain had slept with sex workers and given his wife VD...He was a traitor when he was a POW in Vietnam...*

*He had been brainwashed and turned into a Manchurian Candidate...Cindy
had mob ties.*

It was a toxic mix of innuendo and conspiracy theories. Reports circulated of anti-McCain telephone push polls in which the caller would make a
derogatory statement about McCain—it could be a scurrilous allegation—
and ask the recipient if that might affect how she or he votes. One story went
around of a caller asking, "Would you be more or less likely to vote for John
McCain if you knew he had fathered an illegitimate black child?" It was
tough for reporters to nail down much of this—and who was responsible.
Operatives of the state GOP machine backing Bush? Bob Jones activists?
Freebooters?

The Bush campaign, not surprisingly, said, *It's not us*. But Bush and Rove
did not condemn the vicious smear campaign or call for its cessation. Plenty
of political observers in South Carolina assumed a nod and a wink had
come from the Bush camp.

The Christian Coalition, Bob Jones University, the shadowy smear-
spreaders, Thurmond, the bare-knuckled machine schemers, Confederate
flag lovers—they came through for Bush. He triumphed in South Carolina
with 53 percent of the vote to McCain's 42 percent. Bush, who had tried
to distance himself from conservative extremists, had hooked up with the
party's intolerant wing to save his campaign.

Republican strategists fretted aloud that Bush had too tightly bound himself to the zealots and haters and would pay for that in the general election.
"He makes it much harder with these Bob Jones and Pat Robertson episodes," complained Rich Bond, a former chair of the Republican National
Committee.

McCain went into overdrive. In a speech at a high school in Virginia
Beach, Robertson's hometown, the day before that state's primary, the former POW blasted Robertson and Falwell as "agents of intolerance" and
warned the GOP against "pandering to the outer reaches of American politics." He called Bush a "Pat Robertson Republican" and proclaimed, "We
are the party of Abraham Lincoln, not Bob Jones." This was tough stuff—an
attempt to delegitimize Bush and his religious right compatriots in the eyes
of moderate Republican voters ahead of the next batch of primaries. McCain
pointed out he was not critical of conservative religious voters; his beef was
with "a few of their self-appointed leaders." But this was more than a rebuke
of a few men. Robertson, Falwell and the Christian right had powered GOP
politics for more than two decades, and McCain assailed this partnership.

No top Republican contender had called out the party's extremists in such a sharp manner perhaps since Rockefeller did so with the Birchers in 1964.

Bush pounced and accused McCain of dividing "people into camps" and playing on "religious fears." Rove—sticking to his rule of turning incoming criticism into outgoing assaults—slammed McCain: "This is a reprehensible attempt to bring religion into American politics in a very ugly way." Political scientist Mark Rozell observed, "It's a risky strategy [for McCain] because the Christian conservatives are a huge part of the Republican voting base in Virginia."

McCain's aides called this speech the "defining moment" of the campaign. The next day, their candidate sharpened the blade. Referring to Falwell and Robertson, McCain told reporters on his campaign bus, "To stand up to the forces of evil, that's my job, and I can't steer the Republican Party if those two individuals have the influence they have on the party today." For calling the pair "evil," McCain was forced to apologize, but he stood by his previous speech.

Defining moment—perhaps, but not in the way McCain and his aides wished. He lost Virginia by nine points. After that, Bush bagged every primary except for a few in New England. The "agents of intolerance" and the "forces of evil" prevailed. Bush demonstrated that the religious right, racists, homophobes, and Confederate flag fans were instrumental elements of the party. "What used to be outside is now in," remarked Kevin Phillips, the onetime Republican strategist.

———

After enlisting and pandering to the far reaches of the party to preserve his political hide, Bush had no hesitation in jilting them. He would spend the rest of the campaign presenting himself as an amiable, reasonable, and nonthreatening conservative who wanted the American Dream to touch every heart. A uniter not a divider—he reminded voters repeatedly. He welcomed the endorsement of moderate Republicans, including Colin Powell, and didn't seem to mind the barbs from social conservative leaders who continued to question his commitment to their causes. Such squabbles probably helped Bush by distracting attention from his wintertime flirtation with Robertson and Bob Jones University.

When a leaked video showed an NRA leader bragging that with a Bush win "we'll have a president where we work out of their office," Bush took the opportunity to indignantly assert he was no puppet of the gun group. He also noted that NRA leader Wayne LaPierre "may have gone too far" when he claimed that President Clinton purposefully accepted a level of gun violence to shape the gun debate in the Democrats' favor. Yet Bush, whose policy stances largely lined up with the NRA's wishes, welcomed the group's support.

At the NRA's annual convention, its president, actor Charlton Heston, revved up the extreme rhetoric. Holding a musket over his head, he exclaimed to a crowd of twenty thousand cheering delegates, "Our gun rights are truly in peril...Who wins the election will determine our freedoms into the next century." The group vowed to spend between $10 million and $15 million to defeat Vice President Al Gore, the presumptive Democratic nominee, and other Democrats. It declined to endorse Bush, but given the bad press the NRA had received in the 1990s for seeming to encourage extremist violence, this was probably best for Bush. The NRA's on-the-ground organizing was more important than its stamp of approval.

When the GOP convention in Philadelphia rolled around in the summer, social conservatives were willing to hold their tongues. Bush was anti-abortion, promised tax cuts for families, and vowed to bring "honor and integrity" to the presidency. He had selected Dick Cheney, a tried-and-true conservative and abortion foe, as his running mate. Even better, his wife, Lynne Cheney, was a critic of liberal feminism and academia.

If Bush wasn't screaming for an immediate end to abortion and wailing about the threat of gay rights, the Christian rightists could live with that, given he was their best shot at tossing the Democrats out of the White House that Clinton had defiled. No harsh talk of a culture war? They could accept that, too. Bush said he wanted to avoid a repeat of the 1992 convention and its "negative tone" and "divisive message." The rightists would not get in the way of Bush's attempt to frame himself as a "different kind of Republican."

In a way, this was a sign of success for the Christian right. It had become part of the GOP establishment. Its people were delegates, party leaders. That prompted pragmatism. The Republican Party was *their* party, and they had a big stake in seeing its nominee succeed. Combs explained it simply to a reporter: "We now have a place at the table. We are a part of what is going on. Our role is to go into the convention united and to come out of the convention united." Falwell told the *New York Times*, "Our crowd needs to get into the battle, keep their mouths shut and help this man win."

The Bush team nixed convention appearances by Robertson, Forbes, Bauer, and other social conservative favorites. Instead, the event featured Powell, national security expert Condoleezza Rice, professional wrestler Dwayne "the Rock" Johnson, and performances from Black and Latino singers and dancers. "Where did the meanness go?" *New York Times* reporter E. J. Dionne Jr. wondered. For the past six years, the Democrats had depicted the Gingrich-headed GOP as a nasty and greedy outfit slashing programs for the needy and the elderly, shutting down the government, spreading noxious rhetoric, and mounting cutthroat attacks and puritanical crusades against Clinton and his party. That was all off the agenda this week.

At the convention, the Christian Coalition held a rally for members and supporters. About three thousand people turned out. Robertson sniffed at news stories claiming the convention demonstrated the religious right had lost its clout. Wait for the fall, he said. The plan—despite the coalition being $1.5 million in debt—was to hand out 75 million voter guides that would favor Bush and to operate registration and get out the vote drives through churches. At the convention, Falwell talked up Bush, claiming, "I haven't sensed this much excitement among religious conservatives since Ronald Reagan."

In his acceptance speech, Bush noted "good people" disagree on abortion. He cited his adherence to a "compassionate conservatism" that serves "justice and opportunity." He did not bash government. He hailed the civil rights movement. "I believe in tolerance, not in spite of my faith, but because of it," he told a crowd of delegates that included many who distinctly opposed tolerance. (Some delegates had protested the speech of Representative Jim Kolbe, the only openly gay Republican in Congress.)

Bush did not sound like the warriors of the right who railed against big government, Democrats, liberalism, secularism, feminists, gays, and all the other forces supposedly destroying the nation: "I will not attack a part of this country because I want to lead the whole of it." Yet he channeled the right's disgust with the Clinton years, vowing to uphold the "dignity" of the presidency. It was a bravura performance. He addressed the far right's animosities and apprehensions without employing its incendiary rhetoric. The Republican Party had tamed the extremists within its ranks and figured out how to exploit them without bearing their blemish.

After the convention. Bush skipped the annual Christian Coalition conference. Though Robertson had in recent months managed to limit his overheated and occasionally bonkers oratory, he did on the final night of the conference return to form and claim that an alliance of feminists, gays, atheists, and communists were ruining the nation. And he was ready to send out those pro-Bush voter guides. As the New York Times reported, his group, the NRA, and assorted antiabortion organizations were "pouring millions of dollars into phone banks, commercials and voter drives" to assist Bush.

———

With the help of the Christian Coalition, the NRA, and other right-wing groups, Bush reached a virtual tie with Gore in the election. On Election

Day, the vice president received 530,000 more votes than Bush (half a percentage point of the national tally). But the Electoral College results hinged
on Florida, where Bush led by 1,784 votes. The next five weeks would be
filled with various recounts and lawsuits, with Bush's slim margin of victory narrowing. And it would be the action of a mob—and the threat of
violence—that helped determine who would lead the United States.

Two weeks into the postelection mess, Miami–Dade County began a
recount of 10,750 ballots. The Gore campaign believed this particular review
could benefit it the most. The Bush team took fierce measures to stop it.
Brad Blakeman, a Bush campaign operative dispatched to Miami to combat
Democratic efforts, was running messaging operations asserting the Democrats, by requesting recounts, were trying to overturn a national election.
Representative Lincoln Diaz-Balart, a Florida Republican, complained,
"The presidential election is being stolen." Cuban Americans in Miami who
supported Bush held protests that equated recounts with a political coup.
Rick Sanchez, a local Cuban American television news anchor (who voted
for Bush), later said Republicans were "manipulating the situation."

When Miami–Dade County workers began the hand count on the eigh-
teenth floor of the downtown government center, a crowd of irate protesters
gathered outside. They had been urged to come by Republican phone banks
and Radio Mambi, an influential Spanish-language station in Miami. Then
a mob of angry Bush supporters entered the building and began banging
on the doors that led to the counting room. "Stop the count!" they shouted.
"Stop the fraud!" They tried to push their way into the room. County workers feared this melee could become violent.

This was not a protest mounted by local citizens. The demonstrators
were GOP operatives flown to Florida to win the recount street battle. They
included Capitol Hill staffers, Bush-Cheney campaign workers, and lobby-
ists. "All seasoned operatives," Blakeman later said. They had been deployed
by Blakeman to disrupt the recount.

When asked by reporters to identify themselves, the protesters didn't tell
the truth. One who was an aide to a New Mexico congresswoman said she
was a Virginian on vacation in Miami. Staffers for House Majority Whip
Tom DeLay and Senate Majority Leader Trent Lott were part of the manu-
factured swarm. A reporter overheard a protester saying he had been in contact with Rove. According to the *Wall Street Journal*'s Paul Gigot, who was
on the scene, when the recount was moved to a room with computerized
ballot-scanning machines that could speed up the count, Representative
John Sweeney, a New York Republican at the site, issued a command to the
GOP ruffians: "Shut it down." (Years later, Roger Stone, the notorious dirty

trickster, would claim credit for organizing what would become known as the Brooks Brothers Riot, but Blakeman insisted Stone was "full of shit" and had nothing to do with it.)

When a local Democratic official showed up to obtain a sample ballot, the protesters accused him of stealing one of the votes under examination. They shoved and pushed him, and police had to escort him to safety. Another Democratic observer claimed he was punched and kicked. Meanwhile, the faux demonstrators continued to demand the recount be halted and tried to storm into the inspection room. People were trampled, kicked, and punched. One security officer believed this disturbance "could escalate out of control." At that point, David Leahy, the supervisor of elections, suspended the review and shortly after that called off the entire Miami-Dade recount. He told reporters that the protests had factored in the decision, though later he maintained the canvassing board had not been intimidated by the GOP mob.

The scheme—and the threat of violence—did the trick. "It was well thought-out and preplanned," Blakeman boasted years later. GOP hooligans in khakis had perhaps won Bush the presidency.

Over the next three weeks, recounts in other counties dropped Bush's margin to 537 votes. More legal wrangling ensued until December 12, when five justices of the US Supreme Court, each appointed by a Republican president, issued an unprecedented and controversial decision that shut down the remaining recounts. The election was over.

Though Bush had tried to win the election by appealing to moderates, he had lost 65 percent of the secular vote and had needed the Robertson army to succeed. As Robertson noted, "Without us, I do not believe that George Bush would be sitting in the White House." Yet four million registered evangelical voters had not bothered to go to the polls. (It's possible some were turned off by the late-breaking revelation that Bush had been arrested for driving under the influence of alcohol in 1976.) Looking ahead to 2004, Karl Rove took note of these absent voters.

———

Bush's presidency paid off for the Robertson-Falwell crowd. He reinstated a ban on US aid to international organizations that performed abortions. He halted federal funding for new stem cell research. He created an office that would hand out millions of dollars to religious groups that supplied social services—a policy some legal experts criticized as unconstitutional. Robertson's Operation Blessing received a $1.5 million, three-year, faith-based grant.

Bush appointed many evangelical Christians to jobs. He selected John Ashcroft, a darling of the religious right, to be his attorney general. His education secretary would declare his preference for Christian schools. His interior secretary had previously supported discredited gay reparative therapy. Kay Coles James, a former vice president of the Family Research Council and a former dean at Pat Robertson's Regent University, was placed in charge of the Office of Personnel Management. (A few years earlier, she had published a book in which she likened homosexuality to drug addiction, adultery, alcoholism, and "anything else sinful.") Bush named Christian right activists to scientific advisory panels. He appointed to his AIDS advisory council an antigay activist who had called homosexuality "a sinful death-style" and advocated efforts to "rescue the homosexual" through Christian proselytization. (The nomination was eventually withdrawn.) The Reverend Lou Sheldon, a virulent antigay crusader, became an adviser to a White House summit on faith-based initiatives.

White House aides regularly attended Weyrich's weekly meetings of Christian right strategists. When the Bush administration held an HIV Prevention Summit, it invited representatives of religious right organizations to join public health experts at the event. These social conservatives described homosexuality as a mental illness, called for a resolution opposing homosexuality, and proposed pulling all federal dollars from HIV prevention efforts and spending the money on programs that supposedly turned gay men straight. The White House also supported and funded abstinence and marriage-protection programs operated and advocated by the religious right that had lousy track records.

Bush's main initiatives were a tax bill with reductions largely tilted toward the wealthy and a controversial education reform bill increasing the emphasis on standardized testing. But he conveyed policy legitimacy upon the Christian right, including its antigay fanatics, its science deniers, and its charlatans. No administration had been as overtly evangelical. Weyrich, who two years earlier had advised social conservatives to give up on politics, gushed to the New York Times, "The [Bush White House] effort to communicate with conservatives and to understand our concerns and address our concerns and involve us in the process is the best of any of the Republican administrations, including Ronald Reagan."

A few months into his presidency, when the Council for National Policy held its twentieth-anniversary conference in Washington, Bush and Rove hosted a private meeting in the White House for members of its Gold Circle Club. His overall message to the Christian right was clear: I am on your side.

CHAPTER 19

What We Deserve

Two days after al Qaeda terrorists piloted airliners into the World Trade Center towers and the Pentagon—killing three thousand Americans—Jerry Falwell and Pat Robertson tried to turn the horrific attack into a new front for the Christian right's culture war.

With fires still burning at Ground Zero in Lower Manhattan, Falwell appeared on Robertson's television show and offered an explanation: "What we saw on Tuesday, as terrible as it is, could be minuscule if, in fact, God continues to lift the curtain and allow the enemies of America to give us probably what we deserve." *What we deserve.* He went on to say, "The abortionists have got to bear some burden for this because God will not be mocked. And when we destroy 40 million little innocent babies, we make God mad. I really believe that the pagans, and the abortionists, and the feminists, and the gays and the lesbians who are actively trying to make that an alternative lifestyle, the ACLU, People for the American Way, all of them who have tried to secularize America, I point the finger in their face and say, 'You helped this happen.'" *You helped this happen.*

Robertson agreed: "I totally concur, and the problem is we have adopted that agenda at the highest levels of our government."

These two leaders of the religious right, long courted and afforded respectability by the Republican Party and its presidents, now castigated liberals as the enemies of God and blamed them for the worst terrorist assault in modern history.

The pair were widely criticized. The Bush White House issued a statement repudiating their remarks. Falwell apologized and said, "I had no intention of being divisive." But he had spent decades preaching divisiveness and claiming his foes sought (and would cause) the destruction of America. Even while apologizing he continued to claim liberals threatened the existence of the nation. In an interview with CNN, he asserted the ACLU and other organizations, "which have attempted to secularize America, have removed our nation from its relationship with Christ on which it was founded. I therefore believe that that created an environment which possibly has caused God to lift the veil of protection which has allowed no one to attack America on our soil since 1812." (He forgot about Pearl Harbor.)

———

With the attack of September 11, 2001—which occurred thirty-six days after Bush received an intelligence report headlined "Bin Ladin Determined to Strike in US"—the political battles over many issues would be superseded by trauma and the new war on terrorism. Priorities would shift, the Bush presidency reshaped. One paramount question was whether the assault would unify or further divide the country. Would it fuel extremism or help the nation become closer in common purpose?

Six days after the attack, Bush visited the Islamic Center of Washington and tried to tamp down anti-Islamic sentiment. "Islam is peace," he said. "These terrorists don't represent peace. They represent evil and war." He praised the contribution of Muslim Americans to the nation and decried anti-Muslim violence. He quoted the Koran: "In the long run, evil in the extreme will be the end of those who do evil." Speaking to Congress, he reiterated, "The enemy of America is not our many Muslim friends." Bush's words would not persuade his Christian fundamentalist allies.

Extreme actions, it turns out, yield extreme reactions. The mass killings of September 11 would prompt harsh and angry rhetoric—as well as feed bigotry and hate—on the right and create fault lines in American politics that Republicans would soon exploit.

Weeks after the attack, Franklin Graham, the son of legendary evangelist Billy Graham and a Christian right leader who had delivered the invocation at George W. Bush's inauguration, proclaimed Islam "a very evil and wicked religion." In the coming year, Robertson would say that Muslims were "worse than the Nazis" and aimed to exterminate Jews, and Falwell would refer to Muhammad as "a terrorist." The Reverend Jerry Vines, a Florida pastor and a past president of the Southern Baptist Convention, would call Muhammad a "demon-possessed pedophile," with the New York Times citing this remark as an example of "how hate speech against Muslims had become a staple of conservative Christian political discourse." In 2003, the Reverend Richard Cizik, a top official of the National Association of Evangelicals, would tell the Times, "evangelicals have substituted Islam for the Soviet Union. The Muslims have become the modern-day equivalent of the Evil Empire." Something to fear and despise.

Bush would tread a fine line between the noble views he expressed at the Islamic Center and political realities, as the Republican Party tried to capitalize upon the prejudice and paranoia sparked by 9/11. He didn't reproach or break with Robertson, Falwell, and the religious right as they promoted anti-Islam bigotry. The Defense Department invited Franklin Graham to deliver a Good Friday homily at the Pentagon. When a video emerged of Lieutenant General William Boykin, a deputy undersecretary of defense, declaring that the US military was "a Christian army" engaged in a "spiritual battle, not a physical battle" against jihadists and Satan, Defense Secretary Donald Rumsfeld praised his "outstanding record."

Bushworld would accept the Christian right's rhetorical war against Muslims. They needed the evangelical voters who had stayed home to come out in 2004. And Bush administration policies—the use of torture, expanded surveillance and racial profiling, and the invasion of Iraq—would reinforce the far right's demonization of Islam.

After 9/11, Islamophobia and terrorism-related fearmongering took root within conservative and Republican soil—and became daily fare on Fox News (especially for top-rated host Bill O'Reilly) and political ammunition for the GOP. Despite Bush insisting that the fight against terrorism should not be a partisan battle, Rove told a meeting of the Republican National Committee that the party should push the message that Republicans "do a better job...of protecting America." (Bush at that point had overseen a military operation in Afghanistan that chased the al Qaeda–supporting Taliban out of power but failed to capture al Qaeda leader Osama bin Laden.) It was a throwback to the old Republican pitch that Democrats could not be trusted to defend the nation.

Months later, a computer disk containing a private PowerPoint presentation Rove had cooked up for Republican candidates was found in the park across from the White House. A key talking point for the GOP contenders: "Focus on the war." And as the midterm contests drew near, the campaign got nasty. Georgia Republican Representative Saxby Chambliss, who was challenging incumbent Democratic Senator Max Cleland, a decorated Vietnam War veteran who had lost three limbs on the battlefield, ran a television ad that displayed Cleland's photo alongside bin Laden and Iraqi dictator Saddam Hussein. It declared Cleland did not have the "courage" to defend the nation from these men. Though John McCain spoke out against the ad, most Republicans remained mum. In South Dakota, GOP Representative John Thune fired off a spot at Senator Tim Johnson, another Democratic incumbent, that referred to Saddam and al Qaeda while excoriating Johnson for being weak on defense. Thune lost by 524 votes, but the reprehensible ad in Georgia helped elect Chambliss—and that win helped give Republicans narrow control of the Senate.

————

It was inevitable that 9/11 would spark an endless flow of conspiracy theories. *It was an inside job…Mossad knew in advance and warned all the Jews who worked at the World Trade Center…There was no plane at the Pentagon…Bush and Cheney allowed it to happen so they would have a pretext for war.* All traumatic events catalyze conspiracism. But after 9/11, the most dangerous conspiracy theories were the ones that infected the Bush administration.

Three days after September 11, the conservative American Enterprise Institute hosted a press briefing with Gingrich, former UN ambassador Jeanne Kirkpatrick, and other conservative thought leaders. To explain the horrendous event, Kirkpatrick called on Laurie Mylroie, a onetime Harvard assistant professor who was now an AEI fellow. Mylroie cast doubt on the widespread assumption that al Qaeda had mounted the attacks. But if they were the evildoers, she added, it was "next to impossible" they had pulled off 9/11 without assistance from Saddam.

For years, Mylroie had peddled the convoluted conspiracy theory that Saddam was the mastermind behind most anti-American terrorism in the world. For her, this traced back to the 1993 bombing of the World Trade Center that had been executed by a small band of Islamic militants and that had killed six people. Mylroie concocted a complicated tale of double identities for the key suspect and claimed Iraq orchestrated that operation. The FBI and the CIA debunked her analysis. But she pressed on, claiming that the Oklahoma City bombing in 1995 was also an Iraqi attack.

Top national security experts thought she was off the rails—a crackpot. But Paul Wolfowitz, a leading neoconservative, bought it, and in 2000 he provided a laudatory blurb for her book alleging Saddam was a diabolical puppet master covertly engineering terrorism against the United States. Her theory fit well with the grand idea that neoconservatives had advocated for years: If Saddam could be gotten rid of, democracy would flourish in Iraq and spread through the Middle East, enhancing US influence in the oil-rich region and bolstering the security of Israel.

On September 11, Wolfowitz was deputy secretary of defense. He and other administration officials who believed Mylroie's unsubstantiated and discredited theory about Saddam immediately pressed for a counterattack on Iraq. Bush focused on Afghanistan and the Taliban instead—that is, for several months. But after US forces routed the Taliban and al Qaeda soldiers out of Kabul in November, Bush asked Rumsfeld to draw up a war plan for Iraq.

In the coming year, the Bush-Cheney White House would wage a relentless campaign to convince the public that Saddam was a threat who had to be taken out. How much Mylroie's nutty conspiracy theory drove this crusade was hard to determine. Bush and the hawks had an assortment of motivations: to remake the Middle East, to finish the job left over from the first US war against Iraq, to protect Israel, to seek revenge for a purported (and unproven) Iraqi assassination plot against George H. W. Bush, and to persuade the American public after 9/11 that Bush and Cheney would do whatever (they thought) it took to safeguard the nation.

In the summer of 2002, Vice President Dick Cheney publicly presented a frightening assessment: "There is no doubt that Saddam Hussein now has weapons of mass destruction. There is no doubt he is amassing them to use against our friends, against our allies, and against us." Yet no US intelligence analysis had reached that conclusion. Cheney was making it up.

The line between conspiracy theories, lousy intelligence, and outright lies blurred. Cheney publicly cited the allegation that Mohamed Atta, the lead 9/11 plotter, had met with an Iraqi intelligence officer in Prague—though the CIA had discredited this report. The Bush administration claimed Saddam had purchased aluminum tubes for producing weapons-grade uranium, but top government scientists had concluded otherwise. Bush asserted Saddam was in cahoots with al Qaeda, yet no solid intelligence backed this up. Cheney promoted a report that Iraq had acquired uranium from Niger—but this story had originated with forged documents peddled by an Italian con man. And so on. The White House put out a stream of flimsy or unfounded assertions, some the direct result of administration officials conspiring to conjure up evidence for a case for war.

Yet no matter the evidence (or lack thereof) of a WMD threat from Saddam or an operational link between al Qaeda and Baghdad, Bush, in his public statements, repeatedly mentioned Saddam and 9/11 in the same breath, conflating the two and characterizing Saddam as an immediate danger to the United States. He was capitalizing on fear and falsehoods—and his push for war was echoed and amplified nonstop by Fox News and other right-wing media. A few weeks before the US invasion of Iraq in March 2003, a *Washington Post* poll found that 70 percent of Americans believed the false premise that Saddam was "personally involved" in the 9/11 attack.

———

The war went well…until it didn't. The March 2003 invasion succeeded in driving Saddam, a corrupt and brutal tyrant, out of power. Eventually, he would be captured and executed. But the Bush administration barely had a plan for the subsequent occupation and failed to arrest the instability and vicious sectarian warfare that ensued. In the coming years, an estimated 200,000 Iraqi civilians or more would be killed in the strife. Thousands of American soldiers would lose their lives. No WMDs would be found in Iraq. This long stretch of violence and chaos would give rise to a new threat to the region: the Islamic State, or ISIS, a militant Islamic group. Bush and Cheney eliminated Saddam, but they created tremendous misery and a geostrategic mess.

In the United States, support for the war plummeted. A fair question was whether Bush had exploited post-9/11 fear to con the public. A year after the invasion, a *Washington Post*/ABC News poll found that 54 percent of Americans believed Bush had lied or deliberately exaggerated the WMD case to justify the war. His presidential approval rating dropped from 71 percent at the start of the war to 50 percent.

With the war becoming increasingly unpopular, to win reelection Bush would need plenty of help, and that would come to include the assistance of right-wing conspiracy theorists and, once again, the intolerant forces of the Christian right.

———

After 9/11, Bush had continued to cater to the religious right, including its most extreme voices and leaders who were still demonizing political enemies and fighting the divisive culture war. He nominated to the federal bench an Alabama attorney general who, in a brief filed for a Supreme Court case concerning anti-sodomy laws, compared homosexuality to necrophilia, bestiality, incest, and pedophilia. Another of Bush's judicial appointees, a leading antiabortion activist, had compared abortion-rights advocates to Nazis, claimed conceptions from rape were nearly impossible, and declared a wife should "subordinate herself to her husband." Both were eventually confirmed by the GOP-controlled Senate.

When the Supreme Court declared anti-sodomy laws unconstitutional in June 2003, Robertson, lamenting that the court had "opened the door to…even incest," called on his millions of followers to pray for the deaths of liberal justices. James Dobson in August condemned the "liberal elite," federal judges, and "members of the media" for being "determined to remove every evidence of faith in God from this entire culture."

But that fall, social conservatives had reason to celebrate. Dobson, Falwell, Sheldon, and representatives of the Christian Coalition, and other religious rightists gathered for a ceremony at the Ronald Reagan Building and International Trade Center, where Bush signed into law a ban on late-term abortions, the first national prohibition on an abortion procedure since the *Roe v. Wade* decision in 1973. It was a major Bush-enabled victory for the Christian right.

About that time, another critical fight arose. In November 2003, the Supreme Court of Massachusetts issued an order paving the way for same-sex couples to marry. Three months later, San Francisco and a few other jurisdictions began issuing marriage licenses to same-sex couples. The Christian right was in an uproar. This was a doomsday scenario. Dobson wrote to his supporters that the fight against same-sex marriage was "our D-Day, or Gettysburg or Stalingrad." The religious right demanded Bush stop this catastrophe by supporting a constitutional amendment banning gay marriage.

Throughout his presidency, Bush had avoided endorsing the gay-bashing and anti-Muslim bigotry of the Christian right. He had ducked supporting such an extreme move as a constitutional ban on same-sex marriage. Now, in an election year in which Bush needed the four million evangelical voters who had not shown up in 2000, it was crunch time. A Pew Research poll found that gay marriage had become a "make-or-break" issue for evangelical Christians. Republican pollster Dick Wirthlin in a 2003 memo had identified same-sex marriage as "an ideal wedge issue." After failing for decades to end abortion, restore school prayer, beat back pornography, or censor the teaching of evolution, the social conservatives had an issue—opposing same-sex marriage—in which they were in line with what was then majority sentiment. Weyrich noted that recruiting new members for the religious right had been flat until gay marriage started "turning things around." It was a boon for the gay-hating social conservatives.

With a tough reelection fight looming—the Iraq War was not going well—Bush decided to encourage and utilize the antigay fervor of the right. In February 2004, he announced his support for a constitutional amendment "defining" marriage "as a union of man and woman as husband and wife." And his campaign would capitalize on the issue.

In the past two decades, the US electorate had grown more divided. Twenty years earlier, about one-fifth of the voting population consisted of what political professionals called "persuadables"—independent or swing voters who could end up casting a ballot for either the Democratic or Republican presidential contender. Campaigns traditionally devoted much energy and resources to winning over these Americans. This year, Bush campaign strategists calculated persuadables at about 6 percent, perhaps lower. That led them to a new game plan: Motivate the base. It didn't mean forget about persuasion. But if in years past campaign efforts were divided 80 to 20 percent in favor of coaxing the in-betweens, in 2004 the Bush campaign significantly changed that balance. Media appearances, ads, campaign mail, phone-banking, Bush's travel—all were predicated on a strategy of base motivation and mobilization.

A critical bloc were those four million Christian-right voters Rove had been chasing since the last election, as well as conservative Catholics. Energizing these voters was a top priority, too important to be left to the Christian Coalition—especially since the group, following Robertson's departure as its head in 2002, had been struggling with fundraising and organizational issues. The Bush squad would directly recruit the religious right into its endeavors. With the energetic and canny Ralph Reed leading the way, the campaign forged connections with churches and pastors across the country. At the Southern Baptist Convention in June 2004, Reed signed up one hundred far-right ministers who pledged to endorse Bush, mount voter registration drives, and reach out to other pastors. A key target was the 850 Protestant megachurches that had sprung up in suburbs and exurbs across the country and that had a combined total of three million congregants.

The Bush team intended to squeeze the Christian right dry, and it did have help. Social conservative activists were placing antigay marriage measures on the ballot in states across the country, including four swing states: Arkansas, Michigan, Ohio, and Oregon. This crusade would drive angry evangelicals and conservative Catholics to the polls—just the type of voters Bush and Rove wanted.

———

On July 29, 2004, Senator John Kerry, a Massachusetts Democrat, strode onstage at the Democratic convention in Boston to accept his party's presidential nomination. Surrounded by veterans who had served with him in Vietnam, he gave a military salute and declared, "I'm reporting for duty." It was a reminder of his tour as a Swift boat commander that had earned him a Silver Star, a Bronze Star, and three Purple Hearts. The delegates cheered. They were thrilled that during the first post-9/11 presidential campaign, with national security a top concern, they had a genuine war hero as their standard bearer. (During the Vietnam War, Bush had served in the Texas National Guard, and there were credible questions as to whether he ended up there thanks to his father's string-pulling and subsequently ducked out on his Guard obligation.)

Kerry's Vietnam experience and his subsequent protest against that war were a crucial part of his personal story, evidence he was commander in chief material. Yet this tremendous asset was about to come under fire in a Republican-backed campaign steered, in part, by a bigoted, flim-flamish, right-wing extremist.

A week after Kerry's speech, a group called Swift Boat Veterans for Truth aired an ad featuring Vietnam veterans who claimed he had lied about his military record and his medals. "John Kerry is no war hero," one asserted. The ad sparked condemnation from the editorial boards of major newspapers but drew much media notice. A week later Regnery, a conservative publishing house, released a book, *Unfit for Command: Swift Boat Veterans Speak Out Against John Kerry*, by John O'Neill and Jerome Corsi, which accused Kerry of fabricating his medal-winning accounts.

O'Neill had served as a Swift boat commander in the same unit in Vietnam as Kerry but after Kerry had left the war zone. Corsi, a longtime friend of O'Neill, was a financial adviser who in 1995 had guided twenty people into a shadowy investment deal in Poland that went bust and lost $1.2 million. The FBI investigated the venture, but no charges were filed. Corsi also had worked undercover with the FBI (or so he claimed) to penetrate the Vietnam Veterans Against the War, a group Kerry had helped to lead in the early 1970s. More recently, Corsi had posted infantile Red-baiting, misogynistic, and bigoted comments on a right-wing website called FreeRepublic.com

Corsi was a regular commentator to this internet forum, which provided a platform for racist and violent rants and assorted conspiracy theories. In posts to the site, Corsi defamed Islam as "a worthless, dangerous Satanic religion" and bashed Muslims as "RAGHEADS [who] are Boy-Bumpers." He referred to Hillary Clinton, now a US senator, as a "FAT HOG" who "couldn't keep BJ Bill satisfied" and asked, "Not lesbo or anything, is she." He suggested that "boy buggering" was "okay with the Pope."

In other posts, Corsi expressed deep hatred of Kerry, whom he called "Anti-Christian, Anti-American." He declared that if Kerry were to be elected president, "there will be no end to how much of America we can destroy." He falsely claimed Kerry had become a practicing Jew and repeatedly called him a "commie," asserting the senator had a "plan to hand America over to our nation's enemies."

Corsi saw commies everywhere. Bill Clinton? An "anti-American communist." NBC broadcast journalist Katie Couric? "Little Katie Communist." He called MSNBC a communist news outlet. He defined a "Perfect Liberal" as "lesbian, self-absorbed, hates America." In other writings, Corsi insisted that Kerry and the VVAW had "coordinated their [antiwar] efforts with Communists" and that Kerry, when an antiwar activist, believed that "Communists were right in maintaining that American values were corrupt and that the only solution was for America to capitulate so Communism could continue to spread."

As the Swift Boat offensive against Kerry spread, the prominent role of a disreputable extremist in the effort received minimal coverage. O'Neill even lied and insisted Corsi was "simply an editor" and not his coauthor—though Corsi's name was on the book and promotional material cited Corsi as a coauthor who had conducted interviews for the book. (O'Neill also claimed he was not a Republican, but he had donated money to GOP candidates and causes.) The involvement of a racist fringe rightist did not slow the attack. Top Republican funders—including Texas GOP megadonor Bob Perry, a friend of Rove—poured millions of dollars into the Swift Boaters' coffers for more ads, which included blasts against Kerry's antiwar activism.

Right-wing media, bloggers, and internet sites amplified the assault, even as it was discredited. A *Washington Post* investigation of the Swift Boat allegations found the group had "failed to come up with sufficient evidence to prove [Kerry] a liar." The *New York Times* noted, "The accounts of Swift Boat Veterans for Truth prove to be riddled with inconsistencies. In many cases, material offered as proof by these veterans is undercut by official Navy records and the men's own statements."

Despite the debunking, the Swift Boat allegations—essentially, an unproven conspiracy theory—dominated this stretch of the campaign and followed one of Rove's political rules: Attack your enemy's strength. The Bush-Cheney campaign denied it had any connection to this blitz—which many political observers found hard to believe. (A member of the Bush-Cheney campaign's veterans committee appeared in a Swift Boat ad, and a top lawyer for the Bush reelection effort provided legal assistance to the Swift Boaters.) Moreover, Bush and the GOP refused to condemn the Swift Boat operation. (President George H. W. Bush called the Swift Boat ads "rather compelling," and First Lady Laura Bush said there was nothing unfair about them.) With the Kerry campaign initially reluctant to respond to charges it considered phony and scurrilous—for fear that would grant them more attention—the Swift Boat smear became a case study in the ability of a false narrative to take hold. And it seemed to take a toll. At the start of August, Kerry had a slight lead over Bush in the polls; at the end of the month, Bush edged ahead of Kerry.

─────────

As delegates milled about at the Republican convention, which opened in Madison Square Garden on August 30, many carried the Corsi-cowritten *Unfit for Command.* At a breakfast meeting of Republicans featuring Rove, Representative Curt Weldon of Pennsylvania praised the book. Morton Blackwell, the veteran New Right leader, handed out bandages that read, "It was just a self-inflicted scratch, but you see I got a Purple Heart for it."

Two attacks originating with extremists were animating Bush's campaign—the war on same-sex marriage and the Swift Boat smear—but neither featured prominently on the podium at the convention. Decades earlier, GOP officials worried about being tarred by their far-right confederates. Now the Republican Party knew how to encourage them without being burdened. In his acceptance speech, Bush spoke one line about same-sex marriage ("I support the protection of marriage against activist judges") without mentioning a constitutional amendment. He devoted only one sentence to abortion ("we must make a place for the unborn child") without calling for outlawing the procedure. He hailed the war in Iraq and pounded Kerry as a tax-and-spend, flip-flopping Democrat who was soft on national security. He said nothing about Kerry's war record. In the week after the convention, Bush opened an eight-point lead over Kerry, the largest Bush advantage in the campaign.

─────────

The Republicans were seeking to harness the culture war sentiments of the extreme right. Just not too obviously. The Swift Boat attack fit this strategy. Kerry was a liberal. He couldn't be a real war hero. He was a fraud who had desecrated and betrayed the US military with his Vietnam protest, and that showed he opposed the true-blue American values of honor, decency, and patriotism. This fit into the long-standing far-right/GOP template—from McCarthy to the Birchers to Gingrich—that the Democrats were the enemy within. On one broadcast, Limbaugh implied Kerry nurtured procommunist sympathies. On another, he exclaimed, "If you want the terrorists running the show, then you will elect John Kerry." (Earlier in the year, Limbaugh had talked up unfounded rumors about Kerry's personal life.) The rhetoric was less blunt than that of previous eras, but the story was the same: Far-right conservatives were calling the Democrats anti-American and anti-God, and the GOP was affirming that animus to gain from it. The Republican Party even sent out mass mailings in West Virginia and Arkansas with the alarming (and false) claim that liberals and Democrats intended to ban the Bible.

The Christian Coalition scaled back its distribution of voter guides. But at its annual conference, speakers described the election as a holy war. GOP House Speaker Dennis Hastert bellowed that "we will not allow [judges] to redefine the American family." (Years later he would be convicted of having sexually molested several boys when he was a wrestling coach and be imprisoned for thirteen months.) Arkansas Governor Mike Huckabee declared America was collapsing. Falwell boasted that the religious right controlled the Republican Party.

Sticking to its plan and not relying on the coalition, the Bush reelection campaign stayed in direct touch with Christian right church leaders across the country. Rob Brendle, an associate pastor at New Life Church in Colorado Springs—an eleven-thousand-member congregation led by Pastor Ted Haggard, the president of the National Association of Evangelicals—told a *New York Times* reporter, "We've been in regular contact with Karl Rove."

The antigay marriage ballot propositions were fully synced up with the Bush campaign. In Ohio, a crucial swing state, the proponents of the measure distributed 2.5 million leaflets through 17,000 churches and made 3.3 million phone calls targeting 850,000 supporters. Simultaneously, the Christian Coalition in the state handed out two million voter guides that favored Bush. By one estimate, several thousand Christian right activists volunteered with the state GOP and the Bush campaign to turn out religious conservatives for Bush. Automated get-out-the-vote phone calls were recorded by the Muslim-bashing Franklin Graham.

Much of the political activity nationwide boosting the antigay ballot measures was coordinated by a collection of Christian right outfits called the Arlington Group. Its members—many who were also part of the Council for National Policy—included the usual fire-breathing, antigay crusaders: Weyrich, Dobson, Bauer, and several dozen others. J. Kenneth Blackwell, the Republican secretary of state in Ohio, participated, and so did Haggard. (Two years later, Haggard would resign as president of the National Association of Evangelicals and be dismissed as leader of his megachurch after a Denver man claimed to have engaged in drug-fueled sex romps with him.) The group's chief organizer, Donald Wildmon, the head of the American Family Association, had blasted gay rights activists in 2001 "for working diligently to overthrow the traditional values of Western civilization." This coordinating outfit held weekly conference calls with White House staffers. Its member organizations poured about $2 million into assorted state efforts. More than half of this money went to Ohio.

Not surprisingly, neither the Bush campaign nor Christian right leaders acknowledged that the ballot measures had been designed to help Bush's reelection. But Blackwell, an honorary cochair of Bush's Ohio reelection campaign, did send a letter to 1,500 state GOP members in August 2004 saying gay marriage would be important in "determining where Ohio's electoral votes will go."

Simultaneously, the Swift Boat Veterans—flushed with cash from major Republican moneymen—were spending about $20 million on ads claiming Kerry was a fake. About a quarter of that went to buy time in Ohio.

On Election Day, the preliminary exit polls pointed toward a Kerry win, but as results came in both campaigns realized the contest would depend on Ohio. When the networks at 1:00 a.m. called Ohio for Bush—a win by 118,000 votes—Bush was the overall victor with 286 electoral college votes to Kerry's 252. He had pocketed 50.7 percent of the popular vote. The election had been a close call for Bush, the narrowest victory for an incumbent president in US history. The Republicans gained four seats in the Senate and three in the House.

As with all elections, multiple forces influenced the outcome: the economy, national security, the mood of the nation, the performance of the candidates. This was the first presidential race after 9/11, and many voters still felt at risk. The Iraq and Afghanistan wars were dragging on, but the economy was expanding, with unemployment and inflation at moderate levels. And Bush and Rove had succeeded in pumping up the Christian right vote. Born-again or evangelical Christians had comprised 23 percent of the electorate. Seventy-eight percent of them voted for Bush, a big increase from 68 percent four years earlier.

Political scientists and pollsters would argue what impact—if any—the antigay marriage ballot measures had on the presidential contest. Yet with the small vote margin in Ohio, the referendum in the state, which passed with 62 percent of the vote, was likely one of several critical factors. Writing in the *New York Times,* historian Garry Wills observed, "This election confirms the brilliance of Karl Rove as a political strategist. He calculated that the religious conservatives, if they could be turned out, would be the deciding factor...President Bush promised in 2000 that he would lead a humble country, be a uniter not a divider, that he would make conservatism compassionate. He did not need to make such false promises this time. He was reelected precisely by being a divider, pitting the reddest aspects of the red states against the blue nearly half of the nation." Bush had again conquered the old Goldwater problem: making political use of extremists without being accused of extremism.

Rove had once dreamed of masterminding a political realignment that would establish the Republican Party as the dominant party for years to come. He failed to pull off such a transformation. But in 2004, Bush had managed to hang on to power—thanks in part to the forces of fundamentalist intolerance and a right-wing smear job.

———

After the election, the fundamentalists and Bush went back to the same push-me/pull-you relationship. During his second term, the Christian right would not win its cherished constitutional amendment blocking gay Americans from marriage. But Bush did appoint two conservatives to the Supreme Court—John Roberts and Samuel Alito—and he vetoed a stem cell bill.

The favorite issues of the social conservatives were overshadowed by other matters. The Iraq and Afghanistan wars remained nightmares and geopolitical failures. (Limbaugh kept insisting that Iraq had possessed weapons of mass destruction—though multiple investigations concluded this was not true.) The Bush administration's incompetent handling of the Hurricane Katrina disaster that struck New Orleans in August 2005 became a national disgrace, and Bush's effort to partially privatize Social Security flopped. A variety of scandals—influence peddling, personal misconduct, illegal campaign finances—struck congressional Republicans. In the 2006 midterm elections, social conservatives did not come to the GOP's rescue. The Democrats won control of both chambers of Congress.

The unpopular and ongoing calamity in Iraq dominated the last half of Bush's second term. His attempt to pass immigration reform—which included a provision to legalize 12 million undocumented immigrants—failed, much because of the vociferous opposition of Limbaugh and other far-right voices. Then came the financial and housing crisis of 2007 and 2008 that triggered the Great Recession. Bush signed a $700 billion bailout plan for failing financial institutions—the largest economic rescue package in US history. In Bush's last week in office, his approval rating, as charted in a CBS News/*New York Times* poll, was 22 percent—the lowest final rating for an outgoing president since such polling began seven decades earlier. His deals with the Christian right and other extremists—sub rosa and overt— had helped him win and retain the White House, but they had not saved his presidency.

———

A week before moving out of 1600 Pennsylvania Avenue, Bush, who had become president claiming to be a compassionate conservative, a uniter not a divider, and a new kind of Republican, hosted Limbaugh for lunch at the White House. A few months earlier, the talk show host had celebrated his twentieth anniversary of broadcasting harsh and often misogynistic, racist, misleading, and tribalistic rhetoric. Bush had called in then, with his father and brother Jeb, and told Limbaugh that they "really appreciate the contribution you've made."

At this farewell lunch, Limbaugh had salmon over rice, and Bush ate a peanut butter and jelly sandwich. Then stewards brought in a chocolate birthday cake adorned with four candles and a chocolate microphone. The president of the United States sang "Happy Birthday" to Limbaugh.

CHAPTER 20

Going Rogue

John McCain took the stage at the packed Memorial Hall in Cincinnati before hundreds of cheering supporters. Eight weeks into the 2008 Republican presidential contest, the Arizona senator who had lost his previous presidential bid was the presumptive nominee. He had vanquished his chief rival, former Massachusetts governor and private equity magnate Mitt Romney, and could start looking toward the November election. McCain and everyone in the room knew the 2004 election had been decided in Ohio. And McCain and his advisers realized Bush had earned that slim victory partly by motivating conservative Christian voters.

With this in mind, the McCain campaign had pulled off a key endorsement. Standing next to McCain was the Reverend Rod Parsley, a prominent televangelist and pastor who led the World Harvest Church of Columbus, a supersize Pentecostal institution that featured a 5,200-seat sanctuary and a television studio, where he taped a weekly show broadcast around the world. His congregation boasted twelve thousand members. In 2004, his church registered and delivered thousands of voters to the polls for Bush.

Parsley praised McCain as a "strong, true, consistent conservative." McCain called the minister "one of the truly great leaders in America, a moral compass, a spiritual guide."

It was almost eight years to the day that McCain, during the 2000 campaign, had slammed Jerry Falwell and Pat Robertson as "agents of intolerance" and had warned his party not to pander "to the outer reaches of American politics." That was then.

Since that time, McCain had transformed from a maverick insurgent to a front-runner who believed the way to the Republican nomination was to work with the party's establishment and court its base, including the Christian right. In 2006, he had patched things up with Falwell. On *Meet the Press*, he said he no longer considered Falwell an "agent of intolerance" and hailed the Christian right as a crucial part of the GOP. This rapprochement had left political observers wondering what had happened to the straight-talking

McCain. (He also had sucked up to Limbaugh, calling the right-wing blow-hard "a voice that is respected by a lot of people who are in our party.")

After Falwell's death in 2007 of cardiac arrest, McCain continued to woo religious right leaders he had once scorned. Parsley was a major grab for him. And on February 27, 2008, the day after the Cincinnati rally, McCain bagged another prominent fundamentalist: Pastor John Hagee, the leader of a Texas megachurch. Yet Parsley and Hagee would become political mill-stones for McCain, for each man was an extremist and, as the old McCain might have said, an agent of intolerance.

In his books and sermons, Parsley, who referred to himself as a "Chris-tocrat," bemoaned the "spiritual desperation" of the United States, blam-ing the usual suspects: activist judges, civil libertarians, the entertainment industry, and homosexual "culture." He had founded an organization that called for prosecuting people who committed adultery, and he had com-pared Planned Parenthood to Nazis.

Parsley reserved his most venomous rhetoric for Islam. In a 2005 book, he warned there was a "war between Islam and Christian civilization," writing that part of the American mission was to eradicate Islam: "I do not believe our country can truly fulfill its divine purpose until we understand our historical conflict with Islam . . . The fact is that America was founded, in part, with the intention of seeing this false religion destroyed." He described Allah as "a demon spirit" and noted that Islamic "extremists" represented "the very heart of Islam." He considered September 11 a call for a holy war to obliterate Islam.

Hagee had a long history of a different sort of prejudice: anti-Catholic bigotry. The head of a San Antonio church with seventeen thousand mem-bers, he had denigrated the Catholic Church as "the great whore" and a "false cult system." He claimed that the Pope was the Antichrist and that Hitler's antisemitism was caused by his education at a Catholic school. He asserted that Hurricane Katrina was the act of a vengeful God to prevent "a homosexual parade" scheduled in New Orleans. Like Parsley, Hagee depicted Islam as a faith of violence, contending that those who follow the Koran "have a scriptural mandate to kill Christians and Jews."

The Catholic League called on McCain to renounce Hagee's support. McCain countered that he was "very proud of Pastor John Hagee's spiritual leadership" and added that Hagee's endorsement "does not mean that I sup-port or endorse or agree with some of the things that Pastor John Hagee might have said." After more criticism, McCain took another step backward and repudiated "any comments . . . if they are anti-Catholic or offensive to Catholics." It was a mealy-mouthed response; he did not disavow Hagee.

(All this was occurring about the time Senator Barack Obama, the leading Democratic presidential contender, was being assailed for harsh and angry comments criticizing the United States made by the pastor at his Chicago church, the Reverend Jeremiah Wright.)

Hagee's anti-Catholic animus drew much more media notice than Parsley's Islamophobia. McCain's embrace of a pastor who urged the abolition of Islam received almost no coverage until early May when *Mother Jones* posted video of a 2005 sermon in which Parsley called Islam "the greatest religious enemy of our civilization and the world" and asserted that the United States must see "this false religion destroyed." During this sermon, Parsley blamed Islam for 9/11 and lamented the existence of 1,209 mosques in America.

Several news outlets carried stories about McCain and the Muslim-bashing pastor. But the candidate refused to break with Parsley.

Two weeks later, a new story about Hagee emerged: In the late 1990s he had preached that Hitler and the Holocaust had been part of God's plan to drive the Jews from Europe to Palestine. Finally, McCain threw the two pastors overboard. He issued a statement dumping Hagee. And he told the Associated Press he was now refusing Parsley's support. The *New York Times* editorial on McCain's better-late-than-never renunciations was headlined, "Sen. McCain's Agents of Intolerance."

McCain had tried to forge an alliance with Christian fanatics and failed. Instead, he ended up unintentionally calling attention to the bigotry of these fundamentalists. Nixon, Reagan, and both Bushes had depended on racists, bigots, or extremists to chart their ways to the White House. Though it seemed at this juncture McCain would not be able to follow the same course, his campaign would soon find itself relying on a different form of extremism and demagoguery.

———

By this point in the 2008 contest, the contours of the race were set. Obama, having defeated Hillary Clinton in the Democratic primary contest, would be the first Black man chosen by a major political party as its presidential aspirant. He was dynamic and fresh, an advocate and symbol of hope. McCain was literally an old war-horse. Obama boasted of his early opposition to the Iraq War. McCain was a high-profile advocate who continued to support the US presence there. Obama promised "change you can believe in." McCain offered patriotism and dependability. The overall context for the race did not favor McCain: The slog-like wars in Iraq and Afghanistan continued, as did the decline of the US economy, hit hard by the housing and financial crisis.

Come the start of August, Obama led by two or so points in the polls. The Democratic convention in Denver was a smash. Bill and Hillary Clinton delivered rousing speeches, as did Senator Ted Kennedy, recently diagnosed with a lethal brain tumor. Obama's acceptance speech, presented before one hundred thousand people in a football stadium, blasted McCain as out of touch with the nation's problems. He punched back at the negative campaign McCain had been waging against him—which suggested Obama cared more about being a celebrity than serving the nation's interests—and said, "I've got news for you, John McCain. We all put our country first."

The Republican convention in St. Paul, Minnesota, was about one thing, and it was not McCain. Feeling his campaign was flagging, McCain and his advisers yearned for a vice presidential pick who would be a game changer, and through a slapdash process they landed on Sarah Palin, the little-known, first-term Republican governor of Alaska, who had been championed by a small group of Washington conservatives, particularly Bill Kristol. She was archly right-wing, photogenic, and the first woman placed on a GOP ticket. But she was highly inexperienced in national security and public policy—and erratic, not too bright, and not up to the job.

At the Republican gathering, though, Palin was the star. Social conservatives were delighted. The religious right had not been thrilled with McCain. Robertson told one reporter the evangelical community was unmotivated this year. But Christian rightists now could adore one half of the ticket. Members of the Council for National Policy were "electrified," according to Tom Minnery of Focus on the Family.

In public, Palin displayed spunk and pizzazz. Her convention speech had bite, as she snidely dismissed Obama as a grandstander, an elitist, and just another of those tax-and-spend-and-appease Democrats. Michael Reagan, Ronald Reagan's son and a conservative talk show host, raved, "I watched the Republican national convention on television and there, before my very eyes, I saw my dad reborn; only this time he's a she."

Palin was an instant political phenomenon. Four days after the GOP convention, McCain led Obama by almost three points in an average of major polls. It was to be his highwater mark.

———

On the campaign trail, the GOP faithful treated Palin as a hero. But she muffed big media interviews. Her answers to basic questions of policy were incoherent or shallow. She became an object of scorn and satire. And the Palin story line—and whatever boost she provided McCain—was quickly eclipsed by the deepening financial crisis. On September 7, the federal government was forced to take over Fannie Mae and Freddie Mac; then Lehman Brothers, the nation's fourth-largest investment bank, imploded. A complete meltdown of the credit markets seemed imminent. A downturn greater than the Great Depression was possible.

Through these terrifying days, as the stock market tanked and the Bush White House and congressional Democrats and Republicans scrambled to forestall a total crash of the American and global economies, McCain came across as unsure and unsteady, without much of a clue as to how to lead in this emergency. He declared, "The fundamentals of the economy are strong." They weren't. Obama projected calm and confidence and soundly steered the Democrats, as a bipartisan $700 billion bailout deal was cobbled together. He demonstrated he could be more than an inspirational leader; he could be a steady governing hand. The polls switched back in Obama's favor.

It was then that Palin stirred the furies of extremism—with the full approval of McCain headquarters.

Appearing on Fox News, Palin claimed Obama should be disqualified from serving as president because he had once denigrated US troops stationed in Afghanistan. She had dusted off and mischaracterized a remark Obama had made a year ago in which he had said the US ought to deploy enough troops in Afghanistan "so that we're not just air-raiding villages and killing civilians, which is causing enormous problems there." Western forces had killed nearly three hundred civilians in the first half of 2007. Afghan president Hamid Karzai had complained about that, and Bush had noted, "We share those concerns."

There was nothing to this attack on Obama. But the following day, Palin intensified the assault.

The *New York Times* had recently published a long piece on Obama's relationship with Bill Ayers, a cofounder of the Weather Underground, the 1960s radical group that had engaged in bombings. As the paper reported, Obama met Ayers, then an education professor, in 1995 "at a lunchtime meeting about school reform" and "their paths have crossed sporadically since then." The paper noted "the two men do not appear to have been close," and Obama had called Ayers "somebody who engaged in detestable acts forty years ago, when I was eight." For Republicans, however, Ayers was an opportunity to mine the suspicion that Obama had a stealth, radical, anti-America agenda.

The McCain campaign sent Palin an email with a command: Rip into Obama as "someone who sees America as imperfect enough to pal around with terrorists who targeted their own country." Though Palin at times was accused by McCain aides of going rogue and not abiding by campaign decisions, in this instance she enthusiastically accepted her marching orders. At a Colorado fundraiser, she let loose this accusation: "He's palling around with terrorists who would target their own country." With a quick fact check, CNN pronounced this allegation false: "There is no indication that Ayers and Obama are now 'palling around'... Also, there is nothing to suggest Ayers is now involved in terrorist activity." It was a completely bogus charge. Obama called this the "launching of swiftboat-style attacks on me" and an attempt to divert attention from the failing economy.

Palin stuck with it. The next day, she repeated the "palling around" line at a California fundraiser and insisted Americans don't know "the real Barack Obama." McCain and Palin were amplifying a racist notion that had spread through the conspiratorial fringes of the far right: Obama was not what he appeared to be; he was covering up a secret and troubling past.

It all began in 2004, when Obama ran for the US Senate in Illinois. Andy Martin, a columnist for an inconsequential website and perpetual failed candidate, claimed Obama was a covert Muslim. Two years later, as Obama was preparing to run for president, anti-Muslim blogger Debbie Schlussel published a post maintaining Obama "feels some sort of psychological need to prove himself to his absent Muslim father." In a conflict with Islamic jihadists, she insisted, Obama would not be loyal to the United States.

In late 2007 and early 2008, versions of an anonymous email titled "Who Is Barack Obama?" began circulating. These emails repeated the claim Obama was a secret Muslim and alleged that when he was a child living with his American mother in Indonesia, he attended a madrassa, a Muslim school that taught Wahhabism, a radical form of Islam "followed by the Muslim terrorists who are now waging Jihad against the western world." The emails asserted that during his swearing in a senator, Obama used the Koran instead of the Bible and that he never would recite the Pledge of Allegiance. None of this was true. The emails ended with a warning: "The Muslims have said they plan on destroying the US from the inside out, what better way to start than at the highest level—through the President of the United States."

The growing internet made it easier for this disinformation to spread quickly and widely. And soon the right-wing media was amplifying the secret Muslim conspiracy theory. *Insight* magazine, owned by the Unification Church, published a story that claimed Obama "was educated in a Madrassa... and has not been forthcoming about his Muslim heritage." Fox

News broadcast a report based on the *Insight* story. Within days, a CNN reporter visited the Indonesian school Obama had attended. It was not a religious school; the facility educated students of various faiths.

The whispers continued. Conservative talk-show hosts spread insinuation. Limbaugh claimed he got "confused" between Obama and Osama bin Laden. In November 2007, the Obama campaign felt compelled to post a memo on its website titled "Obama Has Never Been A Muslim, And Is a Committed Christian." When a Clinton volunteer in Iowa forwarded an Obama-is-a-Muslim email, the Clinton campaign fired this person.

Like a virus, the smear mutated. One new version of the email falsely claimed the Book of Revelation contained a prophecy that the Antichrist will be a man in his forties of Muslim descent who will "promise false hope and world peace" but who "will destroy everything." Another email that was attributed to Christian missionaries who had worked in Kenya alarmingly reported, "Obama IS a muslim and he IS a racist and this is a fulfillment of the 911 threat that was just the beginning...He is not an American as we know it."

In the spring of 2008, a new anonymous email presented a fresh charge: "Barack Obama's mother was living in Kenya with his Arab-African father late in her pregnancy. She was not allowed to travel by plane then, so Barack Obama was born there and his mother then took him to Hawaii to register his birth." Thus started birtherism—the conspiracy theory that Obama, the first Black candidate with a credible shot of becoming president, was not a natural-born citizen and, consequently, not qualified under the US Constitution to become America's chief executive.

The Obama campaign fought back against this conspiratorial allegation that carried a racist stink. He denounced "the kind of politics that uses religion as a wedge, and patriotism as a bludgeon—that sees our opponents not as competitors to challenge, but enemies to demonize." His campaign unveiled a website called "Fight the Smears" to challenge the false accusations, and it posted a certification of live birth, issued by the Hawaiian department of health, that showed he entered this world in Honolulu in 1961.

That should have ended the matter. It didn't. Right-wing and conspiracy bloggers questioned the document's legitimacy: It wasn't signed, there was no raised seal, it lacked a crease, it was a "certification" not a "certificate." The racist theory proliferated. A mid-July Pew Research poll found that 12 percent believed Obama was a Muslim.

Late that month, a researcher discovered a birth announcement for

Obama that had appeared in the *Honolulu Advertiser* on August 13, 1961. Still, the birther conspiracy theory stayed alive. Jerome Corsi, the Red-baiting and bigoted coauthor of the debunked bible of the Swift Boaters, emerged as a prominent birther and went on Fox News to declare the birth certification was "fake." (That month, Corsi, according to a report of the Anti-Defamation League, appeared on a talk show hosted by white suprem-acists that regularly featured Holocaust deniers.)

Researchers for FactCheck.org examined the Hawaii certification and bat-ted away all the baseless claims about the document. The website concluded this record "meets all of the requirements from the State Department for proving U.S. citizenship." It stated, "The evidence is clear: Barack Obama was born in the USA."

Birtherism, though, was here to stay. In mid-August, Philip Berg, a for-mer deputy attorney general of Pennsylvania and a conspiracy theorist who claimed 9/11 had been an inside job, filed a lawsuit asserting Obama was born in Kenya and the birth certification a forgery. The case—which Lim-baugh talked up—would soon be dismissed as "frivolous." But there would be others.

In early October, as McCain descended in the polls, Palin, with her attacks associating Obama with terrorism, was channeling the underlying force propelling birtherism and the secret-Muslim smear: Obama was not a *real* American, he was foreign, he could not be trusted, he was a threat to the nation. In fact, a convergence occurred the day after Palin first accused Obama of "palling around" with terrorists, when Andy Martin appeared on Sean Hannity's show on Fox News and asserted—without any proof—that Obama's stint as a community organizer in the mid-1980s was "training for a radical overthrow of the government." He warned that if Obama were elected president, "we're basically going to be... in the throes of a socialist revolution, which attempts to essentially freeze out anybody who's not part of this radical ideology."

The othering of Obama proceeded at full speed—with its proponents spreading conspiracy theories and exploiting paranoia and racism—and the Republican vice presidential nominee led the charge. She was bringing to the fore a new form of presidential politics in which hatred, tribalism, and rage based on fearmongering, paranoia, and false accusation could be openly expressed as acceptable discourse.

At a rally in Jacksonville, Florida, Palin repeatedly assailed Obama for his connection to Ayers. A conservative radio host who addressed the crowd exclaimed Obama "hangs around with terrorists." Attendees wore shirts and held up signs reading No COMMUNISTS! A supporter in the crowd yelled, "Treason." During an event in Clearwater, Palin said of Obama, "I am just so fearful that this is not a man who sees America the way you and I see America." (At this rally, an attendee shouted a racial epithet at a cameraman.)

Palin served up a toxic blend of lies and xenophobia. An Associated Press analysis didn't hold back: Palin's "attack was unsubstantiated and carried a racially tinged subtext that John McCain himself may come to regret." It noted that "portraying Obama as 'not like us' is another potential appeal to racism." In an article endorsing Obama, Christopher Buckley, the novelist, *National Review* columnist, and former speechwriter for the first President Bush, explained his decision with a reference to his recently deceased father, William Buckley: "Dear Pup once said to me, 'You know I've spent my entire lifetime separating the right from the kooks.'"

When Palin mentioned Obama's link to Ayers at a campaign event, the crowd booed and one man in the audience yelled, "Kill him!" Speaking to a crowd of supporters in New Mexico, McCain asked, "Who is Barack Obama?" One person shouted, "Terrorist." The audience laughed; McCain did not challenge that. On air, Limbaugh amplified the Ayers story, suggesting that Ayers had written Obama's books because Obama was not smart enough to do so.

An attendee at a McCain town hall in Waukesha, Wisconsin, exclaimed, "I'm really mad. It's not the economy. It's the socialist taking over our country." He urged McCain to strike harder at "Obama, [House Speaker Nancy] Pelosi, and the rest of the hooligans." The crowd seconded the sentiment and chanted "USA." (Limbaugh hailed this Republican voter as a hero and chastised McCain for not forcefully attacking Obama: "The people of this country are dead scared about what we face if you lose.") Another man in the audience voiced the paranoia infecting the right: "Why is Obama where he's at? Everyone in this room is stunned. We are all a product of our associations." Something malevolent, he suggested, was afoot. Some in the crowd asserted Obama, this mysterious and diabolical pretender, was engineering voter fraud. McCain did not address the dark suspicions. He was riding the wave his campaign had triggered but now could not control.

McCain's camp even leaned into the suspicion with ads ominously asking, "Who is the real Barack Obama?" The spots ostensibly aimed to sow doubts about the Democratic nominee's experience and policy stands. But this line reinforced the smears and conspiracy theories that targeted Obama's race, religion, and patriotism. Another McCain ad was more explicit: "Barack Obama and domestic terrorist Bill Ayers. Friends. They've worked together for years. But Obama tries to hide it." It was a clear suggestion Obama was in active cahoots with a terrorist.

McCain-Palin rallies transformed into versions of the Two Minute Hate in George Orwell's *1984*, except longer. Crowds in Pennsylvania and Wisconsin shouted, "Off with his head." Warm-up speakers at McCain-Palin events railed against "Barack *Hussein* Obama."

The anger at these events kept rising. Journalists who had covered politics for years had not seen such hatred at campaign gatherings. Something different was occurring. The Republican base was enraged and, thanks to Palin, felt empowered to vent its ire. There was a tone of menace. Attendees would scream and curse at reporters and demand to know why they were not telling the world about Obama's terrorist and Marxist connections. They waved posters calling Obama a communist and proclaiming, BARACK BIN LYIN. They wore T-shirts featuring Obama and a hammer and sickle.

One memorable moment occurred during an event at a high school in Lakeville, Minnesota. A man told McCain he was "scared" of an Obama presidency. McCain responded with respect and kindness: "I have to tell you, he is a decent person and a person that you do not have to be scared of." The crowd didn't buy that and booed. Later a woman said she could not trust Obama because he was an "Arab." McCain replied, "No, ma'am, he's a decent family man, citizen, that I just happen to have disagreements with." Still, at this event, McCain criticized Obama for associating with Ayers.

The right was leaning on McCain to trash Obama and contributing its own conspiratorial twaddle. Floyd Brown, who cooked up the Willie Horton ad in 1988, claimed that Obama was a clandestine Muslim in league with billionaire George Soros, a Jewish financier, to sack the US economy. Former Reagan Pentagon official Frank Gaffney charged the Obama campaign had received between $30 million and $100 million from the Mideast, Africa, and other places "where Islamists are active," with some of these funds coming from jihadists. Donald Wildmon, the Christian right leader, warned that with an Obama victory, "America as we have known it will no longer exist.... [It] will be replaced by a secular state hostile to Christianity." Hysteria was on the march.

McCain and Palin were feeding the worst and most irrational (and perhaps racist) instincts of their voters. With the polls worsening for their man, McCain's strategists believed they had no option but to play to and stoke fear. "It's a dangerous road, but we have no choice," a McCain strategist told the New York *Daily News*. "If we keep talking about the economic crisis, we're going to lose." Reflecting on the campaign years afterward, Obama observed, "Through Palin, it seemed as if the dark spirits that have long been lurking on the edges of the modern Republican Party—xenophobia, anti-intellectualism, paranoid conspiracy theories, an antipathy toward Black and brown folks—were finding their way to center stage."

In the closing days of the campaign, McCain and Palin went full Red-baiting. They pointed to Obama's proposal for more progressive taxation and called him a socialist, maintaining he was hiding a secret anti-America agenda. At a Virginia rally, enraged supporters of the GOP ticket confronted reporters and demanded to know why they were covering up the Ayers-Obama link. Then they began chanting, "Socialist, socialist!" At an Iowa rally, ten days before the election, where attendees howled "Socialist!" at the mention of Obama's name, Palin compared his economic plan to the policies of communist tyrannies: "It leads to...government and politicians and, kind of moving in as the other half of your family to make decisions for you. Now they do this in other countries where people are not free."

At another event, Palin declared, "now is not the time to experiment with socialism." (She was the governor of a state where residents collectively owned the oil resources and received an annual check from the state with a share of the revenue.) PolitiFact called her claim that Obama would "experiment with socialism" a "Pants-on-Fire!" lie. Yet top Republicans joined the chorus, pronouncing Obama a socialist and insisting the election was a referendum on socialism.

For decades, the Republicans had tried to capitalize on tribal sentiments and convince voters that the Democratic presidential nominee of the moment did not embrace American values and was not a *real* American. George McGovern was an anti-military liberal and not a real American. Bill Clinton was a counterculture Boomer and not a real American. Michael Dukakis was a soft-on-crime ACLUer and not a real American. Obama was another in this long line. Republicans were seeking to encourage and profit from the baseless paranoia and suspicions toward Obama that had proliferated on the right. They were legitimizing rage among their faithful. It was no coincidence the target was a Black man. "For those voters," Obama remarked later, "I was no longer just a left-of-center Democrat who planned to broaden the social safety net and end the war in Iraq. I was something more insidious, someone to be feared, someone to be stopped."

McCain and Palin's effort to tap into fright, resentment, and racism—to spin paranoia and suspicion into an electoral majority—failed. On November 4, the people of the United States elected Obama president. His victory was decisive: 53 percent of the popular vote and 68 percent of the electoral votes. Democrats boosted their majorities in both houses of Congress. A postelection study found that Palin had cost McCain about two million votes.

The Palin pick had been a long shot—a Hail Mary that turned into a nightmare for the McCain campaign. And McCain had done more than lose an election. He unleashed—or boosted—a new force. Not just Palin herself, but Palinism: a combination of smear politics, conspiracism, and know-nothingism. McCain "took a disease that was running through the Republican Party—anti-intellectualism, disrespect for facts—and he put it right at the center of the party," author David Brooks observed years afterward. McCain and Palin were defeated, but this brand of demagoguery took root—and it could spread easily through the internet and the expanding right-wing information ecosystem. It was an extremism that interlaced mainstream conservatives, the Republican Party, and the right's conspiratorial fringe and that would influence GOP politics and bedevil the nation for years to come.

A week after the election, Representative Paul Broun, a Georgia Republican, compared Obama to Hitler and Marx and said he feared that Obama, once in office, would establish a Gestapo and impose a communist dictatorship. Right-wing radio host Michael Savage booked as a guest a onetime German member of the Hitler Youth to discuss the similarities between the rise of Nazism and America under Obama.

This stuff was not going away.

CHAPTER 21

Feed the Beast

On January 20, 2009, a bitterly cold day in Washington, Barack Obama stood on a platform on the west side of the US Capitol. The nation remained mired in two wars overseas. The economy was in a freefall. About 1.5 million jobs had been lost since Election Day. Gazing at the massive crowd on the National Mall, the forty-fourth president of the United States called for the country to work together to repair itself: "We gather because we have chosen hope over fear, unity of purpose over conflict and discord. On this day, we come to proclaim an end to the petty grievances and false promises, the recriminations and worn-out dogmas that for far too long have strangled our politics.... In the words of Scripture, the time has come to set aside childish things."

That evening, about fifteen of the top Republicans in town—Representatives Eric Cantor, Paul Ryan, and Kevin McCarthy, Senators Jim DeMint, Jon Kyl, and Tom Coburn, pollster Frank Luntz, former House Speaker Gingrich, and others—met for dinner at the Caucus Room, a ritzy restaurant. They were not there to put aside grievances and recriminations. They were plotting how to block Obama and his agenda, especially the $800 billion stimulus package he was developing to restore the economy. In a time of economic emergency, with Obama's presidency only hours old, they resolved to say no to whatever Obama proposed. That would, they believed, position them best to take the House and Senate in 2010 and the White House two years later. As they departed, Gingrich told his compatriots, "You will remember this day."

There would be no honeymoon. The Republicans would be the party of absolute opposition—pushed in this direction by the far-right voices on talk radio and Fox News. But they didn't realize they were about to be both aided and challenged by a new form of conservative extremism.

―――

In mid-February, Congress passed Obama's stimulus bill, with not a single House Republican and only three GOP senators voting for it. (The measure would eventually create or save three million jobs.) Two days after Obama signed it into law, Rick Santelli, a CNBC commentator, exploded on air while on the floor of the Chicago Mercantile Exchange. He assailed Obama's plan to assist financially pressed homeowners, branding it Cuban-style statism. Why help *losers* pay for their mortgages? With no sense of irony—the traders egging on Santelli had jobs because the government had rescued the financial system—he urged a new Tea Party to rebel against big government bailouts and spending. (The original Tea Party had been a protest against unelected officials overseas imposing onerous taxes. In the stimulus package, Obama provided middle-income Americans a tax cut.)

Santelli's rant went viral. In the new age of social media, the sharing of outrage had become nearly instantaneous. So, too, organizing. Soon groups in and out of Washington were setting up Tea Party rallies in dozens of cities. A major player in this effort was a libertarian-minded outfit called Freedom-Works, which was linked to right-wing billionaire brothers David and Charles Koch (whose father, Fred, had been a founding member of the John Birch Society). The new movement might have looked like a spontaneous explosion of grassroots rage, but not too far behind the scenes big-money, right-wing, corporate-backed outfits were astroturfing the fury to advance their own anti-government, anti-regulations, and tax-cutting agenda.

Two months later, on April 15, Tea Party protests—promoted by Fox News, other conservative media, and long-established rightist organizations, including the Young Republicans and the Heritage Foundation—were held in more than two hundred cities and drew several hundred thousand people. The mad-as-hell events had a goofy side: suburbanites dressing up in colonial outfits. There was also a disturbing element: signs depicting Obama as the bloody-smiling Joker or Hitler. And others: OBAMA IS THE ANTI-CHRIST. THE AMERICAN TAXPAYERS ARE THE JEWS FOR OBAMA'S OVENS. STAND IDLY BY WHILE SOME KENYAN TRIES TO DESTROY AMERICA?... HOMEY DON'T PLAY DAT!!!

At some rallies, Confederate flags waved. Attendees shared with reporters assorted conspiratorial beliefs that probably could be summed up in one overarching and ominous right-wing fantasy: Obama was a secret Muslim born in Kenya who was in league with shadowy elites and purposefully trying to destroy the nation by increasing the deficit and forcing an economic collapse he could exploit to impose a totalitarian regime.

The protest participants included a crazy quilt of the right: anti-government advocates, militia people, Christian nationalists, abortion rights foes, opponents of gun safety measures, libertarians, birthers, social conservatives, and veterans of the Patriots movement of the 1990s. A bit of the old New Right and the Christian right—with even more anger. They didn't like bailouts and government spending, particularly Obama's stimulus. But the central organizing principle appeared to be hatred of Obama and a fear of impending tyranny and doom. This was a sequel to the alarming McCain-Palin rallies of the previous fall.

Representative Kevin McCarthy, a California Republican, brought Representative John Boehner, an Ohio Republican who was the party's House leader, to the Tea Party rally held that day in Bakersfield. No rabble-rouser, Boehner was a country-club conservative, crafty and well-skilled in the political games of Capitol Hill. The son of a barkeep, he fancied cutting deals and then hitting the links or repairing to a saloon where he could enjoy a cigarette and a glass of merlot. This event was a wake-up call—or a warning. As journalist Robert Draper later put it, "Boehner had never seen anything like it—an outcry of anti-Washington vitriol bordering on the elemental—and immediately recognized that he could either board this train or be flattened by it." These folks were not looking for the Republicans to legislate. Many Tea Partiers considered the GOP part of the turncoat establishment that was betraying the nation. They yearned for Republicans willing to wage all-out war against Obama, the commie libs, the corrupt elites, and whoever the hell else was destroying their US of A.

An ugly and raw nerve had been struck. But the new Tea Party movement and the GOP were heading toward a marriage of convenience—or perhaps a shotgun wedding—in which the Republicans would accept and encourage foul and conspiratorial currents to achieve power.

In July, congressional Democrats introduced Obama's major health care reform bill, eventually called the Affordable Care Act. It would establish a government-run clearinghouse for private insurance plans to allow tens of millions of uninsured people to obtain coverage and would implement numerous reforms to constrain health care costs and boost quality. Insurers would no longer be able to deny coverage due to preexisting conditions. The right immediately blasted the proposal, which was largely based on a plan once advocated by the Heritage Foundation and implemented by Mitt Romney when he was governor of Massachusetts, as a government takeover of the health care industry—a false charge.

One particularly phony allegation would come to define the right-wing assault on this initiative: the act would create mandatory counseling sessions for seniors during which they would be pressured to end their lives. This charge of so-called "death panels" ricocheted through the traditional conservative media echo chamber—the *New York Post*, Fox News, Limbaugh, the *Wall Street Journal*—and the increasingly influential social media world of Facebook and Twitter, where much Tea Party networking and conspiracy-mongering was occurring. Far-right Representative Virginia Foxx, a Virginia Republican, exclaimed on the House floor that the plan would "put seniors in a position of being put to death by their government." Boehner echoed this untrue allegation. (The plan would set up only *voluntary* end-of-life counseling.) But it was Sarah Palin who turned this disinformation into a national panic.

After the 2008 election, Palin returned to Alaska, where her approval rating had fallen nearly forty points. In July 2009, fed up with her job as governor, she abruptly resigned. Perhaps to cash in—she was reportedly making speeches for $100,000 an appearance—or to prepare for a presidential bid. She remained a hero for the far right.

In early August, she published a Facebook post asserting Obama was setting up a "death panel" in which "his bureaucrats" would judge "the sick, the elderly, and the disabled" on their "level of productivity in society" and determine "whether they are worthy of health care." She called this "downright evil."

Her fraudulent charge triggered a media frenzy. Senator Lisa Murkowski, a moderate Alaska Republican who Palin's political action committee supported, criticized her: "It does us no good to incite fear in people by saying that there's...these 'death panels'...There is no reason to gin up fear in the American public by saying things that are not included in the bill." But conservatives were drawn to her lie. Limbaugh backed Palin: "She's dead right." (PolitiFact would months later brand death panels the "Lie of the Year.")

Within weeks, 30 percent of Americans believed death panels were real. (Among Republicans, that number was 47 percent.) And there was a new political force to grab hold of this inflammatory and inaccurate accusation: the Tea Party.

To their list of grievances, Tea Partiers added Obamacare and the death panels. At congressional town hall meetings, right-wing activists voiced their ire. During one such event, Representative John Dingell, a Michigan Democrat, was booed and heckled. A man with a son afflicted with cerebral palsy screamed at Dingell that the new bill would mean the end of his son's life. As Dingell tried to explain that was not true, the constituent yelled, "Fraud! Liar!" Republicans eagerly capitalized on this baseless fear. At a constituent meeting in Iowa, Senator Chuck Grassley told the crowd, "We should not have a government program that determines you're gonna pull the plug on Grandma."

Throughout the summer, Tea Partiers railed about "socialistic" medicine. They compared Obama's administration to the Soviet Union, communist China, and the Nazis. They screamed at Democratic and Republicans: *We want our country back.* Violence was a theme. At a town hall meeting

Obama held in New Hampshire, a man bearing a pistol (legally) held a banner that said, IT'S TIME TO WATER THE TREE OF LIBERTY. (This was an allusion to a Thomas Jefferson quote: "The tree of liberty must be refreshed from time to time with the blood of patriots and tyrants.") At a constituent event hosted by Democratic Senator Ben Cardin in Hagerstown, Maryland, a man held up a sign that read DEATH TO OBAMA. (The US government and public-interest watchdog groups noticed that right-wing militia activism, after declining in the late 1990s, was on the rise.) A popular T-shirt at Tea Party gatherings said PROUD RIGHT-WING EXTREMIST.

During the first year of Obama's presidency, Limbaugh did his share to whip up the hate and paranoia. He pronounced Obama an "extremist tyrannical president." He claimed the president was pushing socialism and "fascism." He told his audience that the Obamacare logo was "close to a Nazi swastika," that Obama and the Democratic Party planned "to impose Nazi-like socialism policies on this country," and that the Obama White House was "sending out thugs to beat people up" at town hall meetings.

Limbaugh's swill was incessant. Obama and the Democrats were destroying cities so Republicans would move out and Democrats could control them. They were "purposefully" ruining the US economy in order to gain "total control" of the nation. Limbaugh pushed one conspiratorial notion after another, playing to his audience's prejudices and making millions: Obama was an "authoritarian imperialist"; he had "sympathy for dictators" because he "inherited his father's Marxism"; his goal was to become "emperor." And this radio agitator kept promoting birtherism. Obama was "more African in his roots than he is American," he bleated, and was "behaving like an African colonial despot."

Republicans still loved Limbaugh. He claimed he constantly heard from members of Congress who wanted him to promote their efforts. One poll found that 11 percent of Republicans considered this radio chest-thumper the leader of their party. He was the voice of the GOP.

The racist notion that Obama was not an American had not been erased by his election as president. In fact, it seemed to gain ground—including within the Republican Party. Following Election Day, lawsuits were filed in several states challenging the certification of Obama's victories on the false claim he had not been born in the United States. They were all tossed out. But birtherism was being encouraged by prominent Republicans. Senator Richard Shelby, an Alabama Republican, expressed doubt about Obama's birthplace, saying "I haven't seen any birth certificate."

Representative Bill Posey, a Florida Republican, introduced a bill that would require presidential candidates to disclose their birth certificates— and he refused to say whether he believed Obama had been born in the United States. Conservative Republicans began signing on to the bill, including Representative Randy Neugebauer of Texas, who said of Obama's citizenship, "I don't know. I've never seen him produce documents that would say one way or another." (The Obama campaign had produced a certification of birth.) The two Republican senators of Oklahoma each made birtherish comments. When Representative Mike Castle of Delaware said at a town hall meeting that Obama was a citizen, an angry crowd of his constituents booed him. A poll taken in July showed that only 42 percent of Republicans believed Obama was born in America. Twenty-eight percent said that he was not, and 30 percent were unsure.

One unlikely conservative voice advising the right to refrain from birtherism was Glenn Beck. The Fox News host told his audience to forget about Obama's citizenship—he assumed Obama was a natural-born American. Birtherism, he said, was being used to "marginalize" Obama's critics: "It makes them look like flat-earthers." He counseled his viewers to focus on the Red threat, claiming Obama was "appointing Communists."

Beck joined Fox in January 2009 and doled out a poisonous stew of inflammatory rhetoric and conspiratorial demagoguery. He was an immediate hit, soon drawing huge audiences of millions. Through his Fox broadcast and his daily radio show, he peddled Bircher-like apocalyptic paranoia. Beck— once derided by novelist Stephen King as "Satan's mentally challenged younger brother"—hounded Obama appointees he depicted as hair-raising threats to the nation and elevated a crazy rumor that the Obama administration was using the Federal Emergency Management Agency to set up concentration camps for its political enemies. "We are a country that is headed towards socialism, totalitarianism, beyond your wildest imagination," he declared. Obama—a "socialist" or a "full-fledged Marxist"—had plans to create a "dictorial" [sic] and "fascist" state. Beck warned Obama was setting up a "civilian national security force" and "this is what Hitler did with the SS." He also called Obama a "racist" who had "a deep-seated hatred for white people."

Beck's mission was to terrify his audience. For Beck—a professed fan and promoter of the crackpot conspiracy theorist W. Cleon Skousen—there were plots everywhere: The US government intended to seize land in order to back a new currency. The government wanted access to your home thermostats so it could control you and your family. The message he repeated ad nauseum: Obama is an existential threat to the nation, and they are coming for *you*.

Beck's rise at Fox coincided with the birth of the Tea Party, and he became a favorite of the movement. Tea Partiers held Beck-watching parties in local restaurants. They bought the distorted right-wing history books he hawked. They hung on his every delusion. If outrage and paranoia were the measurement, Beck outdid Limbaugh in feeding the animosity of Republicans and conservatives who feared the Black man in the Oval Office.

In Beck's telling, a civil war was practically at hand—or might need to be to save the nation from Obama. And this merchant of lies, suspicions, and false horrors was fully validated by the GOP and the conservative movement. Republican leaders—Rove, Palin, and GOP chair Michael Steele—regularly appeared on his show. His guests included Senators Hatch, DeMint, and Judd Gregg and Representatives Boehner, Michele Bachmann, and Darrell Issa. In a video tribute to an unaccredited Utah-based college that promoted the works of Skousen, Romney hailed Beck as "a man who is really making an impact in our entire country" and called him "a statesman in his own right." All these Republicans were providing credibility to an unhinged conspiracy theorist who demonized Obama, sowed political discord, and bolstered hate, terror, and distrust within the American public.

Beck, Limbaugh, other right-wing media, Tea Partiers (and their big-money underwriters), and Republicans were creating a dangerous narrative: America was under attack from the inside. Anyone who listened to all this and believed these sources had reason to be profoundly afraid. In late August, on his radio show, Beck informed his followers the situation was calamitous: "Most of America doesn't have a clue as to what's going on. There is a coup going on. There is a stealing of America, and the way it is done, it has been done through the guise of an election, but they lied to us the entire time. Some of us knew! Some of us, we're shouting out, you were: 'This guy's a Marxist!' 'No, no, no, no, no, no.' And they're gonna say, 'We did it democratically,' and they are going to grab power every way they can. And God help us in an emergency."

On September 12, Beck's troops assembled in the nation's capital, with Tea Partiers and other right-wingers gathering for what was billed as the Taxpayer March on Washington, an event he had energetically promoted.

The rally—organized by the corporate-sponsored FreedomWorks—drew a crowd of tens of thousands (as the media reported) or one million (as the organizers claimed). Limbaugh insisted two million people were present.

It was a festival of loathing. Speakers railed against an Obama-guided descent into socialism and a loss of the "American way." Signs compared Obama to Hitler and promoted extreme messages: TREASON. PARASITE-IN-CHIEF. OBAMMUNISM IS COMMUNISM. The protest was laced with racism. People carried posters depicting Obama as an African witch doctor. One woman held a placard reading THE ZOO HAS AN AFRICAN LION AND THE WHITE HOUSE HAS A LYIN' AFRICAN! Another person had a sign that said SOMEWHERE IN KENYA A VILLAGE IS MISSING AN IDIOT. Audience members waved GLENN BECK FOR PRESIDENT signs. One woman told a reporter that "people are here because they're afraid of the death camps that are coming."

Attendees complained about illegal immigration, the Obama administration appointing "czars" to oversee key policy areas, the purported climate change hoax, and the health care bill. And this hodgepodge of animosity, conspiracy, and false accusations was blessed by Republicans. Speakers included former House Majority Leader Dick Armey, Senator DeMint, and Representatives Mike Pence, Marsha Blackburn, and Tom Price. Pence declared that "Americans want health care reform, but they don't want government takeover."

The GOP's base, racked with Tea Party fever, was losing touch with reality. In October, a focus group study of conservative Republicans in the Atlanta area found that these people believed that Obama was ruthlessly advancing a secret agenda to wreck the United States to expand government control of the citizenry and that he was fronting for evil forces that had underhandedly maneuvered him into the White House. And though the Republicans were encouraging such fact-free and irrational opinions, these conservatives believed the GOP was not mounting a fierce enough opposition. Instead, they relied on Glenn Beck, Fox News, and the Tea Party. To gain their support, the GOP would have to destroy Obama.

A month later, Bachmann called the Tea Party foot soldiers to Capitol Hill for an event that would fuse the GOP to the Tea Party and its extremism.

A second-term House member from Minnesota, Bachmann had developed a reputation as one of the more bizarre legislators in the nation. A spokesperson for the paranoid right, she was a proponent of death panel disinfo. Earlier in the year, she had said she would refuse to fill out the US census form for 2010 because the information collected could be used to set up internment camps. She also had accused Obama of attempting to establish "reeducation camps" for young people. (She was referring to a community service program.) During the 2008 campaign, she had expressed concern that Obama "may have anti-American views" and called for the media to "take a great look at the views of the people in Congress and find out are they pro-America, or anti-America." Bachmann was a Tea Party star.

As the Obama health care package moved through Congress, approaching votes, Bachmann, appearing on Fox News, urged Tea Partiers to trek to the Capitol for a last-ditch attempt to kill the measure. Several thousand heeded her call and flocked to a protest outside Congress. (Many attendees had been bused in by Americans for Prosperity, a conservative organization started by the Koch Brothers.) They carried signs depicting Obama as Sambo. One placard said OBAMA TAKES HIS ORDERS FROM THE ROTHSCHILDS—a new take on a persistent antisemitic trope. There were posters referencing birtherism.

The crowd roiled with anger. Most notably, GOP leaders basked in the rage and cheered on a movement partly powered by racism and antisemitism. Only a few days earlier, while Obama was delivering a speech to Congress, Representative Joe Wilson, a South Carolina Republican, had shouted at the president "You lie!" The speakers that day shared Wilson's hostility.

After Bachmann addressed the assembled—and the crowd yelled, "Kill the bill! Kill the bill!"—top House Republicans Boehner, Cantor, and Pence each made his way to the microphone, as did other GOP legislators. They all wanted a piece of this action. Fully in the mood, Boehner called the bill, "the greatest threat to freedom I have ever seen." (Greater than Jim Crow?) TV actor John Ratzenberger claimed the Democrats were propelled by ideas that come from "overseas." Hollywood legend Jon Voight warned Obamacare was a step toward national socialism. In the front of the crowd, a protester held an enormous sign that equated Obamacare with Holocaust death camps. At the mention of Democrats, the crowd shouted, "Nazis! Nazis!"

The rally marked the House Republicans' complete embrace of the Tea Party—with all its ugly extremism. They had placed their imprimatur upon a fury-driven movement fired up by bigotry. Boehner clearly believed he could ride this tiger to the majority and attain his dream of becoming speaker. He and his comrades were feeding a beast.

———

The Republicans soon had reason to believe their dreams of a Tea Party–fueled victory could come true. In January 2010, Massachusetts Republican state Senator Scott Brown defeated Democratic state Attorney General Martha Coakley to fill the US Senate seat left open by the death of Ted Kennedy.

Brown had vowed to vote against Obama's health care initiative. The media labeled Brown's win the Tea Party's first electoral triumph.

A few weeks later, one of the movement's leading groups, Tea Party Nation, held the first national Tea Party convention in Nashville. TPN was a for-profit corporation, and it charged $549 a ticket, presumably pocketing a good chunk of the revenue. That prompted grumbling among Tea Partiers about grifting within their movement. One speaker warned that Obama and his crew were using climate change to seize control of Americans' lives and impose "a one-world government."* Judge Roy Moore, a conservative hero, claimed Obama wanted "a UN guard stationed in every house." There was much discussion about Obama's birth certificate. Palin, who recently had pronounced birtherism "a fair question," headlined as the keynote speaker. Conservative writer Jonathan Kay, who was in attendance, complained, "It has become clear to me that the movement is dominated by people whose vision of the government is conspiratorial and dangerously detached from reality."

Downplaying the fringe-right paranoia on display, the organizers of the event insisted they had a more mature goal: electing a Tea Party Congress later that year. In essence, taking over the Republican Party.

The hate kept coming. On March 20, 2010, as House Democratic leaders worked to round up the votes needed for final passage of the Affordable Care Act, hundreds of angry Tea Party activists gathered outside the Capitol. When Representative John Lewis, a Georgia Democrat and civil rights icon, passed by, demonstrators yelled "nigger" at him. Representative Barney Frank, an openly gay Massachusetts Democrat, received similar treatment, as protesters shouted "faggot" and "homo." Representative Emanuel Cleaver, a Missouri Democrat and a Black man, entered the Capitol, and a protester spat at him.

The bill, which paved the way for 20 million people to obtain health insurance, passed the next day on a 219–212 vote. All 178 Republicans opposed it. "Get down on your knees and pray," Beck told his people. "Pray. It's September 11th all over again."

———

The Tea Party was not exactly a brand-new political phenomenon. It was essentially the GOP's right-wing base on steroids. This was an old whine in

---

* Climate change was a key target of right-wing and Republican conspiracism. A few weeks earlier, Senator James Inhofe, an Oklahoma Republican who was a GOP point man on the issue, told me that climate change was a hoax cooked up by radical environmentalists and Hollywood liberals who had managed to hoodwink scientists, legislators, and policy advocates around the world. The cabal, he said, was led by Barbra Streisand. He was serious.

a new bottle. The movement comprised mostly white men over the age of forty-five, with almost two-thirds of its supporters identifying as conservative Republicans. Sixty-three percent watched Fox News. They tended to believe that "too much has been made of the problems facing black America" and that Obama favored Blacks over whites. Fifty-nine percent doubted Obama's American nationality. Polls showed a deep antipathy among Tea Partiers for undocumented immigrants. Many identified with the religious right. And, no doubt, they recoiled at a host of overlapping social and demographic forces affording more influence to the urban, the young, the secular, Latinos, and Asians.

This was the GOP core riled up and operating within an enclosed and self-reinforcing information ecosystem of right-wing bloggers, websites (including the relatively new *Breitbart News*), social media, talk radio, and Fox. Hofstadter, Lipset, and other chroniclers of far-right extremism had concluded it was often propelled by the fear of declining social status in a shifting world. As political scientists Christopher Parker and Matt Barreto would note, "People are driven to support the Tea Party from the anxiety they feel as they perceive the America they know, the country they love, slipping away, threatened by the rapidly changing face of what they perceive as the 'real' America: a heterosexual, Christian (mostly) male, white country."

These people were becoming a powerful electoral force within the GOP. And Palin led the way. Following passage of Obamacare, her political action committee identified congressional Democrats to defeat in the upcoming midterm elections, and the group produced a map with crosshairs designating the targeted congressional districts. One belonged to Representative Gabrielle Giffords of Arizona. To fire up her Tea Party followers, Palin issued a tweet urging, "Don't Retreat, Instead—RELOAD!"

Liberal commentators attacked Palin's use of violent imagery. Giffords responded in an interview: "We're on Sarah Palin's targeted list, but the thing is that the way that she has it depicted has the crosshairs of a gun sight over our district, and when people do that, they've got to realize there are consequences to that action."*

———

It was a spring of discontent for Republicans not in line with the Tea Party and the extremist paranoia, hate, and bigotry the GOP was normalizing.

———

* On January 8, 2011, Jared Lee Loughner, a troubled young man, shot Giffords in the head during a constituent event and opened fire on the people lined up to meet her—injuring fourteen and killing six. Giffords survived but was severely injured; she later resigned from Congress. Loughner had no apparent partisan motive.

Representative Bob Inglis, a Republican from South Carolina, discovered this when he traveled to his district and met with donors to his previous campaigns. Though Inglis had a 93 percent lifetime rating from the American Conservative Union, he faced a challenge in the GOP primary from a local prosecutor backed by the Tea Party, and his longtime financial supporters were not ponying up for his reelection. "They were upset with me," Inglis later recalled. They were Beck fans and during the meeting, as Inglis recounted, "They say, 'Bob, what don't you get? Barack Obama is a socialist, communist Marxist who wants to destroy the American economy so he can take over as dictator. Health care is part of that. And he wants to open up the Mexican border and turn [the US] into a Muslim nation.'" Inglis was stunned. He hadn't realized how deep his constituents had fallen into the pit.

Inglis consulted with Boehner. What should he do? The top House Republican advised him to tell these people that things were not quite that bad and that Inglis did disagree with Obama on the issues. "Hold on, Boehner," Inglis responded. "That doesn't work. Let me tell you, I tried that and it did not work." He told Boehner, "If you're going to lead these people and the fearful stampede to the cliff that they're heading to, you have to turn around say over your shoulder, 'Hey, you don't know the half of it.'" That is, reinforce their anger and paranoia.

On the campaign trail, fighting for his political life, Inglis, who had served six terms in Congress, was pressed repeatedly to call Obama a "socialist." He wouldn't. He considered that a lie.

At one point, he met with a dozen Tea Party activists. "I sat down," he recalled, "and they said on the back of your Social Security card, there's a number. That number indicates the bank that bought you when you were born based on a projection of your life's earnings, and you are collateral. We are all collateral for the banks. I have this look like, 'What the heck are you talking about?' I'm trying to hide that look and look clueless. I figured clueless was better than argumentative. So they said, 'You don't know this?! You are a member of Congress, and you don't know this?!' And I said, 'Please forgive me. I'm just ignorant of these things.' And then of course, it turned into something about the Federal Reserve and the Bilderbergers and all that stuff. And now you have the feeling of antisemitism coming in, mixing in."

Death panels, birtherism, global conspiracies—Inglis heard it all. Voters echoed Beck and Limbaugh and hailed Palin. Inglis ruefully saw this as a celebration of ignorance. The "flame-throwers" of the right, he subsequently said, "were causing people to run with fear and panic," and his fellow Republican officials were "afraid of being run over by that stampeding crowd." His colleagues could not "summon the courage" to say no to Beck, Limbaugh, and the Tea Party. Boehner had made his strategic calculation: Play to the extremists.

What Inglis witnessed was occurring throughout the land. On May 8, Tea Party activists at the Republican state party convention in Utah mutinied against incumbent Senator Bob Bennett, mocking him as "Bail-Out Bob" for having voted for the huge TARP financial rescue plan. And the Tea Partiers didn't appreciate that he wouldn't label Obama a "socialist." They supported an attorney named Mike Lee for the Senate nomination, and Bennett came in third. He was out of a job.

That same month, Rand Paul, a far-right conservative activist and ophthalmologist who shared the conspiratorial bent of his father, Representative Ron Paul, defeated a moderate Republican in the party's primary for US Senate in Kentucky. Rand Paul had regularly appeared on the radio show of Alex Jones, a loony anti-government conspiracy theorist and one of the more prominent cheerleaders for the idea that the Bush administration was complicit in the 9/11 attacks. On one show, Paul agreed with Jones when the host called the TARP financial rescue package "fascism" and claimed an Obama climate change bill would establish an "army of armed EPA agents— thousands of them" who would burst into residences to determine if they were meeting energy-efficiency standards. Paul joined Jones (and validated him) in declaiming the "New World Order," which in Jones's world was code for a cabal of globalists and international financiers plotting to undermine, if not destroy, the United States for their own gain. (Jones believed a key part of this plot was to create a "scientific dictatorship" that would exterminate the "useless eaters," aka 80 percent of the human population.)

In Maine, Tea Party activists at the Republican Party state convention replaced a middle-of-the-road platform with one that dismissed climate change as a myth, called for the abolition of the Federal Reserve and the Department of Education, and expressed concerns about "one world government." In Nevada, Sharron Angle, a Tea Party-backed candidate and oddball who had called for abolishing Social Security and decried black football uniforms because they suggested satanic influence, defeated a former chair of the state GOP for a US Senate nomination. (Weeks later, she spoke at a conference cosponsored by the John Birch Society.) During the general election against Senate Majority Leader Harry Reid, she would talk of the possible need for "Second Amendment remedies" to reform Congress—which to many seemed an endorsement of violence.

In late June, Inglis was drubbed by his Tea Party opponent, Trey Gowdy, 71 to 29 percent.

Since the mid-1990s, the percentage of Republicans who called them-selves "very conservative" had been rising. (It would go from 19 percent to 33 percent by 2015.) They were not only more conservative regarding ideology and policy; they were more die-hard in sentiment. They desired confronta-tion and looked to have their rage, grievances, and suspicions—even irra-tional and unfounded beliefs—validated and championed. It was a politics of feeling. E. J. Dionne Jr. called it "the steady radicalization of American conservatism." And Inglis was on the wrong side of this.

Afterward, Inglis noted that his party had been hijacked by Beck, Lim-baugh, and the extreme right: "We're being driven as herd by these hot micro-phones…that are causing people to run with fear and panic." He said it was difficult for Republicans in Congress to "summon the courage" to say no to these talkers and the Tea Party wing. "We're failing the conservative move-ment," he remarked. "We're failing the country." He disparaged Boehner's attempt to use the Tea Party to win the House: "It's a dangerous strategy to build conservatism on information and policies that are not credible."

Credibility and policy were not priorities for the GOP and the right. Out-landish stances, allegations, and conspiracy theories were the imperatives. This was a politics of hyperbole. The redder the meat the better. Beck con-stantly claimed an evil New World Order—the long-held bugaboo of Skou-sen, Robertson, and other conspiracists—was practically at hand under the dictatorial reign of Obama. (In July, one Beck viewer assembled an arse-nal of guns and headed to shoot up the San Francisco office of a small, lib-eral foundation that Beck had identified as a linchpin in this conspiracy to destroy capitalism. On his way there, the gunman was stopped by police and after a shoot-out apprehended.) On one show, Beck read from a 1948 antisemitic book commissioned by poet Ezra Pound that claimed Jewish-led bankers had created the Federal Reserve to dominate the world. Former Republican Representative Tom Tancredo declared Obama "a more serious threat to America than al Qaeda." Former Arkansas Governor Huckabee claimed Obama's "worldview is dramatically different than any president, Republican or Democrat, we've had," explaining (or so he thought), "He grew up more as a globalist than an American."

The conspiracism and ridiculous narratives never ended. It was good for ratings and business and profitable fodder for fundraising letters. Writing in *Forbes*, far-right commentator Dinesh D'Souza served up a delusional sce-nario. Starting with the false premise that Obama's actions "are so bizarre that they mystify his critics and supporters alike," D'Souza contended that the two most popular explanations—Obama is "clueless" or a "European-style socialist"—were insufficient. What accounted for Obama's decisions, he insisted, was a fierce "anticolonialism" that Obama had inherited from the Kenyan father he had barely known. "Obama learned to see America as a force for global domination and destruction," D'Souza insisted, and he was committed to thwarting it. In a statement bordering on racist, D'Souza asserted, "The U.S. is being ruled according to the dreams of a Luo tribesman of the 1950s." (Obama's father had received an M.A. in economics from Harvard.)

D'Souza had created a high-class version of the Obama-as-witch-doctor signs displayed at Tea Party rallies. It was birtherism nonsense taken to a new level. Yet it had Gingrich's endorsement. He called D'Souza's article the "most profound insight I have read in the last six years about Barack Obama." Gingrich waxed, "What if [Obama] is so outside our comprehension, that only if you understand Kenyan, anti-colonial behavior, can you begin to piece together [his actions]? That is the most accurate, predictive model for his behavior."

This marked the apex—or nadir—of the Republican and conservative attempt to *other* Obama and portray him as not a real American, and it buttressed the message pushed by Beck, Tea Partiers, and others that the country was endangered by a subversive internal enemy. Years later, Obama would reflect, "The Tea Party and its media allies had accomplished more than just their goal of demonizing the healthcare bill. They had demonized me."

———

Early in October, one set of Tea Party leaders met with members of the Council for National Policy, which now included Palin and Armey among its several hundred participants. The Tea Partiers shared a secret strategy memo that outlined their $675,000 get-out-the-vote effort for the midterm elections. It also noted a grander ambition: to "renew the commitment to limited government and free markets in the hearts and minds of at least 60 percent of the American public over the next 40 years."

The Tea Party had continued to demonstrate its electoral muscle. In Florida, Marco Rubio, the former speaker of the Florida House of Representatives and a Tea Party–backed candidate, scared GOP Governor Charlie Crist out of the race for the Republican US Senate nomination. Rick Scott, a Tea Party–favored political novice who had once headed a giant health company fined $1.7 billion for defrauding Medicare and other federal programs, beat Representative Bill McCollum, an establishment Republican, in the state's GOP gubernatorial primary. In the Republican Senate primary in Delaware, the Tea Party raised hundreds of thousands of dollars for social conservative activist Christine O'Donnell. She had defaulted on personal loans and been pursued by the IRS for failing to pay taxes but had racked up endorsements from Palin, Limbaugh, and the NRA. She defeated nine-term Representative Mike Castle. (When Karl Rove on Fox News pronounced O'Donnell's statements "nutty" and called her unelectable, Palin, Limbaugh, and other right-wingers berated him. He soon was back on the air endorsing O'Donnell.) After giving speeches at Tea Party rallies, Ron Johnson, the CEO of a plastics business in Wisconsin, won the GOP senatorial nomination. In October, the New York Times identified 129 House candidates and nine Senate contenders affiliated with the Tea Party, each one a Republican.

Boehner was delighted to exploit the Tea Partiers. He had McCarthy draw up a "Pledge to America" for GOP congressional candidates—their version of Gingrich's Contract with America. It addressed core Tea Party issues: repeal Obamacare, halt all tax increases, cut federal spending by $100 billion. The Tea Party—with up to 1,400 loosely knit groups across the country—was now driving the conservative movement and the Grand Old Party. At the same time, money poured into the campaign. Republican outside groups dumped almost $200 million into Senate and House races, more than twice what was coming from pro-Democratic sources.

Election Day was a massacre for Obama and the Democrats. The party in charge of the White House tends to take a hit in midterms. And Main Street was still reeling from the economic devastation caused by the financial meltdown of the Bush-Cheney years, while 180,000 American troops remained deployed in unpopular quagmires in Iraq and Afghanistan. Obama had passed a financial reform bill over Wall Street objections—but it had generated little political steam for him. A hard-to-contain massive oil spill in the Gulf of Mexico had been a political drag on Obama. With all this, the White House had expected to lose thirty or so House seats. But the Republicans picked up a whopping sixty-four seats to win control of the lower chamber. The Democrats lost six Senate seats but held on to the majority. Conservatives and extremists—including Rand Paul and Ron Johnson—rode the Tea Party wave into Congress. Two fringe Tea Party Senate contenders, Angle and O'Donnell (who was compelled to air an ad in which she declared, "I am not a witch"), lost contests that establishment Republicans likely would have won. In a less-noticed development, Republicans gained more than seven hundred state legislature seats across the nation. Obama conceded the election was a "shellacking."

A month later, Obama, meeting with labor leaders in the White House, complained the GOP had become impossible to work with: "It used to be that you could govern by peeling off a couple of Republicans to do the right thing. Now Palin and Beck are the center of the Republican Party—and there is no cooperation." He noted that the Democrats were losing white male voters to the voices of extremism: "Fed by Fox News, they hear Obama is a Muslim 24/7, and it begins to seep in...The Republicans have been at this for forty years."

As for Boehner, his strategy—harness the power of the Tea Party to grab political control—had panned out. Now, like the dog who catches the car, he had to figure out what to do with it.

The third year of Obama's presidency would be shaped by the extremists and Tea Partiers who had gained power in the House. They would not achieve their core objectives. Obamacare would not be repealed. The stimulus and the bailouts that had prevented economic collapse would not be undone. One hundred billion dollars would not be slashed from that year's budget. Whole chunks of the federal government would not be abolished.

They would, however, succeed in forcing the political debate in Washington to focus on deficit reduction instead of economic growth and, most of all, they would precipitate unnecessary crises, first by opposing passage of legislation to fund the federal government (which threatened a government shutdown) and then by refusing to go along with the routine procedure of raising the debt ceiling so the government could pay its bills (which threatened a federal default that could spark a global financial emergency).

In each of these episodes, Boehner, now the House speaker, was inhibited by the new Tea Party members of the GOP House caucus from striking the split-the-difference compromises he fancied as a legislator. Obama, while conceding certain spending cuts (but not the draconian decreases the Tea Party allies and conservatives demanded), prevented the Republicans from blowing up (or burning down) the nation's fiscal house and perhaps the overall economy.

The Tea Partiers, operating as hostage takers, created chaos (which they didn't mind). But the government did not shut down, nor did it default— though the irresponsible conflict spurred by the House Republicans caused a downgrading of the credit rating of the United States, which could raise the cost of borrowing.* Reflecting on the debt-ceiling fiasco, Mike Lofgren, a veteran Republican congressional staffer, wrote, "To be sure, like any political party on Earth, the GOP has always had its share of crackpots...But the crackpot outliers of two decades ago have become the vital core today."

The new Tea Party House members had little interest in governing. They had come to Washington to shout, "Hell, no!" Years later in his memoir, Boehner, looking back on this class of 2010, would say, "They didn't really want legislative victories. They wanted wedge issues and conspiracies and crusades." A chief concern was how their actions played on Fox News or on social media. They were, according to Boehner, "just thinking of how to fundraise off of outrage or how they could get on Hannity that night."

The Tea Party and its supporters would score a smashing success in one area: increasing the tribalist toxicity of American politics.

---

* My 2012 book, *Showdown: The Inside Story of How Obama Battled the GOP to Set Up the 2012 Election*, covers the budget and debt-ceiling battles and other conflicts between Obama and the Tea Party–driven Republicans.

CHAPTER 22

The Fever Doesn't Break

On February 10, 2011, the ballroom at the Wardman Park Marriott Hotel in Washington was filled to capacity. Excited conservatives crammed the entrances to get in. Donald Trump, the New York City developer and reality television star, was speaking.

This was Trump's first appearance at the annual Conservative Political Action Conference, a get-together of right-wing activists, Republican officials, and presidential wannabes. The self-centered celebrity had not been a regular on the conservative circuit. He had run for president in 2000, seeking the Reform Party nomination, but that venture lasted only a few months before he withdrew from the race. At different times, he had been registered as a Republican, a Democrat, a member of the Independent Party, and unaffiliated. These days murmurs spread that the bombastic gossip-column favorite was considering another shot at the White House. He told the assembled he would let them know by June. And he intimated there was something troubling about Obama: "Our current president came out of nowhere—in fact I'll go a step further. The people who went to school with him, they never saw him, they don't know who he is. It's crazy."

Trump was playing the birther card. He didn't mention the president's birthplace. He was, though, repeating the calumny pitched during the 2008 campaign: this guy wasn't who or what he appeared to be. But Trump was not one to engage only in insinuation. Soon after, he went full birther.

This was his gambit to jump to the head of the GOP pack. He could read the numbers: A Public Policy Polling survey found that 51 percent of Republican voters now believed the lie that Obama was not born in the United States. And he was being egged on by Roger Stone, a conspiracy theorist and longtime Trump adviser.

On *Good Morning America*, Trump said that he was skeptical of Obama's citizenship and that anyone who shared this view should not be dismissed as an "idiot." He pushed his baseless Obama's-a-mystery rubbish: "Growing up no one knew him. The whole thing is very strange." A week later, on *The View,* he went further: "Why doesn't he show his birth certificate?" On Fox News, he declared, "I want to see his birth certificate." And on the *Today* show, he said, "I'm starting to think he was not born here." Trump the Birther was now a full-fledged media obsession, especially on Fox News, where he became a regular fixture as the top champion of this racist conspiracy theory. He demanded Obama release the long-form version of his birth certificate. He suggested the 1961 birth announcement that appeared in a Honolulu newspaper was fake and speculated (aloud, of course) that Obama's long-form birth document listed his religion as Muslim.

Trump maintained he had sent investigators to Hawaii to look into all this: "I have people that have been studying [the birth certificate issue] and they cannot believe what they're finding... It's one of the greatest scams in the history of politics and in the history, period. You are not allowed to be a president if you're not born in this country. Right now, I have real doubts." He promised to release his tax returns once Obama disclosed his birth certificate. On CNN, he asserted, "I've been told very recently... that the birth certificate is missing. I've been told it's not there and it doesn't exist." He hawked other Obama conspiracies. Bill Ayers, he insisted, was the true author of Obama's book *Dreams from My Father.*

It was all crap. No bona fide investigators in Hawaii. No missing birth certificate. Trump was spewing hogwash. Not only was he getting away with it—he wasn't ostracized by the media for flogging lies—he was rewarded with attention and GOP support. Privately, Trump told people that the more he peddled birtherism, the higher he went in the GOP presidential polls—a reflection on both him and the Republican electorate.

During Trump's birther spree, Boehner said he believed Obama was born in Hawaii, but when pressed on why he wouldn't stand up to this nonsense, he remarked, "It's not my job to tell the American people what to think."

Obama watched all this with dismay and mystification. "It was clear that Trump didn't care about the consequences of spreading conspiracy theories that he almost certainly knew to be false," Obama later wrote. As far as Obama was concerned, this was a continuation of the Republican practice of deploying unfounded accusations to deter him: He was pushing death panels; he was trying to bankrupt the nation. "In fact," Obama observed, "the only difference between Trump's style of politics and theirs was Trump's lack of inhibition. He understood instinctively what moved the conservative base most, and he offered it up in an unadulterated form."

The Republican hardliners ate it up. After two months of Trump promoting birtherism, a Fox News poll found 24 percent of Americans thought

Obama was not a citizen. A PPP poll showed Trump leading all the potential GOP presidential contenders.

———

Obama had enough. He instructed his White House counsel to dig up the long-form birth certificate, and, on April 27, as the document was released, he appeared in the White House briefing room to decry the media fixation on this matter and other trivialities. "We're not going to be able to solve our problems if we get distracted by sideshows and carnival barkers," the president said, adding, "We do not have time for this kind of silliness."

Trump did not acknowledge his opportunistic silliness. Rather, he declared victory, bragging that he had forced Obama to release the long-form certificate and the nation could thank him for "getting rid of the issue." He did not keep his promise to release his tax returns.

Three days later, Trump and Obama had a historic encounter at the annual White House Correspondents' Association dinner, a schmooze-fest that brings together thousands of journalists, politicians, and government officials—and a smattering of Hollywood celebrities. During his remarks, Obama lacerated the reality TV celebrity, who was present as a guest of the *Washington Post*: "No one is happier, no one is prouder to put this birth certificate matter to rest than The Donald. And that's because he can finally get back to focusing on the issues that matter—like, did we fake the moon landing? What really happened in Roswell? And where are Biggie and Tupac?" He made fun of Trump's "breadth of experience," citing a recent episode of his show *Celebrity Apprentice* in which Trump had "fired" actor Gary Busey: "These are the kind of decisions that would keep me up at night. Well handled, sir. Well handled." (The joke became more pointed a day later, after news broke that US special forces had assaulted a compound in Pakistan and killed bin Laden. No one in the audience knew that Obama by then had given the order for the raid.)

Through Obama's remarks, Trump scowled in silence. Many in the audience believed they were witnessing a public humiliation that would undermine Trump's standing. Perhaps this was the end of birtherism . . . and Trump. Obama wasn't so sure. "The same reporters who laughed at my jokes would continue to give him airtime," he subsequently observed. "Their publishers would vie to have him sit at their tables. Far from being ostracized for the conspiracies he'd peddled, he in fact had never been bigger."

Two weeks after the dinner, Trump announced he would not run for president. "Business is my greatest passion and I am not ready to leave the private sector," he said in a statement. Yet even with the long-form certificate release and Trump wing-clipped, birtherism was not dead. Birther lawsuits kept being filed—and kept being dismissed. Jerome Corsi released a book claiming Obama was not eligible to be president, insisting the long-form birth certificate was a forgery. The birthers would never yield—nor be expunged from Republican circles.

On February 2, 2012, Mitt Romney stood in the lobby of the Trump International Hotel in Las Vegas, waiting for its owner.

The second-place finisher in the 2008 Republican primaries was now the front-runner in his party's presidential sweepstakes. But it had not been an easy path for Romney. He had been declared the winner of the Iowa caucuses a month earlier, but further counting would show he ended up thirty-four votes behind Rick Santorum, a former senator from Pennsylvania and rabid social conservative perhaps best known for likening homosexuality to bestiality and pedophilia. Though Romney had bagged decisive wins in New Hampshire and Florida, he had been thrashed in South Carolina by Gingrich, who was running as a Tea Partier, urging a civil war between the true believers and the GOP establishment, and lambasting Romney as a predatory capitalist who looted companies and left behind "broken families, broken towns and people on unemployment."

It had been one of the oddest presidential primary campaigns. The main energy source for the GOP remained its Tea Party base, and a series of fringe candidates had leaped to the top of the field, only to crash and burn. Bachmann led at one time and then quickly fell back. Herman Cain, the former CEO of Godfather's Pizza and a Tea Party activist, hit the number one spot and faded (after accusations of sexual harassment surfaced). Texas Governor Rick Perry tried to muscle his way into the lead with a Tea Party–friendly proposal to abolish three federal departments. Asked to name them during a debate, he only managed to come up with two. "Oops," he said. He slid in the polls. And Gingrich had campaigned erratically, generating stupid controversies. When asked by a Christian Broadcasting Network interviewer about his well-known infidelities, he attributed his past extramarital adventures to the fact that he was "driven by how passionately I felt about this country" and "worked too hard." In other words, patriotism made him cheat on his wives. Gingrich had his moment in first place and then dimmed. (Palin had opted not to run.)

None of the Tea Party–ish candidates were sticking. A movement awaited a fire-breathing Obama-basher preaching an apocalyptic message, but it had only attracted inconsistent and not-ready-for-prime-time candidates.

Through it all, Romney had been a slow, steady, and unflashy campaigner with a penchant for dumb remarks that made him seem like an out-of-touch plutocrat. A former chief executive of the Bay State and onetime finance executive—in 2002 he had proclaimed he was "moderate" and "progressive"—he was the GOP establishment's best hope. He clumsily lurched to the right on immigration (calling for "self-deportation"), contraception, gay rights, and other issues to remain viable in the Tea Party–ruled GOP cosmos, without fully embracing the lunacy animating much of the Republican world and conservative movement. He had not joined the birthers. He did not rail against Obama as a socialist or a secret Muslim. He was the adult in the Republican room. But Romney had devised a more subtle way of exploiting the right's paranoia and extreme hatred of Obama. His message: Obama wasn't truly part of America.

In a campaign book titled *No Apology: The Case for American Greatness* and released in 2010, Romney had slammed Obama for apologizing for "American misdeeds, both real and imagined." (Romney didn't explain what was wrong with apologizing for real misdeeds.) And in May 2011, he had taken a harsh swipe at the president, declaring, "The Obama Administration fundamentally does not believe in the American Experiment." That was a sizable criticism to hurl at the biracial son of a Kenyan and Kansan who became the first Black president of the United States.

On the stump, several months later, Romney remarked, "I just don't think that President Obama understands America. I say that because this week...he said that Americans are lazy. I don't think that describes America." (Obama had not called Americans lazy.) Campaigning in New Hampshire, days ahead of its primary, Romney blasted Obama as a man who didn't comprehend "the nature of America." And while he eschewed affixing the S-word to Obama, he devised a close substitute, declaring that Obama "wants us to turn into a European-style welfare state." (Gingrich went all the way and claimed Obama intended to transform America into a "secular" and "radical European socialist" nation, and Santorum wailed that if Obama were reelected, "America as we know it will be gone.") Without questioning the location of Obama's birth, Romney was embracing the fundamental impulse of birtherism: *otherism*. Obama was foreign to the idea and image of America—even after serving years as president.

With this in common with Trump and Tea Partiers, Romney ended up in the vainglorious developer's hotel. In the lobby, Trump, who ten months earlier had denigrated Romney for buying and selling companies and "getting rid of jobs," affixed his seal of approval to the GOP front-runner: "He's not going to continue to allow bad things to happen to this country." Romney giddily responded, "There are some things that you just can't imagine happening in your life. This is one of them. Being in Donald Trump's magnificent hotel and having his endorsement is a delight." With this event, not only was Trump vouching for Romney; the GOP's likely nominee was wrapping his arms around a bigoted conspiracy-pusher. A signal went out: Trump was an influential player within the GOP.

It would take Romney another three months to beat back the challenges from Santorum and Gingrich, and he would continue to *other* Obama. "He doesn't fathom that America is unique," Romney asserted. "Our president doesn't have the same feelings about American exceptionalism that we do." Obama shot back: "It's worth noting that I first arrived on the national stage with a speech at the [2004] Democratic convention that was entirely about American exceptionalism and that my entire career has been a testimony to American exceptionalism."

At a rally in late April in New Hampshire, Romney trotted out his version of Palin's 2008 claim that Obama would turn the United States into a socialist nightmare. Under Obamacare, he warned, "government will come to control half the economy, and we will have effectively ceased to be a free enterprise society." This phony, fear-inducing factoid had been cooked up by Romney's campaign staff to appeal to the Beck-watchers and Tea Partiers. Romney was portraying Obama as a foe of the American system, wherever he was born.

———

The fever on the right would not abate. Representative Allen West, a Florida Republican and Tea Party darling, declared that "there's about 78 to 81 members of the Democratic Party that are members of the Communist Party." At the annual NRA convention, Ted Nugent, a washed-up rocker and far-right bad boy, called Obama's administration "vile, evil, and America-hating." He urged Romney supporters "to ride into that battlefield and chop their heads off." (His violent rhetoric was a reprise of his comments from the previous presidential election, when he held up two machine guns at a concert and told Obama to "suck on" them, adding, "Hillary, you might want to ride one of these into the sunset, you worthless bitch.") Romney accepted Nugent's endorsement. John Sununu, a top surrogate for Romney and former New Hampshire governor, huffed, "I wish this president would learn how to be an American." Later in the campaign, he would ridicule Obama as "lazy."

Romney didn't call Obama a commie. He didn't declare that Obama hated America. But Romney welcomed the backing of those who made such claims. And with his own words, he reinforced the idea that Obama was not truly part of the nation he led. He affirmed for Republican voters and the right-wing extremists that they were right to see Obama as an illegitimate holder of the presidency.

———

After the Republican National Committee pronounced Romney the presumptive nominee in late April, his campaign proceeded almost as if the Tea Party no longer existed. During the primary, Romney had kowtowed to conservatives. Now he fixated on selling himself as a Mr. Fix-It for the still-ailing economy, blaming Obama for the nation's woes, and warning a second-term Obama would steer the nation toward statism and more government control. Obama and his crew pounded Romney for his career at Bain Capital, where he oversaw corporate buyouts and investments that in some cases led to massive firings or outsourcing of jobs overseas.

The Obama campaign was obsessed with motivating its base constituencies by targeting them with specific messaging, while the Romneyites did not go to great lengths to fire up the Tea Party. The Romney gang figured these Obama-hater voters were on their side. But Romney's aides felt compelled to invite Palin to speak at the Republican convention. They were relieved when she declined. They also felt it necessary to hand a speaking slot to Trump, who after endorsing Romney had recorded robocalls and hosted a fundraiser for him.

Trump was scheduled to address the convention in Tampa on opening night, and the Romney gang shuddered in anticipation. What the hell might he say? Fortunately for the Romney campaign, a tropical storm bearing down on Florida forced the cancellation of the first day. No Trump, no problem.

There were other problems, including the acceptance speech of Romney's running mate, Representative Paul Ryan, the conservative budget policy wonk who had previously proposed severe domestic spending cuts, the abolition of the Medicare guarantee, and tax cuts for the well-heeled. He blasted Obama for reductions in Medicare spending that he had supported. He blamed Obama for the closing of an auto plant in Wisconsin that was shuttered before Obama became president. And placing an Ayn Rand–ian twist on the classic fearmongering of the right, Ryan claimed Obama's vision was "a dull, adventureless journey from one entitlement to the next, a government-planned life, a country where everything is free but us." This was over-the-top, Beck-ish agitprop, a sop to Tea Party hysterics. The speech was panned for being hyperbolic and misleading.

The next night, Romney's speech was overshadowed by a bizarre appearance from actor-director Clint Eastwood, who delivered a rambling and off-color talk in which he addressed an empty chair that symbolized Obama.

During the final weeks, the two campaigns adhered to their established lines of attack. And Romney and Republicans tried to exploit a horrific assault on the US diplomatic facility in Benghazi, Libya, which killed four Americans, including Ambassador Christopher Stevens, claiming the White House had purposefully misled the public about the tragedy—a charge subsequent investigations did not confirm. The GOP contended the incident demonstrated that Obama was not serious about defending the nation from terrorism.

Obama's case that Romney was an uncaring billionaire who didn't understand the hardships of middle- and low-income Americans was bolstered in mid-September when *Mother Jones* posted a surreptitiously recorded video of Romney at a big-dollar Florida fundraising dinner denigrating 47 percent of Americans as people "who are dependent upon government, who believe that they are victims, who believe the government has a responsibility to care for them, who believe that they are entitled to health care, to food, to housing, to you-name-it...And the government should give it to them." He added, "My job is not to worry about those people. I'll never convince them they should take personal responsibility and care for their lives."

Two years after the Tea Party blew up the political order, it was not a decisive factor in this election. Come Election Day, Obama crushed it. He bested Romney 51 to 47 percent in the popular vote and 332 to 206 in the Electoral College, with his party adding two seats to its Senate majority and boosting its House numbers by eight seats.

That night, right-wing billionaire and Fox News owner Rupert Murdoch commented to an associate, "Our nation is ruined." As soon as the results were in, Trump tweeted, "This election is a total sham and a travesty. We are not a democracy!"

The Obama playbook had succeeded. Exit polls showed Romney had scored better than Obama on key qualities: "strong leader," "shares my values," and "vision for the future." But when asked if the candidate "cares about people like me," Obama topped Romney 81 to 18 percent. The GOP othering of Obama—playing to the fears and angers of the Tea Party base—didn't triumph.

Earlier in the campaign, Obama, in an interview with *Rolling Stone*, had mused that a reelection victory could mark a turning point for the Republican Party and its dependence on extremism and paranoia: "My hope is that if the American people send a message to [Republicans], there's going to be some self-reflection going on—that it might break the fever. They might say to themselves, 'You know what, we've lost our way here. We need to refocus on trying to get things done for the American people.'"

———

The fever didn't break.

After the election, Reince Priebus, the chair of the Republican Party, commissioned an autopsy of the GOP defeat. In the past six presidential elections, the party had collected a majority of votes only once. Something was wrong, the party elders thought.

In March 2013, the RNC released the resulting one-hundred-page report. The GOP, it said, was "marginalizing itself, and unless changes are made, it will be increasingly difficult for Republicans to win another presidential election in the near future." It observed that "public perception of the Party is at record lows. Young voters are increasingly rolling their eyes at what the Party represents, and minorities wrongly think that Republicans do not like them or want them in the country." The autopsy offered an obvious remedy: "We need to campaign among Hispanic, black, Asian, and gay Americans and demonstrate we care about them, too." It also had to deal with its women problem: "When it comes to social issues, the Party must in fact and deed be inclusive and welcoming." Priebus summed up what the party needed: broader outreach and a softer tone.

Much of the party and its voters didn't get the memo.

As pundits paged through the autopsy report, the Tea Partiers of the GOP were rebelling against a grand immigration deal—legalization of millions of undocumented residents *and* enhanced border security—that a bipartisan group of Democrats and Republican legislators was stitching together. So much for reaching out to Latino voters. Leading the renegades was Representative Steve King of Iowa, a racist birther who had called Obama "very, very, urban," accused him of favoring "the black person," and asserted that the president's middle name, Hussein, carried a "special meaning" for Islamic radicals. King organized a Capitol Hill protest opposing the immigration legislation, and it felt like a Tea Party revival. Glenn

Beck pumped up the crowd. King exclaimed, "We're going to defend our way of life." Bachmann held up a white baby and declared, "Say hello to America's future." One sign in the crowd read SHUT THE DOOR. Another said PROUD AMERICAN CHRISTIAN. A third proclaimed IMMIGRATION REFORM = LEGALIZED INVASION.

King and Bachmann won this battle. The opposition mounted by the Tea Party, Beck, Fox News, and other right-wing media prompted Boehner to scuttle the legislation. Declaring victory, King referred to the undocumented minors who now would not be granted legal status: "For every one who's a valedictorian, there's another one hundred out there who weigh 130 pounds and they've got calves the size of cantaloupes because they're hauling 75 pounds of marijuana across the desert." The gravitational pull of bigotry within the GOP was immense.

A few months later, the Tea Party wing in the House, demanding the defunding of Obamacare, forced a two-week government shutdown and nearly triggered another debt ceiling crisis. Through the entire year, ultraconservatives had been generating hysteria over the health care measure. Bachmann claimed, "It literally kills women, kills children, kills senior citizens." (False.) Representative Louie Gohmert of Texas maintained that a "guy out there making $14,000" would have to pay "several thousand dollars for an Obamacare policy." (False.) Senator Rand Paul exclaimed that "you will go to jail" if you don't purchase health insurance and refuse to pay the tax penalty. (False, too.) This was performative politics that boosted paranoia among the base. Obamacare survived—and went on to become a popular program that did not kill or imprison anyone.

Paranoia and fear were the coin of the Republican realm—and GOP leaders did little to change that. Boehner wanted immigration reform to succeed, and he wished to put aside the Obamacare fight, but he had no control over Republican House members who heeded the rants of Limbaugh, Beck, and assorted Fox contributors. These legislators feared the wrath of Limbaugh's "ditto-heads" and Fox viewers more than any admonition from Boehner or Priebus. With most of these members hailing from gerrymandered districts that heavily favored a Republican, they worried more about facing challenges from the right in primary contests than prevailing in general elections. Their worst political nightmare was to be targeted by the Tea Party for insufficient loyalty to its fanaticism.

Boehner could not separate the GOP from the zealots and kooks: These people were his voters and, now, his fellow House members. At a dinner, Rupert Murdoch asked Eric Cantor, "What happened to immigration reform? Why not pass the bill?" Cantor, no doubt restraining himself, replied, "Rupert, have you *watched* your network?"

In April 2014, Boehner met for coffee in New York City with Fox chieftain Roger Ailes. He was sick of watching the crazies of his caucus—Bachmann, King, Gohmert, and others—being amplified by Ailes's network. Good ratings for Fox created anarchy for the House speaker. Ailes tried to wave off Boehner's concern. But Boehner had come with something of a bribe in hand. He gave Ailes a heads-up: He would soon be launching a special committee to investigate Secretary of State Hillary Clinton's handling of the terrorist attack in Benghazi. Talk about red meat for Ailes's Obama-*and*-Hillary-hating audience. Now couldn't the network exec help him out by cutting back on the appearances of the knuckleheads?

At the mention of Benghazi, Ailes detonated. He became agitated and told Boehner that there was a plot to destroy Ailes. It involved Obama, who *was* a Muslim and who had not been born in the United States. The White House, Ailes insisted, tracked his every move. But the sly media man had acquired a security detail and set up "safe rooms" to defeat the surveillance. Boehner later described this encounter to author Tim Alberta as "the most bizarre meeting I'd ever have in my life. He had black helicopters flying all around his head that morning. It was every conspiracy theory you've ever heard...I began to realize that Ailes believed in all this crazy stuff." The man in charge of this all-important echo chamber for the right—where the looniest ideas germinated and spread—was himself cracked, and his network was holding the GOP hostage. As Alberta noted, "The Speaker had come with hopes of quieting the furor on Fox News. He left more concerned than ever about the threat it posed to the country."

Yet Boehner had no compunction about throwing oil on the flames. Ever since the Benghazi assault, an assortment of congressional committees had investigated the tragedy. A primary issue was whether the Obama administration had characterized the raid as a spontaneous reaction to an anti-Islamic film posted on YouTube—and not a preplanned terrorist action—to dodge responsibility for not having been better prepared. Republicans cried cover-up; Democrats claimed bureaucratic miscommunication. Republicans also charged that Hillary Clinton's State Department had delayed a decision to rescue the Americans in the facility, though the GOP-led House Armed Services Committee had found no evidence of that.

An independent review board had issued a report criticizing the State Department for providing insufficient security to the mission—and the department had accepted the findings and pledged to implement reforms.

Still, Republicans and Fox shouting heads found Benghazi too delicious to let go. They promoted a variety of unfounded allegations and conspiracy theories. Bachmann claimed the CIA had ordered its officers not to help those under attack. (Untrue.) Beck, Fox News, and Rand Paul were pushing the unsubstantiated notion that Ambassador Stevens had run weapons for the Obama White House from Libya to Turkey for use in the Syrian civil war.

Boehner wanted the crazies to shut up. But Benghazi was their baby, and for the paranoia-mainlining, Fox-following GOP base, another sign of Obama fecklessness, nefariousness, or both. Best of all, it held potential for tarring Clinton, the likely Democratic nominee in 2016. Boehner's special Benghazi committee, chaired by Tea Party fave Trey Gowdy, would keep the issue alive. (In 2015, after over a year of more Benghazi headlines, Representative Kevin McCarthy would say the quiet part aloud: "Everybody thought Hillary Clinton was unbeatable, right? But we put together a Benghazi special committee, a select committee. What are her numbers today? Her numbers are dropping.")

A few months after the creation of the special committee, the House intelligence committee released a comprehensive report shooting down various Benghazi conspiracy theories and finding that extensive efforts were made to save the Americans at the compound. Still, Boehner's keep-Benghazi-alive panel continued. Ultimately, the committee would uncover no big Benghazi secrets. But it would trigger a whole other scandal by asking for Clinton's emails when she served as secretary of state. That request yielded a revelation that would have a deep impact on the 2016 presidential contest: She had used a private server for her emails while at Foggy Bottom, and after she left the State Department she had destroyed thirty thousand emails on this server that were deemed personal. The right's fixation on uncovering a Clinton conspiracy had led to an actual problem for her.

As 2014 headed toward the midterm elections, the Republican establishment tried to have it both ways. The old crowd—of which Boehner was a member—was directing money toward more traditional Republican candidates in primary battles against Tea Party–ish insurgents. Yet Boehner, with his Benghazi move, was pandering to renegades and the party's Fox-addicted followers.

One tough race that advertised the party's problem with extremism was occurring in Mississippi. Senator Thad Cochran, a septuagenarian Republican incumbent widely seen as off his game, had a primary challenge from state Senator Chris McDaniel, an anti-Washington rebel and social conservative who had bagged endorsements from Trump, Tea Partiers, and right-wing groups, including the Club for Growth and Jim DeMint's Senate Conservatives Fund. He was also a supporter of a local chapter of the Sons of Confederate Veterans, a Confederacy-celebrating outfit that advocated for Mississippi's present-day secession from the Union. Its newsletter compared the Obama years to Reconstruction (when white supremacists were booted out of power in the South). It occasionally put up billboards declaring "Happy birthday, President Jefferson Davis."*

McDaniel campaigned alongside a conspiracy theorist named Wayne Allyn Root, who alleged Obama was a "Manchurian candidate" and part of a secret plan to "destroy the country." Root stumped for McDaniel throughout the state on a bus paid for by the Tea Party Express. Palin joined him on the trail, as well. This was the new GOP.

Despite his association with outright bigotry and bizarre conspiracism— or because of it—McDaniel almost won. Cochran hung on by a mere 7,700 votes.

In Virginia a more improbable Tea Party target fell: Eric Cantor, the House GOP's second-in-command. The Tea Party and right-wing talk radio had rallied behind the modest campaign of Dave Brat, an economics professor at Randolph-Macon College. He pummeled Cantor as a career politician who favored "amnesty" for undocumented residents because the legislator had touted the immigration reform package that included providing citizenship to minors. Far-right radio host Laura Ingraham traveled to Cantor's district to star at a Brat rally, where she decried Cantor as an ally of Obama and Pelosi, declaring, "We are slowly losing our country." On June 14, Brat squashed Cantor by eleven points. He would go on to win the general election handily.

As the November elections approached, Democrats braced for another blow. The economy had slowly improved, and Obamacare (after a botched rollout) was up and running, and a withdrawal of troops in Afghanistan had begun. But real median household income remained about eight percent

---

* A few months later, the news would break that Representative Steve Scalise, a Louisiana Republican and the House majority whip, had spoken in 2002 at a gathering of white-supremacist leaders when he was a state representative. He appeared at the convention of the European-American Unity and Rights Organization that had been founded by former Ku Klux Klan leader David Duke and was affiliated with racists and neo-Nazis. His office claimed he had been unaware at the time of the group's racist ideology. It seemed that every couple of years a controversy emerged about a top Republican and an extremist group. In a 2010 interview, Mississippi Governor Haley Barbour had warmly reminisced about his hometown's local chapter of the segregationist Citizens' Council.

lower than 2007, and the rise of the jihadist ISIS in Iraq was a cause for national security worries. And Obama, mainly due to Republican obstruction, had failed to achieve progress on key priorities, such as gun violence, climate change, and immigration reform. His job approval rating dropped to about 40 percent on Election Day.

The Republicans had thrown the post-2012 autopsy into the trash can. Widening the party's stance on social issues, reaching out to Black, Latino, and women voters—they did none of that. The party had evolved into an entity split into two overlapping parts: establishment conservatives who railed against taxes, government spending, and regulations, and Tea Party conservatives who railed against taxes, government spending, and regulations *and* who embraced various forms of extremism, political paranoia, and conspiracy theory. The net result was that in these midterm elections, the Republicans expanded their House majority and with nine new Senate seats won control of the upper chamber. The GOP would have its largest Senate majority in eighty years; the House Democrats would sink to their lowest point in decades.

Though the GOP was divided, the ascendant power seemed on the side of the Tea Partiers and the fringe right. Boehner would not last another year as speaker. He would skedaddle out of the House a few steps ahead of a Tea Party mutiny. The beast he had fed to attain the speakership was now looking to devour him. Cantor had been an appetizer.

Five years earlier, Boehner, the top Republican in the nation, had signed a devil's bargain. He mirrored the hyperbolic hysteria about Obamacare and did little to douse the flames of birtherism and other conspiratorial fantasies of the right. This had won him the speaker's gavel—but at the cost of affirming the irrationality and paranoia of the right.

When Boehner had heard about Cantor's loss to Brat, he thought to himself that he was finished. He was right. The party was no longer his. He had helped it reach this troubling point. And it was going to get worse.

CHAPTER 23

"I Am Your Voice"

It seemed like a stunt, a novelty act, another bizarre joke in American culture: Donald Trump gliding down an escalator in the lobby of the Trump Tower, past a *small* crowd of cheering supporters, including actors paid to fill out the audience, with Neil Young's "Rockin' in the Free World" on the P.A., to announce he was running for president. But on this day, June 16, 2015, a man embodying the forces of extremism was placing the GOP on the road to becoming a party that not only flirted with hatred, racism, and paranoia but that fully accepted, embraced, and depended upon the dark matter of America.

In a long and rambling speech, Trump lamented, "Our country is in serious trouble." The onetime birther-in-chief quickly struck a racist note, calling undocumented Mexican immigrants "rapists." He claimed he would, if victorious, build a border barrier and "have Mexico pay for that wall." He asserted that he had opposed the Bush-Cheney invasion of Iraq. (False.) He noted that gross domestic product had dipped below zero for the first time ever. (False.) He said, "Our nuclear arsenal doesn't work." (False.) He insisted the United States had an enemy within: "losers" and "people selling this country down the drain." He proclaimed that "the American dream is dead" and that he would "make America great again."

Trump was widely dismissed as a contender. After all, he was an egomaniacal publicity hound with a sordid past of bankruptcies, mob ties, shady business deals, scandalous personal conduct, and racist and misogynistic comments—not to mention an inveterate liar and a champion braggart. He was no conservative and barely a Republican. He had supported the Clintons, endorsed abortion rights, criticized free trade, and opposed entitlement cuts.

To many observers, it looked as if the race would eventually boil down to a contest between an establishment Republican (probably former Florida Governor Jeb Bush) and a Tea Party Republican. This would be a rerun of an all-too-familiar story: the insiders' favorite versus a hardcore conservative insurgent. In such a face-off, Trump was a sideshow.

Yet Trump knew the Republican base better than the party's leaders. For decades, the GOP and the conservative movement had encouraged and capitalized on the apprehension, anger, paranoia, and grievance that existed on the right. They often did so in a manner that afforded them a measure of plausible deniability by using coded language, narrowcasting their fearmongering appeals, or twinning messages of dread with more uplifting rhetoric. Though not always. Sarah Palin's campaign of hate in 2008, the Tea Party rebellion—each accepted and fanned by the GOP establishment—had validated irrationality, animus, racism, and resentment within the Republican electorate and whetted the appetite of those voters for a politics propelled by animosity and rage. They had blazed the path for Trump.

The reality TV loudmouth who had used birtherism as a test run knew this. The voters who cheered on Palin and the Tea Party, who believed the conspiracy theories of Glenn Beck, who relished the cruel and false monologues from Rush Limbaugh, who worshipped Fox News, who were revved up by outrage spread on social media, who saw Obama and the Democrats not as political foes but evildoers bent on decimating the nation (death panels! secret Muslims! concentration camps!) needed a stronger fix in the 2016 race, and Trump would give it to them. This onetime steak salesman was the king of red meat. His campaign would be a political abattoir.

In the first weeks of his campaign, the real estate mogul lifted pages from Nixon's playbook, just as he had swiped Reagan's "Make America Great Again" slogan. "There's a silent majority out there," he declared at a rally in South Carolina. "We're tired of being pushed around, kicked around, and acting and being led by stupid people." Following a shooting in Chattanooga, Tennessee, which claimed the lives of five service members, Trump exclaimed, "We're losing law and order."

Trump traded in negative passions, not political discourse. That was the point. Prior to his campaign launch, Trump and a few close aides had concocted a theory. Trump's name identification was close to 100 percent. Most voters already had a well-formed view of him—the good and the bad. They knew he was mean-spirited and uncivil, a pompous and unrelenting self-promoter, a businessman of slippery repute, and a moral reprobate. His campaign wouldn't be about delivering the correct policy pronouncements. The question was, did GOP primary voters want a bombastic amplifier of rage—a political shock jock who didn't give a damn about rational and informed policy debate—to lead the nation and fight for their *idea* of America? Someone who would give the finger to the powers that be—the elites, the politicians, the politically correct crowd, the experts, and whoever else pissed them off. If enough Republican voters craved a son of a bitch—*their* SOB—in the White House, Trump had a chance.

In years past, the dilemma for the Republican Party was to what extent it would accept, cater to, or embrace extremists on the right—the people whom Goldwater, Reagan, Buckley, and other conservatives had called the "kooks." Now the issue for the GOP was the inverse: What should the party do when a kook tries to storm the castle and steal the throne?

———

Republican regulars breathed a sigh of relief when Trump, weeks into his campaign, insulted the venerated John McCain by saying, "He's not a war hero...I like people who weren't captured. (Trump had eluded the Vietnam draft with five deferments, including one for bone spurs in his heel. In a 1998 interview he called avoiding sexually transmitted diseases his own personal "Vietnam.") Certainly, this unconscionable blast against the former POW would demonstrate to GOP voters that Trump did not possess a temperament suitable for serving as commander in chief. Yet his standing in the polls—he already led a large herd—was unaffected. Trump and his advisers were delighted that establishment Republicans were aghast at this comment, for it demonstrated they had no idea that many Republican voters yearned for a bastard willing to offend the folks in charge.

During the first debates, Trump did just that. He was crude and rude. When Fox News host Megyn Kelly pressed him on his long record of misogynistic remarks, he refused to apologize—and later suggested Kelly only posed this query because she had been menstruating. He derided his rival Republicans. Jeb Bush was "low energy." Rand Paul was ugly. Trump compared Ben Carson, a noted neurosurgeon, to a child molester.

It was soon apparent that the rules of politics—and polite society—didn't apply to Trump. His rallies attracted thousands—sometimes tens of thousands—of supporters, almost all white. These events drew extensive live media coverage. (By the end of the primary contest, Trump received an estimated $3 billion worth of free media attention from broadcast and cable news channels.) Following the first GOP debate, 82 percent of the online conversation about the event focused on Trump.

Trump's campaign—marginally managed by a handful of second-raters—combined outrage culture with modern politics. The guy tweeted out all the dark notions of his id and couldn't restrain the impulses of his ego. He didn't put out policy papers. He claimed he had all the answers. How to juice up the economy, revive manufacturing, negotiate tremendous trade deals, provide great health care, rid the world of terrorism? Just elect him. He was a killer.

And he knew the enemy. Hillary Clinton, the leading Democratic contender, was a crook. Obama was a duplicitous and diabolical pretender. Trump was a mad-as-hell candidate just right for the radicalized GOP electorate that had been weaned on Limbaugh, Beck, and Fox and that had for decades been told the nation was being ruined from within by various elites and unseen forces.

The anti-immigrant, anti-Obama, anti-establishment sentiment Trump was tapping ran deep within the Republican electorate. Right-wing groups constantly sent out fundraising emails contending Obama planned to confiscate all guns, suspend the Constitution so he could run for a third term, relinquish American sovereignty to the United Nations, and mount a military operation within the United States to subdue any opposition to him. Conservative media peddled such stories repeatedly. The GOP did nothing to discourage the creation of this fact-free alternative reality. In fact, it regularly validated the purveyors of such claptrap. Consequently, it was no surprise that many of its voters wanted a candidate who understood what was *really* happening. A poll found that 54 percent of Republicans believed Obama was a secret Muslim. Over 60 percent said they felt "betrayed" by GOP officeholders.

———

Trump was addressing the anger, resentments, and sense of marginalization within the party's base. Ticked off about pushing 1 for English and 2 for Spanish? Trump got it. His core argument was about American identity. It was truly us versus them. Undocumented Latino immigrants, Muslims, the Black community, and the elites who protected or coddled them—he was against all of them.

At a September 17, 2015, Trump town hall in New Hampshire, a man in the audience yelled, "We have a problem in this country; it's called Muslims. We know our president is one." This attendee referred to Muslim "training camps" and asked, "When can we get rid of them?" Trump did not seek to disabuse this fellow of these racist and false notions or calm him. He affirmed his concern: "We're going to be looking at a lot of different things. You know, a lot of people are saying that, and a lot of people are saying that bad things are happening out there." On Fox Business, he said he would "certainly look at" the idea of shutting down mosques in the United States.

Trump was mainstreaming extremism and bigotry—without using coded language or any tricks. After a November terrorist attack in Paris that killed more than 130 people, he proposed monitoring mosques and setting up a government database to track Muslims in the United States. When an ISIS-inspired terrorist gunned down fourteen people in San Bernardino, California, Trump called for "a total and complete shutdown of Muslims entering the United States until our country's representatives can figure out what is going on." That would be illegal—but polls showed a significant majority of Republicans agreed. He proposed reinstating torture for terrorist suspects and killing their wives and children. Trump tweeted out the false racist claim that 81 percent of white murder victims were killed by Black people. (The correct number was 15 percent. Most whites are killed by other white people.)

Here was the out-in-the-open culture war that many conservatives and extremists had long yearned for, a combination of populism, nativism, and nationalism mixed with racism and pandering to the religious right. One big applause line at Trump's events was his vow to end the nonexistent "war on Christmas" and have people say "Merry Christmas" instead of "Happy Holidays."

But he was not winning over the leaders of the Christian right. During a speech at the Council for National Policy in October, Trump lost his way and began talking about his hair. Marjorie Dannenfelser, a veteran antiabortion activist, turned to Bill Walton, the CNP's president, and complained, "This is insulting." But at the end of this session, when Trump offered to have his photo taken with CNP members, the line extended out the ballroom. A short time later, she and other antiabortion activists wrote an open letter to Iowa voters maintaining, "America will only be a great nation when we have leaders of strong character who will defend both unborn children and the dignity of women. We cannot trust Donald Trump to do either."

Pundits noted the obvious: Trump was succeeding because he reflected the anger of a large swath of voters. A postelection analysis by political scientists John Sides, Michael Tesler, and Lynn Vavreck found his fans were dissatisfied with politics and the economy but the "most important" factor underlying their support for Trump was "attitudes about racial, ethnic, and religious groups and racially charged issues." This transcended economic concerns, they noted: "There was a powerful idea that 'my group'—in this case, white Americans—was suffering because other groups, such as immigrants or minorities, were getting benefits that they did not deserve. This idea, which was common among Republican voters, also predated Trump. He just leveraged it to his advantage." These academics observed that "the roots of Trump's appeal were hiding in plain sight. He capitalized on an existing reservoir of discontent about a changing American society and culture."

Trump's campaign, they concluded, was "a vehicle for a different kind of identity politics—one oriented around some white Americans' feelings of marginalization in an increasingly diverse America." Not surprisingly, affection for Trump spread among white nationalists, neo-Nazis, and other racist extremists. And when David Duke, the former Klan leader, endorsed Trump, the Republican front-runner was slow to renounce Duke.

Trump was selling this message of grievance at the right time. The Tea Party had made the battle against immigration reform and opposition to amnesty for undocumented people a top priority. And according to polls, racial resentment among white Republicans had been on a steady and sharp rise since the Reagan days. Trump's potential audience had grown—and it was susceptible to a campaign of BS and rage. Two GOP strategists wrote in a memo, "Trump voters are exceedingly low-information voters. They do not read the *Washington Post* or even conservative blogs. They do not watch cable news rigorously."

But these voters knew they were angry.

———

Trump's outlandish actions and remarks kept establishment Republicans shaking their heads and telling themselves he wouldn't last. Yet nothing impeded him. He mocked a disabled reporter. He praised Vladimir Putin, the repressive and murderous Russian leader. He couldn't explain the basics of the nuclear triad.

Could the party accept a candidate so extreme in his personal prejudice, vulgarity, and ignorance? Trump's rivals took their shots. Rick Perry called him a "cancer on conservatism." Louisiana Governor Bobby Jindal said he was a "madman." South Carolina Senator Lindsey Graham remarked, "You know how you make America great again? Tell Donald Trump to go to hell. He's a race-baiting, xenophobic, religious bigot. He doesn't represent my party."

By and large, though, party officials treated Trump gingerly, afraid he might bolt the GOP, run as an independent, and destroy the Republicans' chances to retake the White House. His bad business deals, his potential conflicts of interest, his defrauding of students at Trump University, his refusal to pay bills, his overseas manufacturing of Trump-branded products, his assorted policy flip-flops, his past and present racist remarks, his narcissistic and boorish conduct—most of this was generally left alone by his opponents in the race. Which gave Trump plenty of running room. By the end of the year, he still led the polls, generally reaching between 25 and 40 percent, with the dozen-plus other-rans dividing the rest. It was not until mid-December that Jeb Bush, who languished in the single digits in the surveys, took a swing at Trump, calling him "unhinged" and a "chaos candidate." It didn't matter.

Playing to bigots and wackos, Trump demonstrated he had the nerve to say anything. He insisted that on September 11 he had witnessed "thousands and thousands" of cheering Arabs in New Jersey celebrating the collapse of the World Trade Center. No such thing happened. But when challenged, Trump maintained he saw it on television. Fact-checkers scored Trump the most prodigious liar of the GOP pack. That, too, didn't matter.

Nor did it matter that Trump embraced the most prominent conspiracy theorist in the nation: Alex Jones, the 9/11 truther and proprietor of a website called InfoWars. Jones had become notorious in recent years for claiming that the horrific 2012 mass shooting at Sandy Hook Elementary School in Newtown, Connecticut, in which twenty children and six adults were killed, was a "giant hoax" and a "false flag" operation concocted by the government to spur support for gun control. (He also asserted that the government used secret chemicals to make people gay.) More recently, Jones had spread the crazy idea that a planned military training exercise in Texas and other states called Jade Helm 15 was a front for a military occupation of the Lone Star State.

Trump appeared on Jones's online talk show, and Jones hailed him as a modern-day George Washington who could save the nation before it collapsed, calling his campaign "epic." Trump repaid the compliment, telling Jones, "Your reputation is amazing. I will not let you down." The man leading the Republican parade had endorsed one of the country's biggest kooks.

Trump was signaling to the paranoid right that he was one of them. Earlier in the campaign, he had backed the baseless theory that vaccinations caused autism. In the months ahead, he would share an assortment of conspiratorial notions: ISIS was plotting a "military coup" in the United States; there was something fishy about the death of Supreme Court Justice Antonin Scalia; Senator Ted Cruz's father was involved in the assassination of John Kennedy; Vince Foster's suicide was a cover story for some foul act. He was practically a modern-day Bircher.

Trump's initial success was the logical extension of the decades-long GOP project of whipping up suspicion and paranoia for political gain. Other contenders in the race were engaged in similar conduct. Ben Carson, who in December experienced a surge and topped Trump in a few polls, was an outright fan of W. Cleon Skousen, the conspiracy-monger whom the

National Review characterized as a "nutjob." Carson believed secret Marxists were plotting to destroy the nation by infiltrating all its institutions. And Ted Cruz, a favorite of social conservatives, courted the loony right by noting he understood "the reason for concern and uncertainty" regarding the Jade Helm 15 military exercise "because...the federal government has not demonstrated itself to be trustworthy." He (and Huckabee and Jindal) attended a "religious liberty convention" hosted by a pastor who called for lesbians and gay people to be executed. Florida Senator Marco Rubio voiced unfounded charges about Benghazi and repeatedly asserted Obama was purposefully trying to debase the nation and plotting to confiscate all guns from Americans.

In seeking to exploit extremism, Trump was no loner among the Republicans. He was just better at it than the others—and more committed. And Trump seemed surprised by how easy it was to turn bombast, bigotry, and paranoia into impressive poll numbers. At a campaign stop at Dordt University in Sioux Center, Iowa, on January 23, 2016, he blurted out, "I could stand in the middle of Fifth Avenue and shoot somebody, and I wouldn't lose any voters, OK? It's, like, incredible."

———

For months, worried Republican officials had been saying, just wait until voting starts. Then Trump's latest reality TV show would crumble. They were wrong. Trump won three out of the four early primaries—New Hampshire, South Carolina, and Nevada—and seven of the eleven states on Super Tuesday on March 1. The twice-divorced, profane wheeler-dealer who was rarely seen in church fared well with evangelical voters. The self-proclaimed billionaire with a long history of stiffing his contractors and manufacturing his products overseas won the votes of blue-collar Reagan Democrats. His campaign of rancor and resentment—with its brazen antipathy to Muslims, undocumented immigrants, Blacks, liberals, Hollywood, Obama, George W. Bush, his Republican rivals, and the party establishment—had become a hostile takeover of the Republican Party.

After decades of milking extremism for votes, how could the GOP turn off the pump? Following Super Tuesday, Mitt Romney took a stab at it. In a speech, he assailed the Republicans' top vote-getter: "Donald Trump is a phony, a fraud. His promises are as worthless as a degree from Trump University. He's playing members of the American public for suckers." Yet Romney was quite the imperfect messenger. He had enthusiastically accepted Trump's endorsement during the 2012 race and elevated him. Only *now* he realized that Trump was a con man?

GOP Representative Mike Pompeo, a Tea Party conservative who had endorsed Rubio, warned his fellow Kansans that Trump was an immoral man with dictatorial tendencies and posed a serious threat to the nation. Rubio prophesized catastrophe should Trump succeed: "Every moment in human history that has been built on a foundation of anger and fear has been cataclysmic in the end." He warned, "Don't give in to the fear. Do not allow the conservative movement to be defined as anger." Yet Rubio, in a way, reinforced Trump's basic message, asserting, "Every traditional institution in America is failing you." He cited the media, education, business, and "your politicians and political parties."

Trump presented a moment of reckoning for the GOP. "We should have basically kicked him out of the party," Lindsey Graham moaned, too late. Nebraska Senator Ben Sasse said that if Trump were nominated, he would leave the GOP. (He didn't.)

Political commentators often talk about the fight for the soul of a party. But what was now at stake was the Republican Party's fundamental identity. A man with allegiance to no ideological principles—conservative or otherwise—was carjacking the party. Glenn Beck, who had endorsed Cruz, huffed that Trump represented a "crisis for conservatism." He compared the developer to Hitler and warned that Trump was a possible "extinction-level event" for American democracy and capitalism.*

Menace hung in the air at Trump rallies, reminiscent of the McCain-Palin gatherings, though his crowds were larger and more agitated. Attendees wore T-shirts proclaiming, TRUMP THAT BITCH and HILLARY SUCKS BUT NOT LIKE MONICA. Trump supporters verbally assaulted members of the media, echoing Trump's unrelentingly vicious and dangerous attacks on the "dishonest" reporters and "fake news."

At one rally, Trump encouraged attendees to beat up a protester. "I'd like to punch him in the face." (He had earlier said he would pay the legal fees of any supporter who would "knock the crap out of" a protester.) At another, several white men attacked a Black man; Trump shouted, "Get him out of here. Throw him out." At a rally in Fayetteville, North Carolina, when a group of protesters started shouting, the crowd got riled up. "Go home, niggers!" someone yelled. A white man in a cowboy hat sucker-punched one of the Black protesters and later declared, "We don't know who he is, but

---

* After Trump won, Beck, acknowledging his own responsibility for boosting the politics of paranoia, said, "If you want to blame me for him, that's fine." But then in 2018, he embraced Trump and endorsed him for reelection.

we know he's not acting like an American. The next time we see him, we might have to kill him." Trump seemed to justify this attack, saying, "In the good old days this doesn't happen because they used to treat them very, very rough." The crowd cheered. Days later, he remarked, "The audience hit back and that's what we need a little bit more of." Trump was turning violence into entertainment.

With Jeb Bush departed from the race—he fled after the first four contests—the party establishment rested its hopes on Rubio and then Cruz to thwart Trump's raid on the GOP. Trump engaged in various bouts of slimy political mud wrestling with Rubio and Cruz. Rubio derided Trump as a "con artist," and he and the developer got into an argument over the size of Trump's penis. Cruz disparaged Trump as a "maniac," a "narcissist," "fundamentally wrong," "a pathological liar," and "utterly amoral."

After Trump crushed Rubio in Florida, the senator's home state, Rubio quit the race. On May 3, Trump trounced Cruz in Indiana, and the Texan gave up. The contest was over. A party that had long maintained a relationship with extremism—and that had managed since 1968 to not be defined by this—now had an undeniable extremist as its presidential nominee.

———

Over the years, the Republicans had weaponized paranoia for political gain. They had mendaciously demonized opponents as threats to the nation and sidled up to and exploited the worst parts of America's nature: fear, xenophobia, tribalism, bigotry, and racial animus. Trump did all of that to win the GOP nomination. He wasn't going to stop now that he was essentially the de facto leader of the party. Hillary was still Crooked Hillary. Insults flew. Tweets kept coming.

When a federal judge named Gonzalo Curiel issued rulings against Trump in a lawsuit that accused him of conning students at the for-profit Trump University, Trump castigated Curiel, claiming he had an "inherent conflict of interest" because the judge was "of Mexican heritage." (Curiel was born and raised in Indiana.) Republicans, still believing they could impose guardrails for their presumptive nominee, condemned Trump. Representative Paul Ryan, the Wisconsin Republican who had replaced Boehner as House speaker, called Trump's attack on Curiel "the textbook definition of a racist comment."

Yet slowly, the establishment began to come to terms with this megalomaniac. Trump met with House Republicans in Washington. Many left the meeting praising him—even members of the Tea Party–ish Freedom Caucus, who claimed to stand for conservative ideological purity, a description that did not fit Trump. He was campaigning as a rabid protectionist and vowing he would not reduce entitlement programs. And he was making irresponsible and reckless statements every day, claiming that Clinton had done nothing to try to help Ambassador Stevens and the others in the Benghazi compound, that foreign governments had hacked her email server, that she believed in open borders, that the United States was the highest-taxed nation in the world, that hundreds of recent immigrants had been "convicted of terrorist activity."

The party caved. Ryan offered a tepid endorsement of Trump. Rubio signed on. Perry did the same.

Trump, though, had yet to seal the deal with social conservatives and the Christian right. He had collected a lot of religious right votes but had not won over the leadership. Jerry Falwell Jr. had joined the Trump bandwagon at the start of the year. But in South Carolina, James Dobson had tried to rally Christian right voters to Cruz's side—and failed. The Christian right voters who George W. Bush had depended upon were now as radicalized as many other Republican voters.

In mid-May, Trump released a list of his potential Supreme Court nominees—each of them a jurist or an elected official who would make a religious rightist's heart flutter. The next month, at a summit of social conservatives in Times Square organized by Council for National Policy member Bill Dallas, Trump told the leaders of the movement that he owed Christianity "so much" because "the evangelical vote was mostly gotten by me." In other words, he had a transactional relationship with Christ. When Franklin Graham compared Trump to the biblical David, some in the audience winced. Trump rambled on about his electoral victories and the media coverage of the election, but he tossed out the phrases the evangelicals longed to hear, particularly "pro-life judges," and vowed to be a battler for the Christian right. A year earlier, a Supreme Court decision had legalized same-sex marriage across the nation. The religious right, once more, believed it was losing the culture war. If a liar and a cheat—a man who had publicly said he had never asked God for forgiveness—was promising to be their defender, in return for votes, they'd take that deal. A relationship of convenience was born.

———

Trump's convention in Cleveland was a tribute to division and extremism. On display was a GOP fully in the grips of Trumpmania. Previous party leaders—McCain, Romney, and both George Bushes—skipped the gathering. The event was chockful of hate. Trump supporters and delegates wore

T-shirts and buttons calling for Clinton's imprisonment. On the convention floor, delegates waved HILLARY FOR PRISON signs. A Trump adviser and delegate named Al Baldasaro said in a radio interview that Clinton "should be put in the firing line and shot for treason." Roger Stone and Alex Jones held rallies and events supporting Trump and promoting a variety of conspiracy theories. (Two years earlier, Stone had tweeted, "Hillary must be brought to justice—arrested, tried and executed for murder.") One night, Jones entered the arena wearing a badge identifying him as a "special guest" of the Republican Party.

Ben Carson, in his speech to the delegates, linked Hillary Clinton to Lucifer. When retired Lieutenant General Michael Flynn, Trump's top national security adviser, spoke and slammed her for using private email while secretary of state, the crowd chanted, "Lock her up!" Flynn joined in. Calling for imprisoning a political foe was unprecedented in modern political conventions.

Trump's speech was loud and angry. He asserted the nation faced "a moment of crisis" and that "our very way of life" was threatened by crime and terrorism. He called himself the "law and order candidate." He proclaimed, "No longer can we rely on those elites in media, and politics, who will say anything to keep a rigged system in place." He boasted, "Nobody knows the system better than me. Which is why I alone can fix it."

"I am your voice," Trump shouted. That was a true statement. His was the voice of the Republican Party.

———

While the Democratic convention proceeded the following week, Trump continued to pound the drums of hate. He attacked Khizr Khan, a speaker at the Democratic gathering whose son, an Army captain, had been killed by a suicide bomber in Iraq, and he uttered an anti-Muslim comment about Khan's wife. Republicans reprimanded Trump. He didn't care. Responding to the reports that Russian operatives had hacked the Democratic National Committee computer servers and, through WikiLeaks, released the pilfered internal documents to disrupt the Democrats' convention, Trump encouraged Russia to hack Hillary Clinton to find the thirty thousand personal emails she had removed from the private server she had used while secretary of state. (Hours afterward, Russian operatives did try to penetrate Clinton's email.)* A week later, Trump suggested Clinton could be targeted for

———

* During the Democratic convention, Trump advisers—including Donald Trump Jr. and campaign chairman Paul Manafort—denied Russia was trying to sabotage the 2016 election. Yet a month earlier, Trump Jr., Manafort, and Trump son-in-law Jared Kushner, ahead

assassination by "the Second Amendment people," if she were elected president. He absurdly called Obama "the founder of ISIS" and tagged "crooked Hillary Clinton" as a "co-founder." The lock-her-up chant was a persistent soundtrack at his rallies.

In mid-August, Trump replaced Paul Manafort, his campaign's chief executive, with Steve Bannon. (Manafort had been tied to sleazy business dealings with Putin-friendly Ukrainian politicians.) Bannon ran *Breitbart News*, the conservative site, which he proudly declared was "the platform for the alt-right." The alt-right was an extreme wing of the conservative movement that ranted against immigrants, Muslims, the globalist agenda, and multiculturalism and that was linked to white nationalism and antisemitism. With this move, Trump interlocked his campaign with a beyond-the-pale slice of the conservative world. It was as if Goldwater had selected a top John Birch Society official to manage his campaign.

Clinton saw an opening to brand Trump an extremist. "The de facto merger between *Breitbart* and the Trump campaign represents a landmark achievement for this group, a fringe element that has effectively taken over the Republican Party," she said. And she kept up this attack. At a New York City fundraiser, she exclaimed, "You could put half of Trump's supporters into what I call the basket of deplorables. Right? The racist, sexist, homophobic, xenophobic, Islamophobic—you name it." She added that Trump "tweets and retweets their offensive hateful mean-spirited rhetoric. Now, some of those folks—they are irredeemable, but thankfully they are not America." The other half of Trump's base, Clinton said, "feel that the government has let them down" and are "desperate for change." These voters, she noted, "are people we have to understand and empathize with as well."

Clinton's numbers might have been inexact, but the sentiment was accurate. Trump was appealing to the worst—with little subterfuge or no apology. But insulting voters was not a good look for a normal candidate. The Trump campaign accused Clinton of revealing "her true contempt for everyday Americans." The political press covered her remarks as an unforced error. In an effort to troll Clinton, Donald Trump Jr. retweeted a photoshopped image titled "The Deplorables" that showed his father, himself,

---

of a secret meeting in Trump Tower with a Kremlin emissary who supposedly possessed dirt on Hillary Clinton, were informed that Moscow wanted to covertly help Trump win. Still, throughout the campaign, Trump and his crew aided and abetted Russia's attack on the United States by either denying its existence or downplaying it. Michael Isikoff and I chronicle the Kremlin's assault on the election and the Trump camp's involvement in our book *Russian Roulette: The Inside Story of Putin's War on America and the Election of Donald Trump*.

Roger Stone, Alex Jones, Ben Carson, Rudy Giuliani, New Jersey Governor Chris Christie, and other Trump supporters standing with a cartoon character called Pepe the Frog. Pepe was an alt-right symbol associated with white supremacy.

Unconventional interlopers helped Trump's campaign of hate. Fake news sites generated disinformation that boosted his campaign: *Pope Francis endorsed Trump. Clinton sold arms to ISIS. An FBI agent who leaked her emails was found dead.* And Russia was running a secret operation to flood US social media with false and phony messages designed to exacerbate political division in the United States and boost Trump's prospects. A 2019 Senate intelligence committee report noted that operatives of the St. Petersburg–based Internet Research Agency used social media posts "to deceive tens of millions" of Americans in a campaign that was part of Putin's "covert support" for Trump. The Kremlin's trolls especially targeted Black Americans.

During a mid-September press conference, Trump took his first steps to shy away from the racist birtherism that had set the foundation for his romancing of the angry and paranoid right. In a terse, one-sentence statement, he said, "President Barack Obama was born in the United States, period." Not surprisingly, he issued no apology. But he falsely claimed the Hillary Clinton campaign in 2008 had initiated birtherism. He excused one lie with another.

––––––

At the start of October, Trump, after a lousy performance in his first debate with Clinton, trailed in the key swing states. Republicans in Washington were saying—privately—they would only have to grin and bear this nominee for another four weeks. Then the GOP could get back to being the GOP. Limbaugh complained that in the Trump-Clinton face-off there was no true conservative on the ballot. But Marjorie Dannenfelser, the antiabortion activist who had once urged Iowa voters to not support Trump, signed on as national chair of Trump's Pro-Life Coalition.

On October 7, the oddest US presidential election got odder. That afternoon, the Obama administration released a report officially confirming that Russia had been secretly intervening in the US election with its hack-and-leak operation. White House officials expected this news to be a bombshell. But an hour later, the *Washington Post* revealed outtake footage from a 2005 episode of the television show *Access Hollywood* in which Trump crudely boasted of pursuing a married woman and sexually assaulting women. ("Grab 'em by the pussy. You can do anything.") That became the headline of the day... until about thirty minutes later, when WikiLeaks released the first trove of emails and documents Russian hackers had stolen from Clinton campaign chair John Podesta.

The race was in a state of unprecedented turmoil. Republicans saw their chance to undo Trump's hostile takeover. Several called on him to quit the campaign. Ryan phoned GOP chair Reince Priebus and demanded the party dump Trump—though there was no official mechanism for doing so. Indiana Governor Mike Pence, whom Trump had selected as his running mate, went AWOL. Trump grudgingly apologized (sort of) and vowed to remain in the race.

Two days later at the second debate, Trump pulled a stunt. He showed up with Paula Jones and two other women who had accused Bill Clinton of sexual assault. During the debate, Trump insisted, "I have great respect for women." Hillary Clinton called him unfit to serve. Trump vowed that if elected he would appoint a special prosecutor to investigate Clinton. It was a nasty confrontation.

Ryan wanted to withdraw his endorsement of Trump. But with the party's voters enthralled with Trump's brand of extremism, the GOP couldn't easily break with Trump. Representative Kevin McCarthy talked Ryan out of it, explaining that could hurt other Republicans on the ticket. When Ryan condemned Trump in a conference call with all the House Republicans, he was shocked to see that members were irate that he had publicly criticized Trump. The Access Hollywood video had not turned the GOP tide against Trump—not even as numerous women came forward to allege Trump had sexually harassed or assaulted them. Women showed up at his rallies wearing a T-shirt that proclaimed TRUMP CAN GRAB MY...with an arrow pointing toward the crotch. Conservatives stood by him. Christian right leaders, desperate for the antiabortion judges Trump promised, were eager to make excuses and stand by him.

During the third debate, Clinton accused Trump of being a "puppet" for Putin. "No puppet. No puppet," Trump replied. "You're the puppet." He charged that the election was being "rigged" to ensure his loss, and he hinted he might not accept the results. No modern presidential candidate had ever done that.

The closing weeks of the campaign were marked by WikiLeaks' daily dissemination of Democratic emails and memos stolen by Russian operatives— which triggered a steady flow of mini-controversies that impeded the Clinton camp from advancing its own messaging. (In a significant media failure, the political press barely covered Russia's intervention in the election.) In the polls, Trump slowly gained back the ground he had lost after the Access Hollywood video. Eleven days before Election Day, FBI Director Jim Comey

revived the Clinton email scandal. In July, he had cleared her of any criminal conduct, though noting Clinton and her aides had been "extremely care-
less" in handling classified information. Now he notified Congress that a
new set of her emails might be on a laptop that had come into the FBI's possession. That turned out not to be the case. But another round of headlines
about emails created a strong headwind for Clinton in the final week of the
campaign.

By now, the hate and extremism at Trump events were no longer news-
worthy. At a rally in New Hampshire, a Trump supporter shouted, "Assassinate that bitch!" No one reacted. Chants of "Lock Her Up" became ho-hum.
The Republican nominee's brazen exploitation of fear, suspicion, and paranoia was standard operating procedure.

———

On Election Night, Clinton pocketed more votes, but Trump, with narrow
margins in Pennsylvania, Michigan, and Wisconsin (totaling 77,744 votes),
won those swing states, and the election. He had no coattails. Democrats
netted six House and two Senate seats, as the Republicans maintained control of both chambers.

After the race was called, Trump hit the stage at the Hilton Midtown in
Manhattan. "Now it's time for America to bind the wounds of division,"
said the great divider.

Right-wing activists and autocratic leaders around the world expressed
joy. Internet Research Agency employees in Russia celebrated. According to
a message intercepted by US intelligence, one of these Russians reported,
"We uncorked a tiny bottle of champagne... took one gulp each and looked
into each other's eyes... We uttered almost in unison: 'We made America
great.'"

Trumpism didn't start with Trump. It might have been a tough truth
for Republicans and conservatives to handle. But the party had frequently
relied on racial resentment and patriotic animus to power its way into office.
Sometimes it had done so behind a veil of euphemisms and smiles. Yet with
Trump as the Republican nominee, the party exchanged a dog whistle for
a megaphone. Trump had openly displayed bigotry, validated hatred, and
fueled paranoia and xenophobia. He had unapologetically engaged in
demagoguery and spread disinformation and fear to rally and rile up supporters. He had emboldened extremists and kooks. He had encouraged and
exploited the worst elements of American life. And the party—its leaders
and its voters—yielded to him. Trump was not an aberration. He was the
soul of the party.

CHAPTER 24

Very Fine People

President Donald Trump sat at the conference table in the Treaty Room on the second floor of the White House residence, where President Ulysses Grant once conducted cabinet meetings. Christopher Wray, the new FBI chief, Attorney General Jeff Sessions, and Homeland Security Adviser Tom Bossert had come to brief Trump and his new chief of staff, John Kelly, on the murder of an American citizen.

Three nights earlier, on August 11, 2017, nearly seven months into the Trump presidency, scores of white supremacists and neo-Nazis bearing tiki torches had assembled in Charlottesville, Virginia, and marched through the University of Virginia campus chanting, "White lives matter" and "Jews will not replace us." This parade of hate was a prelude to a Unite the Right rally, organized by white nationalists, to be held the following day to protest the proposed removal of a statue of General Robert E. Lee.

The next morning, a Saturday, Klansmen, right-wing militia members, neo-Confederates, and other racist extremists waving Confederate flags and Nazi banners gathered before the rally. Some were armed with semiautomatic weapons. Some wore Trump's signature red baseball cap proclaiming MAKE AMERICA GREAT AGAIN. Counterprotesters arrived in the downtown area as well. Fighting broke out between the groups. Riot police tried to clear the scene. Before the counterprotesters were gone, a white nationalist drove his Dodge Challenger into a group of them, killing thirty-two-year-old Heather Heyer and injuring thirty-five others.

Trump was at his golf club in Bedminster, New Jersey, when news of Heyer's death hit. He zapped out a tweet that mentioned it as a sidenote: "Charlottesville sad!" A little while later, he read a statement condemning "this egregious display of hatred, bigotry, and violence." Then he ad-libbed: "On many sides, on many sides." *On many sides?* This weak response drew a flood of criticism. Republican Senator Cory Gardner tweeted, "Mr. President— we must call evil by its name. These were white supremacists and this was domestic terrorism."

On Monday, in the Treaty Room with Wray, Sessions, and Bossert,

Trump expressed no interest in the federal investigation of Heyer's murder. According to an account published years later by journalist Jonathan Karl, Trump complained the protesters were being treated unfairly, noting they were right to oppose the removal of the statue. Sitting at Grant's table, he declared Lee "the greatest strategic military mind perhaps ever." He called the KKK and neo-Nazis "bad" but was on their side regarding the statue: "Next will be Washington and Jefferson."

Wray said it was important for Trump to state that the Klan and neo-Nazis were responsible for the violence. Yet Trump continued to rave about the talents of the Confederate generals. An American president was hailing the traitors of the Civil War and going soft on racist fascists.

After the meeting, Trump read a statement forced on him by his aides: "Racism is evil. And those who cause violence in its name are criminals and thugs, including the KKK, neo-Nazis, white supremacists, and other hate groups." That was not the end of this.

At a press conference the next day, Trump defended *all* his comments on Charlottesville, decried the removal of Confederate statues, and said of the protesters, "Not all of those people were neo-Nazis, believe me. Not all those people were white supremacists by any stretch." He observed that there had been "very fine people on both sides." Referring to the Unite the Right demonstrators, he remarked, "You had a lot of people in that group that were there to innocently protest."

The reaction was harsh. "There are no good neo-Nazis," Senate Majority Leader Mitch McConnell said. Republicans and pundits piled on. Meanwhile, former Klan chief David Duke tweeted, "Thank you President Trump for your honesty & courage to tell the truth." And white nationalist leader Richard Spencer—who after Trump's election had held a meeting where neo-Nazis gave the Nazi salute and shouted, "Hail Trump!"—called Trump's statement "fair and down to earth."

The forty-fifth US president had provided aid and comfort to Nazis and racists. This was as extreme as modern American politics had ever been.

———

In the opening months of his presidency, Trump governed as he had campaigned—chaotically and divisively. At his inauguration, he depicted America as a dystopian hellhole. There was "carnage" across the land, the citizenry was betrayed by a small group of elites, and only he could save the nation. In his first days as president, Trump moved to implement the racism-driven initiatives he promised as a candidate. He signed an executive order banning foreign nationals from seven predominantly Muslim countries from entering the United States. He approved an order to build a border wall.

His administration busted good-government norms and ran on disorder, suspicion, and disinformation. Senior Trump adviser Kellyanne Conway claimed the White House presented "alternative facts." But even the conservative editorial board of the *Wall Street Journal* decried the unprecedented level of presidential prevarication, citing Trump's "seemingly endless stream of exaggerations, evidence-free accusations, implausible denials, and other falsehoods."

Though previous Republican presidents had routinely rewarded far-right allies with jobs, Trump placed extremists within his inner circle and legitimized the white nationalism–friendly alt-right. Bannon was named his chief strategist, marking a first: a self-proclaimed supporter of the arguably racist alt-right serving in the White House. Trump hired Stephen Miller, a top campaign aide, as a senior policy adviser. Before joining the Trump campaign, Miller, an avowed restrictionist on immigration, had regularly circulated material from white nationalist sites to Bannon's *Breitbart*, and in emails to the publication he had promoted a racist French novel popular among neo-Nazis and white supremacists who believed the "great replacement" theory (which held that white people were purposefully being displaced throughout the Western world). Julia Hahn, a former *Breitbart* correspondent who associated with white nationalists, was hired as White House deputy policy strategist.

Another denizen of the alt-right world, Sebastian Gorka, a *Breitbart* and Fox News contributor with a history of vilifying Muslims, was appointed deputy assistant to the president for counterterrorism. Shortly after he began working at 1600 Pennsylvania Avenue, the *Forward* revealed Gorka "had close ties...to Hungarian far-right circles, and has in the past chosen to work with openly racist and anti-Semitic groups and public figures." (Both Bannon and Gorka would be gone from the White House by the end of August.) Trump selected Michael Flynn, who had collaborated with Muslim-bashing extremists, as his national security adviser—but Flynn was forced to resign twenty-three days into the administration for lying about conversations he had with Russia's ambassador to the United States.

Trump also paid back Christian right leaders and voters who had rescued him during the campaign. He ended US funding for international organizations that promoted or performed abortions and rescinded protections for transgender students. He nominated Judge Neil Gorsuch, a favorite of social conservatives, to the Supreme Court.

An extremist was in the White House. Trump spewed a never-ending stream of mean, angry, and divisive tweets. He retweeted an account loaded with anti-Muslim, antisemitic, and white supremacist material. He claimed undocumented immigrants were slicing up teenage girls with knives because they didn't "want to use guns because it's too fast and it's not painful enough." (The story was false.) He encouraged police officers to handle suspects roughly. He ratcheted up his war on reporters, referring to the news media as "the enemy of the people," a term used during the French Revolution and in Nazi Germany and Stalinist Russia to justify execution and imprisonment.*

Through the opening months of the Trump presidency, the Russia scandal hung over the new president. Trump continued to falsely deny that Putin had intervened in the election, calling the ongoing investigations a "hoax" and a "witch hunt." In March, FBI Director Jim Comey announced the bureau was investigating Putin's attack on the 2016 election and interactions between the Trump campaign and Russia. Two months later, Trump fired Comey. The next week, former FBI Director Robert Mueller took over the Trump-Russia investigation as special counsel.

To distract from the various Russia probes, Trump deployed an old trick: paranoia. He accused Obama of wiretapping him in Trump Tower, tweeting, "This is Nixon/Watergate. Bad (or sick) guy." No wiretapping had occurred. Trump was once again making up stuff and provoking the worst suspicions on the right. Simultaneously, Bannon and the conservative media started assailing what they called the Deep State—supposedly a secret cadre of anti-Trump officials within the intelligence community and other government agencies who schemed against the president. It was a familiar tactic: the enemies-within scare-mongering that Republicans and right-wingers had recklessly employed since McCarthyism.

The Trump White House was a circus—or a zoo. Senior aides lasted only months, sometimes less. Trump's poll numbers were awful: 36 percent approval rating, the lowest six-month mark in seventy years. But the chaos, mess, and never-ending controversies did not shake Trump's iron-grip hold on the Republican Party. He was scoring 90 percent among GOP voters.

Trump used the flood of criticism he received to support the us-versus-them

---

* In 2016, CBS correspondent Lesley Stahl asked Trump why he constantly attacked the media. Years later at a journalism forum, she recounted his reply: "I do it to discredit you all and demean you all, so when you write negative stories about me no one will believe you."

framework he sold his followers. Speaking to a gathering of Christian conservatives, he declared, "We're under siege," meaning his administration *and* the religious right. That was a resonant message for conservatives who continued to view themselves as victims oppressed by modern America and the loathsome libs. At a Council for National Policy meeting, a CNP leader—who was not identified in leaked material from the session—called liberals "evil" and said, "The activists on the left and the people who fund them are out to destroy everything you hold dear. Your families. Marriage. Your businesses. Your freedom of speech. Your freedom of religion. Everything." Members of the CNP and the Conservative Action Project, a related right-wing group, met almost every week with Trump administration officials.

As Jim McLaughlin, a GOP pollster, put it, "In many ways, Donald Trump is the conservative movement right now."

———

Two months after the killing in Charlottesville, former President George W. Bush delivered a speech targeting Trump without mentioning him by name. "Bigotry seems emboldened," he said, noting, "Our politics seems more vulnerable to conspiracy theories and outright fabrication." Bush was trying to steer the GOP away from a complete surrender to Trumpism. Republican Senators Bob Corker, Jeff Flake, and John McCain raised similar points, with Flake and Corker doing so only after deciding to not seek reelection. (McCain had been diagnosed with brain cancer and would die the following summer.) The way that moderate Republicans once warned of extremism infecting the party from the outside—from the Birchers, the New Right, the religious right, or the Tea Party—a handful of Republicans now warned that the extremism within and at the top of the party threatened the GOP. They made no headway.

Most Republicans fully capitulated. They feared Trump's wrath and lived in terror of getting on the wrong side of a Trump tweet or a Fox News segment. His former rivals who had denigrated him during the 2016 election— Lindsey Graham, Ted Cruz, and others—now marched in lockstep with the GOP's dear leader. "Virtually every Republican," *Axios* proclaimed, "is now a Trump Republican."

———

In early December, Trump made what for any other politician would have been a shocking endorsement: He backed Roy Moore, a far-right former Alabama judge running in a special election to fill the US Senate seat Sessions had vacated. Moore, a birther and a fierce social conservative tied to neo-Confederate groups, was an extremist who would have once been dismissed as a kook. He had been expelled as chief justice of the state after refusing to implement a federal court order to remove a five-thousand-pound Ten Commandments monument from a courthouse. Moore called for banning Muslims from serving in Congress, bashed gays, and praised Putin. He believed Obama was a secret Muslim.

In early November, he won the GOP primary—another sign of how radicalized the GOP base had become, Afterward, Moore was credibly accused of having chased after and in some cases sexually assaulted teenage girls when he was in his thirties. Taking a page from Trump's playbook, Moore denounced the allegations as "fake news" orchestrated by the liberal, anti-Trump elite. As these revelations caused national Republicans to distance themselves from him, Trump declared his support for Moore. Republicans then dialed down their criticism of Moore, and the Republican National Committee invested money in the race.

This episode demonstrated Trump's increasing sway over the party. He conveyed his blessing upon an alleged child molester and a fringe-right extremist, and the party went along. Trump was in control. (Moore would lose narrowly, but 68 percent of white voters backed this alleged sex offender.)

—————

Trump provided hardcore Republicans a few policy wins to cheer. He ended the DACA program that prevented undocumented minors from being deported. He passed a tax cut that was heavily tilted toward the wealthy and estimated to add $1 trillion to the deficit. He also, over Republican objections, slapped extensive tariffs on imported steel and aluminum and imposed a stiff tariff on a wide variety of Chinese exports, triggering a trade war. And he approved a budget that would produce large deficits, much of it driven by record amounts of military spending. None of this hurt him with the party's base.

Nor did scandalous revelations, such as the news that his personal attorney Michael Cohen had illegally paid $130,000 in hush money to a porn star named Stormy Daniels for keeping quiet about her alleged extramarital affair with Trump. (Trump had instructed Cohen to make the payment—and lied about that.) Another former top Trump aide, Paul Manafort, was found guilty on tax fraud and bank fraud charges related to the work he had done in Ukraine for Putin-friendly politicians.

Through all the controversies, Republicans stood by Trump. He referred to African nations and Haiti as "shithole countries." He implemented a "zero tolerance" program for undocumented immigrants, separating nearly two thousand migrant children from their parents, sparking public outrage over "kids in cages." He engaged in an erratic diplomatic pas de deux with North Korean dictator Kim Jong-un. He appeared at a joint press conference with Putin in Helsinki and accepted Putin's phony denial of intervention in the 2016 election, siding with a foreign adversary over his own intelligence community.

Senator Corker described the situation bluntly: Republicans had become "cultish" and "fearful" under Trump. Trump had transformed the party into an organization with only one mission: him. As Corry Bliss, executive director of the Congressional Leadership Fund, a super PAC supporting House GOP candidates, explained, "It's not about ideology anymore. It's only about Trump. Are you with him or are you against him? That's the only thing that matters to voters in the Republican base." The GOP had become a cult of personality.

———

In October 2018, Trump spotted a racist opportunity too obvious to ignore. A group of Central American migrants was heading through Mexico toward the US border. Caravans were routine, and this one was a thousand miles away. But here was a chance to terrify voters prior to the midterm elections. He declared this band of migrants—mainly people fleeing violence, political repression, and poverty—was "an invasion of our country" by "gang members" and "unknown Middle Easterners," and conservative media and his fellow Republicans issued similar hyperbolic warnings. Asked for evidence the caravan included Middle Easterners, Trump acknowledged, "There's no proof of anything. But they could very well be."

Trump tweeted out an ad his campaign produced that showed mobs of brown-skinned people and that claimed the migrant caravan was filled with "dangerous illegal criminals." The spot focused on a Mexican man who had killed two California police officers, and it asserted, "Democrats let him in our country. Democrats let him stay." This was a lie. This criminal had been deported during the Clinton administration and reentered the United States during the George W. Bush years. The misleading ad was widely denounced as racist and compared to the infamous Willie Horton commercial; NBC, Facebook, and even Fox News pulled it off the air.

In a White House speech loaded with falsehoods, Trump repeated a conspiracy theory spreading on the right: Left-wing donors were financing the caravans from Central America. This tied it all together for Trump's base: the libs, dangerous immigrants, and terrorists. Some versions of this reckless charge claimed eighty-eight-year-old billionaire George Soros, a Hungarian American Holocaust survivor, funded the migrant caravan. Representative Matt Gaetz, a Florida Republican and Trump fan-boy, posted a video on Twitter of a man supposedly handing cash to migrants and claimed this was a payment to join the caravan and "storm the US border @ election time." He asked, "Soros?" Trump tweeted out this video, too.

This was dangerous stuff. The Soros conspiracy theory apparently motivated Cesar Sayoc, a Florida Trump devotee who mailed more than a dozen bombs to people and organizations Trump had criticized, including Soros, Barack Obama, and Hillary Clinton. Robert Bowers, the accused killer of eleven people at the Tree of Life synagogue in Pittsburgh on October 27, had been obsessed with the caravan and described it as "invaders" on a social media account.*

Trump and the GOP's dissembling and fearmongering failed. The Democrats, who mounted a canny campaign exploiting Trump's unpopularity without turning him into the number one issue, netted forty seats and won the House. Their gains, which came mostly in suburban areas, were seen as a decisive referendum on Trump, though the Republicans picked up two seats in the Senate. Trump claimed the election as a "Big Victory."

———

The end of Trump's second year in office was marked by a budget fight that led to a monthlong government shutdown. Trump demanded $5 billion from Congress to build the wall on the Mexican border. He insisted that terrorists had been caught at the border. But his own State Department reported there was no "credible information" indicating this. Congress said no to his funding request.

After thirty-five days of shutdown, Trump caved and announced a deal that did not include $5 billion for his wall. The next month, Michael Cohen testified before Congress and flipped on his former boss. Trump, he said, "is a racist. He is a con man. He is a cheat." He prophesized that if Trump lost the 2020 election, "there will never be a peaceful transition of power."

On April 18, 2019, the Justice Department released a redacted version of Mueller's final report of his Russia probe. He did not uncover evidence that Trump and his campaign had criminally conspired with the Kremlin's

---

* On August 3, 2019, a far-right gunman shot up a Walmart in El Paso, Texas, killing twenty-three people, the deadliest attack on Latinos in modern American history. One reason for the massacre, the alleged shooter noted in a screed, was the migrant "invasion" being orchestrated to "replace" white culture and import illegal voters to dilute the political power of the right.

attack on the 2016 election that was waged in part to help Trump. But the report included damning findings: The Trump campaign tried to collude with Moscow, sought to benefit from the Russian attack, and aided and abetted Putin's operation by echoing and amplifying Moscow's false denials. It documented multiple contacts between Kremlin operatives and associates of the Trump campaign, showed that Trump had lied about his business dealings in Russia when he ran for president, and revealed numerous (and perhaps illegal) Trump attempts to obstruct the investigation.* But by now, Republicans had been trained by Trump to scream "hoax" and "witch hunt" whenever the subject of Russia arose. Few Republicans were troubled or disgusted by Mueller's conclusions—or by an adversary's assault on the United States. They cared more about serving Trump.

———

Onstage in the Amway Center in Orlando, Florida, on June 18, before thousands of adoring supporters wearing red MAGA hats, Trump officially announced he was running for reelection. He rehashed the usual resentments, complaining about the "witch hunt" Russia investigation, the treasonous news media, and "crooked Hillary." The crowd yelled, "Lock her up!" Trump denigrated the Democrats as an "angry, left-wing mob" and declared that the 2020 election would be a "verdict on the un-American conduct of those who tried to undermine our great democracy, undermine you." In the manner of an aspiring autocrat, he equated his personal trials and grievances with those of his supporters and proclaimed his political opponents to be enemies of the state. He was *othering* half of the nation.

Trump said nothing he hadn't bellowed hundreds of times already. But this was a reminder that Trump was the Republican Party's unrestrained extremist in chief, mining veins of suspicion, paranoia, bigotry, xenophobic enmity, and rage-driven tribalism for votes. What the party years ago did sub rosa Trump paraded into the open. He had legitimized the GOP's exploitation of hatred and fear. The game plan for remaining in the White House was more of the same.

———

On July 30, Donald Trump retweeted a crazy account that pronounced the Democrats "the true enemies of America." This account had previously

---

* A bipartisan Senate intelligence committee report, released in 2020, would reveal the disturbing fact that Manafort, while chief executive of the Trump campaign, repeatedly interacted with a suspected Russian intelligence officer who was possibly involved in Moscow's attack on the 2016 election.

pushed the bizarre QAnon conspiracy theory. With a president helping to promote one of the most loony and dangerous notions in American public life, here was a new frontier of political extremism.

The fundamental QAnon view was a conspiracist's dream (or nightmare): A clandestine and wicked global cabal of satanic elites who ate babies and trafficked children for sex—a group that included Hillary Clinton, international bankers, CEOs, Hollywood power brokers, and others—was scheming to control the world, and Trump was engaged in a clandestine battle to thwart them. The origins of this warped belief included a Michael Flynn tweet.

Days before the 2016 election, Trump's top campaign national security aide tweeted a story from a junk website falsely claiming that a new batch of Hillary Clinton emails showed she had engaged in money laundering and sex crimes with children. Two days later, conspiracy theorist Alex Jones said that Clinton had "personally murdered and chopped up and raped" children. Meanwhile, users of a conspiracy-minded site who had pored over the John Podesta emails stolen by Russian hackers maintained they had uncovered coded language indicating prominent Democrats were part of a satanic cult of baby eaters and child traffickers that operated out of the basement of a Washington pizzeria. This led to the ludicrous Pizzagate conspiracy theory, promoted by far-right bloggers, which prompted one believer to show up armed at the restaurant (which had no basement) and fire off a shot before being arrested.

With Pizzagate dribbling along in the fringes of the fringe, a far-right message board in October 2017 posted an anonymous message from a supposed Deep State insider—identified only as Q—who recycled the Pizzagate basics and expanded the conspiracy theory to a wider transnational plot involving villains beyond Hillary Clinton and her gang. With more "Q drops" and an increasing number of fanatics trading unhinged QAnon theories online—John F. Kennedy Jr. wasn't dead; he was working with Trump to defeat the globalist sex-trafficking bad guys!—this conspiracy movement grew, becoming popular with anti-government activists, militia groups, and Trump supporters. QAnoners started showing up at Trump rallies, holding Q signs and waving QAnon banners and flags. Trump had created fertile ground for this paranoid and preposterous irrationality.

In May 2019, the FBI field office in Phoenix released an intelligence bulletin warning that "conspiracy theory–driven domestic extremists" were a growing threat, specifically citing QAnon. It noted these conspiracy theories would "occasionally" drive "groups and individual extremists to carry out criminal or violent acts." In fact, there had already been QAnon-related violence. Cesar Sayoc, who had mailed bombs to Democrats and Soros prior to the 2018 midterms, was a QAnon believer.

The president of the United States was assisting this dangerous, delusion-based movement. He intermittently retweeted the accounts of QAnon pushers—as did Donald Trump Jr. and others in the Trump universe. A Trump campaign ad featured QAnon signs from rallies. At a Trump rally in Cincinnati, a warm-up speaker recited the slogan of the QAnoners: "Where we go one, we go all." Were these secret signals to the fringe nutballs? Maybe not. But the QAnoners could be forgiven for reading them as such. Trump never waved them off. QAnon crazies became part of his political base.

Trump encouraged all sorts of conspiracism. His Twitter feed was full of retweets of conspiracy-mongers and racists (as well as accounts tied to Russian, Chinese, and Iranian intelligence services). He described the world in terms that resonated with the paranoid: Sinister forces were conspiring against him and his supporters. The Deep State was spying on him and subverting his presidency. He readily echoed barmy allegations. He cited the debunked claim that MSNBC host Joe Scarborough had been mysteriously involved in the death of an intern when he was a member of Congress. He referred to terrorist attacks that had not happened. He repeated the false story spread by white nationalists that white farmers were being massacred in South Africa. He hinted that the Clintons were involved in the jailhouse death of sex trafficker Jeffrey Epstein.

One conspiracy theory particularly haunted Trump, and his belief in it would lead him to become only the third president ever to be impeached.

———

On July 25, 2019, Trump called Ukrainian president Volodymyr Zelenskyy. The Ukrainian requested more Javelin anti-tank missiles that could be used in his country's fight against pro-Russian forces in eastern Ukraine. Trump grabbed the moment to muscle Zelensky and replied, "I would like you to do us a favor." He then referred to a baseless conspiracy theory related to the Russia investigation that claimed Ukraine, not the Kremlin, engineered the cyber break-in of the Democratic National Committee computers in 2016 and that the DNC servers had been whisked away to Ukraine to cover up the *real* story. He pressed Zelenskyy: "I would like you to find out what happened with this whole situation."

Trump was looking for information to discredit the multiple investigations that had concluded that Moscow subverted the 2016 election to help Trump. He desperately wanted to undermine a narrative he could not live with: He had been elected president with Kremlin assistance. Trump also pressured Zelenskyy to investigate Joe Biden and his son Hunter, who had served on the board of a Ukrainian energy company, and manufacture dirt on the former Democratic vice president, who was running for president and leading Trump in the polls. Trump allies—and pro-Russia disinformation operatives—had been circulating the disproven allegation that Biden had forced the dismissal of a Ukrainian prosecutor to smother an investigation of Hunter.

Trump's shocking attempt to lean on a foreign leader to produce derogatory information on a political rival triggered impeachment proceedings in the House. During impeachment hearings, GOP legislators repeatedly referred to the Ukrainian conspiracy theory and other wild and unproven Deep State–related notions to protect Trump and deflect from his wrongdoing. Fiona Hill, who had been the top Russian expert in the Trump White House, tried to shut this down, testifying, "Some of you on this committee appear to believe that Russia and its security services did not conduct a campaign against our country and that perhaps, somehow, for some reason, Ukraine did. This is a fictional narrative that has been perpetrated and propagated by the Russian security services themselves. I would ask that you please not promote politically driven falsehoods that so clearly advance Russian interests." Her plea didn't work. The Republicans kept at it—and Trump did, too. The next day on Fox News, he prattled on about Ukraine covertly possessing the servers. He was advancing Russian disinformation.

The Democratic-controlled House voted to impeach Trump for abuse of power and obstruction of Congress, without one Republican supporting either charge. The absence of a single GOP vote prompted media stories about Trump's complete dominance of the party. The *New York Times* noted that Trump was wearing "a political coat of armor built on total loyalty from the GOP activists and their representatives in Congress." The impeachment trial in the Senate ended on February 5, 2020, predictably with Trump being acquitted, as all fifty-three Republicans sided with him but one: Mitt Romney, now a senator from Utah. Trump's approval rating among Republicans was a record 94 percent.

The night before Trump's acquittal, during his State of the Union speech, the president falsely claimed, "Our economy is the best it has ever been." He praised Rush Limbaugh, who had recently been diagnosed with Stage 4 lung cancer, and awarded the radio man who had been hurling falsehoods and sowing discord for more than thirty years the Presidential Medal of Freedom. The moment had its own logic: Limbaugh's brash, bombastic, divisive, and grievance-fueling rhetoric had cleared the way for Trump.

Trump's speech contained only two sentences about the deadly coro-

navirus spreading in China, and he played down the risk. He didn't mention the warning he had received from his national security adviser,
Robert O'Brien: This virus would "be the biggest national security threat"
of Trump's presidency.

———

Trump's narcissistic, disruptive, divisive, demonizing, confrontational
politics—now fully normalized within the Republican Party—resulted in
the preventable deaths of thousands of Americans.

As the COVID-19 pandemic struck the United States, Trump made a
series of misguided and false statements diminishing the danger at hand.
"We have it totally under control," he said on January 22. He claimed the
virus would likely vanish in April with warmer weather. He compared
COVID to the flu. Always pushing a paranoia-colored Manichean view of
the world, he called the pandemic the "new hoax" of the Democrats—after
the Russia investigation and the Ukraine impeachment. Donald Trump Jr.
claimed that Democrats hoped the virus would kill "millions of people"
so Trump's presidency would fail. Trump's comrades in the conservative
media joined in. Limbaugh told his millions of listeners the "coronavirus is
the common cold" and was being "weaponized" by Trump's political enemies to bring him down. Trump and his allies were turning this crisis into
yet another clash in the political civil war that he relished inflaming.

Trump imposed bans on travel from China and Europe. With the virus
spreading, the stock market reeling, and the economy grinding to a halt, he
declared a national emergency and proposed a stay-at-home plan to slow the
spread. But he set a poor example. He did not vigorously encourage social
distancing. He dismissed the importance of testing, fearing extensive testing would reveal more cases and harm him politically. He did not follow the
recommendation to wear a mask—and would deride those who did.

Together these missteps created a new front in the culture war, with
far-right and Tea Party–ish activists challenging lockdowns and mask
wearing. In one poll, nearly one in five respondents said they believed the
Centers for Disease Control and Prevention was exaggerating the serious-
ness of the virus to undermine Trump's presidency. Trump allowed—even
encouraged—the pandemic to become another battle in the long-running
right-wing assault on expertise and science.

In late March, Trump seemed to take a stand against his administration's own policy, when he started calling for a quick return to normal,
and tweeted, "WE CANNOT LET THE CURE BE WORSE THAN THE
PROBLEM ITSELF." In mid-April, he issued tweets declaring "LIBERATE

MINNESOTA," "LIBERATE MICHIGAN," and "LIBERATE VIRGINIA"—largely seen as encouragement to the right-wing protesters feverishly (and sometimes violently) opposing the stay-at-home orders state officials had implemented.

Trump alleged his enemies were trying to "inflame" the coronavirus "situation" to damage his reelection prospects.

The far right got the signal. Sean Hannity exclaimed, "This scaring the living hell out of people—I see it, again, as like, let's bludgeon Trump with this new hoax." Jerry Falwell Jr. prematurely called students back to his evangelical Liberty University. Glenn Beck exclaimed, "I would rather die than kill the country." Conservative pundit Dennis Prager compared prudent public health measures to the appeasement of Nazi Germany. Conservative activists Diamond and Silk claimed that the rising death count was a media plot to undermine Trump. Wild conspiracy theories about the origins of the pandemic and unproven treatments spread. Dr. Anthony Fauci, the director of the National Institute of Allergy and Infectious Diseases and a top coronavirus adviser to Trump, who came to be seen as the leading advocate of COVID restrictions, began to get death threats.

Trump's White House repeatedly interfered with decisions and pronouncements made by public health agencies and failed to set up an effective testing system or meet the needs of the health care system for personal protective equipment. With Congress, Trump did provide economic relief to Americans thrown out of work and businesses hobbled, and he initiated a program supporting the rapid development of vaccines. But he talked up ineffective and unproven remedies—including the possible "injection" of bleach—and continuously declared greater progress was being achieved than was occurring. He boasted of the high ratings his televised coronavirus news conferences received and displayed little empathy for those who had lost loved ones or jobs due to COVID-19. "All he could think about was the [reelection] campaign," former New Jersey Governor Chris Christie, a close Trump adviser, later said. "He didn't talk much about anything else."

With his inconsistent messaging, Trump fostered an atmosphere in which tribalistic politics shaped Americans' attitudes toward COVID-19. Polls showed that many more Democrats than Republicans considered it a serious threat. Later, researchers would conclude that Trump's erratic management of the crisis led to hundreds of thousands of deaths that could have been avoided with a more rigorous, robust, and consistent response. His initial handling of the pandemic laid the foundation for subsequent right-wing skepticism toward the COVID-19 vaccines, which would result in much higher death rates in red states than in blue states.

That Trump and the right turned a public health emergency into polarized political conflict was hardly surprising. Then Trump had another chance to exacerbate the Great American Divide—and he seized it.

On May 25, a Minnesota police office held his knee on the neck of George Floyd for more than nine minutes, killing the forty-six-year-old Black man. The murder triggered protests across the nation against racism and police brutality under the banner of Black Lives Matter. Most were peaceful; some led to violent confrontations between protesters and police or counterprotesters and to looting. Trump did little to calm the nation; he urged governors to "dominate" the Black Lives Matter demonstrators. "When the looting starts, the shooting starts," he tweeted. In meetings with advisers, Trump called for deploying US troops to defeat the protesters—a proposal his aides resisted.

When several hundred mostly peaceful protesters gathered at Lafayette Square across from the White House, law enforcement officers in riot gear violently moved in and used pepper balls and chemical spray to clear the crowd. From the White House, Trump declared, "I am your president of law and order"—reviving the old call of George Wallace and Richard Nixon—and then he trotted to a church next to the park, accompanied by top aides, including the defense secretary and the chairman of the Joint Chiefs of Staff, and held up a Bible for two awkward minutes.

James Mattis, who had resigned as Trump's first secretary of defense a year and a half earlier, could not contain his outrage at this "bizarro photo op" Trump had staged with "military leadership standing by." In a statement, he said, "Donald Trump is the first president in my lifetime who does not try to unite the American people—does not even pretend to try. Instead, he tries to divide us. We are witnessing the consequences of three years of this deliberate effort."

Mattis was not entirely correct. Other presidents had been purposefully divisive when it served their political interests. He was right, though, that Trump didn't bother to pretend.

Fear and division was Trump's strategy for his 2020 reelection effort. At his opening campaign rally in a Tulsa arena—which was less than half-full—Trump signaled he would base much of his reelection bid on the exploitation of white backlash against Black Lives Matter. He told the crowd he was the defender of "our heritage" and decried the razing of Confederate statues. He insisted on calling the coronavirus "Kung flu"—a term that had been labeled an anti-Asian slur. He warned that if the anti–police brutality protesters prevailed, a law-abiding citizen could easily become the victim of a "very tough hombre," associating crime with Latinos. He subsequently tweeted out videos of Black rioters punching white people and retweeted a video of Trump supporters that included one shouting "white power." He called Black Lives Matter "a symbol of hate."

None of this was subtle. Trump had been sending out fundraising emails to supporters warning that America was being overrun by "violent thugs" and "anarchists" and that he would end "this madness" and "restore LAW AND ORDER." At a July 3 speech at Mount Rushmore, Trump pressed his core message that the country was besieged by forces eager to annihilate the United States. "Our nation," he said, "is witnessing a merciless campaign to wipe out our history, defame our heroes, erase our values, and indoctrinate our children. Angry mobs are trying to . . . unleash a wave of violent crime in our cities." The goal of this supposed "left-wing cultural revolution" was to "destroy" civilization and impose "new far-left fascism." In a White House speech, he proclaimed, "We are now in the process of defeating the radical left, the Marxists, the anarchists, the agitators, the looters." Once again, according to Trump, America was on the verge of carnage that only he could prevent.

Trump's campaign—and other GOP endeavors—relentlessly dispatched emails to millions of Republicans alerting them that Biden, the Democrats' presumptive nominee, and his party had a secret plan to impose "radical socialism" on the nation. In 2008, Palin and McCain had assailed Obama as a "socialist" for proposing a more progressive tax system. In 2012, Romney went with a more nuanced formulation: Obama was turning the United States into a "European-style welfare state." Trump shot far beyond all that with a smear claiming the Democrats were cop-hating commies aiming to impose "far-left fascism."

As he and the GOP fomented fear, Trump also promoted a self-protective conspiracy theory: The election would be stolen from him. Months earlier, he had begun planting the seeds, sending out emails to supporters saying it was "no secret that the Democrats are trying to steal the Election out from under me." He claimed that the Democrats were "plotting against me from the very beginning" and "trying to rig the game" and would "create chaos" with "voter fraud." (And, of course, the email recipient should send him money so he could combat this scheme.) Now he railed against the use of mail ballots during the pandemic—though there was no indication such voting could not be conducted fairly. In a tweet, he predicted the election would be "the most INACCURATE & FRAUDULENT Election in history." It was a classic move of a would-be authoritarian, especially one who worried about losing: Undermine faith in the democratic system.

———

Due to the pandemic, the presidential nominating conventions were mostly highly produced television shows. The Democrats fixated on Trump's mishandling of the coronavirus crisis. Former First Lady Michelle Obama registered the deepest cut. Referring to a recent Trump remark about the horrendous death toll of the pandemic—"It is what it is"—she noted simply, "He cannot meet the moment. He simply cannot be who we need him to be." With nearly two hundred thousand Americans dead due to COVID, Biden, in his acceptance speech, contended that Trump "has failed in his most basic duty to this nation. He failed to protect us." He took aim at Trump's terror-drenched message: "Too much anger. Too much fear. Too much division...I will be an ally of the light, not of the darkness." This election, he said, was about winning "the soul of America."

Trump stuck to the low road of fearmongering and demagogic demonization. Delivering his convention speech from the White House before 1,500 guests (in violation of both tradition and social distancing recommendations), he slammed Biden as a "Trojan horse for socialism." With violent unrest that week in Kenosha, Wisconsin, following the police shooting of a Black man, Trump proclaimed that a vote for Biden would "give free rein to violent anarchists, agitators, and criminals who threaten our citizens." This election, he said, "will decide whether we will defend the American way of life or whether we allow a radical movement to completely dismantle and destroy it."

Throughout the fall campaign, Trump expanded on his brazen campaign of fear and vilification, and virtually no one in the Republican Party took public exception. His handling of the COVID-19 crisis, his harsh response to the Black Lives Matter protests, his ugly and divisive rhetoric, his baseless claim that the election would be stolen from him—nothing Trump did caused a problem within the GOP. Candidates sought to campaign with him. The donations poured in. The party stood for one thing: Trump. He would brook no dissent on this point, and there was none.

Trump continued to find ways to ratchet up the hate. He tweeted, "If I don't win, America's Suburbs will be OVERRUN with Low Income

Projects, Anarchists, Agitators, Looters, and of course, 'Friendly Protesters.'" A Biden victory, he predicted, would lead to far-left antifa protesters
and terrorists flooding suburban America. He raised the prospect of vicious
thugs subsuming white neighborhoods and "crime like you've never seen
before." It was all-out race-baiting. Simultaneously, he offered happy talk
about the pandemic. The coronavirus—the "China virus," as he called it—
would soon be gone and vaccines widely available before the end of the year
(though his advisers told him none of this was true).

And then Trump did something no candidate had done. Asked by
a reporter if he would commit to a peaceful transfer of power "win, lose,
or draw," he replied, "We're going to have to see what happens." The next
day, he said he was "not sure" the election could be honest. A president was
threatening to not abide by the election results.

Trump also refused to distance himself from the extremists of the right.
At the first debate, Biden accused him of using "everything as a dog whistle
to try to generate racist hatred, racist division." He pressed Trump to condemn white nationalists. Trump initially declined. Then he petulantly said,
"Give me a name." Biden shot back, "The Proud Boys"—referring to the
chauvinistic white nationalist–allied group that had attacked Black Lives
Matter protesters. "The Proud Boys," Trump said, "stand back and stand
by." This was hardly a renunciation; more like an invitation.

Two weeks later, in mid-October, Trump, who had recently recovered
from COVID-19, was interviewed at a televised town hall by Savannah
Guthrie of the *Today* show. He did decry white supremacists and antifa. But
when Guthrie asked Trump to denounce QAnon, he declined, saying, "I
know nothing about QAnon." That was highly unlikely. Two months earlier, he had been asked about QAnon during a press conference, and he had
replied, "I don't know much about the movement other than I understand
they like me very much, which I appreciate." He then had added, "I have
heard that it's gaining in popularity. I've heard these are people that love
our country." *Love our country.* This sounded like an endorsement. In fact,
QAnon had seeped into the GOP, with several supporters of this wacko conspiracy theory running for Congress as Republicans. That included Lauren
Boebert in Colorado and Marjorie Taylor Greene in Georgia. (Greene possessed a record of making racist and antisemitic comments and boasted a
Trump endorsement.) Now Trump told Guthrie he was unfamiliar with this
internet phenomenon, but he said, "I do know they are very much against
pedophilia. They fight it very hard." Another endorsement.

Guthrie followed up by asking Trump why he had tweeted out a QAnon
conspiracy theory that claimed Obama and Biden had Navy SEALs killed to

cover up the fake death of Osama bin Laden. "That was a retweet," Trump said, adding, "I'll put it out there. People can decide for themselves." The president was justifying the spreading of bogus information. "You're the president," Guthrie replied. "You're not, like, somebody's crazy uncle who can just retweet whatever."

But Trump had been pushing a variety of unproven conspiracy theories throughout the campaign. He claimed antifa was being funded by Soros. On Fox, he told Laura Ingraham that Biden was controlled by "people that you've never heard of, people that are in the dark shadows." At his rallies, he encouraged "Fire Fauci" chants—essentially validating unfounded COVID-19 conspiracy theories, which often focused on Fauci—and reinforced right-wing antipathy toward science and public health expertise.

Trump was the GOP's—and the nation's—crazy uncle. He was campaigning on hatred, bigotry, conspiracism, paranoia, and rage—exploiting apprehension and irrationality and threatening to deny the election results and move the nation toward autocracy. And he continued pushing an alternative and false reality. At the second debate, he claimed the virus was disappearing. Yet the nation was approaching 250,000 COVID deaths, with hundreds of thousands more to come.

On Election Night, shortly after 2:00 a.m., Trump appeared in the White House and launched his latest and most dangerous conspiracy theory. He declared the election was a "fraud." The race was too close to call at that point, though the trendlines favored Biden. Citing no proof, Trump claimed the vote count was being rigged against him. "Frankly, we did win the election," he stated. It was the beginning of an unprecedented and treacherous attack on democracy in which the Party of Lincoln and the conservative movement would eagerly and loyally serve as Trump's enablers and coconspirators.

The extremist in the White House, who had adopted and perfected the long-standing Republican practice of weaponizing grievance, racism, and suspicion to become the most powerful person in the nation, now intended to harness these forces to wreck the American system.

The Aftermath

L ate in the evening of January 6, 2021, after the rioters incited by the nineteenth Republican president had been cleared out of the Capitol, Senator Lindsey Graham took to the well of the Senate. Graham embodied the GOP's relationship with Trump. During the 2016 campaign, he had assailed Trump as a "race-baiting, xenophobic, religious bigot" who should be kicked out of the party, yet once Trump was president, Graham became a sycophant slavishly devoted to him. "Trump and I, we've had a hell of a journey," an agitated Graham huffed. "I hate it to end this way. Oh, my God, I hate it. From my point of view, he's been a consequential president. But today, the first thing you'll see, all I can say is count me out. Enough is enough."

Enough is enough. That seemed to be true for numerous Republicans. A large bloc of Republicans—147 House members and eight senators—had stuck with Trump's Big Lie in the aftermath of the insurrectionist assault and voted to support baseless objections to the certification of electoral votes, but party leaders saw an opportunity to pry the GOP from Trump's grip.

In the days following the attack, Senate Republican leader Mitch McConnell appeared almost giddy with the thought that Trump had discredited himself and become politically vulnerable. "If this isn't impeachable, I don't know what is," he said to advisers. Two of Trump's Cabinet members—Secretary of Education Betsy DeVos and Secretary of Transportation Elaine Chao (McConnell's wife)—quit in supposed disgust. Three Northeastern GOP governors urged Trump to resign. In conversations with fellow House Republicans, Representative Kevin McCarthy declared what Trump had done was "atrocious and totally wrong." He told his colleagues he was considering pushing Trump to resign, noting, "I've had it with this guy." Some Republican officials pondered whether Trump should be removed from office using the Twenty-Fifth Amendment.

This was the GOP establishment's best chance to separate itself from Trump since the *Access Hollywood* video emerged in 2016. The moment didn't last long.

When House Democrats offered an impeachment resolution a week after the riot, Representative Liz Cheney of Wyoming, the third-highest-ranking Republican in the House, tried to rally support within her party for the measure. Here was a way for the GOP to de-Trumpify. Were Trump convicted in an impeachment trial, the Senate could vote to bar him from holding any federal office in the future. Impeachment, conviction, disqualification—the Republican Party had an escape route.

In a fierce statement, Cheney blasted Trump: "The president of the United States summoned this mob, assembled the mob, and lit the flame of this attack. Everything that followed was his doing. None of this would have happened without the President. The President could have immediately and forcefully intervened to stop the violence. He did not. There has never been a greater betrayal by a President of the United States of his office and his oath to the Constitution."

Her fellow House Republicans disagreed.

Cheney persuaded only nine others to join her in voting with all the Democrats for impeachment. Though McCarthy stated that Trump "bears responsibility" for the "attack on Congress by mob rioters," he voted against the measure. Two weeks afterward, McCarthy visited Trump, who was now out of office, in Mar-a-Lago, his Florida retreat, and posed for a photo with the former president, both men smiling. Months later, McCarthy declared that Trump had "no involvement" in the January 6 attack.

McConnell followed a similar course. He and forty-two other Republicans voted to acquit Trump in his second impeachment trial. A bipartisan majority supported conviction, yet fell ten votes shy of the required two-thirds. Following the vote, McConnell delivered a fiery speech calling Trump "practically and morally responsible for provoking" the January 6 riot. He fiercely condemned Trump: "The people who stormed this building believed they were acting on the wishes and instructions of their president. And their having that belief was a foreseeable consequence of the growing crescendo of false statements, conspiracy theories, and reckless hyperbole which the defeated president kept shouting into the largest megaphone on planet Earth." Trump, McConnell exclaimed, had deployed "wild falsehoods" to encourage "terrorism" and had been "determined to either overturn the voters' decision or else torch our institutions on the way out." He said he had voted to acquit only on technical grounds, citing the dubious argument that a president out of office could not be placed on trial for impeachment.

After this passionate anti-Trump outburst, McConnell shared no further criticism of Trump. Twelve days later, he essentially said never mind, noting he would "absolutely" support Trump should he become the party's presidential nominee in 2024. And McConnell and McCarthy each opposed the creation of a bipartisan independent commission to investigate the assault on the Capitol. After their initial blasts at Trump, the two top officials of the Republican Party had sussed out the obvious: Most Republicans—especially Republican voters—were standing by the man who had attacked American democracy and caused a violent raid on Congress. So they decided to move on as if nothing had happened.

The party that Trump had bent to his will remained his. He still dominated fundraising for the Republicans, having collected hundreds of millions of dollars in the months since the election with his false claims. Casting him aside would be a blow to GOP finances. It would also enrage the base of Republican voters who continued to regard Trump as their beloved—and now wronged—champion. With the House Republicans only seven seats away from gaining control and the Senate split evenly, GOP officials dared not alienate the die-hard Trump voters prior to the 2022 midterm elections. The party couldn't turn on Trump without blowing itself up. Not even his incitement of extremist violence as part of an attempted coup could change that.

———

Trump had led the Republican Party and many of the seventy-four million Americans who voted for him on November 3, 2020, into a deep hole. For years, he had been convincing his followers to believe lies. He had engaged in a style of disinformation similar to that attributed to Moscow—the firehose of falsehood: a steady stream of untruths that, in the words of one expert, "entertains, confuses, and overwhelms the audience." Throughout his presidency, Trump kept the bullshit flying, according to the *Washington Post*, uttering more than 30,573 false or misleading statements. *The economy was the strongest it had ever been. The Russian investigation was nothing but a Deep State hoax. He handled the coronavirus masterfully. His phone call with Zelenskyy was perfect.*

On Election Night 2020, Trump added his biggest lie to the pile: that he was reelected by millions of votes and victory was stolen from him by the Democrats, the media, and other evil schemers. In the official count, Biden thrashed Trump by seven million votes, but only beat him narrowly in the crucial swing states to score a 306 to 232 win in the Electoral College.

In the subsequent days and weeks, Trump repeatedly brayed that the race had been rigged. His campaign and its allies pursued recounts and dozens of legal challenges. A group of lawyers and activists led by Rudy Giuliani and an attorney named Sidney Powell—dubbed the "crazies" by other Trump advisers—began pitching the wildest conspiracy theories involving manipulated voting machines, Italian hackers, software developed for Venezuelan leader Hugo Chavez (who died in 2013), vote-counting farms in Germany, money from Cuba and China, bamboo paper ballots, and, of course, Soros and the CIA. Their claims zipped across QAnon-related websites. Michael Flynn, Trump's disgraced first national security adviser (whom Trump pardoned at the end of November), encouraged Trump officials to seize voting machines and force a rerun of the election. At one point, he advised Trump to declare martial law. It was a spree of nuttiness propelled by kooks, conspiracists, and extremists—all of it blessed by Trump for his supporters who had been conditioned to believe his most outlandish fabrications.

Giuliani and other Trump allies lost spurious lawsuits in one court after another, eventually being defeated in sixty cases. They never produced any evidence of significant wrongdoing or fraud.

Despite the absence of proof, top Republicans echoed Trump's lies and rushed to the battlements for him. "President Trump won this election," McCarthy declared. The Texas attorney general, a Republican, filed a baseless lawsuit with the Supreme Court to invalidate the electoral votes from Georgia, Michigan, Pennsylvania, and Wisconsin, and GOP attorneys general in seventeen other states joined the lawsuit. They were seeking to disenfranchise millions of voters. Trump hailed the effort with a tweet: #OVERTURN. One hundred and twenty-six House Republicans signed on to an amicus brief in favor of the bogus suit. The Supreme Court tossed the case aside.

With the party apparatus and right-wing media bolstering his big con, Republican voters lapped up the propaganda. A mid-November Reuters/Ipsos poll found that half of Republicans believed Trump "rightfully won" and only 29 percent said Biden was the legitimate victor. In a Monmouth University survey, three-quarters of Trump's voters said they believed Biden had triumphed only due to fraud.

Conservative leaders feverishly embraced the cause. Steve Bannon asserted the election was a "mass fraud" and spread assorted conspiracy theories. (He also called for beheading Fauci and Wray: "I'd put the heads on pikes.") Multiple Stop the Steal groups popped up on social media. "Clean your guns," declared the organizer of one. FreedomWorks, the conservative advocacy group bankrolled by corporate donors that ginned up the Tea Party movement, sponsored protests against the election results. Far-right militia groups joined the effort. Matt Schlapp, a lobbyist and chairman of the influential American Conservative Union, trekked to Nevada, where he claimed thousands of illegal votes cast had been cast. (A "pants on fire" lie, concluded PolitiFact.) Ginni Thomas, a prominent right-wing activist and wife of Supreme Court Justice Clarence Thomas, sent text messages promoting QAnon-ish conspiracy theories about the election to White House chief of staff Mark Meadows. Fox News, *Breitbart*, One America News Network, Newsmax, and other far-right outlets covered Trump's fake reality as if it were true and promulgated the hysteria.

Influential conservative groups and Council for National Policy members planned Stop the Steal events, including a large gathering in the nation's capital scheduled for January 6. Women for America First, a dark-money outfit operated by Amy Kremer, a former leader of the Tea Party Express, was the main organizer for this rally. Other right-wing organizations promoting the event included Turning Point Action, the student-oriented band of Trump enthusiasts run by Charlie Kirk, the opening speaker at the Republicans' 2020 convention, and Phyllis Schlafly Eagles, the outgrowth of the group founded by far-right hero Phyllis Schlafly.

Trump had transformed the Republican Party and virtually the entire conservative movement into a robot army for his authoritarian crusade to invalidate an election and crush democracy. Both party and movement existed only to serve Trump. The cult of personality continued.

On December 1, Attorney General Bill Barr, up to now a fierce Trump protector, publicly declared that Trump's claims of a stolen election were completely false: "To date, we have not seen fraud on a scale that could have effected a different outcome in the election." His statement did nothing to slow down the march of Trump's lie or to persuade millions of Americans they had been flimflammed by Trump. (When Barr next met with Trump, the president told him, "You must hate Trump.") For Trump's zealous followers, nothing could undermine the word of their Dear Leader.

———

Trump's assault on democracy was not limited to crazy talk and half-baked lawsuits. He pursued crafty—and perhaps illegal—schemes behind the scenes to subvert the election. He pressured Republican state election officials and legislative leaders to annul the results in key states. (They resisted.) In a call to Georgia's Republican secretary of state, Brad Raffensperger, Trump said, "I just want [you] to find 11,780 votes, which is one more than we have [to get]." Raffensperger said no. State election officials and GOP officeholders who defied Trump's attempts to subvert the election received death threats from Trump fanatics inflamed by the defeated president.

After Barr resigned in disgust at Trump's refusal to accept his loss, Trump pressed the Justice Department to announce that the voting results were fraudulent, telling acting Attorney General Jeffrey Rosen to state "the election was corrupt and leave the rest to me and the Republican congressmen." He meant Representatives Marjorie Taylor Greene, Mo Brooks, Jim Jordan, Scott Perry, and other far-right Republicans who were secretly colluding with Trump to overturn the election. Rosen refused. Top department officials resisted and threatened to resign en masse when they discovered Trump planned to replace Rosen with a lackey who intended to use the Justice Department to keep Trump in power.

Trump's final gambit was for Pence and Trump loyalists in Congress to block the certification of the Electoral College votes on January 6. Trump told Pence, "You can either go down in history as a patriot or you can down in history as a pussy." Pence declined to join his boss's Constitution-defying plot. That day, Trump assembled his mob of extremists, and his lies led to hand-to-hand combat at the US Capitol between domestic terrorists screaming "fight for Trump" and guardians of the citadel of democracy.

Yet Trump was not the fundamental source of the crisis. Nor were the Republican Party, the conservative movement, or the right-wing media that spread Trump's disinformation and joined his war on democracy. The problem was Republicans—the voters, the people. Not just those few thousand in the January 6 rage-driven mob, but the millions who accepted Trump's reality-free and irrational assertions, who looked to this dissembling, power-mad egotist for the truth. Republican officeholders devoted themselves to Trump because he owned the allegiance of these voters. He had won the Republican masses. His prejudices, his lies, his resentments were theirs. Millions loved Trump for that. Their fervor was the real threat to the nation.

There is a vast ocean of academic literature exploring why human beings believe conspiracy theories, hold fast to false premises, and are susceptible to tribalism and drawn to authoritarians. Many of the explanations relate to issues of identity and status. "Right-wing extremist movements in America have all risen against the background of economic and social changes which have resulted in the displacement of some population groups from former positions of dominance," Seymour Martin Lipset and Earl Raab wrote half a century before QAnoners, Christian nationalists, Proud Boys, neo-Nazis, militia members, white supremacists, and others stormed the Capitol. A wide variety of theories address the relationship of resentment and grievance to politics and the association between psychological concerns and political ideology. And in the age of the internet, experts debate and explore the role of media, social media, online networks, and disinformation in shaping the public square and influencing (or perverting) discourse. Yet in the real world, for politicians seeking to exploit and encourage irrationality, unease, and animus, the explanations don't matter. What counts is that the politics of fear and unreason can work. Not always. But often.

Many voters are susceptible to stories and messages aimed at their worries, insecurities, hatreds, and ignorance. Republicans have long realized this. From McCarthyism to the Southern strategy to the New Right to the Tea Party—the GOP told Americans they were being victimized and the country was being subverted by other Americans. Did Republicans prey upon existing apprehensions (addressing demand) or stir anxieties that otherwise might remain in check (creating supply)? Both. The Republican Party encouraged Americans to believe the worst, and it affirmed the worst beliefs held by Americans. It operated a feedback loop that caused and reinforced animosity and suspicion. It bred extremism; it cynically profited off extremism.

Republicans might dismiss this judgment with a both-sides-do-it argument and point to instances of unfair Democratic attacks. The GOP has often complained the Democrats typically deride it as a party of cold-hearted, racist, corporate-lackey villains eager to rob Americans of their Social Security checks and Medicare benefits. (A progressive group—not a Democratic Party outfit—in 2011 produced an ad showing a Paul Ryan figure throwing a wheelchair-bound granny off a cliff.) But there has been no Democratic equivalent of McCarthyism, the Southern strategy, Pat Robertson's Satan-baiting, or the Tea Party. Michael Dukakis did not demonize George H. W. Bush; he said his policies were wrong.

The left has concocted conspiracy theories about the right and Republicans—say, 9/11 was an inside job—but top elected Democrats have not endorsed or exploited these notions. These ideas did not become fundamental components of Democratic dogma and strategy. Yet the GOP has repeatedly absorbed, legitimized, and advanced bizarro beliefs for political gain. Here is one way to look at it: The Vince Foster conspiracy theory was bunk; the Russian attack on the 2016 election was real.

The political use of fear and the exploitation of extremism has been an asymmetrical endeavor. Goldwater worked with Birchers. The left of the 1960s was no friend of the Democrats. Prominent Democratic officials have generally not accused Republicans of conspiring with sinister global forces to cook up clandestine plans to purposefully destroy the United States from within. The GOP has proffered that argument regarding Democrats for more than seventy years.

And then there was Trump. No national Democrat in recent decades has openly courted voters with explicit bigotry and enmity. No Democratic president had made direct common cause with extremists, spread so many lies, and bolstered conspiracism. Trump's style of politics was a hopped-up version of the paranoid style of politics. He found a home for it within the Republican Party. What does it say about the GOP that it could be subsumed by a demagogic political novice who played to bigots, racists, and other extremists?

With belligerent rhetoric, Trump told voters they were right to—they ought to—see political opponents and Americans who hold different views and values as vicious evildoers who endangered the country. In an America starkly divided by political passions, he deliberately splashed gasoline and lit match after match—even during a pandemic that was claiming thousands of American lives a week. Republican voters cheered and joined his legion; Republican Party officials signed up as loyal lieutenants or lapdogs.

The Party of Lincoln, which was formed in 1854 to protect democracy, became the Party of Trump, which after the 2020 election assumed one overriding mission: to sabotage democracy to keep a rogue in power.

———

After the January 6 riot, the Republican Party did not change. It became even more of a Trump-über-alles entity, adopting the Lost Cause of the 2020 election as its driving force. A Reuters/Ipsos poll found that half of Republicans said the January 6 siege was "largely a non-violent protest" or the work of left-wing agitators "trying to make Trump look bad." More than half of Republicans bought a false narrative and dismissed or downplayed an act of domestic terrorism that had threatened the Constitution. John Geer, a public opinion expert at Vanderbilt University, told Reuters, "Republicans have their own version of reality. It is a huge problem. Democracy requires accountability and accountability requires evidence."

To be a Republican was to be a Trump devotee, and that meant accepting Trump's propaganda about the election. This became the party's loyalty oath. Trump would endorse only adherents of the Big Lie and those who shared his quest to undermine democracy. He vowed vengeance against those who would not carry this banner. The GOP candidates who parroted Trump's lies tended to win Republican primaries. Adhering to the truth often meant a death sentence in Trump's GOP. As Ruth Ben-Ghiat, an autocracy expert and history professor at New York University, observed, Trump had transformed the Republican Party: "He's changed the party to an authoritarian party culture. So not only do you go after external enemies, but you go after internal enemies. You're not allowed to have any dissent."

———

In the stretch after January 6, with the GOP more subjugated than ever to Trump, extremism within its ranks flourished. If Trump and the party could get away with a violent attack on the Capitol, it seemed practically anything, any hardcore or extremist position, was possible. Trump-worshipping conservatives expressed skepticism about the new COVID-19 vaccines, with Republican officials, such as Florida Governor Ron DeSantis, opposing mask and vaccine mandates, even fighting against private businesses establishing such requirements. One result: The COVID death toll in counties Trump carried in 2020 was significantly higher than in Biden counties.

Within weeks of Biden's inauguration, Republican state lawmakers proposed 361 bills in 47 states to impose new voting restrictions and to hand more control over elections to Republican state legislatures. (One of those laws allowed Georgia Republicans to kick Black Democrats off county election boards.) Numerous GOP advocates of Trump's Big Lie began running for state positions in charge of elections. Republicans mounted a concerted effort to dominate the vote-counting system and to obtain the power to do in the future what Trump had failed to achieve: overturn elections.

The party became more QAnonish. Marjorie Taylor Greene and Lauren Boebert, onetime QAnon supporters just elected to the House as far-right Republicans, drew much media notice. Greene's record, in particular, came under scrutiny. She had previously called for executing prominent Democrats, including Nancy Pelosi, Hillary Clinton, and Barack Obama; pushed the conspiracy theory that the 2018 school shooting in Parkland, Florida, was a "false flag" operation; and peddled a bizarre antisemitic theory about a California wildfire being caused by a space laser controlled by a corporate cabal that included the Rothschild banking firm. She also had moderated a Facebook page that promoted the John Birch Society (which still existed in a much-diminished capacity). But when Speaker Pelosi moved to strip Greene of her committee assignments, the House GOP stood by Greene and even applauded her during a meeting.

Dozens of other QAnoners campaigned as Republicans for congressional seats and other offices. Trump endorsed several. A PRRI poll found that 23 percent of Republicans believed the QAnon conspiracy theory. Republicans, including Representative Louie Gohmert and Texas GOP state chair Allen West, attended QAnon-affiliated conferences. At one QAnon-ish event, Michael Flynn seemed to call for a military coup in the United States. Donald Trump Jr. posted QAnon-associated tweets and memes on social media.

In the post–January 6 period, wacko Republicans seemed emboldened. Greene and Representative Paul Gosar, an Arizona Republican, each spoke at a white nationalist conference organized by Holocaust revisionist and Hitler fan Nick Fuentes. At this event, the crowd approvingly chanted, "Putin! Putin! Putin!" (Prior to Putin's brutal and illegal invasion of Ukraine in 2022, Bannon and Fox News host Tucker Carlson declared they were rooting for Putin.) Gosar circulated an anime-style video that featured a character that looked like him killing Democratic Representative Alexandria Ocasio-Cortez. The House voted to censure Gosar; only two Republicans supported the measure. Boebert maligned Representative Ilhan Omar, a Minnesota Democrat and Somali immigrant, with an anti-Muslim slur, calling her part of the "jihad squad." When the Capitol was evacuated due to a bomb threat, Representative Mo Brooks expressed sympathy for the bomb-threat suspect, saying he understood "citizenry anger directed at dictatorial Socialism."

As the GOP further Trumpified, its social conservative base hardened. The party cynically pushed one panic after another, ginning up overheated controversies about transgender issues, the canceling of Dr. Seuss (which didn't happen), the discussion of homosexuality in classrooms, and critical race theory. After GOP-appointed conservative justices on the Supreme Court overturned *Roe v. Wade*, Republicans moved forward with abortion bans without exceptions for rape, incest, or protecting the life of the mother. (The court's decision ending the constitutional right to an abortion was the culmination of decades of continuous plotting and political organizing by social conservative fanatics that tracked back to the rise of the New Right in the 1970s and the subsequent alliance forged by the GOP with religious right extremists.) Republicans and Trump backers now raised the prospect of challenging same-sex marriage and contraception use.

Republicans flirted with the "great replacement" theory—the racist conspiracy theory promoted by white nationalists that claimed white people in the United States were purposefully being replaced by people of color. When Carlson on a broadcast asserted that Democrats were "trying to replace the current electorate...with new people, more obedient voters, from the Third World" to dilute the political power of other Americans (read: white Americans), he was widely criticized for promoting a view propounded by racists. Yet the Republican National Committee quickly sent out a fundraising email declaring Carlson was "absolutely right."

The GOP also opened a new front in the culture war against Democrats: pedophilia. During the confirmation hearings for Ketanji Brown Jackson, the first Black woman ever nominated to the Supreme Court, Republican senators alleged she had been unusually lax in sentencing people convicted of child-pornography crimes. This was a false and reckless charge. But Donald Trump Jr. tweeted that Democrats were "really doing their best to secure the pedophile vote for future elections." And Marjorie Taylor Greene declared, "The Democrats are the party of pedophiles." Here was more proof that many Republican voters would swallow any swill about the Democrats served them by Trump and his team. An *Economist*/YouGov Poll found that 49 percent of Republicans believed it definitely or probably true that "top Democrats are involved in elite child sex-trafficking rings." Only 13 percent said this was false, with 39 percent unsure. A *Washington Post* article called the GOP's adoption of pedophilia-baiting "the new red scare." The party and its voters were truly divorced from reality and off the rails.

———

For decades, Republicans and the right-wing media had told voters to be scared and suspicious. The world was a treacherous place, full of hidden foes: commies, radicals, Black protesters, secularists, foes of the American family and so-called traditional values, secret Muslims, antifa. Gingrich ripped Bill Clinton as the "enemy of normal Americans." Birchers and Tea Partiers saw conspiracies in every nook and corner. Politicians played on existing fears within the polity but also created fears. (Migrant caravans full of terrorists!) It was all fueled by hate. And after January 6, the hate kept coming—from Trump and others.

During a meeting of House Republicans a few weeks following the riot, Representative Andy Biggs, a far-right Arizonan, declared that Democrats "are not just an opponent. They're an adversary that's trying to wipe this country out and change it forever." This sentiment was a driving force in Trump's GOP. Florida Senator Rick Scott claimed that Democrats and the "militant left" had a "plan" to destroy patriotism, capitalism, free speech, and the nuclear family, and he asked, "Is this the beginning of the end of America?" Ohio Republican Senate candidate and author J. D. Vance asserted, "The professors are the enemy." On his podcast, Bannon proclaimed, "We have a chance, once in our lifetime, to destroy the Democratic Party as an institution. We cannot let this slip from our grasp." When the user of a social media site set up by Trump seemingly called for "Civil War," Trump shared that post.

In his second inaugural address, delivered forty-one days before he would be assassinated, Lincoln declared, "with malice toward none, with charity for all." Trump had turned Lincoln's party into an enterprise of malice. He was a stress test—for the GOP and for the US political system. The Republican Party failed the exam. It could not resist the gravitational pull of his demagoguery or its voters' demand for a politics of malice and extremism. As former GOP consultant Stuart Stevens observed in his memoir, the party had "legitimized bigotry and hate as an organizing principle." He added, "Trump has served a useful purpose by exposing the deep flaws" of the Republicans. The political system fared better than the GOP in that it resisted and survived Trump's efforts to undermine a national election, retain power illegitimately, and steer the country toward authoritarianism—though Trump had come close.

With Trump firmly in control of the Republican Party, the opportunity for a course correction for the GOP appeared limited to nil. Cults of personality are not easily ended. Their destruction often requires the complete discrediting of the leader—and even that may not do it. Conspiracy theories are tough to debunk. Challenging such notions tend to make adherents angry or defensive, and they cling more firmly to their misguided beliefs.

Trump and his followers shared a grand delusion—the myth of the stolen election. It was as if Republicans were experiencing a form of shared psychosis, in which people in proximity to a person suffering psychosis—that is, a person experiencing delusions or engaging in conduct indicating a detachment from reality—start to experience the same symptoms. Even though top aides told him there had been no significant voter fraud, Trump insisted his false contentions about the election were true. A paranoid narcissist and would-be autocrat, he might have believed they were. But whatever he thought, millions of his followers regarded his fiction as fact, reinforced by a conservative media still enthralled with Trump. One treatment for shared psychosis is obvious: separating the secondary patients from the primary source. That was not likely to happen with Trump and the Republican Party.

Losing can cause a political party to reflect upon its standing and consider changes. The Republicans did that after the 2012 election—and then ignored the proposed recommendations. But after Trump's defeat in 2020, his call for revenge and restoration became the raison d'etre for the party. Neither his loss nor January 6 forced the Republicans into a reckoning. Perhaps demographic trends would undermine the GOP over time; Trump's most vehement supporters remained older white guys who would not be around forever. And the same was true for Trump. But the rise and success of Trump-emulating politicians was a sign that Trumpism without Trump could be the Republican Party's future.

On January 6, 2022, when the House of Representatives convened for a session to commemorate the first anniversary of the attack on Congress, only two Republicans attended: former Vice President Dick Cheney and his daughter, Representative Liz Cheney. The rest of the GOP wanted nothing to do with a ceremony marking the Trump-inspired insurrectionist raid on the Capitol. The wounds of that day had not healed. The lies that fed the violence had not been defeated. A recent ABC/Ipsos poll had found that 52 percent of Republicans believed the people involved in the January 6 attack had been "protecting democracy." That meant half of the GOP electorate saw the violent extremists who had assaulted law enforcement officials, threatened to kill the vice president, and tried to overturn a legitimate election as heroes. The party was cracked.

In Statuary Hall, a chamber near the House floor, which had been briefly occupied by the marauders a year earlier, President Joe Biden delivered a speech and for the first time in his presidency let loose on Trump: "The former president of the United States of America has created and spread a web of lies about the 2020 election. He's done so because he values power over principle, because he sees his own interests as more important than his country's interests and America's interests, and because his bruised ego matters more to him than our democracy or our Constitution." Trump, he said, had held "a dagger at the throat of America."

Trump had planned to conduct a press conference that day, but his aides had talked him out of it. Instead, in a statement, he complained that Biden had "used my name today to try to further divide America." (Biden had not cited Trump by name.) And he added, "The Democrats want to own this day of January 6th so they can stoke fears and divide America. I say, let them have it because America sees through theirs [*sic*] lies and polarizations." The great divider and fearmonger who had tried to overthrow the nation's constitutional order was accusing the other side of his own sins.

Trump noted he would have more to say soon at a rally in Florence, Arizona. And he did. Before an enthusiastic crowd of fifteen thousand, he proclaimed he had won in 2020. He called the media's characterization of his false election claims as the "Big Lie" a "lot of bullshit." He referred to the January rioters who had been arrested as "political prisoners." He excoriated Biden and the Democrats, exclaiming, "The country is being destroyed." And he hinted at a "historic comeback," suggesting he intended to run again in 2024. When he left the stage, the P.A. system played the 1966 soul hit "Hold On, I'm Comin'."

In 2020, a majority of the American public rejected Trump and his politics of conspiracism, racism, tribalism, and authoritarianism, but the demagogic Trump, with his constant spewing of reality-distorting disinformation, maintained a fierce hold on the Republican Party and tens of millions of its voters. Thirty percent of Americans still supported the Party of

Trump, and polls showed he had a shot at regaining power in the next presidential election. In the footsteps of McCarthy, Goldwater, Nixon, Reagan, George H. W. Bush, George W. Bush, McCain, Palin, Romney, and other Republicans, Trump had embraced, empowered, and tapped the menacing forces of far-right extremism. He did it more extensively, more cynically, and more explicitly than his predecessors—and he did so to commandeer the party. Under Trump's control, the Grand Old Party was consumed and conquered by the extremism, rage, and hatred it had long exploited. Formed 168 years earlier to save the nation from the expansion of slavery, the Republican Party, now infected with a political madness, had become a threat to the republic. A critical question for the days and years ahead was whether American democracy would overcome the danger it posed.

Acknowledgments

Writing history can be a lonely *and* a communal endeavor. You are focused on years long ago—lost in time and separated from the trials and tribulations of today—but dependent on the chroniclers who have come before. While I worked on this project in my home office during a pandemic, my colleagues were those historians and journalists who had strived in the past to capture, preserve, and explain important aspects of American life and whose efforts made this book possible. Many are listed in the bibliography. As I wrote *American Psychosis*, I felt they were by my side, and I thank them all.

Profound thanks always go to Gail Ross, a superb agent and a fierce advocate for her authors and their books. For thirty-three years, she has been a guide and a friend, always generous and frank with insights ("that idea won't sell") and enthusiastic in her encouragement ("that's the book to write!"). The publishing industry is fortunate to have her as an ally, as am I.

Sean Desmond, my editor and the editorial director at Twelve, deserves a solid round of applause. This is not our first rodeo together. As I knew from our previous project, he is a supportive coach with a sharp eye. Through the process, he displayed patience, shared his optimism and faith, nudged without pushing, and caused me to believe that this book was the most important one in his stable. That all helped a lot. His perceptive reading of the manuscript greatly improved the book. Many thanks to the entire Twelve team: Zohal Karimy, Megan Perritt-Jacobson, Estefania Acquaviva, Bob Castillo, Jim Datz, and Ben Sevier, the publisher of Grand Central. And thanks to copyeditor Mark Steven Long and cover designer Jarrod Taylor.

You would not be holding this book in your hand—or reading it on a device—were it not for the hard work of two indispensable and diligent research assistants who unearthed, sorted through, and organized decades' worth of material: Jeremy Fassler and Delphine d'Amora. Corrine Worthington spent hours in an archive collecting much-needed documents. Amarins Laanstra-Corn acquired important material when not tending to her studies at college. Madeleine Nephew and Jon Corn provided essential assistance in compiling the source notes and the bibliography. I thank them all.

A heartfelt thanks goes to Ernie Lazar, an independent researcher of right-wing movements and anticommunism who assembled an online archive of thousands of documents. He plucked out and forwarded numerous records related to the John Birch Society and overloaded me with material—which is what an author wants. His contribution to this book and to scholarship overall has been immense.

Michael Beschloss, Norman Ornstein, and Lawrence Rosenthal offered early—and important—advice and encouragement that was much appreciated.

The staff at the main reading room of the Library of Congress was cheerfully helpful—what a wonderful place to work, even during a pandemic—and the staff at Columbia University's Rare Book and Manuscript Library did me an important favor. My deepest appreciation to both.

I am grateful for my colleagues at *Mother Jones*. It's a privilege and a pleasure to work with them every day to produce kickass journalism. To name-check a few: Monika Bauerlein, Clara Jeffery, Daniel Schulman, Marianne Szegedy-Maszak, James West, Jahna Berry, and Madeleine Buckingham. Schulman was so kind as to read the manuscript and, of course, he found ways to make it better (as he often does with my copy). Also, a special thanks to the team that works on my *Our Land* newsletter: Rob Pjetri, Dylan DiSalvio, Daniel King, Robert Wise, Emily White, and Amber Hewins. (You can check out the newsletter at www.davidcorn.com.) King applied his copyediting prowess to the galleys and improved this book.

I am proud to be part of the MSNBC team. A thank-you to all my colleagues at the network, including the producers, bookers, and, particularly Joy Reid, Ari Melber, Lawrence O'Donnell, and Rachel Maddow.

You truly learn who your friends are during a pandemic—mainly because you miss them dearly. During this tough stretch, I was fortunate to receive much-needed support and friendship (even if remotely) from the Cheat Mountain Club gang: Sally, Stephen, Garret, and Larkin Kern; Reid, Dio, and Gabel Cramer; Martha Weiss and Josh, Annie, and Isabel Rosenthal; Jenny Apostol and Marco, Nico, and Lyla DiPaul; and Angela Coyle and Andrew, Brendan, Maya, and Ryan Fontanez. Sonya Cohen is always in my (and our) memory.

My basement (or backyard) band provided shelter from the storm of book writing; thanks to David Grinspoon, Adam Brookes, Sam Kittner, and Larry Nittler. Friends who checked in on me when I was often too overwhelmed to check in on them and friends who have always been by my side, even when we have been apart, include Eric Scheye, Steven Prince, Steve Earle, Nils Lofgren, Jay Roach, Joe Pichirallo, Julie Burton, Ted Mankin, James Grady, Bonnie Goldstein, Tim Weiner, Kate Doyle, Tony Alfieri, Ellen Grant, Chris Harvie, Claudia Harvie, Ricki Seidman, Lynn Sweet, Margaret Nagle, Darren Criss, Christina Sevilla, Steve Rochlin, and Joe Cirincione. As always, a special shout-out to Peter Kornbluh, who offered much encouragement and who gave the manuscript a careful vetting. A thank-you goes to Michael Isikoff for our past collaborations, which taught me much about writing books. Of course, thanks to all my Twitter pals. You know who you are. And thanks to lawyer/friend Peter Kaufman for his navigational help.

Several generous friends opened their lovely homes to me while I was working on this book and could be only a subpar houseguest: Bobby Shapiro and Liz Nessen, and Sara Nichols and Frank Arentowicz. Many thanks to Karen Mark and A. M. Tucker for camaraderie and neighborly assistance.

I am ever grateful for the love and support from Ruth Corn Roth, Gordon Roth, Barry Corn, Steven Corn, Amy Corn, Samantha Corn, Sarah Corn, and Jon Corn. Jon continues to inspire me (and others) with his grit and determination.

Once more, I end by thanking the most important collaborators in my life: Amarins, Maaike, and Welmoed. With each book comes a new acknowledgment of my gratitude for their love and support and of my appreciation for their own impressive achievements. I have watched Amarins and Maaike grow into confident and independent-thinking women, and while writing this book, I witnessed them crafting their own lives, determined to make our society more just and beautiful. Welmoed, talented and brilliant, has been the creative director of our family, doing much to help each of us pursue our own dreams, while she has been highly successful in a career dedicated to spreading art and culture in a world that needs more of both. They have my love and admiration. With this book, I spent much time gazing backward in time. Now that it's done, I look forward to peering ahead and seeing what the future holds for the four of us.

Source Notes

Not long after I arrived in Washington, DC, in 1987, I visited a small office downtown. The lighting in it was poor. The office was crammed with many gray filing cabinets. Inside each were hundreds of files containing information on right-wing groups and individuals. The two people who worked in this office—Wes McCune and Gladys Segal—had for many years been collecting literature, newsletters, pamphlets, and mailings from conservative organizations, clipping newspaper and magazine articles about the right, and maintaining an extensive index card system charting every entity and person. Their outfit was called Group Research, Inc.

McCune, a former journalist and executive assistant to President Truman's secretary of agriculture, initiated this project in 1962, with support from labor unions. He kept it going until 1996. Through all those years, he published a mimeographed newsletter called *Group Research Report* that tracked significant developments and scuttlebutt within the world of the right: the formation of new groups, personnel changes, fundraising and financial information, the publication of books and reports, accounts of conferences and other events, and interactions between the far right and politicians and government officials. At first, this newsletter was published semimonthly, in later years, monthly or quarterly. It was a treasure trove of information, and cumulatively it is a history of the modern right.

At the start, conservatives despised McCune's enterprise, assailing it as a cross between a spying operation and a blacklist. The FBI in the mid-1960s investigated him and then closed its probe when it found no sign that Group Research, Inc. was a communist-backed scheme. It was merely a monitoring project that reviewed public material. Anyone could subscribe to the report, and McCune was delighted to help reporters and congressional investigators who came seeking assistance.

The back issues of *Group Research Report* were an invaluable source for this book. The Library of Congress has a partial collection of the newsletter. But the vast files of Group Research and every issue of *Group Research Report* are now part of the Rare Book and Manuscript Library of Columbia University. I wish McCune, who died in 2003, was alive today, so I could tell him how much this book benefitted from his endeavors.

Another wonderful source was Rick Perlstein's series of magisterial histories of American politics that covers the 1950s through 1980: *Before the Storm*, *Nixonland*, *The Invisible Bridge*, and *Reaganland*. Many chapters in this book were informed by Perlstein's monumental work.

This book examines the decades-long relationship between the GOP and extremists of the right, and I was fortunate that others have written insightful histories of the modern conservative movement, such as E. J. Dionne Jr.'s *Why the Right Went Wrong: Conservatism—from Goldwater to the Tea Party and Beyond*; John S. Huntington's *Far-Right Vanguard: The Radical Roots of Modern Conservatism*; and Jonathan M. Schoenwald's *A Time for Choosing: The Rise of Modern American Conservatism*.

The bibliography lists the other works I relied on. Additionally, I reviewed hundreds of contemporary newspaper and magazine stories. A large portion of the second half of the book focuses on subjects and events that I covered as a reporter. For me, much of this is living history that I witnessed and chronicled. Below I cite particularly important sources for each chapter.

Introduction: Two Mobs

You can watch part of Nelson Rockefeller's speech at the 1964 GOP convention on You-Tube: https://www.youtube.com/watch?v=VXDVclImqJ8. Accounts of his speech and the convention can be found in Thomas J. McIntrye's *The Fear Brokers: Peddling the Hate Politics of the New Right* (see the introduction by Mark Hatfield); J. William Middendorf II's *A Glorious Disaster: Barry Goldwater's Presidential Campaign and the Origins of the Conservative Movement*; Stephen Shadegg's *What Happened to Goldwater?: The Inside Story of the 1964 Republican Campaign*; Richard Norton Smith's *On His Own Terms: A Life of Nelson Rockefeller*; Theodore H. White's *The Making of the President, 1964*; and Richard Hofstadter's *Anti-Intellectualism in American Life, The Paranoid Style in American Politics, Uncollected Essays 1956–1965*. (See the essay "Goldwater and His Party.") The account of the January 6, 2021, attack is drawn from extensive news reporting. The *New York Times* produced a marvelous video recounting the assault: https://www.nytimes.com/video/us/politics/100000007606996/capitol-riot-trump-supporters.html.

Chapter 1: Backstory I: The Rise and Decline of the Grand Old Party

Two of the best histories of the Republican Party are Heather Cox Richardson's *To Make Men Free: A History of the Republican Party* and Lewis L. Gould's *The Republicans: A History of the Grand Old Party*. I also consulted Jill Lepore's *These Truths: A History of the United States*; David W. Blight's *Frederick Douglass: Prophet of Freedom*; John A. Farrell's *Richard Nixon: The Life*; Greg Mitchell's *Tricky Dick and the Pink Lady: Richard Nixon vs. Helen Gahagan Douglas—Sexual Politics and the Red Scare, 1950*; Stephen Kinzer's *The True Flag: Theodore Roosevelt, Mark Twain, and the Birth of American Empire*; and William Bragg Ewald Jr.'s *Who Killed Joe McCarthy?* Robert A. Slayton's "When a Catholic Terrified the Heartland" in the *New York Times* (December 10, 2011) is a good account of Catholic bigotry and the 1928 election.

Chapter 2: Backstory II: Fear and Loathing in America

There is a rich literature regarding paranoia, extremism, and conspiracy theory in American public life. Hofstadter's work, collected in the volume cited above, is essential, as is *The Politics of Unreason: Right-Wing Extremism in America, 1790–1970*, by Seymour Martin Lipset and Earl Raab. I also relied on Andrew Burt's *American Hysteria: The Untold Story of Mass Political Extremism in the United States*; Jesse Walker's *The United States of Paranoia: A Conspiracy Theory*; and Kathryn S. Olmsted's *Real Enemies: Conspiracy Theories and American Democracy, World War I to 9/11*. The account of the Ku Klux Klan's involvement in the 1924 election is based on David M. Chalmer's *Hooded Americanism: The First Century of the Ku Klux Klan, 1865–1965*; Rory McVeigh's *The Rise of the Ku Klux Klan: Right-Wing Movements and National Politics*; and Wyn Craig Wade's *The Fiery Cross: The Ku Klux Klan in America*. Other sources for this chapter included William E. Leuchtenburg's *Franklin D. Roosevelt and the New Deal, 1932–1940*; Josh Zeitz's "When America Hated Catholics" in *Politico* (September 23, 2015); Wayne S. Cole's "The America First Committee" in the *Journal of the Illinois State Historical Society* (Winter 1951); and David Gordon's "America First: the Anti-War Movement, Charles Lindbergh, and the Second World War, 1940–1941," a resource guide compiled for a Historical Society and New York Military Affairs Symposium in 2003.

Chapter 3: The General and the Scoundrel

The account of Dwight D. Eisenhower and Joe McCarthy's campaign trip is based on Ewald's *Who Killed Joe McCarthy?* and Robert Griffith's "The General and the Senator: Republican Politics and the 1952 Campaign in Wisconsin" in the *Wisconsin Magazine of History* (No. 1, 1970). Ewald also chronicled the subsequent behind-the-scenes feuding between the Eisenhower White House and McCarthy. Other sources for this chapter included Hofstadter's *Anti-Intellectualism in American Life*; Lipset and Raab's *The Politics of Unreason*; Burt's *American Hysteria*; Lepore's *These Truths*; Olmsted's *Real Enemies*; Perlstein's *Nixonland*; and *The Radical Right*, a collection of essays edited by Daniel Bell.

Chapter 4: No Good Birchers

There are many good histories of the rise of the right and the John Birch Society in the 1950s, including Perlstein's *Before the Storm*; Schoenwald's *A Time for Choosing*; Huntington's *Far-Right Vanguard*; John A. Andrew III's *The Other Side of the Sixties: Young Americans for Freedom and the Rise of Conservative Politics*; Arnold Forster and Benjamin R. Epstein's *Danger on the Right: The Attitudes, Personnel and Influences of the Radical Right and Extreme Conservatives*; D. J. Mulloy's *The World of the John Birch Society: Conspiracy, Conservatism, and the Cold War*; and Edward Miller's *A Conspiratorial Life: Robert Welch, the John Birch Society, and the Revolution of American Conservatism*. Correspondence regarding the John Birch Society from Robert Welch and Barry Goldwater comes from a massive archive of Bircher-related material assembled by independent researcher Ernie Lazar. A guide to his archive can be found at http://archive.org

/details/lazarfoia. For William F. Buckley's involvement with the Goldwater campaign and the Birchers, see John B. Judis's *William F. Buckley Jr.: Patron Saint of the Conservatives*; Alvin S. Felzenberg's *A Man and His Presidents: The Political Odyssey of William F. Buckley Jr.*; and Buckley's own account: "Goldwater, the John Birch Society and Me" in *Commentary* (March 2008).

Chapter 5: In Your Heart

The account of the 1964 presidential campaign draws on Perlstein's *Before the Storm*; White's *The Making of the President, 1964*; F. Clifton White's *Suite 3505: The Story of the Draft Goldwater Movement*; Shadegg's *What Happened to Goldwater?*; Andrew's *The Other Side of the Sixties*; and Schoenwald's *A Time for Choosing*. Phyllis Schlafly's involvement in the race is covered in Donald Critchlow's *Phyllis Schlafly and Grassroots Conservatism: A Woman's Crusade* and Carol Felsenthal's *The Sweetheart of the Silent Majority: The Biography of Phyllis Schlafly*. Her secret Bircher membership was revealed in Ronald Radosh's "Phyllis Schlafly, 'Mrs. America,' Was a Secret Member of the John Birch Society" in the *Daily Beast* (April 20, 2020); this story was based on documents obtained by Ernie Lazar through the Freedom of Information Act. J. Evetts Haley's role in the 1964 campaign was examined by William Adler in "A Texan Looks at Lyndon," published in the *Texas Monthly* in September 1987, and John S. Huntington in "'The Voice of Many Hatreds': J. Evetts Haley and Texas Ultraconservatism," which appeared in the *Western Historical Quarterly* in January 2018.

Chapter 6: Keeping the Kooks Quiet

Matthew Dallek's account of Ronald Reagan's 1966 gubernatorial campaign, *The Right Moment: Ronald Reagan's First Victory and the Decisive Turning Point in American Politics*, was an essential source, as was Kurt Schuparra's *Triumph of the Right: The Rise of the California Conservative Movement, 1945–1966* and Gerard J. De Groot's "'A Goddamned Electable Person': The 1966 California Gubernatorial Campaign of Ronald Reagan" in *History* (July 1997). Also see Stuart Spencer's interview in the Ronald Reagan Oral History Project of the Miller Center of Public Affairs Presidential Oral History Program at the University of Virginia. Other sources included Andrew's *The Other Side of the Sixties*; Schoenwald's *A Time for Choosing*; Perlstein's *Before the Storm* and *Nixonland*; the Anti-Defamation League's 1966 report "The John Birch Society–1966"; and Seth Offenbach's 2010 dissertation at the State University of New York at Stony Brook, *The Other Side of Vietnam: The Conservative Movement and the Vietnam War*.

Chapter 7: "Bring Us Together"

The story of the 1968 campaign is well told in numerous books. Richard Nixon's deal with the segregationists is best covered in *American Melodrama: The Presidential Campaign of 1968* by Lewis Chester, Godfrey Hodgson, and Bruce Page. Other sources for this chapter include Lawrence O'Donnell's *Playing with Fire: The 1968 Election and the Transformation of American Politics*; Theodore H. White's *The Making of the President,*

1968; Joe McGinniss's *The Selling of the President*; Philip A. Klinker's *The Losing Parties: Out-Party National Committees, 1956–1993*; Lipset and Raab's *The Politics of Unreason*; and Perlstein's *Nixonland*. Haldeman's notes on Nixon's conversation about exploiting race during the campaign are available in the Richard Nixon Presidential Library and are reported in Farrell's *Richard Nixon: The Life*. Farrell also revealed the notes showing Nixon thwarting the Vietnam peace talks in "When a Candidate Conspired with a Foreign Power to Win an Election," published in *Politico* (August 6, 2017). Also see Jeremy D. Mayer's "Nixon Rides the Backlash to Victory: Racial Politics in the 1968 Presidential Campaign" in the *Historian* (No. 2, 2002).

Chapter 8: Ratfucking America

Perlstein's *Nixonland* and *The Invisible Bridge* cover Nixon's presidency, his reelection, and his fall, as does Farrell's *Richard Nixon: The Life*. For Nixon's continued reliance on the Southern strategy, see James Boyd's "Nixon's Southern Strategy" in the *New York Times* (May 17, 1970). Schoenwald's *A Time for Choosing* examines Nixon's relationship with conservatives. David Paul Kuhn chronicles the hard hat riot in his book *The Hardhat Riot: Nixon, New York City, and the Dawn of the White Working-Class Revolution*. Other sources for the riot: Jefferson Cowie's "Nixon's Class Struggle: Romancing the New Right Worker, 1969–1973" in *Labor History* (No. 3, 2002); Jefferson Cowie's "The 'Hard Hat Riot' Was a Preview of Today's Political Division" in the *New York Times* (May 11, 2020); and Angela Serratore's "The 'Hard Hat Riot' of 1970 Pitted Construction Workers Against Anti-War Protesters" in *Smithsonian Magazine* (May 8, 2020). Theodore H. White reported on the 1972 election in *The Making of the President, 1972*. For excellent accounts of Watergate, see Garrett M. Graff's *Watergate: A New History* and Stanley Kutler's *The Wars of Watergate: The Last Crisis of Richard Nixon*. Also, see Scott J. Spitzer's "Nixon's New Deal: Welfare Reform for the Silent Majority" in *Presidential Studies Quarterly* (September 2012).

Chapter 9: "Make Them Angry"

The best account of the rise of the New Right is Alan Crawford's *Thunder on the Right: The "New Right" and the Politics of Resentment*. For the 1976 campaign, see Perlstein's *The Invisible Bridge*; Jules Witcover's *Marathon: The Pursuit of the Presidency, 1972–1976*; Jonathan Alter's *His Very Best: Jimmy Carter, A Life*; and Kai Bird's *The Outlier: The Unfinished Presidency of Jimmy Carter*. Information about Joseph Coors is drawn from 1975 hearings held by the Senate Committee on Commerce on his nomination to the board of directors for the Corporation for Public Broadcasting. Also see Stephen Isaacs's "Coors Beer—and Politics—Move East" in the *Washington Post* (May 4, 1975). For information on the Pioneer Fund, see the 2017 Southern Poverty Law Center report "From Eugenics to Voter ID Laws: Thomas Farr's Connections to the Pioneer Fund." The Ford campaign memo about the Reagan campaign can be found at the Gerald R. Ford Presidential Library (https://www.fordlibrarymuseum.gov/library/exhibits/campaign/016800303-002.pdf).

Chapter 10: Onward Christian Soldiers

Orrin Hatch's relationship with conspiracy theorist W. Cleon Skousen is based on his own tribute to Skousen in the *Congressional Record* of January 25, 2006 (pages S114–115) and Matt Canham's "The Political Birth of Orrin Hatch" in the *Salt Lake Tribune* (January 31, 2012). Sources for the continuing development of the New Right include Crawford's *Thunder on the Right*; Perlstein's *Reaganland*; Richard Meagher's "Remembering the New Right" (published by Political Research Associates in 2009); and McIntyre's *The Fear Brokers*. For the rise of Jerry Falwell and the religious right, see Michael Sean Winters's *God's Right Hand: How Jerry Falwell Made God a Republican and Baptized the American Right*; Dirk Smillie's *Falwell, Inc.: Inside a Religious, Political, Educational, and Business Empire*; and Frances FitzGerald's "A Disciplined, Charging Army" in the *New Yorker* (May 18, 1981). Alter's *His Very Best* and Bird's *The Outlier* provide excellent accounts of Jimmy Carter's presidency. You can watch Reagan's appearance with Jim Bakker on YouTube: https://www.youtube.com/watch?v=TizWOt9vBaU.

Chapter 11: Let's Make America Great Again

The story of the 1980 presidential election can be found in Perlstein's *Reaganland*; Alter's *His Very Best*; Bird's *The Outlier*; John Brady's *Bad Boy: The Life and Politics of Lee Atwater*; Elizabeth Drew's *Portrait of an Election: The 1980 Campaign*; and Andrew E. Busch's *Reagan's Victory: The Presidential Election of 1980 and the Rise of the Right*. For the role of the religious right in the campaign, see Winters's *God's Right Hand* and Sidney M. Milkis and Daniel J. Tichenor's "Building a Movement Party: The Alliance Between Ronald Reagan and the New Christian Right," published by the UVA-Miller Center (https://millercenter.org/rivalry-and-reform/building-movement-party). Also see Angie Maxwell and Todd Shields's *The Long Southern Strategy: How Chasing White Voters in the South Changed American Politics*; Robert Jones's "How Trump Remixed the Republican 'Southern Strategy'" in the *Atlantic* (August 14, 2016); and Joseph Crespino's "Did David Brooks Tell the Full Story about Reagan's Neshoba County Fair Visit?," posted by the History News Network (November 11, 2007).

Chapter 12: Reaganland

Two good overviews of Reagan and his presidency are Garry Wills's *Reagan's America: Innocents at Home* and Sean Wilentz's *The Age of Reagan: A History, 1974–2008*. Robert Billings's homophobic remarks were reported by Jim Peron in the September 1981 issue of the *Libertarian Review* ("The New Theocracy: Moral Majority's Grab for Power"). The relationship between the Reagan White House and the religious right, particularly Falwell and the Moral Majority, is chronicled in the White House papers of Morton Blackwell archived at the Ronald Reagan Presidential Library. Also see David John Marley's "Ronald Reagan and the Splintering of the Christian Right" in the *Journal of Church and State* (No. 4, 2006). For Falwell's continuing participation in politics, see Winters's *God's Right Hand* and Smillie's *Falwell, Inc.* Good histories and accounts of the start of the Council for National Policy are Robert O'Harrow Jr.'s "God, Trump and the Closed-Door World of a Major Conservative Group" in the *Washington Post* (October 25, 2021) and Anne Nelson's *Shadow Network: Media, Money, and the Secret Hub of the Radical Right*. For more information on LaHaye, see Robert Dreyfuss's "Reverend Doomsday" in *Rolling Stone* (January 28, 2004) and Rob Boston's "Left Behind" in *Church & State* (February 2002). LaHaye's promotional John Birch Society film was reported by Heather Hendershot in *What's Fair on the Air?: Cold War Right-Wing Broadcasting and the Public Interest*. A good primer on the nuclear weapons freeze is Lawrence S. Wittner's "The Nuclear Freeze and Its Impact" in *Arms Control Today* (December 2010).

Chapter 13: Morning (and Nazis) in America

The Richard Darman and Lee Atwater memos can be found in Peter Goldman and Tony Fuller's *The Quest for the Presidency, 1984*. Other good accounts of the 1984 campaign include Brady's *Bad Boy* and Jack W. Germond and Jules Witcover's *Wake Us When It's Over: Presidential Politics of 1984*. For the Reagan administration's and Republicans' connections to the World Anti-Communist League, neo-Nazis, and other extremists, see Scott Anderson and Jon Lee Anderson's *Inside the League: The Shocking Exposé of How Terrorists, Nazis, and Latin American Death Squads Have Infiltrated the World Anti-Communist League*; Russ Bellant's *Old Nazis, the New Right, and the Republican Party*; Joe Conason's "Reagan and the War Crimes Lobby" in the *Village Voice* (May 14, 1985); and Paul W. Valentine's "The Fascist Specter Behind the World Anti-Red League" in the *Washington Post* (May 28, 1978). For more on Falwell's political activity: Winters's *God's Right Hand*. Excellent accounts of the Iran-contra scandal include Jane Mayer and Doyle McManus's *Landslide: The Unmaking of the President: 1984–1988*; Theodore Draper's *A Very Thin Line: The Iran-Contra Affairs*; Malcolm Byrne's *Iran-Contra: Reagan's Scandal and the Unchecked Abuse of Presidential Power*; and *The Iran-Contra Scandal: The Declassified History*, edited by Peter Kornbluh and Malcolm Byrne.

Chapter 14: Not Kinder or Gentler

Good books chronicling the 1988 election include Peter Goldman and Tom Mathews's *The Quest for the Presidency: The 1988 Campaign*; Jack W. Germond and Jules Witcover's *Whose Broad Stripes and Bright Stars?: The Trivial Pursuit of the Presidency, 1988*; Richard Ben Cramer's *What It Takes: The Way to the White House*; and Brady's *Bad Boy*. The George H. W. Bush diary entries can be found in Jon Meacham's *Destiny and Power: The American Odyssey of George Herbert Walker Bush*. For information on Pat Robertson, see Rob Boston's *The Most Dangerous Man in America?: Pat Robertson and the Rise of the Christian Coalition*.

Chapter 15: Spiritual Warfare

The account of Rush Limbaugh's rise as a conservative hero is drawn from John K. Wilson's *The Most Dangerous Man in America: Rush Limbaugh's Assault on Reason*; Zev Chafets's *Rush Limbaugh: An Army of One*; Paul D. Colford's *The Rush*

Limbaugh Story: Talent on Loan from God: The Unauthorized Biography; David Remnick's "Day of the Dittohead" in the *Washington Post* (February 20, 1994); and Lewis Grossberger's "The Rush Hours" in the *New York Times* (December 16, 1990). For Limbaugh and Roger Ailes, see Gabriel Sherman's *The Loudest Voice in the Room: How the Brilliant, Bombastic Roger Ailes Built Fox News—and Divided a Country*. You can listen to Limbaugh's first show on WABC: https://wabcradio.com/episode /100th-anniversary-special-rush-limbaugh-7-4-88-10-03-21/.

For Newt Gingrich and the Viet Cong memo and GOPAC, see Julian Zelizer's *Burning Down the House: Newt Gingrich and the Rise of the New Republican Party*. Bush's diary entries appear in Meacham's *Destiny and Power*. Elizabeth Rickey chronicled her encounter with David Duke and the Billy McCormack episode in a chapter in *The Emergence of David Duke and the Politics of Race* (edited by Douglas Rose). The McCormack story was covered by the *Slow Burn* podcast in an episode titled "David Duke: The Nazi and the Republicans" (Season 4, Episode 3). For the rise of Pat Robertson's Christian Coalition, see the Anti-Defamation League's 1994 report "The Religious Right: The Assault on Tolerance & Pluralism in America"; Sara Diamond's *Roads to Dominion: Right-Wing Movements and Political Power in the United States*; Boston's *The Most Dangerous Man in America?*; Frederick Clarkson's "Inside the Covert Coalition" in *Church & State* (November 1992); and James M. Penning's "Pat Robertson and the GOP: 1988 and Beyond" in *Sociology of Religion* (Autumn 1994). For the 1992 campaign, see Jack W. Germond and Jules Witcover's *Mad as Hell: Revolt at the Ballot Box, 1992* and Peter Goldman and the *Newsweek* team's *Quest for the Presidency, 1992*. You can watch Tom Brokaw's interview of Pat Buchanan here: https://www.youtube.com /watch?v=Z3t4N2lGgo8.

Chapter 16: The Clinton Chronicles

One of the best examinations of the Vince Foster case is Dan E. Moldea's *A Washington Tragedy: How the Death of Vincent Foster Ignited a Political Firestorm*. Joe Conason and Gene Lyons chronicle the right-wing assault on Bill and Hillary Clinton and all the investigations in *The Hunting of the President: The Ten-Year Campaign to Destroy Bill and Hillary Clinton*. Sidney Blumenthal, a journalist-turned-Clinton-adviser, provides the view from inside the Clinton camp in *The Clinton Wars*. For Falwell's role, see Winters's *God's Right Hand* and Smillie's *Falwell, Inc.* For the religious right's continuing involvement in politics, see the Anti-Defamation League's "The Religious Right: The Assault on Tolerance & Pluralism in America"; Diamond's *Roads to Dominion*; Frederick Clarkson's *Eternal Hostility: The Struggle Between Theocracy and Democracy*; and Daniel K. Williams's *God's Own Party: The Making of the Christian Right*. Pat Robertson's "concentration camp" remark was reported by Molly Ivins; see "Un-Christian Behavior by the Religious Right" in the *San Francisco Chronicle* (September 15, 1993). For Newt Gingrich and the 1994 election, see Zelizer's *Burning Down the House*.

Chapter 17: A Vast Right-Wing Conspiracy

The account of Helen Chenoweth's hearing is drawn from Sidney Blumenthal's "Her Own Private Idaho" in the *New Yorker* (July 2, 1995). For the militia movement and the NRA, see Frank Smyth's *The NRA: The Unauthorized History* and Daniel Levitas's *The Terrorist Next Door: The Militia Movement and the Radical Right*. For the Christian Coalition's activity in the mid-1990s, see Williams's *God's Own Party*. For coverage of the Clinton-Gingrich confrontation and the government shutdown, see Elizabeth Drew's *Showdown: The Struggle Between the Gingrich Congress and the Clinton White House* and Zelizer's *Burning Down the House*. Bob Woodward chronicles the 1996 election in *The Choice: How Bill Clinton Won*. For Limbaugh in the Clinton years, see Wilson's *The Most Dangerous Man in America*. Accounts of the continuing Clinton investigations (and right-wing assaults on the Clintons) can be found in Blumenthal's *The Clinton Wars* and Conason and Lyons's *The Hunting of the President*. See also Michael Isikoff's *Uncovering Clinton: A Reporter's Story* and Phillip Weiss's "Clinton Crazy" in the *New York Times* (February 23, 1997). You can read the Clinton "conspiracy commerce" memo at https://www.documentcloud.org/documents/1115427-clinton-the-communication -stream-of-conspiracy.html.

Chapter 18: Fortunate Son

The activity of the Council for National Policy during the 2000 campaign and the George W. Bush years is drawn from O'Harrow's "God, Trump and the Closed-Door World of a Major Conservative Group." For the 2000 primary contest between John McCain and George W. Bush, see Richard Gooding's "The Trashing of John McCain" in *Vanity Fair* (November 2004). Good accounts of the 2000 presidential race include Dana Milbank's *Smashmouth: Two Years in the Gutter with Al Gore and George W. Bush*; James Ceasar and Andrew E. Busch's *The Perfect Tie: The True Story of the 2000 Presidential Election*; and the *Washington Post* political staff's *Deadlock: The Inside Story of America's Closest Election*. The account of the Bush campaign's mob in Miami is drawn from *537 Votes*, an HBO documentary directed by Billy Corben; John Lantigua's "Miami's Rent-a-Riot" in *Salon* (November 28, 2000); and contemporary news reports.

Chapter 19: What We Deserve

The account of the Bush administration presenting a misleading case for the Iraq invasion is drawn from Michael Isikoff and David Corn's *Hubris: The Inside Story of Spin, Scandal, and the Selling of the Iraq War* and Robert Draper's *To Start a War: How the Bush Administration Took America Into Iraq*. Also see Amy Gerhkoff and Shana Kushner's "Shaping Public Opinion: The 9/11-Iraq Connection in the Bush Administration's Rhetoric" in *Perspectives on Politics* (No. 3, 2005). For the Bush administration's relationship with the Christian Coalition and the religious right, see Esther Kaplan's *With God on Their Side: How Christian Fundamentalists Trampled Science, Policy, and Democracy in George W. Bush's White House* and Rob Boston's "Inside the Christian Coalition" in *Church & State* (November 2004). For the Swift Boat Veterans' attack on

John Kerry, see Duncan Black's "MMFA Investigates: Who is Jerome Corsi, Co-author of Swift Boat Vets Attack Book?," posted by Media Matters (August 6, 2004); "The Lies of John O'Neill: An MMFA Analysis," posted by Media Matters (August 24, 2004); Pamela Collof's "Sunk" in *Texas Monthly* (January 2005); Michael Dobbs's "Swift Boat Accounts Incomplete" in the *Washington Post* (August 22, 2004); and Kate Zernike and Jim Rutenberg's "Friendly Fire: The Birth of an Attack on Kerry" in the *New York Times* (August 20, 2004). For the 2004 campaign, these books were essential: Evan Thomas and the *Newsweek* staff's *Election 2004: How Bush Won and What You Can Expect in the Future*; James W. Ceaser and Andrew E. Busch's *Red Over Blue: The 2004 Election and American Politics*; and *The Values Campaign?: The Christian Right and the 2004 Elections*, edited by John C. Green, Mark J. Rozell, and Clyde Wilcox. Also see the interview with Rozell that is part of "The Election of 2004" series of the Collective Memory Project at Southern Methodist University Center for Presidential History; and Sue O'Connell's "The Money Behind the 2004 Marriage Amendments," which was posted on FollowTheMoney.org (https://www.followthemoney.org/research/institute-reports /the-money-behind-the-2004-marriage-amendments).

Chapter 20: Going Rogue

The McCain controversy with Rod Parsley was precipitated by articles I wrote for *Mother Jones*. See "McCain's Spiritual Guide: Destroy Islam" (March 12, 2008) and "McCain's Pastor Problem: The Video" (May 8, 2008). For accounts of the 2008 campaign, see John Heilemann and Mark Halperin's *Game Change: Obama and the Clintons, McCain and Palin, and the Race of a Lifetime* and James W. Ceaser, Andrew E. Busch, and John J. Pitney's *Epic Journey: The 2008 Elections and American Politics*. For an account of how birtherism began, see Ben Smith and Byron Tau's "Birtherism: Where It All Began" in *Politico* (April 22, 2011). I covered the 2008 campaign and witnessed McCain and Palin rallies. Quotes from Barack Obama in this and succeeding chapters are from his memoir, *A Promised Land*.

Chapter 21: Feed the Beast

The meeting of GOP leaders plotting to obstruct President Barack Obama was reported by Robert Draper in his *When the Tea Party Came to Town*. This chapter's account of the rise of the Tea Party draws on several books: Dionne's *Why the Right Went Wrong*; Tim Alberta's *American Carnage: On the Front Lines of the Republican Civil War and the Rise of Trump*; Michael Grunwald's *The New New Deal: The Hidden Story of Change in the Obama Era*. See also *At the Tea Party: The Wing Nuts, Whack Jobs and Whitey-Whiteness of the New Republican Right . . . and Why We Should Take It Seriously*, edited by Laura Flanders; and another collection of essays and articles called *Steep: The Precipitous Rise of the Tea Party*, edited by Lawrence Rosenthal and Christine Trost. Alberta's book is particularly good at chronicling the relationship between Republican elected officials and the Tea Party. Also see David Barstow's "Tea Party Lights Fuse for Rebellion on Right" in the *New York Times* (February 15, 2010); Katie Zernike's "Tea Party Looks to

Move From Fringe to Force" in the *New York Times*, (February 6, 2010); Sean Wilentz's "Confounding Fathers" in the *New Yorker* (October 18, 2010); Vanessa Williamson, Theda Skocpol, and John Coggin's "The Tea Party and the Remaking of Republican Conservatism" in *Perspectives on Politics* (No. 1, 2011); and the Anti-Defamation League's 2009 report "Rage Grows in America: Anti-Government Conspiracies." For an account of the "death panel" canard, see Brendan Nyhan's "Why the 'Death Panel' Myth Wouldn't Die: Misinformation in the Health Care Debate" in the *Forum* (Issue 1, 2010). Limbaugh's reign during the Obama years is covered in Wilson's *The Most Dangerous Man in America*. Also see Simon Maloy's "Limbaugh's Unrivaled Influence on Republican Politics," posted by Media Matters (March 13, 2012). As for Glenn Beck, these articles were particularly useful: Hannah Dreier's "Glenn Beck No Stranger to Conspiracy Theories or Incendiary Rhetoric," posted by Media Matters (September 4, 2009); "The 50 Worst Things Glenn Beck Said on Fox News," posted by Media Matters (June 30, 2011); and Alexander Zaitchik's "Meet the Man Who Changed Glenn Beck's Life" in *Salon* (September 16, 2009). The account of Bob Inglis's 2010 campaign is drawn from my story "Confessions of a Tea Party Casualty" in *Mother Jones* (August 3, 2010). The account of Obama's December 2010 meeting with labor leaders is based on minutes I obtained for my book *Showdown: The Inside Story of How Obama Battled the GOP to Set Up the 2012 Election*, which covers the fights in 2011 between Obama and the Republicans over the budget and the debt ceiling.

Chapter 22: The Fever Doesn't Break

For Donald Trump's birther spree, see Ashley Parker and Steve Eder's "Inside the Six Weeks Donald Trump Was a Nonstop 'Birther'" in the *New York Times* (July 2, 2016). Obama writes about this in *A Promised Land*. Good overviews of the 2012 campaign include Mark Halperin and John Heilemann's *Double Down: Game Change, 2012* and James W. Ceaser, Andrew E. Busch, and John J. Pitney Jr.'s *After Hope and Change: The 2012 Elections and American Politics*. (*Double Down* reveals Rupert Murdoch's reaction to Obama's victory.) I broke the story of the 47 percent video. See "SECRET VIDEO: Romney Tells Millionaire Donors What He REALLY Thinks of Obama Voters" in *Mother Jones* (September 17, 2012) and my eBook *47 Percent: Uncovering the Romney Video that Rocked the 2012 Election*. Alberta's *American Carnage* is a good source for the 2014 campaign and the continuing conflict between GOP leaders and Tea Party Republicans. It also is the source for John Boehner's bizarre conversation with Roger Ailes and Rupert Murdoch's meeting with Eric Cantor. A good resource regarding the Benghazi controversy is Eugene Kiely's "Benghazi Timeline," posted by FactCheck.org (June 30, 2016).

Chapter 23: "I Am Your Voice"

Valuable works covering Trump and the 2016 campaign include Alberta's *American Carnage*; Thomas Lake and the staff of CNN's *Unprecedented: The Election That Changed Everything*; Jonathan Karl's *Front Row at the Trump Show*; Katy Tur's *Unbelievable: My*

Front-Row Seat to the Craziest Campaign in American History; and *Trumped: The 2016 Campaign That Broke All the Rules*, edited by Larry Sabato, Kyle Kondik, and Geoffrey Skelley. *Identity Crisis: The 2016 Campaign and the Battle for the Meaning of America*, by John Sides, Michael Tesler, and Lynn Vavreck, provides an excellent analysis of Trump's success and his relationship with his voters. Also see Lawrence Rosenthal's "Trump, the Tea Party, the Republicans, and the Other," posted on the Other & Belonging website (June 30, 2016). For Trump's interaction with the Council for National Policy and its members, see O'Harrow's "God, Trump and the Closed-Door World of a Major Conservative Group." This chapter is informed by reporting I did during the campaign, particularly on-background interviews I conducted with Trump advisers. For a detailed account of Russia's attack on the 2016 election and interactions between the Trump camp and Russia-related operatives, see *Russian Roulette: The Inside Story of Putin's War on America and the Election of Donald Trump* by Michael Isikoff and David Corn, and the US Senate Select Committee on Intelligence report on "Russian active measures campaigns and interference in the 2016 campaign," particularly Volume 2 ("Russia's Use of Social Media," 2019) and Volume 5 ("Counterintelligence Threats and Vulnerabilities," 2020). The election night quote from the Internet Research Agency employee is found in Volume 2.

Chapter 24: Very Fine People

The account of Trump's handling of the Charlottesville protest is drawn from Karl's *Front Row at the Trump Show*. Valuable histories of Trump's presidency include Alberta's *American Carnage*; Jonathan Karl's *Betrayal: The Final Act of the Trump Show*; Carol Leonnig and Philip Rucker's *A Very Stable Genius: Donald J. Trump's Testing of America* and their *I Alone Can Fix It: Donald J. Trump's Catastrophic Final Year*; and Bob Woodward's *Fear: Trump in the White House* and *Rage*. For Stephen Miller's promotion of white nationalist material, see the report posted by the Southern Poverty Law Center, "Stephen Miller: The Breitbart Emails" (November 12, 2019). For an account of the Trump-Russia scandal during the Trump administration, see Isikoff and Corn's *Russian Roulette*. For Trump's promotion of QAnon supporters, see Alex Kaplan's "Trump Has Repeatedly Amplified QAnon Twitter Accounts. The FBI Has Linked the Conspiracy Theory to Domestic Terror," posted by Media Matters (January 11, 2021). See also Mike McIntire's "In Trump's Twitter Feed: Conspiracy-Mongers, Racists and Spies" in the *New York Times* (November 2, 2019). For Trump and the COVID-19 crisis, see Eugene Kiely, Lori Robertson, Rem Rieder, and D'Angelo Gore's "Timeline of Trump's COVID-19 Comments " on FactCheck.org (October 2, 2020); Kathleen Hall Jamieson and Dolores Albarracin's "The Relation Between Media Consumption and Misinformation at the Outset of the SARS-CoV-2 Pandemic in the US" in the *Harvard Kennedy School Misinformation Review* (April 2020); and Howard Schneider's "U.S. COVID Response Could Have Avoided Hundreds of Thousands of Deaths: Research," posted by Reuters (March 25, 2021).

Epilogue: The Aftermath

Accounts of Trump's postelection efforts to overturn the 2020 election can be found in Karl's *Betrayal*; Bob Woodward and Robert Costa's *Peril*; and Jonathan Martin and Alexander Burns's *This Will Not Pass: Trump, Biden, and the Battle for America's Future*. The hearings held by the House select committee investigating the January 6 riot provided much information on Trump's maneuvers to retain power. Also see Doug Bock Clark, Alexandra Berzon, and Kirsten Berg's "Building the 'Big Lie': Inside the Creation of Trump's Stolen Election Myth" in *ProPublica* (April 26, 2022). For Trump's record of uttering false statements, see Glenn Kessler, Salvador Rizzo, and Meg Kelly's "Trump's False or Misleading Claims Total 30,573 over 4 Years" in the *Washington Post* (January 24, 2021). Also see Michael Kruse's "The One Way History Shows Trump's Personality Cult Will End" in *Politico* (April 16, 2022) and Cass Sunstein's "The Delicate Art of Debunking Conspiracy Theories" in *Bloomberg* (February 10, 2020).

Bibliography

Adler, William. "A Texan Looks at Lyndon." *Texas Monthly*, September 1987.

Alberta, Tim. *American Carnage: On the Front Lines of the Republican Civil War and the Rise of President Trump*. Harper, 2019.

Alter, Jonathan. *His Very Best: Jimmy Carter, A Life*. Simon & Schuster, 2020.

Amend, Alex. "From Eugenics to Voter ID Laws: Thomas Farr's Connections to the Pioneer Fund." *Hatewatch*, December 4, 2017.

American Jewish Committee. *American Jewish Year Book*. Springer, 1964.

Anderson, Scott, and Jon Lee Anderson. *Inside the League: The Shocking Exposé of How Terrorists, Nazis, and Latin American Death Squads Have Infiltrated the World Anti-Communist League*. Dodd, Mead, 1986.

Andrew, John A. III. *The Other Side of the Sixties: Young Americans for Freedom and the Rise of Conservative Politics*. Rutgers University Press, 1997.

Bagdikian, Ben H. "In the Heart of the Right, Goldwater Lives!" *New York Times*, July 18, 1965.

Bailyn, Bernard. *The Ideological Origins of the American Revolution*. Harvard University Press, 1976.

Barstow, David. "Tea Party Lights Fuse for Rebellion on Right." *New York Times*, February 15, 2010.

Barth, Alan. "Report on the 'Rampageous Right." *New York Times*, November 26, 1961.

Beinart, Peter. "Glenn Beck's Regrets." *Atlantic*, January–February 2017.

Bell, Daniel, ed. *The Radical Right: The New American Right, Expanded and Updated*. Doubleday, 1963.

Bellant, Russ. *Old Nazis, the New Right, and the Republican Party*. South End Press, 1991.

Benkler, Yochai, Robert Faris, and Hal Roberts. *Network Propaganda: Manipulation, Disinformation, and Radicalization in American Politics*. Oxford University Press, 2018.

Berg, A. Scott. *Wilson*. G. P. Putnam's Sons, 2013.

Bird, Kai. *The Outlier: The Unfinished Presidency of Jimmy Carter*. Crown, 2021.

Black, Duncan. "MMFA Investigates: Who Is Jerome Corsi, Co-author of Swift Boat Vets Attack Book?" Media Matters, August 6, 2004.

Blight, David W. *Frederick Douglass: Prophet of Freedom*. Simon & Schuster, 2018.

Bloom, Mia, and Sophia Moskalenko. *Pastels and Pedophiles: Inside the Mind of QAnon*. Stanford University Press, 2021.

Blumberg, Jess. "A Brief History of the Salem Witch Trials." *Smithsonian Magazine*, October 23, 2007.

Blumenthal, Sidney. "Her Own Private Idaho." *New Yorker*, July 2, 1995.

Blumenthal, Sidney. *The Clinton Wars*. Farrar, Straus and Giroux, 2003.

Boehner, John. *On the House: A Washington Memoir*. St. Martin's Press, 2021.

Boston, Rob. *The Most Dangerous Man in America?: Pat Robertson and the Rise of the Christian Coalition*. Prometheus Books, 1996.

Boston, Rob. "Left Behind." *Church & State*, February 2002.

Boston, Rob. "Inside the Christian Coalition." Americans United for Separation of Church and State, November 2004.

Bowman, James. "Rush Limbaugh: The Leader of the Opposition." *National Review*, September 6, 1993.

Boyd, James. "Nixon's Southern Strategy: 'It's All in the Charts.'" *New York Times*, May 17, 1970.

Brady, John. *Bad Boy: The Life and Politics of Lee Atwater*. Addison-Wesley, 1996.

Buckley, William F. Jr. "In Search of Anti-Semitism: What Christians Provoke What Jews? Why? By Doing What?—And Vice Versa." *National Review*, December 30, 1991.

Buckley, William F. Jr. "Goldwater, the John Birch Society, and Me." *Commentary*, March 2008.

Burt, Andrew. *American Hysteria: The Untold Story of Mass Political Extremism in the United States*. Lyons Press, 2020.

Busch, Andrew E. *Reagan's Victory: The Presidential Election of 1980 and the Rise of the Right*. University Press of Kansas, 2005.

Byrne, Malcolm. *Iran-Contra: Reagan's Scandal and the Unchecked Abuse of Presidential Power*. University Press of Kansas, 2014.

Canham, Matt. "The Political Birth of Orrin Hatch." *Salt Lake Tribune*, January 31, 2012.

Cantor, David. *The Religious Right: The Assault on Tolerance & Pluralism in America*. Anti-Defamation League, 1994.

Cavendish, Richard. "Senator McCarthy's Crusade Begins." *History Today*, February 2, 2000.

Ceaser, James W., and Andrew E. Busch. *The Perfect Tie: The True Story of the 2000 Presidential Election*. Rowman & Littlefield, 2001.

Ceaser, James W., and Andrew E. Busch. *Red over Blue: The 2004 Elections and American Politics*. Rowman & Littlefield, 2005.

Ceaser, James W., Andrew E. Busch, and John J. Pitney Jr. *Epic Journey: The 2008 Elections and American Politics*. Rowman & Littlefield, 2009.

Ceaser, James W., Andrew E. Busch, and John J. Pitney Jr. *After Hope and Change: The 2012 Elections and American Politics, Post 2014 Election Update*. Rowman & Littlefield, 2015.

Chafets, Zev. *Rush Limbaugh: An Army of One*. Sentinel, 2010.

Chalmers, David M. *Hooded Americanism: The First Century of the Ku Klux Klan, 1865–1965*. Doubleday, 1965.

Chester, Lewis, Godfrey Hodgson, and Bruce Page. *American Melodrama: The Presidential Campaign of 1968*. Viking Adult, 1969.

Clark, Doug Bock, Alexandra Berzon, and Kirsten Berg. "Building the 'Big Lie': Inside the Creation of Trump's Stolen Election Myth." *ProPublica*, April 26, 2022.

Clarkson, Frederick. "Inside the Covert Coalition." *Church & State*, November 1992.

Clarkson, Frederick. *Eternal Hostility: The Struggle Between Theocracy and Democracy*. Common Courage Press, 1997.

Cole, Wayne S. "The America First Committee." *Journal of the Illinois State Historical Society*, Winter 1951.

Colford, Paul D. *The Rush Limbaugh Story: Talent on Loan from God: The Unauthorized Biography*. St. Martin's Press, 1993.

Colloff, Pamela. "Sunk." *Texas Monthly*, January 2005.

Conason, Joe. "Reagan and the War Crimes Lobby." *Village Voice*, May 14, 1985.

Conason, Joe, and Gene Lyons. *The Hunting of the President: The Ten-Year Campaign to Destroy Bill and Hillary Clinton*. St. Martin's Griffin, 2001.

Coppins, McKay. "The Social-Distancing Culture War Has Begun." *Atlantic*, March 30, 2020.

Corben, Billy, director. *537 Votes*. HBO, 2020.

Corn, David. "Evidence Undermines Attack." *Nation*, August 20, 2004.

Corn, David. "Confessions of a Tea Party Casualty." *Mother Jones*, August 3, 2010.

Corn, David. *Showdown: The Inside Story of How Obama Battled the GOP to Set Up the 2012 Election*. William Morrow, 2012.

Corn, David. "SECRET VIDEO: Romney Tells Millionaire Donors What He REALLY Thinks of Obama Voters." *Mother Jones*, September 17, 2012.

Corn, David. *47 Percent: Uncovering the Romney Video That Rocked the 2012 Election*. William Morrow, 2012.

Corn, David. "Sponsors of the Pre-Attack Rally Have Taken Down Their Websites. Don't Forget Who They Were." *Mother Jones*, January 12, 2021.

Corn, David. "How Trump and His Crew Boost Putin's Disinformation." *Our Land*. March 19, 2022 (https://link.motherjones.com/public/27080239).

Cowie, Jefferson. "Nixon's Class Struggle: Romancing the New Right Worker, 1969–1973." *Labor History*, No. 3, 2002.

Cowie, Jefferson. "The 'Hard Hat Riot' Was a Preview of Today's Political Divisions." *New York Times*, May 11, 2020.

Cramer, Richard Ben. *What It Takes: The Way to the White House*. Vintage Books, 1993.

Crawford, Alan. *Thunder on the Right: The "New Right" and the Politics of Resentment*. Pantheon Books, 1980.

Crespino, Joseph. "Did David Brooks Tell the Full Story About Reagan's Neshoba County Fair Visit?" History News Network, November 11, 2007.

Critchlow, Donald T. *Phyllis Schlafly and Grassroots Conservatism: A Woman's Crusade*. Princeton University Press, 2005.

Dallek, Matthew. *The Right Moment: Ronald Reagan's First Victory and the Decisive Turning Point in American Politics*. The Free Press, 2000.

Day of Rage: How Trump Supporters Took the U.S. Capitol. Produced by the *New York Times* Visual Investigations team. *New York Times*, 2021 (https://www.nytimes.com/spotlight/us-capitol-riots-investigations).

De Groot, Gerard J. "'A Goddamned Electable Person': The 1966 California Gubernatorial Campaign of Ronald Reagan." *History*, July 1997.

Diamond, Sara. *Spiritual Warfare: The Politics of the Christian Right.* South End Press, 1989.

Diamond, Sara. *Roads to Dominion: Right-Wing Movements and Political Power in the United States.* The Guilford Press, 1995.

Dionne, E. J. Jr. *Why the Right Went Wrong: Conservatism—from Goldwater to Trump and Beyond.* Simon & Schuster, 2016.

Dobbs, Michael. "Swift Boat Accounts Incomplete." *Washington Post*, August 22, 2004.

Draper, Robert. *When the Tea Party Came to Town.* Simon & Schuster, 2013.

Draper, Robert. *To Start a War: How the Bush Administration Took America into Iraq.* Penguin Press, 2020.

Draper, Theodore. *A Very Thin Line: The Iran-Contra Affairs.* Hill and Wang, 1991.

Dreier, Hannah. "Glenn Beck No Stranger to Conspiracy Theories or Incendiary Rhetoric." Media Matters, September 4, 2009.

Drew, Elizabeth. *Portrait of an Election: The 1980 Presidential Campaign.* Simon & Schuster, 1981.

Drew, Elizabeth. *Showdown: The Struggle Between the Gingrich Congress and the Clinton White House.* Touchstone, 1997.

Drew, Elizabeth. *Whatever It Takes: The Real Struggle for Political Power in America.* Viking Adult, 1997.

Dreyfuss, Robert. "Reverend Doomsday." *Rolling Stone*, January 28, 2004.

Drum, Kevin. "The Real Source of America's Rising Rage." *Mother Jones*, September-October 2021.

Dunn, Geoffrey. *The Lies of Sarah Palin: The Untold Story Behind Her Relentless Quest for Power.* St. Martin's Griffin, 2011.

Epstein, Benjamin R., and Arnold Forster. *The Radical Right: Report on the John Birch Society and Its Allies.* Random House, 1967.

Ewald, William Bragg Jr. *Who Killed Joe McCarthy?* Simon & Schuster, 1984.

Farrell, John A. *Richard Nixon: The Life.* Doubleday, 2017.

Farrell, John A. "When a Candidate Conspired with a Foreign Power to Win an Election." *Politico Magazine*, August 6, 2017.

Felsenthal, Carol. *The Sweetheart of the Silent Majority: The Biography of Phyllis Schlafly.* Doubleday, 1981.

Felzenberg, Alvin S. *A Man and His Presidents: The Political Odyssey of William F. Buckley Jr.* Yale University Press, 2017.

Fisher, Max. "Probing the Tea Party's Conspiracy Theorist Fringe." *Atlantic*, February 11, 2010.

FitzGerald, Frances. "A Disciplined, Charging Army." *New Yorker*, May 18, 1981.

Flanders, Laura, ed. *At the Tea Party: The Wing Nuts, Whack Jobs, and Whitey-Whiteness of the New Republican Right… and Why We Should Take It Seriously.* OR Books, 2010.

Foser, Jamison. "The Lies of John O'Neill: An MMFA Analysis." Media Matters, August 24, 2004.

Foster, Arnold, and Benjamin R. Epstein. *Danger on the Right: The Attitudes, Personnel and Influence of the Radical Right and Extreme Conservatives.* Random House, 1964.

Freedman, Paul B., et al. "Interview with Stuart Spencer," Ronald Reagan Oral History Project. Miller Center of Public Affairs Presidential Oral History Program, University of Virginia, 2001.

Friedersdorf, Conor. "Rush Limbaugh Is Cheating on Conservatism with Donald Trump." *Atlantic,* January 14, 2016.

Fuller, Tony, and Peter Goldman. *The Quest for the Presidency, 1984.* Bantam Books, 1985.

Garrett, Major. *Mr. Trump's Wild Ride: The Thrills, Chills, Screams, and Occasional Blackouts of an Extraordinary Presidency.* All Points Books, 2018.

Germond, Jack W., and Jules Witcover. *Wake Us When It's Over: Presidential Politics of 1984.* Macmillan, 1985.

Germond, Jack W., and Jules Witcover. *Whose Broad Stripes and Bright Stars?: The Trivial Pursuit of the Presidency, 1988.* Warner Books, 1989.

Germond, Jack W., and Jules Witcover. *Mad as Hell: Revolt at the Ballot Box, 1992.* Grand Central, 1993.

Gershkoff, Amy, and Shana Kushner. "Shaping Public Opinion: The 9/11-Iraq Connection in the Bush Administration's Rhetoric." *Perspectives on Politics,* No. 3, 2005.

Goldberg, Robert Alan. *Barry Goldwater.* Yale University Press, 1995.

Goldman, Peter, and Tom Mathews. *The Quest for the Presidency: The 1988 Campaign.* Simon & Schuster, 1989.

Goldman, Peter, et al. *Quest for the Presidency, 1992.* Texas A&M University Press, 1994.

Goldwater, Barry. *The Conscience of a Conservative.* Princeton University Press, 2007.

Gooding, Richard. "The Trashing of John McCain." *Vanity Fair,* November 2004.

Gordon, David. "America First: The Anti-War Movement, Charles Lindbergh and the Second World War, 1940–1941." Resource guide. Historical Society and New York Military Affairs Symposium, September 26, 2003.

Gorenfeld, John. *Bad Moon Rising: How Reverend Moon Created the* Washington Times, *Seduced the Religious Right, and Built an American Kingdom.* PoliPointPress, 2008.

Gould, Lewis L. *The Republicans: A History of the Grand Old Party.* Oxford University Press, 2014.

Graff, Garrett M. *Watergate: A New History.* Avid Reader Press, 2022.

Green, John C., Mark J. Rozell, and Clyde Wilcox, eds. *The Values Campaign?: The Christian Right and the 2004 Elections.* Georgetown University Press, 2006.

Griffith, Robert. "The General and the Senator: Republican Politics and the 1952 Campaign in Wisconsin." *Wisconsin Magazine of History,* No. 1, 1970.

Grossberger, Lewis. "The Rush Hours." *New York Times,* December 16, 1990.

Grunwald, Michael. *The New New Deal: The Hidden Story of Change in the Obama Era.* Simon & Schuster, 2012.

Haldeman, H. R. *The Haldeman Diaries: Inside the Nixon White House.* Publishing Mills, 1995.

Haley, J. Evetts. *A Texan Looks at Lyndon: A Study in Illegitimate Power.* Palo Duro Press, 1964.

Halperin, Mark, and John Heilemann. *Double Down: Game Change 2012.* Penguin Press, 2013.

Hardisty, Jean. *Mobilizing Resentment: Conservative Resurgence from the John Birch Society to the Promise Keepers.* Beacon Press, 2000.

Hatch, Orrin. "Tribute to W. Cleon Skousen." *Congressional Record* 152:5 (January 25, 2006), pp. S114–5.

Heilemann, John, and Mark Halperin. *Game Change: Obama and the Clintons, McCain and Palin, and the Race of a Lifetime.* Harper Perennial, 2010.

Hendershot, Heather. *What's Fair on the Air?: Cold War Right-Wing Broadcasting and the Public Interest.* University of Chicago Press, 2011.

Hofstadter, Richard. *Anti-Intellectualism in American Life, The Paranoid Style in American Politics, Uncollected Essays 1956–1965.* Edited by Sean Wilentz. Library of America, 2020.

Holden, Jeremy. "The 50 Worst Things Glenn Beck Said on Fox News." Media Matters, June 30, 2011.

Howison, Jeffrey D. *The 1980 Presidential Election: Ronald Reagan and the Shaping of the American Conservative Movement.* Routledge, 2014.

Huntington, John S. "'The Voice of Many Hatreds': J. Evetts Haley and Texas Ultraconservatism." *Western Historical Quarterly,* Spring 2018.

Huntington, John S. *Far-Right Vanguard: The Radical Roots of Modern Conservatism.* University of Pennsylvania Press, 2021.

Isaacs, Stephen. "Coors Beer—and Politics—Move East." *Washington Post,* May 4, 1975.

Isikoff, Michael. *Uncovering Clinton: A Reporter's Story.* Three Rivers Press, 2000.

Isikoff, Michael, and David Corn. *Hubris: The Inside Story of Spin, Scandal, and the Selling of the Iraq War.* Three Rivers Press, 2006.

Isikoff, Michael, and David Corn. *Russian Roulette: The Inside Story of Putin's War on America and the Election of Donald Trump.* Twelve, 2018.

Ivins, Molly. "Un-Christian Behavior by the Religious Right." *San Francisco Chronicle,* September 15, 1993.

Jamieson, Kathleen Hall, and Dolores Albarracín. "The Relation Between Media Consumption and Misinformation at the Outset of the SARS-CoV-2 Pandemic in the US." *Harvard Kennedy School Misinformation Review,* April 2020.

Jeansonne, Glen. *Leander Perez: Boss of the Delta.* University Press of Mississippi, 2006.

"The John Birch Society—1966." *Facts.* Anti-Defamation League, February 1966.

Jones, Robert P. "How Trump Remixed the Republican 'Southern Strategy.'" *Atlantic,* August 14, 2016.

Judis, John B. *William F. Buckley, Jr.: Patron Saint of the Conservatives.* Simon & Schuster, 1988.

Kabaservice, Geoffrey. *Rule and Ruin: The Downfall of Moderation and the Destruction of the Republican Party, from Eisenhower to the Tea Party.* Oxford University Press, 2012.

Kaplan, Alex. "Trump Has Repeatedly Amplified QAnon Twitter Accounts. The FBI Has Linked the Conspiracy Theory to Domestic Terror." Media Matters. January 11, 2021.

Kaplan, Esther. *With God on Their Side: How Christian Fundamentalists Trampled Science, Policy, and Democracy in George W. Bush's White House.* The New Press, 2004.

Kaplan, Joshua, and Joaquin Sapien. "New Details Suggest Senior Trump Aides Knew Jan. 6 Rally Could Get Chaotic." *ProPublica*, June 25, 2021.

Karl, Jonathan. *Front Row at the Trump Show.* Dutton, 2020.

Karl, Jonathan. *Betrayal: The Final Act of the Trump Show.* Dutton, 2021.

Kay, Jonathan. "Bachmann, Gaffney, and the GOP's Anti-Muslim Culture of Conspiracy." *Daily Beast*, July 13, 2017.

Kessel, John H. *The Goldwater Coalition: Republican Strategies in 1964.* Bobbs-Merrill, 1968.

Kessler, Glenn, Salvador Rizzo, and Meg Kelly. "Trump's False or Misleading Claims Total 30,573 Over 4 Years." *Washington Post*, January 24, 2021.

Kiely, Eugene. "Benghazi Timeline." FactCheck.org, June 30, 2016.

Kiely, Eugene, et al. "Timeline of Trump's COVID-19 Comments." FactCheck.org, October 2, 2020.

Killian, Linda. *The Freshmen: What Happened to the Republican Revolution?* Westview Press, 1998.

Kinzer, Stephen. *The True Flag: Theodore Roosevelt, Mark Twain, and the Birth of American Empire.* Henry Holt, 2017.

Klinker, Philip A. *The Losing Parties: Out-Party National Committees, 1956–1993.* Yale University Press, 1994.

Kopel, Dave. "Ronald Reagan, Extremist Collaborator." *New Ledger*, October 28, 2010.

Kornacki, Steve. *The Red and the Blue: The 1990s and the Birth of Political Tribalism.* Ecco, 2018.

Kornbluh, Peter, and Malcolm Byrne, eds. *The Iran-Contra Scandal: The Declassified History.* New Press, 1993.

Kruse, Michael. "The One Way History Shows Trump's Personality Cult Will End." *Politico*, April 16, 2022.

Kuhn, David Paul. *The Hardhat Riot: Nixon, New York City, and the Dawn of the White Working-Class Revolution.* Oxford University Press, 2020.

Kutler, Stanley I. *The Wars of Watergate: The Last Crisis of Richard Nixon.* W. W. Norton, 1990.

LaHaye, Tim. *The Battle for the Mind: A Subtle Warfare.* Fleming H. Revell, 1980.

Lake, Thomas. *Unprecedented: The Election That Changed Everything.* Melcher Media, 2016.

Lantigua, John. "Miami's Rent-a-Riot." *Salon*, November 28, 2000.

Leonnig, Carol, and Philip Rucker. *I Alone Can Fix It: Donald J. Trump's Catastrophic Final Year.* Penguin Press, 2021.

Lepore, Jill. *These Truths: A History of the United States.* W. W. Norton, 2018.

Leuchtenburg, William E. *Franklin D. Roosevelt and the New Deal.* Harper Perennial, 1963.

Levin, Josh, host. "The Nazi and the Republicans." *Slow Burn: David Duke*, Season 4, Episode 3. Slate Group, 2020.

Levitas, Daniel. *The Terrorist Next Door: The Militia Movement and the Radical Right.* St. Martin's Press, 2002.

Lewis, Michael. *Losers: The Road to Everyplace but the White House.* Vintage Books, 1998.

Limbaugh, Rush. *The Way Things Ought to Be.* Pocket Books, 1992.

Lipset, Seymour Martin, and Earl Raab. *The Politics of Unreason: Right-Wing Extremism in America, 1790–1970.* Harper & Row, 1970.

Lofgren, Mike. *The Party Is Over: How Republicans Went Crazy, Democrats Became Useless, and the Middle Class Got Shafted.* Penguin Books, 2012.

Lyons, Gene. *Fools for Scandal: How the Media Invented Whitewater.* Franklin Square Press, 1996.

Mak, Tim. *Misfire: Inside the Downfall of the NRA.* Dutton, 2021.

Maloy, Simon. "Limbaugh's Unrivaled Influence on Republican Politics." Media Matters, March 13, 2012.

Marley, David John. "Ronald Reagan and the Splintering of the Christian Right." *Journal of Church and State*, No. 4, 2006.

Martin, Jonathan, and Alexander Burns. *This Will Not Pass: Trump, Biden, and the Battle for America's Future.* Simon & Schuster, 2022.

Maxwell, Angie, and Todd Shields. *The Long Southern Strategy: How Chasing White Voters in the South Changed American Politics.* Oxford University Press, 2019.

Mayer, Jane. *Dark Money: The Hidden History of the Billionaires Behind the Rise of the Radical Right.* Doubleday, 2016.

Mayer, Jane, and Doyle McManus. *Landslide: The Unmaking of the President, 1984–1988.* Houghton Mifflin, 1989.

Mayer, Jeremy D. "Nixon Rides the Backlash to Victory: Racial Politics in the 1968 Presidential Campaign." *Historian*, No. 2, 2002.

McGinniss, Joe. *The Selling of the President.* Penguin Books, 1988.

McIntire, Mike. "In Trump's Twitter Feed: Conspiracy-Mongers, Racists and Spies." *New York Times*, November 2, 2019.

McIntyre, Thomas J., with John C. Obert. *The Fear Brokers: Peddling the Hate Politics of the New Right.* Beacon Press, 1979.

McVeigh, Rory. *The Rise of the Ku Klux Klan: Right-Wing Movements and National Politics.* University of Minnesota Press, 2009.

Meacham, Jon. *Destiny and Power: The American Odyssey of George Herbert Walker Bush.* Random House, 2015.

Meagher, Richard J. "Remembering the New Right: Political Strategy and the Building of the GOP Coalition." *Public Eye*, June 10 2009.

Merlan, Anna. *Republic of Lies: American Conspiracy Theorists and Their Surprising Rise to Power.* Metropolitan Books, 2019.

Middendorf, J. William II. *A Glorious Disaster: Barry Goldwater's Presidential Campaign and the Origins of the Conservative Movement.* Basic Books, 2006.

Milbank, Dana. *Smashmouth: Two Years in the Gutter with Al Gore and George W. Bush—Notes from the 2000 Campaign Trail.* Basic Books, 2001.

Milkis, Sidney M., and Daniel J. Tichenor. "Building a Movement Party: The Alliance Between Ronald Reagan and the New Christian Right," UVA-Miller Center (https://millercenter.org/rivalry-and-reform/building-movement-party). Adapted from Milkis and Tichenor, *Rivalry and Reform: Presidents, Social Movements, and the Transformation of American Politics*, University of Chicago Press, 2018.

Miller, Edward H. *A Conspiratorial Life: Robert Welch, the John Birch Society, and the Revolution of American Conservatism*. University of Chicago Press, 2021.

Mitchell, Greg. *Tricky Dick and the Pink Lady: Richard Nixon vs. Helen Gahagan Douglas—Sexual Politics and the Red Scare, 1950*. Random House, 1998.

Modisett, Bill. *J. Evetts Haley: A True Texas Legend*. Staked Plains Press, 1996.

Moldea, Dan E. *A Washington Tragedy: How the Death of Vincent Foster Ignited a Political Firestorm*. Regnery, 1998.

Mosk, Stanley, and Howard H. Jewel. "The Birch Phenomenon Analyzed: A Report by the California Attorney General's Office Examines the Methods and Speculates on the Motives of the Controversial John Birch Society." *New York Times*, August 20, 1961.

Muirhead, Russell, and Nancy L. Rosenblum. *A Lot of People Are Saying: The New Conspiracism and the Assault on Democracy*. Princeton University Press, 2019.

Mulloy, D. J. *The World of the John Birch Society: Conspiracy, Conservatism, and the Cold War*. Vanderbilt University Press, 2014.

Nelson, Anne. *Shadow Network: Media, Money, and the Secret Hub of the Radical Right*. Bloomsbury, 2019.

"Nixon and School Desegregation: Perspective from George Shultz." Richard Nixon Foundation, February 8, 2017.

Nyhan, Brendan. "Why the 'Death Panel' Myth Wouldn't Die: Misinformation in the Health Care Debate." *The Forum*, Issue 1, 2010.

Obama, Barack. *A Promised Land*. Crown, 2020.

O'Connell, Sue. "The Money Behind the 2004 Marriage Amendments." FollowThe Money.org, January 27, 2006 (https://www.followthemoney.org./research/institute-reports/the-money-behind-the-2004-marriage-amendments).

Offenbach, Seth. *The Other Side of Vietnam: The Conservative Movement and the Vietnam War*. PhD dissertation, Stony Brook University, 2010.

O'Harrow, Robert Jr. "God, Trump and the Closed-Door World of a Major Conservative Group." *Washington Post*, October 25, 2021.

Olmsted, Kathryn S. *Real Enemies: Conspiracy Theories and American Democracy, World War I to 9/11*. Oxford University Press, 2009.

Parker, Ashley, and Steve Eder. "Inside the Six Weeks Donald Trump Was a Nonstop 'Birther.'" *New York Times*, July 2, 2016.

Parker, Christopher S., and Matt A. Barretto. *Change They Can't Believe In: The Tea Party and Reactionary Politics in America*. Princeton University Press, 2013.

"Paula Jones Civil Suit: Chronology." *New York Times*, 1998.

Paul, Christopher, and Miriam Matthews. "The Russian 'Firehose of Falsehood' Propaganda Model: Why It Might Work and Options to Counter It." RAND Corporation, 2016.

Penning, James M. "Pat Robertson and the GOP: 1998 and Beyond." *Sociology of Religion*, Autumn 1994.

Perlstein, Rick. *Before the Storm: Barry Goldwater and the Unmaking of the American Consensus.* Bold Type Books, 2009.

Perlstein, Rick. *Nixonland: The Rise of a President and the Fracturing of America.* Scribner, 2008.

Perlstein, Rick. *The Invisible Bridge: The Fall of Nixon and the Rise of Reagan.* Simon & Schuster, 2015.

Perlstein, Rick. *Reaganland: America's Right Turn, 1976–1980.* Simon & Schuster, 2020.

Peron, Jim. "The New Theocracy: Moral Majority's Grab for Power." *Libertarian Review,* September 1981.

Perry, James M. *Barry Goldwater: A New Look at a Presidential Candidate.* The National Observer, 1964.

Peters, Jeremy W. *Insurgency: How Republicans Lost Their Party and Got Everything They Ever Wanted.* Crown, 2022.

Posner, Sarah. "The Fundamentalist (No. 58)." *American Prospect,* November 19, 2008.

Radosh, Ronald. "Phyllis Schlafly, 'Mrs. America,' Was a Secret Member of the John Birch Society." *Daily Beast,* April 22, 2020.

"Rage Grows in America: Anti-Government Conspiracies." Anti-Defamation League, November 2009.

Raskin, Jamie. *Unthinkable: Trauma, Truth, and the Trials of American Democracy.* Harper, 2022.

Richardson, Heather Cox. *To Make Men Free: A History of the Republican Party.* Basic Books, 2014.

Robertson, Pat. *The New World Order.* World Publishing, 1991.

Rose, Douglas D., ed. *The Emergence of David Duke and the Politics of Rage.* The University of North Carolina Press, 1992. (See Chapter 4, "The Nazi and the Republicans: An Insider View of the Response of the Louisiana Republican Party to David Duke," by Elizabeth Rickey.)

Rosenthal, Lawrence. "Trump, the Tea Party, the Republicans and the Other." Othering & Belonging, June 29, 2016 (http://www.otheringandbelonging.org/trump-the-tea-party-the-republicans-and-the-other/).

Rosenthal, Lawrence. *Empire of Resentment: Populism's Toxic Embrace of Nationalism.* New Press, 2020.

Rosenthal, Lawrence, and Christine Trost, eds. *Steep: The Precipitous Rise of the Tea Party.* University of California Press, 2012.

Rucker, Philip, and Carol Leonnig. *A Very Stable Genius: Donald J. Trump's Testing of America.* Penguin Press, 2020.

Sabato, Larry J., Kyle Kondik, and Geoffrey Skelley, eds. *Trumped: The 2016 Election That Broke All the Rules.* Rowman & Littlefield, 2017.

Schecter, Cliff. "Extremely Motivated: The Republican Party's March to the Right." *Fordham Urban Law Journal,* No. 4, 2002.

Scherstuhl, Alan. "Socialism Starts With Your Kids' Allowance, Preacher W.S. McBirnie Warned in 1965." *Village Voice,* November 8, 2012.

Schlafly, Phyllis. *A Choice Not an Echo: Updated and Expanded 50th Anniversary Edition.* Regnery, 2014.

Schneider, Howard. "U.S. COVID Response Could Have Avoided Hundreds of Thousands of Deaths: Research." *Reuters*, March 25, 2021.

Schoenwald, Jonathan. *A Time for Choosing: The Rise of Modern American Conservatism*. Oxford University Press, 2001.

Schomp, Gerald. *Birchism Was My Business*. Macmillan, 1970.

Schuparra, Kurt. *Triumph of the Right: The Rise of the California Conservative Movement, 1945–1966*. M. E. Sharp, 1998.

Serratore, Angela. "The 'Hard Hat Riot' of 1970 Pitted Construction Workers Against Anti-War Protesters." *Smithsonian Magazine*, May 8, 2020.

Shadegg, Stephen C. *What Happened to Goldwater?: The Inside Story of the 1964 Republican Campaign*. Holt, Rinehart and Winston, 1965.

Sherman, Gabriel. *The Loudest Voice in the Room: How the Brilliant, Bombastic Roger Ailes Built Fox News—and Divided a Country*. Random House, 2017.

Sides, John, Michael Tesler, and Lynn Vavreck. *Identity Crisis: The 2016 Presidential Campaign and the Battle for the Meaning of America*. Princeton University Press, 2019.

Slayton, Robert A. "When a Catholic Terrified the Heartland." *New York Times*, December 10, 2011.

Smillie, Dirk. *Falwell Inc.: Inside a Religious, Political, Educational, and Business Empire*. St. Martin's Press, 2008.

Smith, Ben, and Byron Tau. "Birtherism: Where It All Began." *Politico*, April 22, 2011.

Smith, Richard Norton. *On His Own Terms: A Life of Nelson Rockefeller*. Random House, 2014.

Smyth, Frank. *The NRA: The Unauthorized History*. Flatiron Books, 2020.

Spitzer, Scott J. "Nixon's New Deal: Welfare Reform for the Silent Majority." *Presidential Studies Quarterly*, September 2012.

"Stephen Miller: The Breitbart Emails." Southern Poverty Law Center, November 12, 2019 (https://www.splcenter.org/stephen-miller-breitbart-emails).

Stevens, Stuart. *It Was All a Lie: How the Republican Party Became Donald Trump*. Alfred A. Knopf, 2020.

Stormer, John A. *None Dare Call It Treason*. Liberty Bell Press, 1964.

Sunstein, Cass. "The Delicate Art of Debunking Conspiracy Theories." *Bloomberg*, February 10, 2020.

Sunstein, Cass R., and Adrian Vermeule. "Conspiracy Theories." Public Law & Legal Theory Research Paper Series, Harvard University Law School, January 15, 2008 (http://ssrn.com/abstract=1084585).

Swanberg, W. A. *Luce and His Empire*. Charles Scribner's Sons, 1972.

Sykes, Charles J. *How The Right Lost Its Mind*. St. Martin's Press, 2017.

Thomas, Evan. *Election 2004: How Bush Won and What You Can Expect in the Future*. PublicAffairs, 2004.

Toobin, Jeffrey. "Roger Stone's and Jerome Corsi's Time in the Barrel." *New Yorker*, February 11, 2019.

Toy, Eckard V. Jr. "The Right Side of the 1960s: The Origins of the John Birch Society in the Pacific Northwest." *Oregon Historical Quarterly*, No. 2, 2004.

Tur, Katy. *Unbelievable: My Front-Row Seat to the Craziest Campaign in American History*. Dey Street Books, 2017.

US Senate Committee on Commerce. *Joseph Coors to be a member, board of directors, Corporation for Public Broadcasting*. US Senate, 1975.

US Senate Select Committee on Intelligence. *Russian Active Measures Campaigns and Interference in the 2016 US Election*. US Senate. See Volume 2 ("Russia's Use of Social Media," 2019) and Volume 5 ("Counterintelligence Threats and Vulnerabilities," 2020).

Valentine, Paul. "The Fascist Specter Behind the World Anti-Red League." *Washington Post*, May 28, 1978.

Wade, Wyn Craig. *The Fiery Cross: The Ku Klux Klan in America*. Oxford University Press, 1998.

Walker, Jesse. *The United States of Paranoia: A Conspiracy Theory*. HarperCollins, 2013.

Washington Post political staff. *Deadlock: The Inside Story of America's Closest Election*. PublicAffairs, 2001.

Weiner, Tim. *One Man Against the World: The Tragedy of Richard Nixon*. St. Martin's Griffin, 2016.

Weiser, Benjamin, and Joe Pichirallo. "3 Groups Channeled Arms to Contras After Ban." *Washington Post*, February 26, 1987.

Weiss, Phillip. "Clinton Crazy." *New York Times*, February 23, 1997.

Westin, Alan F. "The John Birch Society." *Commentary*, August 1961.

Westin, Alan F. "Anti-Communism and the Corporations." *Commentary*, December 1963.

White, F. Clifton, and William J. Gill. *Suite 3505: The Story of the Draft Goldwater Movement*. Arlington House, 1967.

White, Theodore H. *The Making of the President, 1960*. Harper Perennial, 2010.

White, Theodore H. *The Making of the President, 1964*. Harper Perennial, 2010.

White, Theodore H. *The Making of the President, 1968*. Harper Perennial, 2010.

White, Theodore H. *The Making of the President, 1972*. Harper Perennial, 2010.

Wiebe, Robert H. *The Search for Order, 1877–1920*. Hill and Wang, 1966.

Wilentz, Sean. *The Age of Reagan: A History, 1974–2008*. Harper Perennial, 2009.

Wilentz, Sean. "Confounding Fathers." *New Yorker*, October 18, 2010.

Williams, Daniel K. *God's Own Party: The Making of the Christian Right*. Oxford University Press, 2010.

Williamson, Vanessa, Theda Skocpol, and John Coggin. "The Tea Party and the Remaking of Republican Conservatism." *Perspectives on Politics*, No. 1, 2011.

Wills, Garry. *Reagan's America: Innocents at Home*. Penguin Books, 2000.

Wilson, John K. *The Most Dangerous Man in America: Rush Limbaugh's Assault on Reason*. St. Martin's Press, 2011.

Winters, Michael Sean. *God's Right Hand: How Jerry Falwell Made God a Republican and Baptized the American Right*. HarperOne, 2012.

Witcover, Jules. *Marathon: The Pursuit of the Presidency, 1972–1976*. Viking Press, 1977.

Witt, Linda. "Reclusive Joe Coors Peddles Beer and a Tough Right-Wing Line." *People*, May 4, 1975.

Wittner, Lawrence S. "The Nuclear Freeze and Its Impact." *Arms Control Today*, December 2010.

Woodward, Bob. *The Choice: How Bill Clinton Won*. Simon & Schuster, 2005.

Woodward, Bob. *Fear: Trump in the White House*. Simon & Schuster, 2018.

Woodward, Bob. *Rage*. Simon & Schuster, 2020.

Woodward, Bob, and Robert Costa. *Peril*. Simon & Schuster, 2021.

Zaitchik, Alexander. "Meet the Man Who Changed Glenn Beck's Life." *Salon*, September 16, 2009.

Zeitz, Josh. "When America Hated Catholics." *Politico Magazine*, September 23, 2015.

Zelizer, Julian E. *Burning Down the House: Newt Gingrich and the Rise of the New Republican Party*. Penguin Books, 2020.

Zernike, Kate. "Tea Party Looks to Move from Fringe to Force." *New York Times*, February 6, 2010.

Zernike, Kate, and Jim Rutenberg. "Friendly Fire: The Birth of an Attack on Kerry." *New York Times*, August 20, 2004.

Index

abortion
  backlash against rights involving, 131
  bans on, 333
  G. W. Bush and, 228, 236, 240
  Hatch and, 126
  McCain and, 222
  Reagan and, 115, 137, 148
  Republican opposition to, 158
  Trump and, 307
Access Hollywood tape, 302, 303
Accuracy in the Media, 193, 208
Acheson, Dean, 23, 40, 63
ACLU, Robertson's blaming of, *230–231*
Adams, John, 17, 25, 26, 27
Adams, John Quincy, *28–29*
Adams, Samuel, 24
Adams, Sherman, 43, 45, 47
Advance magazine, 65
affirmative action, 102
Affordable Care Act (Obamacare), *259–260*,
  265–266, 272, 280, 284
Agnew, Spiro, 96, 99, 102, *103–104*, 108, 113
AIDS crisis, 164, 165, 188, 229
Ailes, Roger, *99–100*, 171, 172, 185, 195, 285
air traffic controllers' strike, 148
al Qaeda, 230, 232, *233–234*
Alarcón, Mario Sandoval, 161
Alberta, Tim, 285
Alexander, Ali, *6–7*
Alexander, Lamar, 103, 189
Alien and Sedition Acts, 26
Alito, Samuel, 243
Allen, Richard, 151
Allen, Steve, 67
Alliance, Inc., 49
"alternative facts," 307
alt-right, 301, 307
America Can Be Saved (Falwell), 133
"America First" slogan, 184
American Alliance, 31

American Center for Law and Justice, 199
American Coalition for Traditional Values, 159,
  165
American Conservative Union (ACU), *117–119*,
  122, 128, 129, 147, 268, 328
American Enterprise Institute, 233
American Family Association, 188, 241
American First Committee, *36–37*
American for Prosperity, 265
American Independence Party, 122
American Jewish Committee (AJC), 75, 76
American Melodrama, An (Chester, Hodgson,
  and Page), 96
American Opinion magazine, 62, 65, 87
American Republican Party, 30
American Revolution, 24
American Security Council, 152
American Spectator, 193, *207–208*
Americans for Goldwater, *56–57*
Anderson, Jack, 110, 163
Anderson, John, 127, 143
Anderson, Jon Lee, *160–161*
Anderson, Martin, 194
Anderson, Scott, *160–161*
Andrews, T. Coleman, 50
Andropov, Yuri, 153
Angle, Sharron, 269, 272
Anti-Bolshevik Bloc of Nations (ABN), 160,
  174
anti-Catholic sentiment, *29–31*, *246–247*
anticommunist crusade, *20–23*, *39–40*, *43–46*,
  48–52, 63, 73, 87, 92, 125, *151–152*. *See also*
  McCarthy, Joe
Anti-Defamation League, 252
anti-German hysteria, *32–33*
anti-immigrant sentiment, 29, 32, 267, *283–284*,
  292–293, 294, 308, *311–312*
Anti-Masons, 28, 29, 30
anti-Muslim sentiment, *231–232*, 238, 246, 247,
  250–251, *292–293*, *306–307*

About the Author

David Corn is a veteran Washington journalist and political commentator. He is the Washington bureau chief for *Mother Jones* magazine and an analyst for MSNBC. He is the author or coauthor of four *New York Times* bestsellers, including the #1 bestseller *Russian Roulette: The Inside Story of Putin's War on America and the Election of Donald Trump; Showdown: The Inside Story of How Obama Battled the GOP to Set up the 2012 Election; Hubris: The Inside Story of Spin, Scandal, and the Selling of the Iraq War*; and *The Lies of George W. Bush: Mastering the Politics of Deception*. He is also the author of the biography *Blond Ghost: Ted Shackley and the CIA's Crusades* and the novel *Deep Background*. He writes the *Our Land* newsletter. He is a Phi Beta Kappa graduate of Brown University.